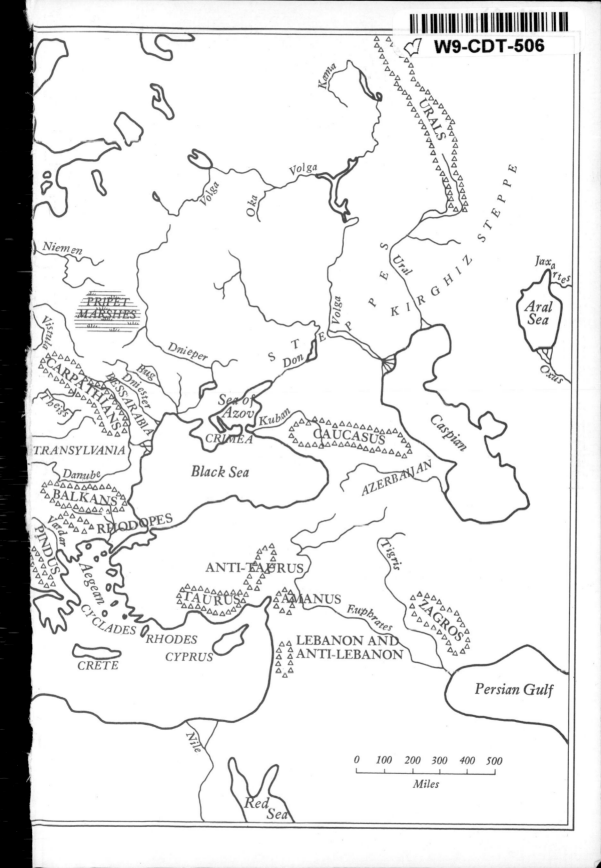

URALS

Kama

Volga

Volga

Oka

Volga

Niemen

S T E P P E S

Ural

KIRGHIZ STEPPE

Jaxartes

Aral Sea

PRIPET MARSHES

Vistula

Dnieper

Don

Volga

Oxus

Bug

CARPATHIANS

Theiss

Dniester

BESSARABIA

Sea of Azov

Kuban

CAUCASUS

Caspian

TRANSYLVANIA

CRIMEA

Danube

Black Sea

AZERBAIJAN

BALKANS

RHODOPES

Vardar

PINDUS

Aegean

Tigris

ANTI-TAURUS

TAURUS

AMANUS

Euphrates

ZAGROS

CYCLADES

RHODES

CYPRUS

LEBANON AND ANTI-LEBANON

CRETE

Persian Gulf

Nile

0   100   200   300   400   500

Miles

Red Sea

History of the Byzantine Empire

The ivory, made in 944, is in the Cabinet des Médailles,
Bibliothèque Nationale, Paris

Jesus crowning the children Romanus II (reigned 959–963) and his first wife (who soon died)

History of the
Byzantine Empire
Mother of Nations

by ENNO FRANZIUS

FUNK & WAGNALLS

NEW YORK

*The author is grateful to the following for
permission to reproduce artwork:*

The American Numismatic Society, New York (pp. 35, 111)

The Ayasofya Museum, Istanbul (pp. 272, 313)

The Ayasofya Museum, Istanbul, and the Byzantine Institute of
America (p. 185)

Bayerische Staatsbibliothek, Munich (p. 368)

Les Belles Lettres, Paris, and Walter de Gruyter, Berlin (p. 166)

Biblioteca Apostolica Vaticana (p. 296)

Biblioteca Apostolica Vaticana and the Dumbarton Oaks Collection,
Washington, D. C. (p. 336)

Biblioteca Estense, Modena (pp. 164, 209, 343, 363)

Biblioteca Nazionale di San Marco, Venice (pp. 231, 259)

Bibliothèque Nationale, Paris (Frontispiece, pp. 284, 295, 389)

The British Museum and Routledge & Kegan Paul, London (p. 418)

The British Museum and Spink & Son Ltd., London (pp. 142, 155,
211, 282)

The Byzantine Museum, Athens (p. 400)

Deutsches Archäologisches Institut, Berlin (pp. 112, 422)

The Dumbarton Oaks Collection, Washington, D. C. (p. 322)

Paul Elek Productions Ltd., London (p. 114)

The Metropolitan Museum of Art, New York (Bequest of Mary
Clark Thompson, 1926) (pp. 11, 108)

Musée du Louvre, Paris (p. 406)

Routledge & Kegan Paul, London (p. 351)

TO

THE GENTLE MEMORY

OF MY WIFE,

Kitty Dallett Franzius

Acknowledgments

To A PERSON who prefers to remain unnamed and to whose good taste the book owes much I am deeply indebted and most thankful for freely given time and criticism.

I am also grateful to Rachel Whitebook of Funk & Wagnalls for many helpful suggestions, and to librarians and libraries on both sides of the Atlantic.

E.F.

Foreword

DESPITE the title of this work, there never was a Byzantine Empire. The body politic whose capital was on or near the Bosporus between 330 and 1453 was the Roman Empire. Descended from a state reputedly founded in 753 B.C. on the left bank of the Tiber, her basic ideal of government derived from Julius Caesar, whose title Emperor expressed the unlimited nature of his authority.

As her borders shrank, the Empire came to be largely Greek-speaking. Yet to her last day her Emperor and her citizens called themselves Romans, and when the Turks seized her land they named it after her—Rum in Asia and Rumelia in Europe. Because of the universal connotation of the word *Roman*, the Empire's foes in the West preferred to call her Greek. Historians have often followed their example or used the term *Byzantine*. As a result, the Empire's continuity, place in history, and relationship to the West are often misunderstood. This book is a modest effort to place in perspective the Roman Empire during the eleven centuries when her capital was in the East.

In referring to emperors who were the first or only members of their family to wear the purple I have usually employed their surnames. This is not meant to reflect on the legitimacy of their title as did the enemies of Napoleon I in calling him Bonaparte or preferably Buonaparte, but because such names as Tzimisces, Vatatzes, or Paleologus seem more readily distinguishable than John I, John III, or Michael VIII. As for proper names and orthography, as far as possible the simpler and more familiar forms are used. This leads to some inconsistency. Thus cities, rivers, and mountains are generally identified by their modern names and regions as they were in the early Empire. Moreover, while most Greek words have been latinized (chiefly by changing the terminal *os* and *on* to *us* and *um*), occasionally it has seemed appropriate to allow the Greek form to stand. With respect to the numbers of armies and casualties, I generally report the figures that have come down the ages. The reader might bear in mind the human tendency to exaggerate such estimates. In the effort to include all the mentioned sites in the maps, noncontemporaneous names and places have often been commingled.

E.F.

Contents

xiv

Contents

Maps

Illustrations

History of the Byzantine Empire

Introduction

c. 1000 B.C.-A.D. 305

PERHAPS a millennium before Christ, Italic tribes (Nordics)[1] descended into the broad Tiber Plain and absorbed the Mediterranean natives. Calling it Latium, they became known as Latins. Generations later, kindred Sabines came down from the mountains and merged with them. In their tribal organization lay the rudiments of the Roman Republic—the annual magistrates, the council of elders, the assembly of property-owning men. They coalesced into a group of city states. Of these, Rome enjoyed a certain prominence by virtue of her possession of the Tiber ford.

In the eighth or seventh prechristian century, Etruscans, whose civilization seems to have had Levantine affinities, gained ascendancy over the Tyrrhenian littoral. In due course an Etruscan prince organized several communities into the city of Rome. A strong army was constituted. A port may have been created at the mouth of the Tiber. Greek and Etruscan artisans were attracted to the city. Industry, commerce, and agriculture flourished.[2]

SENATORIAL RULE

Five centuries before Christ, the Roman Patricians drove out the Etruscan king, restored a republic, but effectively deprived the

[1] To identify peoples consult Appendix on Races.

[2] While the present writer accepts 753 B.C., the traditional date of the founding of Rome, as an approximation, it should be noted that in 1950, after excavations in the Roman Forum, Einar Gjerstad placed the city's founding about 575 B.C.

mostly peasant Plebeians of political power. Yet, in order to secure their support in war the Patricians permitted them to elect tribunes with broad authority to defend their rights. Further concessions followed, and by 300 B.C. the Plebeians had gained practical equality with the Patricians.

This class compromise, stern patriotism, and the alliance of other Latin tribes strengthened Rome, who by fierce wars, the liberal bestowal of local autonomy, and the strategic distribution of colonies of Roman citizens by 270 B.C. brought all Italy south of the Arno under her sway.

She then challenged Carthage, the prime power of the western Mediterranean, and after a shattering quarter-century conflict annexed Sicily, Sardinia, and Corsica. Later she vanquished the turbulent Gauls in the Po Valley and subjected Illyrians on the Dalmatian coast.

In the interim, Carthage had expanded in Spain. When her young military genius, Hannibal, advanced to the Ebro, Rome declared war. In the titanic struggle that followed, Hannibal with a small force annihilated powerful Roman armies, liberating the Gauls of the Po Valley and the Greeks of Magna Graecia. Shaken as never before, the flower of her legions slaughtered, Rome threw all her vitality into the fray and invaded Africa. Hannibal returned to defend his country, only to meet defeat at Zama in 202 B.C. Carthage ceded her Spanish possessions to Rome.

Roman troops moved eastward and after four wars subdued Macedonia. The Greek states came under Roman ascendancy. The Seleucid sovereign was expelled from a large part of Anatolia and his land transferred to allies and friends of the Roman people. Egypt came under Roman influence. Carthage was destroyed, her territory becoming the province of Africa (146 B.C.).

These extensive conquests profoundly affected the Roman people. Contact with Greek individualism tended to weaken Roman patriotism. Moreover, continual warfare kept many farmers in the army for years. Often their farms had been ruined in the Hannibalic War or were absorbed by large estates worked by the slaves whom the victorious legions sent home. Slave labor and imports from Sicily, Africa, and Egypt so cheapened grain that free farmers could not compete. Many drifted into Rome and relied on the state for sustenance. Furthermore, governors, generals, publicans, and speculators exploited provinces and subject states, whose products often relieved or deprived Romans of work. Italy's natural resources were neglected. Without employment many Plebeians became penniless, while their affluent compatriots grew richer on the exploitation of the empire.

It gradually became apparent that the Senate was unfit to rule the Mediterranean World. Originally an advisory body, it had by virtue of its permanence come to dominate the annual consuls and to assume most governmental functions. It was controlled by a group of wealthy families whose members had once been consuls (many of Plebeian origin). They formed a class called noble and jealously guarded their political power.

The first serious challenge to this oligarchy came from Tiberius Gracchus, a noble who was elected tribune in 133 B.C. His assassination inaugurated a prolonged period of intermittent war between the senatorial oligarchy and the popular party as represented by the Assembly.

From the turmoil there rose a great populist leader—Gaius Julius Caesar, a Patrician and assertedly a descendant of Venus, whom he is said to have worshiped with uncommon ardor. In 58 B.C. he assumed the government of Dalmatia, the Po Valley, and transalpine Gaul. Eight years later he had subjected the Gallic tribes to Roman rule. Apparently unappreciative of this great service, the Senate named Pompey, the conqueror of an extensive area in the Levant, sole Consul and in 49 B.C. ordered Caesar to disband his army. Instead, Caesar advanced on Rome. Pompey and most of the nobles embarked for Greece.

Supreme in Rome, Caesar was magnanimous to his enemies. But his situation was precarious, for Pompey controlled most of the empire and had larger forces. Caesar moved into Spain and maneuvered his generals into submission. Then with disconcerting rapidity he crossed the Adriatic and at Pharsalus defeated Pompey. As in Rome and Spain, he pardoned his foes. Pompey fled to Egypt, where he was murdered. After settling affairs in the East, Caesar crushed senatorial armies in Africa and Spain (45 B.C.).

THE EARLY EMPIRE

Lord of the Roman World, Caesar sought to unify the many peoples who had long suffered under senatorial rule. Rome became an orderly city; deserted Italian areas and decaying towns were repopulated; banditry was extirpated; the owners of large estates were constrained to employ some free labor; colonies were sent overseas; agriculture, industry, and commerce were fostered; the calendar was revised; fiscal and judicial reforms were made; and the Po Valley Gauls were enfranchised. The romanization of Italy was completed by a uniform system of local administration, which was later to extend to the provinces, whose financial burdens were lightened and which were protected against officials, speculators, and the military. The Mediterranean World began to pass from exploitation to governance.

For this stupendous task Caesar had assumed the powers of the most important magistracies and centralized all executive authority in himself. The Senate, weakened by new admissions, decreed him life-dictator, pronounced him the father of his country, gave the seventh month of the year his name, and conferred divine honors on him. His title Imperator expressed the unlimited nature of his power and it was thought that he intended to be, like Alexander and other oriental potentates, a god-monarch, whose decrees would be sacred.[3] But in March 44 B.C., on the eve of his departure to attack the Dacians and Parthia, a group of Senators stabbed him to death in the Senate House. So died the greatest Roman, who had freely pardoned his bitterest enemies, given the Mediterranean World just, humane, and intelligent government after years of oppression, and who, had he lived, might have bound the motley races of his empire more closely together and spread Roman civilization far into the quondam realm of Alexander and into the wilds north of the Danube.

Caesar had adopted his grandnephew Octavian, now nineteen, and made him his heir. With Caesar's veterans this youth thwarted Mark Anthony, who seemed to aspire to Caesar's golden throne,

[3] Syme questions this intention. *The Roman Revolution* (Oxford, 1939), pp. 53–55.

cowed the Senate, and became Consul. But when Anthony returned with Lepidus and his legions, Octavian united with them and on the field of Philippi annihilated the assassins of Caesar and the last hopes of the senatorial party (42 B.C.). The victors divided the empire, Anthony obtaining the East, Octavian the West, and Lepidus Africa until eliminated by Octavian a few years later. In 31 B.C. in a naval battle off Actium Octavian put Anthony and the Egyptian Queen Cleopatra to flight. The East submitted to him.

Ruler of his granduncle's entire empire, Octavian in 27 B.C. professedly conveyed the Republic to the Roman Senate and People. The Senate restored it to him, hailed him Prince of the Senate and Augustus, and named the eighth month of the year after him. With control of admissions to the Senate, with the annual consuls now ornamental, and with the Assembly soon to become practically extinct, Augustus consolidated the monarchy. The main fountains of his authority were the imperium (undefined and unlimited military command) and the tribunician power. He was also supreme pontiff. Moreover, his officials were largely his own freedmen, who insensibly assumed the duties of the republican magistrates. Even governors of provinces nominally under senatorial control were accountable to him. Gradually the adopted son of the deified Caesar acquired divine honors, especially in the East, whose peoples were accustomed to semi-celestial rulers.

His long reign brought prosperity to the war-weary Mediterranean World. The provincial resources were developed and uniform land taxes were introduced. Northwestern Spain was pacified. The Roman border was pushed to the Rhine and the Danube, but the effort to stretch it to the Elbe met with shattering defeat. Augustus died in A.D. 14 and was deified by the Senate.

He had adopted his stepson Tiberius and associated him in the tribunician power and the imperium, thus assuring his automatic succession. When Tiberius died in 37, his grandnephew Caligula was acclaimed Caesar by Army and Senate. But the young man seemed unfit for the exalted station, and another power regulated the succession—the Pretorian Guard. Formerly the bodyguards of praetors (generally military provincial governors), they had been transformed into imperial household troops by Augustus and had been established in fortified barracks in Rome by Tiberius. They numbered nine thousand, were at first recruited exclusively in Italy, were commanded by the Pretorian Prefect, and were the only appreciable armed force in or near Rome. In 41 they did away with Caligula and elevated his uncle Claudius, who annexed Thrace, Mauretania, and southern Britain. Upon his demise in 54 they selected his stepson Nero, the last of the progeny of the Caesars.

The legions also turned to emperor-making and brushed Nero aside in 68. After three transitory emperors, Vespasian, the candidate of the combined forces of the East, was master of Rome and the Empire (70). A new dynasty seemed budding when his sons, Titus and Domitian, successively inherited the Empire.

But Domitian was murdered in 96, and the Senate elected the elderly Senator Nerva. Faced with military mutiny, he made the eminent general, Trajan, his colleague and heir. This compromise of Senate and Army and the adoptive system engendered an unparalleled period of domestic concord and good government in the Mediterranean World. The leveling between Italy and the provinces continued. Trajan became sole ruler upon Nerva's death in 98, drove the Dacians beyond the Carpathians, and colonized their land with Romans. Later, haunted by visions of a Roman realm reaching to the Indus, he attacked Parthia. Of his conquests he formed the provinces of Armenia, Mesopotamia, Assyria, and Babylonia. Roman expansion had reached its zenith. But the aging Empire lacked the vigor to maintain his acquisitions, and his adopted son and successor Hadrian abandoned the transeuphratan territory and permitted Armenia to have her own king.

The adoptive era ended in 180 when Marcus Aurelius left the Empire to his son Commodus. After his assassination in 192 civil war between rivals for the purple raged four years. The African Septimius Severus, governor of Pannonia, emerged victorious. He allowed frontier soldiers to live on farms with their families. This step was not taken to foster their domestic virtues, but because the insufficiency of precious metals rendered it necessary to increase the proportion of their pay in kind and to afford them use thereof in their own households. Severus' son Caracalla, who succeeded to the throne in 211, conferred Roman citizenship on all free inhabitants of the Empire, thus completing the political equalization commenced by Caesar.

After his murder in 217 the legions again turned their arms to emperor-making, while pressures on the frontiers increased. In 259

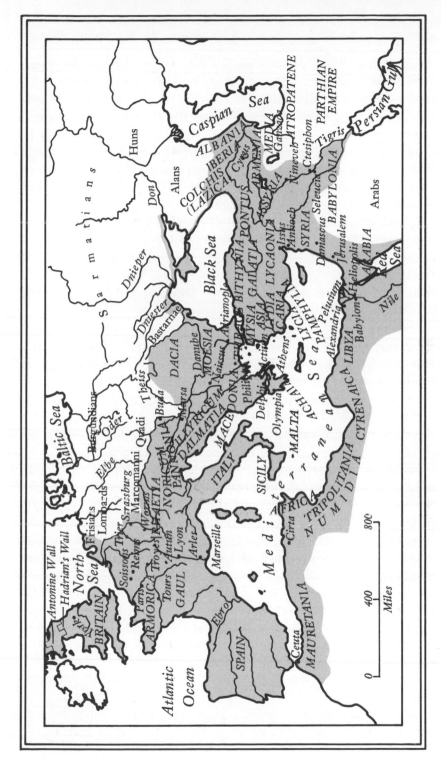

The Empire About 117

the Emperor Valerian was perfidiously captured by the Neo-Persian Sassanid ruler. Never before had an emperor fallen into enemy hands. The Sassanids seemed on the point of reviving the empire of Darius. Germanic tribes crossed the Rhine and the Danube and pillaged in Gaul, Italy, Thrace, Greece, and Anatolia. In Sicily slaves and peasants revolted. Egypt insurged. Famine and pestilence spread. The Empire seemed to be distintegrating. The legions raised a score of regional rulers, who preserved the remnants of Greco-Roman civilization against the invaders.

In 270 Aurelian became Emperor, drove the Goths over the Danube, ceded Dacia to them, expelled other Germanic invaders, suppressed the regional rulers, assumed the diadem and the title of God, and was cut down by his generals (275). The legions resumed their dual function of defending the frontiers and regulating the succession, acclaiming Diocletian in 284.

Diocletian reorganized the Empire, dividing it into smaller units, separating the civil and military authorities, and replacing many Roman institutions with Hellenistic practices. Selecting Nicomedia for his residence, he created Maximian, also an Illyrian who had risen from the ranks, Augustus and entrusted to him the government of the West with Milan as his capital. Later he adopted a Thracian officer, Galerius, made him Caesar, gave him his daughter in marriage, and assigned to him the defense of the Danube with Sirmium for his headquarters, while Maximian adopted an Illyrian officer, Constantius Chlorus, created him Caesar, bestowed on him the hand of his stepdaughter, and committed to him the protection of Gaul, Britain, and Spain with Trier as his seat. Rome sank to the level of a provincial city, her Senate to the rank of a municipal council, and the uniformity of administration planned by Caesar was finally realized.

Closing a reign that by stringent measures had restored comparative order, Diocletian and Maximian abdicated in 305 after investing two new Caesars, Maximin Daia in the East and Valerius Severus in the West, to replace Constantius and Galerius, who now became Augusti.

I

Constantine and New Rome

306–337

ATTENDING Diocletian's abdication on a field near Nicomedia in 305 was a young, stalwart, handsome, Illyrian tribune, Constantine. He was the son of the new, but ailing Augustus of the West, Constantius Chlorus, by the wife whom he had divorced upon accepting the Caesarate and the stepdaughter of Maximian. Constantine hastened to his father, who died a few months later in the palace at York (306). The legions hailed Constantine Emperor and Augustus. Galerius reluctantly accepted his new colleague but granted him only the Caesarate, conferring the title of Augustus on Severus.

The latter confronted the revolt of Maximian's son, Maxentius, in Rome and advanced on the Eternal City. Maxentius induced his father to resume office, and when Severus' troops saw their former commander on the walls of Rome many deserted to him. Severus retreated, later surrendered on condition of generous treatment, and was allowed to commit suicide.

Galerius now invaded Italy. Sixty miles from Rome he halted. Constantine had received from Maximian the title of Augustus and the hand of his daughter Fausta and had moved his forces to the Italian boundary. Galerius had no choice but to withdraw. Yet Maximian was unable to persuade the master of Gaul, Spain, and Britain to strike at his retreating line.

In Rome Maxentius broke with his father. The Pretorians, fearing the discipline of the older man, decided in favor of his son. Maximian retired to Constantine's court at Arles.

In the East the dying Galerius created his friend Licinius Augustus and resigned the Illyrian provinces to him. As a result, Daia, Caesar of the East, exacted the same title. Thus, there were now seven Augusti: Diocletian, who lived in retirement in his palace near Salona (now Split); the apparently restless Maximian; Galerius, who ruled over Greece, Thrace, and Anatolia; Daia, who governed Egypt and Syria; Constantine, the overlord of the West; Maxentius, who held Italy and Africa; and Licinius, who commanded the troops of the Danube.

At Arles, Maximian announced that Constantine had fallen fighting the Franks and resumed the imperium. Constantine returned by forced marches. His father-in-law fled to Marseille, but the troops deserted him when they saw their rightful sovereign before the ramparts. Maximian fell into Constantine's hands and reputedly committed suicide.

In 311 Galerius died. His Asiatic provinces were seized by Daia, while Thrace and Greece fell to Licinius. The latter leagued with Constantine, to whose half-sister Constantia he was betrothed. At the same time Maxentius and Daia drew together. Constantine invaded Italy with a small, mobile force, vanquished two armies, and, encountering Maxentius near the Milvian Bridge, swept him and his cohorts into the Tiber. Alone the Pretorians, sensing that this was their last battle, stood their ground, and the sinking autumnal sun shed a last ray of glory on their crumbling ranks, glittering, defiant, and arrogant to the end.

Rome hailed Constantine, and the Senate decreed the erection of a triumphal arch in his honor, stripping the Arch of Trajan of its sculptures to adorn it. Two months later Constantine went to Milan to attend the marriage of Constantia to Licinius, confer with his elderly brother-in-law, and define their attitude toward the Christians (313).

CHRISTIANITY

At this time the Christians constituted possibly a tenth of the inhabitants of the Empire. Their growth, especially in cities, had been fostered by the decay of national mythologies concurrent with the loss of independence; the yearning for a satisfying religion; the concept of universal fraternity and equality engendered by the Stoic

Colossal marble head of Constantine I (reigned 306–337)

philosophy and the Roman expansion, equalization, and unification; the dissemination of humane Hellenic ideas; the Roman peace; the peerless Roman roads; the protective Roman law and order; the widespread Greek language, which soon displaced the Aramaic of Jesus; and the religious tolerance of the pagans.

Christianity had early emancipated itself from Judaism, which would have bound it to one people, and had resisted Gnosticism, which would have sundered it into a thousand sects. Apostolic tradition and the Holy Script had been declared the sole sources of Christian doctrine. While these sufficed in the Latin West, they seem not to have satisfied the Hellenistic East. Alexandrian divines added methods and principles of an eclectic, but largely Platonic philosophy. Thus, differing theological interpretations of the Greek speculative genius ultimately obscured Christ's teachings and led to dissension, persecution, and bloodshed.

Meanwhile, Saint Paul had given a powerful impulsion to the idea of a universal church uniting all races and classes in Jesus. Moreover, with the delay of the expected Second Advent it became expedient to organize and unite the many Christian communities.

In the democratic apostolic communities there had been no distinction between laity and clergy, and for about a century after the Crucifixion any Christian might address the assemblies of the faithful. A congregation elected a council of elders, the presbyters (whence *priest*), who in turn designated a chairman, the bishop. Imperceptibly the bishops appropriated from their flocks and presbyterian colleagues the right to confirm baptisms, consecrate religious edifices, judge the faithful, ordain the clergy, and administer the Church.

Gradually the bishops of larger cities assumed such titles as High Priest, Sovereign Pontiff, Vicar of Christ, Apostolic Successor. Wielding their right of induction, they extended their authority over rural parishes by installing simple priests. The district thus created formed the bishop's diocese. His presbyterium consisted of the priests, whom he frequently convoked to diocesan assembly.

Similarly, bishops came to meet in provincial synods, to whose resolutions the Holy Ghost was believed to give the force of divine law within the province. These synods were under the presidency of the bishop of the provincial capital. The latter, distinguished by the title of Primate and later of Metropolitan, gained a certain eminence over his colleagues. His sphere came to be known as a metropolitan diocese and he began to assume authority over the bishops within it. But while Rome as the traditional see of Saint Peter and the capital of the Empire, Antioch as the site of the mother church, and Alexandria as the seat of learning were preeminent, yet at the beginning of the fourth century the metropolitan dioceses were bound only by a common faith.

The relations between the Christians and the Empire had not been friendly. Religious intolerance had been almost unknown in the Roman World. There were many gods and religions. Christians, however, indiscriminately insulted other deities. Consequently, when misfortunes befell the Empire many pagans thought that their gods were avenging Christian contumely. Thus, a calamity would often occasion an attack on Christians. It began to appear that the Christians were a disintegrating force, and some emperors endeavored to entice or force them back into the community. But with persons who welcomed martyrdom neither kindly nor harsh magistrates could succeed. Decius, Diocletian, Galerius, Daia, and Severus tried to force Christians to sacrifice to Roman gods or suffer imprisonment, torture, even death. Some performed the perfunctory ceremony. Others refused. But the Church remained a state within a state. Finally, in 311 Galerius issued an edict of toleration.

Such was the situation when Constantine and Licinius met in Milan in 313. Constantine's father had treated the Christians with consideration. Constantine himself apparently in some measure attributed his latest military successes to the Christian God. He and Licinius now annulled all enactments hostile to the Christians and gave their cult a legal status.

The wedding festivities and the imperial conference at Milan were interrupted by the news that Daia had invaded the bridegroom's territory. Licinius hastened eastward and defeated the intruder, who committed suicide. Soon, however, Licinius confronted Constantine, who tore from him his European provinces except for Thrace. This internecine war was followed by foreign invasion. Constantine drove the invading Goths and Sarmatians over the Danube, while Crispus, the son of his first nuptials and now Caesar of Gaul and Britain, thrust the Alamanni over the Rhine. In 324 Constantine defeated Licinius near Adrianople and took Byzantium with the aid of a fleet. Licinius escaped to Anatolia and at Chrysopolis lost his last battle. He abdicated and after a brief internment was killed.

Now sole Emperor, Constantine was the more concerned to preserve Christian unity. He had already tried to impose conformity on the Donatists of Africa and Numidia, who attacked the Church as lax, worldly, and corrupt. His persecution, however, had stimulated the birth of a new sect, the Circumcellions, who defended their creed with huge clubs, inflicting and receiving martyrdom with equal gratification.

In the East a more serious controversy was disrupting the Church—Arianism. Arius, an Alexandrian presbyter, contended that Christ had not eternally coexisted with the Father, but had been created by Him, that Christ was consequently not of the same essence as the Father, but of the substance of created beings. The Primate of Alexandria summoned a provincial synod, whose members were appalled when Arius asserted that Christ was not God and could, if He desired, change, as had Satan. Outraged, they excommunicated him and his partisans and imprecated his doctrines. The dissension inflamed the Levant, and the Emperor finally determined to have the whole Church decide the matter. He convoked the First Ecumenical Council in Bithynian Nice for June 325.

This assembly issued a creed declaring Christ to be of the same substance as the Father and anathematized all those claiming that the Son of God was of a different substance, or that He was created, changeable, or variable, or that "there was when He was not," or that "before He was begotten He was not," or that "He came into existence from what was not."

The Emperor assented to the creed and the anathema and banished Arius and his ecclesiastical adherents. The Council also decided that the Resurrection of Christ be celebrated on the first Sunday after the full moon following the vernal equinox and empowered the Bishop of Alexandria, whose see was still the center of science, to set the date for each year. It further decreed that at least three bishops participate in the ordination of a colleague, that no clergyman exact usurious interest, and that no single churchman have an attractive female in his house, but it rejected a proposal that the clergy be celibate.

During the following year Constantine put to death his son, the

Caesar Crispus, his second wife Fausta, and later the young Caesar Licinius. It would seem that Crispus was executed because he had been accused by his stepmother of seeking to supplant his father and that Fausta paid the supreme penalty when Constantine became convinced of his son's innocence.

The question of Constantine's character and religious views is controversial. He has been variously portrayed as a devout Christian, a syncretic monotheist, a capricious tyrant, a hypocritical *Realpolitiker* using the Christian Church to solidify his power, a genius with the vision to mold the future by fusing the Christian Church with the Roman Empire, and a benighted sovereign who opened the floodgates to the destroyers of the Empire—Christianity and the barbarians. However that might be, like so many of the military, the young Constantine apparently worshiped the sungod. He was possibly more superstitious and more interested in religion than the average pagan officer. In any event, during his advance to the Milvian Bridge and possibly as a result of the success of that campaign, he became convinced that the God of the Christians was more powerful than other gods. While his preference for Christianity dates from that period and while his children were educated as Christians, he was not baptized until the end of his life. This delay may have been for the private purpose of entering the other world purified of sin and the public purpose of not alienating his pagan subjects.

Indeed, although he increasingly favored the Christian Church, he retained the pagan title of Pontifex Maximus, which, however, involved no devotional activities.[1] He may have envisaged the ultimate fusion of the inhabitants of the realm into one religious community with the emperor as its earthly head. He may also have believed that the small body of Christian prelates, who governed units that coincided with imperial administrative districts, was an ideal instrument through which to control his subjects.

In any case, he seems to have felt responsible for the welfare of the Church, especially for its unity. Consequently, when he saw that Arianism was still strong in the East he recalled Arius and induced him to subscribe to a general creed assuaging both conceptions (328). Hoping for complete reconciliation, he sent him to Alexandria to resume his priestly duties. But the Bishop of Alexan-

[1] Jones, *The Later Roman Empire, 284–602* (Norman, Okla., 1964), I, 93.

dria was now Athanasius, young, vigorous, fanatic, and the most eminent exponent of the Nicene Creed. He refused to reinstate Arius. The peace of the Church seemed best served by removing the obdurate pontiff. The Council of Tyre condemned him for some acts of violence and Constantine banished him to Trier (335), while the Council of Jerusalem reinstalled his gaunt, ascetic rival, who was soon poisoned.

While by its marriage to the state, whose sovereign it had accepted as its head at Nice, the Christian Church was growing in terrestrial wealth and might, pagans were pathetically defending their gods from insult, their temples from destruction. They felt that, offended by Christian blasphemy and violence, their gods had departed and abandoned them to drought, famine, pestilence, locusts, and barbarians. The rivers appeared shallower, the mountains lower. Their world seemed sinking. In the general gloom sacrifice, oracle, and atonement yielded to magic, astrology, and demonism. Yet, many pagans came to believe in a universal god above all others, whom they identified with Constantine's supreme deity.

NEW ROME

Rome was too far from the threatened northern and eastern frontiers to direct their defense efficiently, and Constantine considered Sofia, Naissus, Salonica, ancient Troy, and Chalcedon, but finally chose Byzantium as the new capital. Her transformation proceeded rapidly and in May 330 the birth of New Rome or Constantinople was solemnly announced.

This peninsula was already occupied when Megarians, led by the eponymous Byzas, colonized it about 650 B.C. Because of its ichthyic abundance the river became known as the Golden Horn and the exportation of salt fish soon rendered the settlement prosperous. The Byzantines fell under Persian sway about 500 B.C., then joined the unsuccessful Ionic insurrection, and abandoned the city to the avenging Persians. But after the battle of Plataea in 479 B.C. the Spartan King Pausanias ejected the Persians and recolonized Byzantium. Later the city became allied to Athens and again leagued with her in 340 B.C. to repel Philip of Macedon.

During Philip's investment a sudden nocturnal coruscation is said

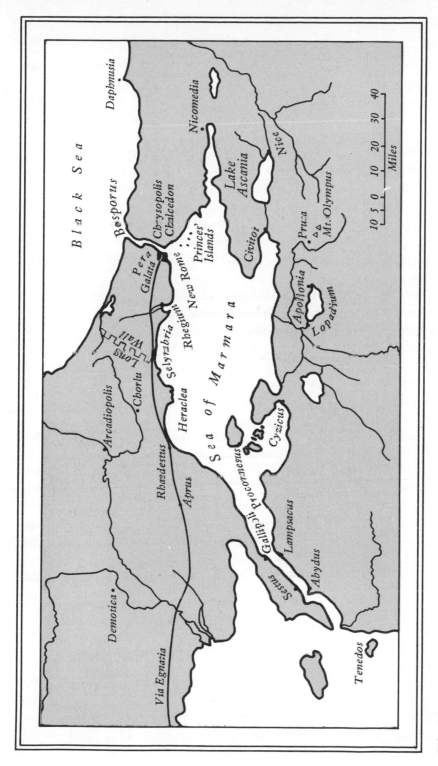

The Marmaran Area

to have revealed his movements and thus saved the city. This op-
portune phenomenon was attributed to the favor of Hecate, in com-
memoration of whom Byzantium adopted the crescent moon as her
emblem. When about 200 B.C. Roman arms appeared in the Levant,
Byzantium became an ally of the Roman People, who gradually
abolished her privileges. But the loss of independence did not affect
Byzantine prosperity, based on fish and tolls. In A.D. 193 the city
espoused the cause of Pescennius Niger, whom the Eastern legions
had elected Emperor and opposed to Septimius Severus. Though
Niger was defeated and killed, the town still bearded the harsh African, who captured it after a three-year siege and razed its cyclopean
ramparts. Later he erected baths, an amphitheater, and a hippodrome.

While Constantine was besieging the rewalled city in 324 he had
occasion to appreciate its almost impregnable site, the deep, sheltered harbor of the Golden Horn, the plethora of fish, the healthful
breezes, the natural control of the Black Sea trade, and the propin-
quity to the troublesome Goths and Persians. He attributed his
selection of the city as his capital to a divine command and in
marking the site of a new wall affirmed that he was following the
steps of an invisible guide.

New Rome's political and ecclesiastical focus was the Augustaeum, a marble forum named after a statue of the Emperor's
mother, the Augusta Helena. From its Golden Milestone imperial
distances were computed.

On the southern side of the Augustaeum an imposing bronze
portal, the Chalke, gave access to the Great Palace, whose buildings
(three distinct groups, the Chalke, the Sacred Palace, and the
Daphne) and gardens sloped gently to the Bosporus.

Also on the southern flank of the Augustaeum lay the popular
pivot of the city, the Hippodrome, begun by Severus in 203 and
completed by Constantine. On its east side was the Kathisma, the
imperial tribune with a raised throne. From here the Emperor could
view the U-shaped race course, the tiers accommodating a hundred
thousand persons, and the promenade at the top. He could be in the
midst of his people, yet not at their mercy, for the Kathisma could
be reached only by a circular stairway from the interior of the
Palace. Renowned relics of Antiquity, such as the horses of Lysippus, embellished the Hippodrome. On the spina, a low wall extend-

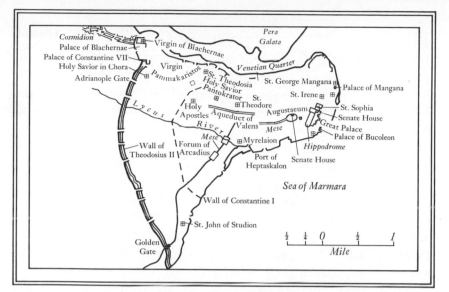

New Rome

ing lengthwise in the middle of the race course, stood among other ancient survivals the bronze, spiral, serpent-headed column dedicated to Apollo by the Greek states after they had repelled the Persians. For eight centuries it had bestridden a sacred rock in the Temple of Apollo at Delphi. Cavernous exhalations had reputedly passed through its hollow interior to convey ambiguous Apollonic oracles to the Pythian priestess, seated above on a golden tripod.

On the eastern side of the Augustaeum, adjoining another palace wing, stood an apsed basilica—the Senate House, for Constantine's son Constantius II established another Senate in New Rome.

On the northern side of the Augustaeum was rising the basilical foundation of the first Church of the Holy Wisdom, Saint Sophia, a name agreeable to both pagans and Christians.

From the Augustaeum the Mese (Middle), the main artery of the capital, led through marble arcades to the colonnaded, elliptical Forum of Constantine, the business center of the city, where the Senate had another theater. Here was a porphyry column. Within its high white marble pedestal were a number of charms to protect the new capital, reputedly the adz with which Noah had constructed the ark, the palladium of Old Rome, the alabaster box of Mary Magdalene, and wood of the crosses of the thieves crucified with Jesus. Standing on the column 120 feet above the ground was a colossal bronze Apollo, said to have come from the genial hands of

Phidias. But Apollo's graceful anatomy was now surmounted by the crowned head of Constantine.

North of the Augustaeum was another basilica, the Church of the Holy Peace, Saint Irene, a name also acceptable to pagans and Christians. Two miles westward, just within the Constantinian Wall, stood a basilica soon to be renamed Church of the Holy Apostles in honor of the supposed remains of a number of apostles enshrined under the altar. Adjoining it was a round mausoleum for the corspes of Constantine, his successors, and the New Roman patriarchs.

Other churches, academies, tribunals, theaters, aqueducts, art treasures, public halls, sumptuous domiciles, palatial reservoirs, and powerful walls (except, for the present, on the Golden Horn, whose mouth was blocked by an enormous chain connecting large wooden blocks) adorned and fortified the city.

Such in brief was the new capital, whose creators sought to imitate the antique. Roman architects had combined the Greek column and entablature with the Etruscan arch and vault. With the arch wide spaces could be spanned without multiplying the points of support, while the use of pozzolana (a volcanic ash, which, mixed with lime, gives a cement of great cohesion) rendered possible vast vaults and domes. Upon brick and cement kernels of imposing proportions was plastered a profusion of decorative materials— porphyry, jasper, agate, marble of all colors, gilt, bronze, frescos, mosaics, and ornamental columns. It was this massive imperial pomp that Constantine impressed on New Rome. Roman sculpture too had insensibly lapsed from the natural and organic into the monumental and architectonic. Even the once expressive busts of the emperors were no longer portraits but monuments.

Letters had become generally turgid, and political orations had degenerated into panegyrics of the monarch in a world that seemed to feel old and to yearn for the heroic age of Hellas. Latin was generally spoken in the western part of the Empire, Greek in the eastern. Yet the Egyptian and Syrian masses clung to their native tongues, while in Gaul some Celtic was still spoken, notably in the Armorican peninsulas. Here in the depth of night in forest recesses furtive descendants of the once powerful Druids still practiced primeval rites. Crushed by the incoming Roman civilization and exorcised by the Christian Church, they blended into the giants and fairies of the Middle Ages.

While in Old Rome gratuitous food, wine, games, and grandiose structures still left the populace the delusion that it ruled the world, in Athens political turmoil had yielded to academic acrimony. Here amid the graceful monuments of a vanished era students from all parts of the Empire participated in scholastic brawls and partook of the learning that the city of Pericles still had to offer. Egypt's venerable monuments and Alexandria, the center of Hellenistic civilization, still attracted scholars and travelers. But the Egyptians were ever ready for obstinate revolts and were generally disliked throughout the Empire.

THE EMPEROR

Although the Empire had developed in to an autocracy, her emperors were not automatically hereditary. If an emperor wished to assure the succession of his son or another he created him Caesar or preferably Augustus. This designated heir acceded to the powers inherent in his title upon the death of his predecessor. In the absence of such an heir the army (generally represented by the guards in the capital) usually proclaimed the new sovereign, the Senate (now consisting largely of imperial officials) concurred in the choice, and the people acclaimed him in the Hippodrome. These bodies resigned to the monarch complete executive, legislative, and judicial authority. Despite this elective process the Christian emperors were not responsible to their subjects but to God, Whose viceregency they claimed.

Pre-Aurelian princes had generally followed Octavian's tactful example and hidden their absolutism behind republican offices. Now, on the contrary, with Sassanian ostentation the emperors sought by despotic divinity to overawe their subjects and, above all, their soldiers, who had so often challenged imperial authority. Diocletian had deified himself with the almighty denomination of Jove; Constantine contented himself with the attributes of the sun god. His head was encircled by a costly diadem, in portraiture even by a nimbus. A silken, gem-studded robe covered his exalted corporeity. Eunuchs, chamberlains, and courtiers encompassed his sacred person. Whoever approached his divine presence was obliged to kneel and permitted to draw the edge of his purple raiment to his lips.

BUREAUCRACY

Court Officials

Court ministers and other personages formed the emperor's council. The most considerable court minister was the Master of the Offices, who received petitions and requests for audiences; conducted the imperial correspondence; administered the arsenals, the postal system, and the extortionate secret service; commanded the palace bodyguard; and appointed the palatine servants.

The Quaestor of the Sacred Palace, generally a man of juristic talent and eloquence, drafted imperial laws.

The Count of the Sacred Largesses received the revenue and disbursed donatives to the army (whence his title).

The Count of the Private Estates attended to the crown property.

The castrated Grand Chamberlain headed a host of emasculated palace menials as well as the Decurions and Silentiaries, whose functions were to guard the monarch and preserve silence in his august vicinity.

Administrative Officials

When emperors took the Roman government from the Senate they placed their slaves and freedmen in administrative control. Even after Hadrian had opened the bureaucracy to the equestrian order (wealthy businessmen) personal service to the emperor remained its motivating purpose. With the admission of the equestrians, however, the civil service grew into a mighty, independent organ of state, whose permanent power was comparable to that of the army. It tended to be conservative and usually maintained a high level of corruption despite vehement edicts of the emperors. Under its weight municipal liberties and institutions gradually suffocated.

The civil administration of the Empire was now divided into about a hundred provinces under governors, who had often purchased their post. Groups of provinces formed twelve dioceses headed by vicars. Superposed on the dioceses were four prefectures, each under the administrative, judicial, and fiscal control of a pretorian prefect, now divested of military command.

In deference to the dignity of Old Rome she was allowed to retain a city prefect, who held the civil and feeble military puissance of the Tiber city. In 359 New Rome also received a city prefect, whose authority was less extensive than that of his Old Roman colleague.

Decorative Officials

The culminal decorative officials were two January Consuls, who gave their names to the year, presided over the Senate, defrayed public games, and were relieved some months later by substitute Consuls.

Of less dignity were the praetors, whose duties were to provide popular divertissement from their own purses and contribute to municipal constructions in course. This ruinous office was inflicted on members of the senatorial order and was required of senators' sons entering the Senate. Praetors were appointed a decade in advance, ostensibly to afford them ample opportunity to protest against the unwanted honor, actually to enable them to gather the necessary funds. Possibly ten years were required to locate a diffident nominee.

The senatorial order, from which most decorative dignitaries were drawn, consisted of several thousand persons diffused over the Empire. It formed a landed aristocracy of wealth and office. Some senators inherited the distinction; others attained it because of high office or rank. Senators were exempted from municipal taxes and subjected to a land assessment more in keeping with their extensive domains. They were, furthermore, constrained to make sizable donations to the monarch on festive occasions, which could easily be multiplied. In the days of the senatorial oligarchy senators had lavishly entertained the public and then recouped their fortunes in the provinces. The first privilege still remained, for if a praetor was unable to sustain his burden the senators were obliged to assume the liability, but senatorial spoliation of the provinces had long since lapsed.

From the senatorial order the city prefects of Rome and New Rome annually selected a hundred persons to deliberate in the senate houses. While a senatorial decree required the sovereign's assent, he often preferred to have the Senate enact unpopular laws or issue mandates that might make him appear petty or vindictive.

Constantine opened to senators many administrative posts from which they had been excluded. Thereafter the equestrian order insensibly disappeared.

The glamor of office in the court, administrative, or decorative service was enhanced by a series of titles, such as Patrician (progeny of the original Patricians having virtually vanished), Illustrious, Most Distinguished, Consular, etc.

ARMED FORCES

The Roman army of the fourth century was not the disciplined, flexible, endurant force that Caesar and Trajan had led from victory to victory. During the long period of internal peace in the second century Romans had grown to dislike the military career. Moreover, the long, voluntary enlistments in the relatively small army had rendered it unnecessary for most citizens to perform military duty. Only when applications lagged had conscription officers proceeded to compulsory enrolments, and such was the Roman aversion to military service that tattoo marks were necessary to discourage desertion.

Consequently, during the third and fourth centuries the Roman armies filled with barbarian offspring and even with Germans from beyond the borders. But the Germans would not submit to discipline, and the iron training and brilliant battlefield evolutions that had brought triumph to Roman arms from the Grampian Hills to the Nubian Desert disappeared. Moreover, when Constantine gave barbarians high military posts, Roman strategy, which theretofore had given Rome an immeasurable advantage over barbarians, also vanished. The Roman army was germanized. The soldiers were permitted to marry and their families were often allowed to follow the train. The fierce barbarian dragon replaced the martial Roman eagle, the raw German battle-cry supplanted the shrill Roman trumpet, the long German sword superseded the short Roman gladius. Only the hovering shadow of Roman training gave the imperial barbarians a degree of superiority over the kinsmen they combatted. Hence, it was necessary to enlarge the army to offset its decline in efficiency, and soldiers' sons were obliged to follow the military vocation.

The army of the fourth century was divided into guards, reserve, Borderers, and Federates.

1. The Federates were foreign tribes in Roman pay, who fought under their own chiefs, in their own manner, and dwelt near the boundaries that they were to protect.

2. The Borderers, who numbered about 250,000 foot and 100,000 horse, were enrolled for twenty-four years and occupied camps, forts, watchtowers, blockhouses, fleets, bridgeheads, sometimes their own huts, houses, or towns on the Roman confines.

3. The reserve troops (or comitatenses) totaled about 150,000 infantry and 50,000 cavalry, were enlisted for twenty years, and were stationed in cities. They received higher emoluments than the Borderers and fought the wars of movement. The foremost regiments enjoyed the invidious ascription of Palatine, or in the case of exclusively barbarian formations, Palatine Auxiliaries. The latter, mostly Germans, were the best troops in the army.

4. The palace guards were also officers' seminaries. There were:

(a) A few thousand mounted Protectors, consisting of exceptionally meritorious veterans and sons of higher officers, who carried golden lances and gem-studded shields.

(b) The Domestics, both foot and mounted. They were young men of eminent and generally military birth, who gradually replaced the Protectors. Veterans ceased to be enrolled and entrance became emptorial. At the head of this corps was the Count of the Domestics, an important officer. If a Domestic took the field, he was commissioned tribune, prefect, prepositus, or, with an independent command, count.

(c) The 2500 mounted Scholarians, who were formed by Constantine to replace the Domestics when absent on duty and were under the control of the Master of the Offices. They were selected for stature, courage, strength, and manly beauty and were mostly Germans. In their midst the Emperor could with comparative impunity charge into enemy ranks.

(d) The Candidates, so called from their white embroidered

uniforms, who came into being soon after the death of Constantine and were also mostly barbarians.

The imperial army was commanded by thirty-five dukes and higher ranking counts, who were subordinate to master generals. The latter commanded the military contingents of one or more dioceses and obeyed two Master Generals in the Presence, who acted as war ministers.

The declining ability to use large numbers of men with tactical address brought a decrease in the size of military units. The old legions of six thousand men were broken into units of five hundred, a thousand, or fifteen hundred men. Military commanders were dependent on provincial governors for their food supply, for if Germans in high military posts gained a commensurate civil power the Empire would be in their hands.

Of the Roman navy little is heard. Three and a half centuries passed between the battle off Actium and the struggle for Byzantium in 324 without a naval encounter. The Mediterranean was a Roman lake and a navy was needed only for police purposes. Rivals for the Empire decided the issue on land, and when Constantine and Licinius fought for Byzantium each had to construct a fleet. This was now easier, for since the defeat of the large triremes of Anthony and Cleopatra by Octavian's lighter vessels in 31 B.C. the trireme had gradually been supplanted by smaller galleys. Such was the Roman contempt for the navy that the light Roman galleys of thirty to fifty oars that patrolled the Channel, the Rhine, the Danube, the Swiss lakes, the Gallic rivers, and the Mediterranean were classed with the Borderers.

TAXES

Since the reign of Augustus there had been an insufficiency of precious metals. Nero began debasing the coin. The practice gradually increased and resulted in economic chaos. Before the middle of the third century the government refused to accept its own specie in payment of taxes. Contracts based on currency were of little value, and the economy of the Empire stagnated.

Nor was Constantine able to restore a unified, elastic, stable currency. He issued the solidus, weighing $\frac{1}{72}$ of a gold pound, which was bought and sold as a commodity with devalued silver and copper coin. Since, however, the foreign commerce of the Empire was small in comparison with her domestic trade, the inflation of money was felt mainly by importers of luxury products (gems and spices from India, rugs and eunuchs from Persia and Armenia, incense and aromatics from Arabia, silks from China, amber from the Baltic, etc.), who were obliged to pay for their purchases in pure gold and silver coins.

Because of the distrust of its own currency the Roman government assessed a large part of its taxes in kind. To simplify the apportionment Diocletian and Constantine enacted laws astricting their subjects to their lands or their occupations. Under the constant pressure of diminishing population and declining prosperity Constantine even gave landowners the right to chain their free tenants to their fields. Moreover, to pay for his large civil and military establishments, his personal indulgences to the army, his apparent laxness with corrupt officials, his new capital, and his subsidies to the Christian Church, Constantine increased the already heavy taxes.

The turmoil of the third century had depopulated large areas of the Empire and harsh taxes brought a further unpeopling. Many farmers fled. Those who remained tended to have fewer children. Yet, while the population and consequently the worth of the land dwindled, taxes were not reduced and weighed more heavily on the survivors.

The middle class was also weakened. The individual who had some wealth was forced into the municipal council, where he and his colleagues were obliged to pay the defaulted taxes of their districts. If a councilor was unable to contribute his share he was first tortured to ascertain whether he had hidden assets, then frequently put to death. Many taxpayers fled to the barbarians, the mountains, the clergy, the masses of the capitals, or to that favored of all havens, the divine hierarchy of corrupt officialdom.

NEIGHBORS

In Britain, Picts harried Hadrian's Wall.

Of more vital import to the Empire were the Germanic tribes, who from the mouth of the Rhine to that of the Danube continually threatened the peace. The barriers that the Empire had erected along these rivers had halted the westward and southward expansion of the West German tribes, who in the fourth century were loosely divided into Alamanni, Franks, Frisians, Saxons, Thuringians, Bavarians, and Lombards. Their growing numbers seemed to render inevitable their continued assault on the Empire with its fertile fields.

While the West Germans had turned from hunting and herding to husbandry to find sustenance in a restricted area, the East German tribes beyond the Oder continued their semi-nomadic existence. Enslaving wild Slavs or driving them into the marshes, they had gradually spread from the Baltic to the Black Sea. They included the Bastarnae, the Gepids, the Rugians, the Heruls, the Scirians, the Vandals, the Burgundians, and the Goths.

The Goths had reached the Black Sea in the second century and had gradually divided into an eastern (the Ostrogoths) and a western branch (the Visigoths), separated by the Dniester. It was probably the pressure of this movement that threw other Germanic tribes against the Danube in the reign of Marcus Aurelius. The Visigoths entered Roman history with violence when they annihilated a Roman army under the Emperor Decius near the mouth of the Danube in A.D. 251. Twenty years later Aurelian ceded Dacia to them. Under Constantine they became Roman Federates, guarded the Danube boundary, and gradually took to husbandry, while the Ostrogoths extended a vague, transitory dominion from the Black Sea to the Baltic.

Continual fratricidal warfare, fomented by Roman gold and intrigue, sapped the Germans' strength. But their growing numbers could no longer find sustenance in their rigorous northern haunts and some tribes were permitted to settle within the Empire and form living barriers against their kin.

Behind the Germans the mixed Sarmatians roamed fretfully over the steppes and beyond them lurked the Huns.

The southern boundary of the commonwealth was protected by the Saharan sands. Only Egypt suffered from Nubian inroads. The disunited Arabian tribes were innocuous.

But in the East the Empire faced a state that also claimed world dominion, the Neo-Persian Sassanian empire. In A.D. 226 the lord of a small Persian state and a descendant of Sassan had overthrown the

Parthians and proclaimed himself King of Kings of the Iranians. But the world had changed since the days of the ancient Persian empire. In the East, Kushana blocked advance to the Indus, while in the West the Romans had penetrated into northern and western Mesopotamia and exerted their influence over Armenia. But the strength of the Sassanid realm lay in the fact that its inhabitants were predominantly Iranian. It was thus essentially a national state. Imbued with the ancient Iranian religion of Zarathustra, the Sassanids entrenched the priestly caste, the magi. Religious intolerance followed. Moreover, the Persian empire was weakened by its powerful aristocrats. Not only was the suzerain largely dependent on them for the administration of his state, but his army consisted mainly of nobles with their retinues. Nevertheless, the Sassanids did not hesitate to engage the compact Roman armies in frequent hostilities, often for hegemony over Armenia.

This mountainous country, whose fertile valleys connect the Iranian Plateau with the harbors of Anatolia, is a conjectural site of the Garden of Eden (on the Araxes) and the supposed resting place of Noah's Ark (on Mount Ararat). It was originally inhabited by Khaldians (Armenoids of the Alpine race, who are noted for the size and curvature of their noses). At an uncertain date, Nordic Phrygians seem to have mingled with them. About 700 B.C. the possibly Iranian Cimmerians invaded the country and merged with the natives. The Armenian nation was born. A century later the Armenians accepted Median ascendancy. The name *Armenia* occurs for the first time in 521 B.C. when the nation was under Persian dominance. But whether under Persian, Seleucid, Parthian, Roman, or Sassanid suzerainty, the Armenians generally had autonomy and their own dynasties.

SUBDIVISION

In 332 Constantine expelled the Goths over the Danube. He also settled in the Empire three hundred thousand Sarmatians, who had been afflicted by a slave rebellion. He divided the Empire among the three young sons of his second nuptials and two nephews, allotting to the Caesar Constantine II Britain, Gaul, and Spain; to the Caesar Constans western Illyria, Italy, and Africa; to the

Caesar Constantius II Syria and most of Anatolia; to his nephew Dalmatius the Caesarate and the future dominion of the greater part of the Balkan Peninsula, which during his lifetime he retained as his own especial sphere; and to his nephew Hannibalianus northern Anatolia with the hand of his daughter Constantina and the titles Nobilissimus and King of Kings of Armenia and other areas.

Sensing his earthly end, Constantine was baptized by the Arian Bishop of Nicomedia. Then, clothed in shining white, he died in May 337 and was enrolled among the gods by the Senate and among the saints by the Church.

II

Christians and Pagans

337-399

FROM the turmoil of the third century and the stabilization of Diocletian and Constantine there had emerged an Empire with a Sassanian court, a barbarian army, a Romano-Hellenistic bureaucracy, an enthralled population, expanding Christianity, declining paganism, vestigial Romano-Hellenistic culture, and a pentarchic sovereignty.

The last feature was soon altered. Constantine's nephews Dalmatius and Hannibalianus and their adherents were murdered, and his three sons partitioned the Empire. Constantine II retained the West, Constantius II the East, the adolescent Constans a middle monarchy. Over him Constantine II declared his guardianship. The stripling did not appreciate this tutelage, and Constantine decided by way of correction to appropriate part of his possessions. He crossed the Alps and was killed in an ambush. His realm was annexed by the youthful Constans. Thus, in the spring of 340 Constantine's quintuple legacy was shared by Constans, who ruled the greater part of the Empire, and Constantius II, who held Thrace and the East.

The reign of Constantius II, who had a long torso, short legs, and solemnly spoke of himself as "My Eternity," was disturbed in 338 when the Persian potentate Shapur II (crowned several months before birth in 310) opened hostilities, threatening Roman influence in Armenia and Roman rule in northwestern Mesopotamia. This fertile tract between the Armenian mountains and the desert bay formed a corridor. The empire that controlled it with the puissant city Nisibis could easily attack the other and with equal facility prevent invasion. Constantine I had perhaps destined his nephew, the King of Kings Hannibalianus, to supplant the Sassanid dynasty and link Persia to the Empire. But his death and the ensuing blood-bath of the imperial family had probably animated Shapur to assail the Empire.

The annals of the long war that followed reveal the deficiencies of the opposing monarchs. Shapur would open the season by invading Roman Mesopotamia, squander his might against the walls of some city or fortress, and withdraw upon Constantius' tardy advance. The latter would then cross the Tigris and devastate Persian territory. Occasionally an indecisive battle would occur, for Shapur lacked the strength to exploit a victory, while Constantius seemed chiefly concerned to preserve his army, the mainstay of his throne.

In 350 Shapur, strengthened by the alliance of vanquished neighbors and the rise of a usurper in the Roman Empire, made a great effort to conquer Roman Mesopotamia. He captured several Roman forts and began the siege of Nisibis. On this populous Hellenistic city, which had twice repulsed him, he determined to visit a wrath worthy of the Brother of the Sun and the Moon. A river that flows through the city was dammed below it. Swollen by melting Armenian snows, it soon encompassed the walls. A fleet armed with catapults attacked but was beaten back. Yet the ingenuity of the King of Kings was not exhausted. He dammed the river above the city and when a large mass of water had collected opened the floodgates. Under the impact of the onrushing waters a portion of the ramparts collapsed. Shapur hurled cavalry, elephants, and archers at the breach. It was stoutly defended by the Roman garrison and even more effectively by mud and water, which soon transformed the assailants into a melee of struggling men and beasts. When the next day dawned the Equal of the Stars was enraged to see a new barrier rising in the gap. He butchered a few of his satraps and lifted the siege to defend his northeastern frontier against Sarmatian invaders, having lost four months and possibly twenty thousand men. Upon his departure Constantius arrived to recompense the valorous Nisibians with his august presence.

Meanwhile, events in the West had led Constantius II to feel that his sacred person would be more useful on the Save than on the Tigris. Constans had in 350 succumbed to Magnentius, a handsome, half-barbarian general, who had been acclaimed Emperor at Autun. Gaul, Spain, Britain, Africa, and Italy had recognized him, while the Illyrian legions had elevated their elderly commander Vetranio.

Apparently Vetranio had accepted the imperial regalia only to preserve the Pannonian and Illyrian forces for the Flavian dynasty. He received a diadem from Constantina, sister of Constantius II and widow of Hannibalianus. When Constantius arrived a dramatic comedy was arranged. On a broad field near Naissus, in the presence of the associated armies Constantius made an address of such touching eloquence that Vetranio's legions, whose most voluble members had been well paid, vociferously acclaimed the son of Constantine unique Emperor. Vetranio, ostensibly yielding to his troops' wishes and Constantius' oratory, placed himself and his diadem at the exalted feet of the Emperor of the East. With the sturdy Illyrian legions at his command Constantius contemptuously rejected the connubial proposals of Magnentius and prepared to contest the sovereignty of the West.

To combat a German invasion of Gaul, instigated by Constantius, Magnentius created his brother Caesar. Constantius conferred the same office, the hand of Constantina, and the surveillance of the Persian confines on Gallus, son of a half-brother of Constantine I.

With the menaced frontiers thus assured, the Eastern and Western armies met near Mursa on the Drave in September 351, thirty-six thousand men under Magnentius, eighty thousand under Constantius, who retired to a chapel. The Drave shielded a wing of each host. On the Easterners' left flank, which extended far beyond the opposing line, was massed the cavalry, several squadrons of which were heavily mailed in Persian fashion. These iron horsemen dispersed Magnentius' cavalry and wheeled against his exposed right wing. Magnentius fled. But his Germans, the flower of his army, resisted so fiercely that thirty thousand Easterners and twenty-four thousand Westerners remained on the Pannonian field.

Magnentius' offer to surrender his dominions on condition of life and liberty was rejected and he fought on. Two years later, cornered in Lyon, the loyalty of his guards wavering, he and his brother committed suicide. His head was hacked off, displayed in the provinces, and vengeance was visited on his actual and suspected adherents.

Meanwhile in Antioch, the young Caesar Gallus and his wife,

apparently intoxicated by their newly acquired power, had instituted a reign of terror, even publicly murdering an official of Constantius, who had remonstrated with them. Constantius feigned in-
dulgence and urged them to come to him, expressing friendship, his
desire to embrace his sister, and his need of the Caesar's counsel.
Constantina died traveling to her brother, and Gallus at length
commenced the journey westward. The honors accorded him diminished as the distance between him and his army increased until
at the Italian border he was deprived of the purple and his head
(354). The customary slaughter of his partisans ensued.

JULIAN

Of the Flavian dynasty there remained only Constantius II and
Julian, half-brother of Gallus. About twenty-four and of medium
stature, Julian had lost his father in the bloodbath of 337. Although
reared a Christian, he was at heart a Neoplatonist. After the execution of Gallus his scholastic beard was shorn, and Constantius replaced his philosopher's cloak with the Caesarean mantle, convey-
ing to him the burdens of the West in the assenting presence of the
troops near Milan and the hand of his sister Helena (355).

That a young man without political or military education or experience should suddenly be given the rule of Spain, Gaul, and Britain resulted from a variety of circumstances. There were simultaneous hostilities on the Rhine, the Danube, and the Euphrates. If the
armed forces needed for the western operations were assigned to a
general he might use them for his own elevation. Moreover, to
confer the Caesarate on an outsider would have violated the dynastic sentiments of Constantius and the soldiers, who venerated his
father's memory. Furthermore, Julian's frankness, awkwardness,
lack of military experience and political ambition recommended
him as an innocuous associate. Yet Constantius surrounded him
with spies, controlled his officials and generals, and limited his personal command to a small bodyguard.

Julian found Gaul devastated, depopulated, occupied by Germans, and oppressed by taxes and corrupt functionaries, while its
legions were diminished and demoralized. This challenge apparently
transformed the unworldly, stoop-shouldered student of philosophy

into an energetic general and administrator. His bravery, endurance, eloquence, and military success endeared him to his soldiers, while his relief measures, defense of the weak, and opposition to excessive taxation and corruption engaged the affection of his subjects. He discomfited an Alamannic host at Strassburg (357), restored the Rhine boundary, built a Rhine fleet, subjected the Salian Franks in the Rhine delta, and reestablished the connection with grain-wealthy Britain.

In the interim, Constantius was occupied with foreign wars. In 358 he crossed the Danube and punished the Quadi. He named a king for the Sarmatians and helped annihilate their former slaves, the Limigantes (Slavs), who during his father's reign had driven their masters from their territory between the Danube and the Theiss.

Enlarged gold solidi of Constantius II (reigned 337–361) and the bearded Julian (reigned 361–363)

The following year Shapur II invaded Mesopotamia at the head of perhaps 100,000 Persians and subject allies and besieged Amida, for whose fall he sacrificed 73 days and possibly 30,000 men. At the end of the season he recrossed the Tigris as he had twenty years before, leaving northern Mesopotamia in Roman hands.

Shapur's belligerence offered the Emperor a pretext for weakening his Caesar, whose popularity alarmed him. He commanded the best troops of the West to march to his standards, although they had enlisted only for service in the Gallic Prefecture, the home of their families, the scene of their victories, the domain of their Caesar. They surrounded Julian's palace in Paris and proclaimed him

Augustus. Julian invited his cousin to confirm his new dignity, recognized him as his senior, and requested only the privilege of appointing his own officers and officials. Constantius refused, again bribed German tribes to invade Gaul, and prepared for war. Julian secured his border, divided his available twenty-three thousand men into three groups, and in an audacious series of stratagems, forced marches, and surprise attacks advanced conquering to the Thracian Pass of Succi, where he awaited the sword or the olive branch. Constantius died and his officers acknowledged Julian sole Emperor (361).

A month later Julian entered New Rome amid jubilation, for his fame had spread throughout the Empire. He dismissed superfluous bureaucrats, palace menials, and secret agents; reduced taxes by a fifth; punished public malefactors of the preceding regime; clarified and accelerated the administration of justice; strengthened the army and the frontier defenses; and aided hard-pressed communities. He rejected the denomination of Dominus, yielded precedence to the January Consuls, attended Senate meetings, and acted in a democratic manner that was no longer understood. Nor did his asceticism enhance his standing, for while the brevity of his slumbers, the floor for a couch, the unheated rooms, his frugal meals, and his sexual abstinence might be matters of public admiration, disapproval, or indifference, his slovenly appearance degraded the purple.

Before recounting his religious labors it may be well to trace the history of the Christian Church since Constantine's death. In 338 Constantius II had been obliged by his brothers to reinstall Athanasius and other exiled Nicene bishops. The two sovereigns of the West could thus appear as champions of the Nicene Creed, which the majority of their subjects professed, and also weaken Constantius, many of whose subjects were Arians. But a council in Antioch found a creed satisfying the Nicenes, yet not offending the Arians, and again expelled Athanasius and other intransigent bishops. After Constans became master of three-fourths of the Empire, however, he convoked a council at Sardica (Sofia), which nullified the Antiochene Creed and restored Athanasius and other Nicene bishops (343). Constantius yielded and the Nicene bishops took over their sees amid violence. But when he became sole Emperor a council condemned Athanasius, who was expelled by imperial soldiers.

With Athanasius and his supporters eliminated, Constantius sought a common creed. He declared the Son to be like the Father without specifying His consubstantiality. In 359 Eastern bishops assembled at Isaurian Seleucia, while Western prelates met at Rimini, for few Levantine priests spoke Latin and almost no Occidental divines knew Greek. They were urged to sign the Emperor's new creed. After some resistance, both in the East and the West, they submitted to his wishes and the Nicene confession of faith was superseded. Thereupon Constantius forbade public pagan sacrifices and closed pagan temples.

His sudden death in 361 changed the situation. Julian, a secret worshiper of the ancient gods, proclaimed religious liberty and bid the pagans reopen or rebuild their temples. Athanasius and his supporters were permitted to return. The Christian Church was required to restore public and temple property. Its judicial authority, the tax exemption of its clergy, and its right to receive legacies were abrogated, while state grants were discontinued. Moreover, Christians were forbidden to be rhetoricians and grammarians, for Julian considered them unworthy to teach the works of the ancient Greeks, whose religion they scorned.

With the Christian Church ousted from its privileged position, Julian commenced to organize the multiple pagan cults into a unified system with a hierarchy of priests and priestesses under himself as Pontifex Maximus. He established convents and monasteries to encourage asceticism and prepare candidates for the ministry, placed public funds for charity into the hands of pagan priests, founded hospitals and poorhouses under religious supervision, and in the temples erected pulpits, whence Neoplatonists expounded their ethical views or interpreted antique myths. He hoped to revive the ancient worship of the gods and the spirit of Hellenism as he understood it. But most pagans of the fourth century did not wish to be disturbed in the placid, perfunctory fulfilment of their ancestral oblations. They were indifferent to the Emperor's fasting, minute performance of religious rituals, and sacrificial slaughter of droves of bulls in his effort to attract the attention of the gods.

Meanwhile, the fame of his arms had spread beyond the Tigris, and Shapur II sent ambassadors to him at Antioch to suggest peace. Julian elected to impose it. With nearly a hundred thousand men he crossed the Euphrates in the early spring of 363. He sent twenty thousand northeastward to join his Armenian ally Arsaces and to engage Shapur's vanguard, which had already broken into Roman Mesopotamia. With the major part of the force Julian marched southeastward. On his flank a thousand ships with provisions and siege machinery floated down the muddy Euphrates. Having crossed the Aboras, the Persian frontier, he devastated plantations, burned villages, and razed cities, butchering inhabitants who resisted and sending those who surrendered to colonize the depopulated Roman Empire.

When he reached the point where the Euphrates and the Tigris were only twenty-five miles apart he cleared for the passage of his fleet a long disused canal joining the two rivers, which Trajan had employed two and a half centuries earlier. It entered the Tigris just above the ruins of Seleucia, the quondam stronghold of Hellenism, founded by the first Seleucid in 312 B.C. and destroyed by the Romans in A.D. 164. It was now a suburb of populous Ctesiphon, which lay opposite, on the east bank of the Tigris, and was the winter residence of the Equal of the Stars. In view of the walls of this Sassanid capital Julian organized games for his soldiers. The same night he crossed the Tigris, scaled its eastern bank, and drove the Persian forces into Ctesiphon.

Since the upper Tigris was not navigable, he burned his ships and marched northward east of the river. He counted on the produce of the fertile Assyrian fields through which he advanced and on the aid of the army of Armenia, which was to cross the northern Tigris and follow the Brother of the Sun and the Moon on his march southward. The Persian host could thus be caught between two armies and annihilated. But the Persians burned their crops and left only a desert of ashes for the legions, while the army of Armenia had not even crossed the Tigris.

Hungry, oppressed by heat and insects and attacked by roving horse archers, the Romans pressed grimly forward, heartened by their Emperor, who shared their pains. On a sultry June day he was leading the van when he learned of an attack on the rearguard. Without buckling on his armor, which he had removed because of the heat, he galloped to the scene of action and put the enemy to flight. Then suddenly he fell from his horse, a javelin in his side, hurled, it was rumored, by a Christian soldier.

In his tent Julian regained consciousness, dwelt on his pleasure at passing from the physical to the ethereal realm, the innocence of his private life, the beneficence of his reign, the foreknown sacrifice of his person, and his motives for not naming a successor. He reproved the tears of his officers and spent his last hours discussing the nature of the soul with the philosophers of his entourage. About midnight the last Flavian expired.

ADRIANOPLE

Julian's officers and officials gathered and selected as his successor the pagan Pretorian Prefect Sallust, for the mostly barbarian troops had unhesitatingly accepted their leader's religion. But Sallust declined, alleging ill health and advanced age, and they chose a young guardsman, Jovian, an Illyrian Christian.

Meanwhile, knowledge of Julian's death had reached the Shah of Shahs. His hopes rose, his elephants trumpeted, his warriors attacked, but faltered before German courage and Roman discipline. Heavy losses convinced the Brother of Celestial Bodies that he could not crush the Roman army. Lest he goad them into the fury of despair, he offered free passage of the Tigris in exchange for Roman transtigran territory; a strip of Mesopotamia, including Nisibis; and liberty of action in Armenia, Albania, and Iberia.

The treaty was solemnly ratified and Jovian led his starving soldiers homeward. He conferred on Procopius, Julian's maternal cousin and the leader of the northern army, the honorific duty of conducting the imperial corpse to its resting place at Tarsus, thus removing a possible rival from his command. He announced his Persian victories to the legions of the West, restored Christianity to its favored position, and issued an edict of toleration to all Christians and pagans. In February 364, before he had reached New Rome, he died, possibly from carbon monoxide poisoning.

The military assembled at Nice and again offered Sallust or his offspring the imperial raiment. The venerable Prefect once more rejected the honor and disparaged the elevation of his inexperienced son. At length the council selected Valentinian, a stalwart Illyrian guardsman in his forty-third year. Valentinian soon conferred the Augustan cloak on his younger brother Valens, gave him the jurisdiction of the Levant, and withdrew to the Occident. Here, after years of warfare he was able to press back the perennial Germans and

The Aqueduct of Valens in Istanbul, completed about 370

reestablish the Rhine and Danube frontiers, while his generals defeated the Saxons and Picts in Britain and the Moors in Mauretania.

In the East, Procopius' relationship to Julian made him a potential rival for the scepter and consequently a hunted man. Eventually, in despair, he appropriated the supreme symbols. New Rome, the Danube provinces, and a large part of Anatolia acknowledged him, while Faustina, the widow of Constantius II, became his wife. But the intrigues of Valens' marshals ended his career.

With his crown assured, Valens devoted a desultory decade to war with Persians and Visigoths when suddenly the Visigothic problem became acute. Oppressed by a wave of Huns coming out of the East, the Visigoths obtained Valens' permission to cross the Danube and settle within the Empire. His intention to fill his shrinking army and the wasted areas of Thrace with Goths was defeated by his generals' cupidity. The Visigoths bribed the imperial officers not to disarm them as agreed. Moreover, they did not receive the sustenance that the Emperor had provided and were not moved to their destined lands. Left in possession of their weapons, detained starving near the Danube, then offered food at exorbitant prices, they became so desperate that, when the southward march finally began, a strong escort was necessary. For it the Danube forts and warships were stripped of their complements, and the Ostrogoths, also pushed by the Huns, invaded the Empire almost unhindered.

In January 377 the Visigoths reached the vicinity of Marcianop-olis. Not allowed within the gates lest they purchase food at lower prices than the imperial officers exacted, they drove the Roman force into the city and plundered the countryside. Joined by slaves, soldiers of their own race, and overtaxed Romans, they made an un-successful attempt to storm Adrianople. Thereupon their leader Fritigern decided to preserve peace with stone walls.

To combat them, Valens, who was occupied with the Persians, dispatched his veterans, who fought a sanguinary but indecisive battle near the lower Danube. Joined by Ostrogoths, Sarmatians, and Huns, the barbarian host grew. The Romans retreated.

Valens appealed for help to his adolescent Western colleague and nephew Gratian, who with his infant half-brother Valentinian II had succeeded their father in 375. But Gratian was occupied with the Alamanni in the Black Forest and sent only his renowned gen-eral, Sebastian. After the latter with a picked force had inflicted a number of defeats on scattered barbarian bands, Valens, insulted by crowds in the Hippodrome for his inaction, took the field.

Although Gratian was hastening to his aid, Valens engaged the barbarians north of Adrianople on a hot August day of 378. The imperial cavalry of the left wing was driving them back when Os-trogothic horsemen appeared from behind parched hills. They were for the first time in recorded history using stirrups. With this secure anchorage the force of their charge scattered the Roman cavalry. From three sides the Roman infantrymen were pressed into so dense a mass that they could hardly wield their weapons. Valens, Sebastian, and the flower of the legions perished. As the long summer afternoon faded and the dying legionaries writhed in dust and blood, the millenary supremacy of the infantry expired. Henceforth, until the invention of gunpowder, cavalry was to dominate.

The Goths pushed on to Adrianople, behind whose bastions the debris of the Roman army had found refuge. After a two-day as-sault Fritigern resumed his peace with stone walls. A view of New Rome's ramparts convinced him of the wisdom of this truce and he led his warriors westward. Nevertheless, the Senate instituted the massacre of thousands of Goths, many of them faithful soldiers of the Empire.

THEODOSIUS

The weight of the Empire now reposed on the youthful Gratian, the infant Valentinian II, and their aged tutor, the poet Ausonius. The appointment of an Eastern colleague seemed indicated. On an estate in Spain an eminent and handsome general, Theodosius, had lived in retirement since the execution of his father. He was recalled by Gratian and in January 379 presented to the troops at Sirmium as Eastern Emperor.

The new monarch reconstituted an Eastern army and extirpated several barbarian bands, who had dispersed to pillage the countryside. Of greater help to the Roman cause was the death in 381 of the able Fritigern. But Roman successes were soon counterbalanced by the throngs of Goths, Huns, Alans, Sarmatians, Vandals, Quadi, and Marcomanni who poured over the unguarded Danube. To expel or annihilate them exceeded the Empire's powers. Consequently, Theodosius enrolled many Goths and allowed others to settle near the lower Danube as Federates. The gradual usurpation of the European part of the Empire by Germanic tribes had begun. Yet these new settlers might also have been romanized but for the fact that they had recently become Arians, largely by the missionary efforts of Ulfilas, a Goth educated at New Rome.

Arians and all other sectaries had been expressly condemned by both Gratian and Theodosius. They had decreed that only those accepting the Nicene Creed be called Catholic Christians and their houses of worship churches. This edict was followed by the Second Ecumenical Council in New Rome in 381. It confirmed and amplified the Nicene Creed, declaring that the Holy Ghost, the Giver of Life, proceeded from the Father. It also accorded the Patriarchate of New Rome equal privileges with and a rank second to that of Old Rome. Amid the customary violence Arian prelates were unseated. Arians and other heretics were driven from their sanctuaries and deprived of civil rights.

Suddenly in Britain, a general, Magnus Maximus, arrogated the imperial devices, crossed to Gaul, and subverted the troops. Gratian was assassinated (383). The new Emperor kept peace with his two colleagues until in 387 he crossed the Alps, ostensibly to help the adolescent ruler of Italy and Africa, Valentinian II, defend his northern frontier. This son of Valentinian I, unpopular in Italy because of his Arian leanings, fled to Theodosius, who assigned him Salonica as residence. A year later Theodosius met Valentinian's beautiful sister Galla, married her, and decided to reseat his youthful brother-in-law. In two battles he defeated Maximus, who was beheaded.

Theodosius restored the Occident to Valentinian II, now seventeen, but sedulously kept him in Gaul, apparently reserving Italy for his younger son Honorius. Meanwhile, Theodosius resided in Milan. When unruly Salonicans murdered the commanding general for imprisoning their favorite charioteer, Theodosius commanded that the crowd be massacred on its next appearance at the races. Seven thousand persons were butchered. The Bishop of Milan, Ambrosius, decided to impose a public penance on the Emperor. The latter tried to avoid it, but the appearance of a large comet convinced him of the need to submit and he attended church services in the garb of a penitent.

He further abolished the Olympic Games because of their pagan association. This venerable festival, based on the principle that cultivation of mind and body pleases the gods, was believed to have been instituted by Hercules. In 776 B.C. the name of an athletic victor was first inscribed. Its fame spread beyond Elis and it became the national celebration of the Greeks, the sacred bond of their common origin, eventually their chronology. Every fourth year during the month in which the Games took place hostilities between Hellenes ceased. Even the political masters of the Greeks aspired to the Olympic olive wreath and the names of Philip of Macedon and Nero are recorded. At the last Olympiad in 393 an Armenian of the Arsacid dynasty won the olive chaplet. The abolition of the Games brought sad times to Olympia. The temple of Zeus was insulted. His famous chryselephantine statue by Phidias was taken to New Rome, where it was consumed by a great fire in 476. But sixteen centuries later the Olympiads were resumed in Athens with twelve nations of three continents participating (1896).

Meanwhile, in Gaul in 392 Valentinian II had been murdered, and the pagan Frankish general Arbogast had appropriated his domain. He draped the purple on the rhetorician Eugene, a Christian with a philosopher's beard. Since Theodosius made no move to take Italy, Eugene took possession and granted the Old Roman Senate's request to restore the ancient cult.

Aroused by the restoration of paganism, Theodosius left New Rome and crossed the Julian Alps unhindered (394). Astonished, he saw beneath him, not far from the rivulet Frigidus, the battle array of the West and a colossal Jupiter pointing an accusing golden thunderbolt at him. His consternation redoubled when he espied enemy troops on the mountain passes behind him. In this desperate situation he sent his Arian Goths forward. They could advance only in small groups and were soon surrounded on three sides by the hesperian forces. When daylight faded ten thousand had perished. During the night Theodosius bribed the detachments on the passes and at daybreak ordered the seemingly hopeless attack. As his men rushed forward to what seemed certain death, there arose behind them a strong wind that blew back on the forces of Jupiter their own spears, blinded them with dust, and rendered their shields unwieldly. Seeing therein a miracle of the Christian God, the Westerners fled to their walled camp, where they surrendered. Arbogast threw himself on his sword and Eugene was beheaded. The last hopes of paganism flickered out.

Four months later, in January 395, the last Roman Emperor to rule alone from Solway Firth to the Euphrates died of dropsy in Milan. He devised the Orient to his son Arcadius, who was seventeen, and the Occident to his son Honorius, who was eleven. To assist the young Eastern Emperor he had appointed the Master of the Offices Rufinius. As regent for the child monarch of the West and military protector of both youths he had named Stilicho, the handsome son of a Vandal officer and the husband of his niece.

Complying with Arcadius' request for armed forces to combat the Huns in Anatolia, Stilicho sent him the Visigothic Federates. But the Goths proclaimed their young leader Alaric king and commenced plundering. They eventually concentrated on the Greek cities but spared Athens, which received Alaric with honor. When Stilicho advanced to chastise the Goths he was ordered out of the East by Arcadius. Meanwhile, having ravaged the Peloponnese and traversed the Corinthian Gulf, Alaric attempted to cross the Pindus into Thessaly but was repulsed by the natives with a reported loss of three thousand men. Soon after, Arcadius created him Master General of the lands that he had just devastated.

As for the Huns in Anatolia, Eutropius, an old eunuch who had succeeded Rufinius, drove them into the Caucasus and Persia and returned to New Rome in triumph (398). The Senate erected statues in his honor and created him January Consul. But within a year a rising of mercenaries, the opposition of the clergy, and the intrigues of the Empress effected the dismissal of the efficient eunuch, who was stripped of honors and property, banished, and executed.

III

Romans and Germans

400–498

THE decline of the birthrate in the Empire resulted largely from plagues, prostitution, war losses, the abandonment of unwanted infants, the enforced celibacy of many slaves, and especially the widespread supersession of prolific free farmers by large estates run by barren slave labor.

In the second century Marcus Aurelius had allowed Germanic tribes to settle on land within the Empire to whose owners they made stipulated payments in kind. Soon many Germans were abandoning their cold and crowded homeland and streaming into the Empire to revivify the failing population and form a bulwark against their kinsmen beyond the borders. The Germans were romanized and Romans were to some extent germanized. The population increased, abandoned lands were transformed into farms, swamps were dried, wild beasts fled, and hardy recruits filled the dwindling ranks of the army. Less propitious for the Empire was the Germanic impatience of restraint, which in the third century contributed to tempestuous risings, emperor-makings, consequent invasion, and renewed depopulation. Moreover, after a few generations the newcomers also became averse to army life. Fresh immigrants were consequently introduced. But they came in such numbers that they could not be romanized and tended to germanize the Empire. Yet, even after the disaster at Adrianople Theodosius increased the rate of barbarian implantations.

As a result, in the army Illyrians yielded to Germans and Roman discipline to barbarian license. Drilling almost ceased and guard duty was relaxed. The Germans refused to wear helmets, knapsacks, or breastplates or to construct fortified camps and hardly differed from their barbarian opponents. Moreover, instead of soldier-emperors who enforced discipline, dynasts living far from camps and battlefields let matters take their course. The barbarian mercenaries came to regard the higher military posts as their domain, viewed the tax-ridden Romans with contempt, and occasionally turned their arms against them to riot and maraud. Their excesses led to a violent Romanist reaction.

VISIGOTHS

About 400 New Rome discontinued the tribute to the Visigothic Master General Alaric. After extensive devastations he traversed the Julian Alps with his whole nation and moved pillaging westward, intending to settle in Gaul. But Stilicho enrolled mixed East German tribes under Radegast, against whom he had been warring in Rhaetia, and hastened to defend Italy. A sanguinary battle, famine, pestilence, and desertions so reduced the Visigoths that Alaric withdrew. As a result of this incursion Honorius removed his court from Milan to Ravenna, which was protected by marshes, powerful walls, and access to the sea. The Gothic inroad, moreover, crystallized in the West the anti-German spirit that had swept the East. Romans enlisted.

In 405 Radegast with a host of Burgundians, Suevi, Vandals, and Alans invaded Italy. Unable to nourish it, he trisected it and advanced with the largest to besiege Florence. Stilicho drove him into the hills around Fiesole, encompassed him, slew him, starved the barbarians into submission, sold some into slavery, and mustered twelve thousand picked men into the Roman army. The two other contingents recrossed the Alps.

The following year Vandals, Alamanni, Quadi, Gepids, Heruls, Burgundians, Alans, Sarmatians, even Romans of lacerated Pannonia crossed the frozen Rhine, defeated the Franks who guarded it, and laid Gaul in ruins. Fearing that Saxons might transport the barbarians into Britain, the island troops created and murdered two emperors and finally elected a soldier named Constantinus (407). Claiming descent from Constantine I, he crossed the Channel, rallied the Gallic troops, and defeated the invaders. Barbarian bands,

Mosaic in the sixth-century church San Apollinare in Classe showing the town and port of Classis, Ravenna's seaport before the Adriatic retreated

however, still roamed the countryside. Indeed, the Burgundians became Roman Federates and in 413 founded the kingdom of Worms.

Meanwhile, Stilicho and Honorius had been planning with Alaric to detach part of the Balkan Peninsula from the Eastern realm. But Constantinus' usurpation led them to renounce the plan and devote themselves to regaining Gaul. Alaric, who had already mobilized his warriors, seized the Julian passes and demanded four thousand pounds of gold as indemnification. Stilicho favored the payment of this sum; the senators, who were to supply it, opposed it. Anti-Germanism swept Senate, court, army, people. Stilicho's officers were cut down, he was decapitated, his relatives and friends were tortured to death, and the wives and children of the barbarian soldiers were butchered (408).

Strengthened by thousands of former mercenaries, embittered by the slaughter of their families, the Visigoths marched on Rome, while Honorius fled to Ravenna. When they appeared before the walls of Rome the Senate decreed the strangulation of Serena, widow of Stilicho and niece of Theodosius. In the ensuing hysteria even pagan sacrifices were secretly permitted in the hope of warding off the barbarian force. Alaric surrounded the city and cut off the African grain supplies. At length the city of the Caesars purchased immunity with five thousand pounds of gold, thirty thousand of silver, four thousand silk robes, three thousand pieces of red leather, three thousand pounds of pepper, and the Senate's promise to urge Honorius to make peace.

Weary of wandering and recurring periods of hunger, the Gothic king desired another master generalship with the revictualment of his people provided by the imperial Prefect or border lands, which the Goths' slaves could cultivate. But safe behind the swamps and ramparts of Ravenna, Honorius, who believed that Constantinus, whom he had recognized as Emperor of Spain, Gaul, and Britain, would send aid, rejected Alaric's proposals.

Alaric consequently returned to Rome and asked the Senate to create an emperor with more pacific inclinations. After some demurral by the Senate and a display of force by Alaric, the scepter was conferred on the aged City Prefect Priscus Attalus who, though an ardent Romanist, was christened an Arian by the Bishop of the Goths. He appointed Alaric and his lieutenant Ataulf respectively Master General and Count of the Domestics jointly with two Romans and inaugurated his reign with a speech claiming senatorial authority over the entire Empire (409). When the new Emperor with a force of Goths had marched as far as Rimini, Honorius recognized him as Augustus and suggested ruling concurrently. Attalus agreed to leave him the maintenance of his court but rejected his continuance in office and invested Ravenna. In despair, Honorius besought New Rome for aid and received from his nephew Theodosius II four thousand men.

These sufficed to suppress any dissidence within the city and to man the walls against Attalus and Alaric. Receiving no more grain from Africa, which remained loyal to Honorius, they raised the siege. Yet Attalus refused to give Alaric the ships to transport a Gothic force to Africa to assure the grain supply. As a result, Alaric stripped him of the purple and engaged Honorius in negotiations, which were broken off after a perfidious attack on the Gothic camp. Unable to take Ravenna, the infuriated Goth moved on

Rome, entered the city during an August night in 410, and sacked it, but with less harshness than might have been expected. He seized all the gold and silver, but finding no food, left after three days, intending to cross to Africa. Unable to traverse the Strait of Messina, he reverted to his former plan of settling in Gaul but died near Cosenza. Captives diverted the course of the Busento, sank his body and the royal treasure into its bed, led the river back into its original channel, and were killed, lest they divulge the grave of the conqueror of Rome.

Alaric was succeeded by Ataulf, who trod impuniously on helpless Italy, while the Roman forces were in Gaul defeating Constantinus, who surrendered on a promise of personal safety and was killed. Ataulf settled in southwestern Gaul in 412 and in 414 married Placidia, his beautiful captive and the sister of Honorius. Like Alaric, he believed that the salvation of Goths and Romans lay in union but was unable to make peace with Honorius. He consequently reinvested Attalus with the supreme mantle. Honorius sent the Patrician Constantius against them. Lacking food, the Goths moved into Spain, already the prey of wandering barbarians. Attalus was captured, adorned the triumph of Honorius, was deprived of a thumb and a finger, and exiled to Lipari.

Soon after, in 415, Ataulf was assassinated and Wallia became King of the Visigoths. With famine ever threatening, he negotiated peace with Ravenna. The Romans supplied six hundred thousand measures of corn. In return, the Goths warred against the Vandal, Alan, and Suevic invaders of Spain and returned Placidia, who reluctantly gave her hand to the Patrician Constantius in 417. After two years of successful warfare in Spain the Goths became Federates and were granted a rich territory between the Loire and the Garonne, receiving a share of the land. The remainder was left in the hands of the Roman inhabitants, over whom the Goths had no legal authority.

Thus, the Empire now contained three stationary German kingdoms, the Salian Frankish and the Burgundian on the Rhine and the Visigothic on the Atlantic. This was not the union of which Alaric, Ataulf, and Placidia had dreamed, but incipient dismemberment. Yet, although Vandal-Suevic war still wasted Spain (which the Vandals were soon to abandon and where the Suevi were to form a

Fifth-century mausoleum of Placidia (d. 450) in Ravenna. The sarcophagi are said to have contained the remains of Placidia, her brother, the Emperor Honorius (reigned 395–423), and her husband, Constantius III (Co-Emperor 421)

kingdom in the northwest), these Germanic kingdoms shielded Gaul, which regained an evanescent tranquillity.

VANDALS

Constantius received the Augustan trophies and died in 421. Apparently Honorius' affection for his twice-bereaved sister Placidia was more than fraternal, and she fled to New Rome with her two children. Upon Honorius' death in 423 a minor official, John, donned the imperial raiment. With Eastern support Placidia took Ravenna by ruse in 425 and became regent for her six-year-old son Valentinian III. John's right hand was amputated. He was then exposed in the circus mounted on an ass and beheaded.

During the reign of Valentinian III two men dominated West Roman destinies—Boniface, the humane Count of Africa, and Aëtius, who in his youth had been a hostage of the Huns.

In 427 Aëtius with Hunnic auxiliaries advanced to defend Roman Gaul against the encroachments of the Federate German kingdoms. He pressed the Visigoths back from the Mediterranean and the Salian Franks into their lands on the Meuse and the Scheldt.

Meanwhile, Placidia suspected that Boniface planned to take over Africa, and Ravennese forces dislodged him. Taking advantage of the internecine strife, Gaiseric, the lame king of the Vandals and germanized Alans, crossed from Spain to Mauretania, while Moors and Donatists uprose. With the African littoral slipping from Roman rule, Placidia made peace with Boniface. It was too late. The Vandals defeated the combined forces of East and West under Aspar and Boniface. Only Carthage and Cirta remained in Roman hands.

Boniface returned to Italy, became Patrician, and was granted the military command of Aëtius. The latter declined to deliver his army. Though Boniface defeated him at Rimini, he died of his wounds. Aëtius with his Huns remained master of the Roman West (434).

Soon he called upon his faithful Hunnic auxiliaries to combat the expanding Federate Burgundians. Their king and twenty thousand warriors were slain. Thus, in 436 the first Burgundian kingdom in Gaul came to a tragic end, to be immortalized in the lay of the Nibelungen.

In 437 Valentinian III, now eighteen, went to New Rome to marry Licinia Eudoxia, daughter of the Eastern monarch, simultaneously transferring Illyrian territory to the Eastern realm, as stipulated when Theodosius II had helped his mother take Ravenna. Her regency was terminated, but the youthful Emperor did not interfere with the government of the Patrician Aëtius.

In 439 a tremor ran through the Roman World. The Vandals took Carthage. Realizing that the Atlas area was lost, Aëtius made peace with Gaiseric. To further ameliorate their relations Valentinian's infant daughter Eudocia was betrothed to Hunneric, son of the Vandal king. This required repudiating Hunneric's wife, daughter of the Visigothic king. Gaiseric decided that she had plotted to poison him, amputated her ears and part of her nose, and returned her to her father. In this unfortunate manner the potential Vandal danger was transformed into alliance and hatred was created between Goths and Vandals. Italy continued to receive grain from Africa, albeit no longer as tribute, while Vandal power spread over northern Africa and to Sardinia, Corsica, the Balearic Islands, and finally Sicily.

HUNS

The Huns, an Altaic people, are described as having small eyes, flat noses, large heads, small bodies, and bow legs. They slashed the cheeks of male sucklings to prevent hirsute growth and render their appearance martial. They often ate and slept on horseback. In 370 they swept westward into the Black Sea steppe. Within five years they had crushed the Alan realm between the Volga and the Don, enrolling some Alans and driving others to the East Germans or into the Caucasus (where as Ossetes they remain to this day); overthrown the Ostrogothic empire, enlisting some Ostrogoths and pressing others westward; and propelled the Visigoths southward into the Empire and northward into Transylvania. An attack on the Empire seemed imminent when suddenly the lunge stopped, possibly because the hordes fell apart. Nevertheless, the Huns remained the dominating people between the Caspian and the Danube.

In 433 Attila, a squat, but haughty individual with broad shoulders, a large head, flat nose, cicatrized cheeks, and small deep-seated eyes, which he would roll fiercely to inspire terror, became head of the western Huns with his permanent camp near modern Budapest. He brought Huns, Germans, and Slavs under his hegemony, even invaded the Sassanid empire, and became supreme from the Caspian to the Rhine. Lest there be any doubt as to the extent of his empire, he entitled himself "Descendant of the Great Nimrod, Nurtured in Engaddi, by the Grace of God King of the Huns, Goths, Danes, and Medes (to mention only the most important), the Dread of the World." When a Christian hermit called him the Scourge of God he delightedly added this agnomen to his collection.

In 445 he ravaged the Danubian provinces and laid the Roman East and West under tribute. Five years later his attention was

drawn to Ravenna by Honoria, the enterprising, triginal sister of
Valentinian III. Lest a husband covet the throne, she had been
obliged to remain celibate. When she accepted a lover he was put to
death and she was betrothed against her will to a harmless Senator.
In despair she appealed to Attila, who demanded her hand with
Gaul as dowry. When his bride was not forthcoming he led a host
of Huns and Germans under their own kings into Gaul (451).

Aëtius rallied the Federates—Franks, the surviving Burgundians
(who had been settled in Savoy), Celts of Armorica, and Visigoths,
the marrow of the Occident. They occupied Orleans. Unable to
dislodge them, Attila ruefully retreated. They followed. On the
plains near Troyes he turned. His Hunnic horsemen swept up the
hill against the Germano-Roman right wing under Aëtius. Theodoric, King of the Visigoths, commanding the Germano-Roman
left, charged into the invaders' right flank. Struck by a javelin, he
fell, but his warriors surged on, disrupted the Huns' right, and
broke through to the center, which under Attila's personal command was engaged with the Alan auxiliaries of the Roman center.
Oppressed by the mighty Gothic charge, Attila fell back to his
wagon camp.

When the next day dawned the once invincible Dread of the
World was at bay behind his wagons, his funeral pyre prepared.
The Goths wanted to surround and starve him into submission. But
Aëtius allowed him to escape across the Rhine, lest the Visigoths'
power be further enhanced.

Still claiming Honoria, the Descendant of Nimrod invaded Italy
the following year, wiped Aquileia from the map, but, troubled by
the twin banes of barbarian hosts, famine and pestilence, did not
cross the Po. A year later he died. Quarrels broke out between
Huns and Germans, and in a titanic struggle near the unknown
Nedao in Pannonia, probably in 454, the Germans crushed the
Huns, who fled over the Carpathians.

WEST ROMAN TWILIGHT

In 454 Valentinian III rewarded the Patrician Aëtius for his long
years' service by assassinating him personally. A half year later two
of Aëtius' German officers cut down the Emperor. Soon after, the

Vandals sacked Rome (455). Elected Western emperors succeeded one another with relative frequence but could not overcome the power of the Gotho-Suevian Patrician Ricimer. He was the successor of Stilicho and Aëtius and the restorer of Germanic influence in the imperial West, where the Romans had again lost control of the army. When Vandal raiders, who even ventured into eastern waters, seemed to require united action Ricimer appealed to the Eastern Emperor Leo for aid. Leo sent an emperor and a thousand ships, but the armada was defeated in 468. Four years later Ricimer died.

His nephew, the Burgundian Gundovald, enthroned an emperor at Ravenna (473). Leo refused to recognize him, adorned Julius Nepos with the Augustan attributes, and sent him to Italy with a military escort. Gundovald withdrew to Burgundy, but the largely East German troops under the quondam secretary of Attila, Orestes, expelled the new monarch (475). Orestes governed Italy in the name of his infant son Romulus Augustulus. Soon the Germanic troops under Odovacar slew Orestes, entered Ravenna, deposed little Romulus, and sent him to live with relatives (476).

They elected Odovacar king. The King of the Germanic troops did not sever Italy from the Empire. As the successor of Stilicho, Aëtius, and Ricimer, he merely wished to preclude the possibility of being hampered or murdered by a Western emperor. He remitted the imperial baubles of Romulus to the Eastern Emperor Zeno, whose suzerainty he acknowledged, requesting for himself recognition as Patrician in Italy. Some land was alienated for the Germanic soldiers, but in general the administration continued as before. The change of government seemed welcome to the Italians, who cooperated with the Patrician in defending Italy against Rugians and Ostrogoths.

In Gaul and Spain the transition from Roman to German rule was also moderate. The Visigothic kingdom expanded to the Rhone and to the Pillars of Hercules. The Burgundian and Frankish kingdoms spread southward. The Romans gave up some of their land, were relieved of the hated imperial tax-collectors, and lived under their own laws. In less romanized Britain, Roman government succumbed to Saxon invaders and by the mid-fifth century had vanished.

Julius Nepos, the last West Roman Emperor, ruled Dalmatia

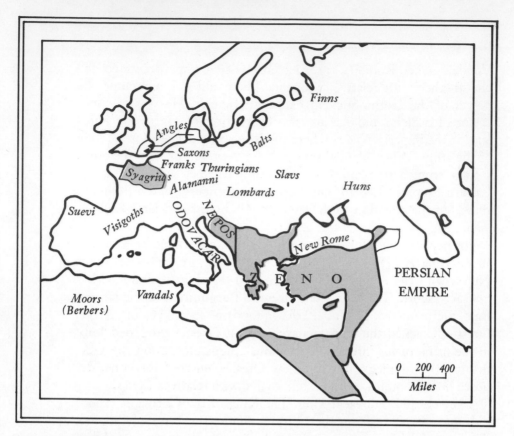

The Empire in 476

and in theory the vestige of Roman Gaul until he was murdered in Diocletian's palace in Split in 480. Dalmatia passed to Odovacar, while the few Roman provinces between the Loire and the Somme nominally reverted to the Emperor. Six years later his master general in Gaul, the King of the Romans Syagrius, was defeated near his capital, Soissons, captured, and murdered by a Frankish king, Clovis. Thus ended five centuries of Roman rule in Gaul.

The collapse of the Roman West was due to the lack of a disciplined Roman army to combat small Germanic groups or tribes. Underlying the want of an army was the absence of funds. Centuries of resistance to Germanic attacks had drained the strength of the imperial West. Indeed, the oppressive taxes imposed to maintain the armed forces required to cope with the Germans had precipitated an agricultural, demographic, and fiscal decline and led to general apathy.

Of the successor states the Frankish was the most solid. This was because, unlike Goths and Vandals, the Franks had not migrated but had simply expanded into Gaul and continued to refill their ranks with kinsmen moving westward; because their rulers had greater authority than other Germanic kings; and because, unlike the Arian Goths and Vandals, the Franks adopted the Nicene Creed and could consequently fuse with the Romans under their rule. Thus the Franks were to defeat or expel other Germanic tribes and transform Gaul into France.

EAST ROMAN REVIVAL

While the history of the Roman West was being impelled by the incoherent blows of unconnected barbarian bands, the East was following a less agitated course. Reviving Romanism bore its first fruits when Thessalians held the Pindic passes against Alaric and when in 399 Anatolian farmers ambushed and massacred plundering Ostrogothic mercenaries. The following year the anti-German Aurelian became Prefect.

Romanist rule was, however, interrupted when Gaïnas, the Gothic commander of the Anatolian regiments, marched on New Rome, replaced Aurelian with a friendly Prefect, transferred the Romanist troops to the provinces, and installed his Goths as masters of the capital and the East. But the populace armed, and Gaïnas fled with most of his Goths, leaving some to be butchered. Yet, to combat Gaïnas, who was preparing to cross to Anatolia, the Goth Fravitta was chosen. His fleet sank his kinsmen as they were crossing the Dardanelles on rafts. Gaïnas escaped, slaughtered the Roman troops serving under him, and with the surviving Ostrogoths crossed the Danube, only to fall in battle against the Huns. Fravitta, the savior of the Levant, was made Consul. Soon after, he was executed when Aurelian and the Romanist party returned to power.

Meanwhile, in 398 John Chrysostom (the Golden Mouthed), a man of fiery eloquence, had become Patriarch of New Rome. An ascetic of irate temperament, fanatically venerated by the populace, he had not hesitated to insult the Augusta Eudoxia publicly. A trial of strength ensued. After a number of councils, intrigue by the offended Empress, fighting, and the formation of a Johannine sect, the Golden Mouthed was finally deposed in 404 and died in exile three years later.

In 408 Arcadius breathed his last and his son Theodosius II, now seven, clambered upon the throne. He seemed destined to a perpetual minority. The Patrician Anthemius, who built a new wall a mile west of Constantine's to meet the capital's growing needs, was regent until 414. Then the Emperor's virginal sister Pulcheria became regent, impressed a cloisteral character on the court, and persecuted Jews, pagans, and heretics. The years passed in relative calm, for the desolated Balkan Peninsula no longer tempted the transdanubian barbarians. In 438 the Theodosian Code, assembling legislation since Constantine I, was published in East and West. Theodosius II, who during his last years seemed under the influence of his chief eunuch, fell from his horse and died in 450. Advised by the barbarian general Aspar, Pulcheria entered nominal nuptials with Marcian, a retired officer, who refused the tribute to the Huns. His wife died in 453, he four years later.

Aspar, a germanized Alan and an Arian, imposed his candidate on the Senate—Leo, a cinquantenarian Thracian tribune. There being no Augustus or Augusta to crown him, the Patriarch did so. This adoption of Sassanian usage became customary and fostered the concept that God was the source of imperial sovereignty. Despite the earthly author of his elevation, Leo combatted Germanic power, which threatened to strangle reborn Romanism in the East as it had in the West. To the external barbarians, who dominated the army, Leo opposed internal barbarians—the Isaurians. Ugly, short, badly armed, but fierce, they had been vaguely hellenized in Seleucid times, but in their inaccessible Anatolian crags had insensibly slipped back into barbarism and frequently raided neighboring provinces. Leo enrolled them in the army and formed an Isaurian palace guard, the Excubitors. He even gave the hand of his daughter to an Isaurian chieftain, Tarasikodissa, who conveniently changed his name to Zeno. By 471 Leo was strong enough to murder Aspar and his son. Three years later he died, having previously appointed his seven-year-old grandson Leo II Augustus.

Little Leo felt the need of a more experienced colleague and in the Hippodrome created his father Zeno Co-Emperor. When the child died some months later, Zeno, who was detested by the populace as an uncouth Isaurian, fled to his native crags. He was replaced by Basiliscus, whose fiscal and religious policies enraged the capital masses. In 476 Zeno reentered the capital and did away with him.

Zeno's reign was troubled by the Ostrogoths. After the fall of Hunnic power in 454 they had become Roman Federates on the Danube. They held off other barbarians, fought among themselves, marauded to the gates of New Rome, extorted gold from the Roman government, and enrolled their sons in the Roman army. Although the young Ostrogothic king Theodoric became Master General in the Presence, Patrician, adoptive son of the Emperor, and January Consul for 484, he occasionally pillaged the Empire. In 488 Zeno induced him to invade Italy.

A year later Theodoric burst into the peninsula with his whole people (perhaps a hundred thousand) and defeated Odovacar. The Senate in Rome ratified him as Patrician in Italy. Odovacar held out in Ravenna until in 493 he consented to share the rule of Italy. Theodoric agreed, entered Ravenna, and slew his sexagenarian rival with a stroke that is said to have cleft him from shoulder to pelvis.

Meanwhile, having crushed a series of Isaurian risings, Zeno had died of an epileptic attack in 491. With the consent of the Senate, the ministers, and the Patriarch, his widow, the Augusta Ariadne, selected a tall, elderly, Illyrian Silentiary, Anastasius, to become her consort and Emperor. He expelled the Isaurians from New Rome and terminated their gold subsidies. They rallied in defense of their prerogatives but were routed by a Roman force with Gothic and Hunnic auxiliaries. The war was protracted several years in Isaurian mountain recesses but in 498 their leader was killed. Many Isaurians were transplanted to the Thracian plains, and the broken nation gradually entered the body of the Empire. Having passed through protective Germanic and Isaurian domination, Romanism had triumphed. A large foreign element remained in the army but was offset by Roman regiments, enrolled from the hardy inhabitants of the Dinaric, Balkan, and Anatolian highlands.

In the West negligible, but frequent barbarian invasions had not allowed Neo-Romanism to grow. Britain had been abandoned and the Atlas provinces were occupied by the Vandals. Gaul, Spain, Italy, and Illyria were in the hands of Federate Frankish, Burgundian, Visigothic, Suevic, and Ostrogothic kings, who acknowledged the nominal overlordship of the Emperor. Thus, Theodoric

Mosaic of the Palace of Theodoric (ruled Italy 493–526) in the sixth-century church San Apollinare in Classe in Ravenna's former seaport

conceded to the Emperor the right to initiate laws and to the Senate of Rome an authority similar to his own. The Romans provided the bureaucracy and the Goths the army, Goths being excluded from the former, Romans from the latter. The Ostrogoths received a share of the land, and Goths and Romans lived in comparative harmony, although no fusion took place because the Goths were Arians.

NESTORIANS

Theodosius I had continued to seek to impose religious uniformity. The Second Ecumenical Council at New Rome in 381 had upheld the Nicene doctrine that Jesus is both God and Man and officially terminated the Arian controversy. Arianism was extirpated among the Romans but lived on among Ostrogoths, Visigoths, and Vandals and shared their destinies.

But Christians in the East did not stress the unity of the Trinity as did the Latin Church. It would seem that they accepted the Nicene identity of Father and Son superficially and continued to think of the Trinity as divided. But with further Trinitarian discussion forbidden, speculation turned to the apposition of the divine and human natures within Christ. The conflict of the Trinity was replaced by that of the Incarnation.

The causes of the controversy were similar. It had been decreed that Jesus possessed perfect divinity and perfect humanity. Periodically churchmen revolted against this doctrine. Some conceived of Him as all Man; others as all God. Other factors accentuated, embittered, and sustained the dispute. The individuals involved were often narrow, fanatic, and irritable ascetics. Moreover, there was rivalry between the patriarchates. Gradually too, in Egypt and Syria, which had not been as deeply hellenized as Anatolia, the basic nationalities rallied behind particular doctrines.

There were sharp differences between Alexandria and Antioch. Alexandria, the center of Hellenistic learning, the birthplace of Neoplatonism, and the city of Clement and Origen, engendered a Platonic theology. Antioch, where in the third century Paul of Samosata had asserted that Christ was merely an exceptional man and where Arius had studied and later found support, developed Aristotelian doctrines. In Alexandria biblical exegesis was free and allegorical, in Antioch literal and historical. While Alexandrian theologians meditated on the heavenly life of Christ, Antiochene scholars studied His earthly existence. Indeed, the struggles over the Trinity and the Incarnation were largely combats between the rival schools of Alexandria and Antioch.

Nestorius, an austere Antiochene monk, became Patriarch of New Rome in 428 and vigorously suppressed heretics within his diocese. Soon, however, he began to express views contrary to the tenets of the ecumenical councils of Nice and New Rome. He believed the two natures of Christ to be contained in two personalities, despite their apparent union in one body. He insisted that Jesus was born human, albeit perfectly so, and that only the indwelling of the Holy Ghost infused Him with divinity. Maintaining that the Holy

Ghost could not be born, he attacked the title *Mother of God*, contending that, being human, Mary could not beget God.

Cyril, Patriarch of Alexandria, came forward to defend the Virgin and the perfect union of the two complete natures within Jesus. In religious persecutions Cyril had a record comparable to that of Nestorius. Exile, mistreatment, or death were the lot of those within his see whose religious views differed from his own. It was during his incumbency that the last prominent pagan, the beautiful Hypatia, was martyred. She occupied a chair of philosophy at the Museum, and her lectures so goaded the Christians that a mob of lay brethren dragged her to a church, stripped off her robes, hacked away her flesh with oyster shells, and tortured her excoriated body with fire until death ended her agony (415).

As for Nestorius, by accusing him of heresy, Cyril could derogate both the Patriarchate of New Rome and the School of Antioch. The controversy shook the Church, and Theodosius II sought to end the discord by convening the Third Ecumenical Council at Ephesus in 431. Cyril and his partisans gathered separately and deposed Nestorius, while Nestorius and his adherents divested Cyril. Theodosius II removed them both. But Cyril managed to effect his own reinstatement and the imperial sanction of his opinions, which were those of the majority, a factor that generally swayed the decisions of the emperors. Nestorius was banished to the Upper Egyptian Desert, where after years of afflictions he died about 450.

For several decades Nestorians clung to Edessa, but in 489 the Edessene school was suppressed and many Nestorians were driven into Persia, where their missionary zeal absorbed the harried Christians. Persian oppression ceased, for the authorities no longer had to deal with Christians bound to the Roman Empire, but with Nestorians expelled by the Empire. Only when the Magian influence increased would persecutions recommence. But even these diminished as the Nestorians consolidated their position in Mesopotamia. Their head, the Catholicos, became an important personage, and the Nestorians flourished until the lethal Mongolian invasions of the thirteenth and fourteenth centuries. The survivors, possibly a hundred thousand, linger on in Iraq, Iran, Syria, Turkey, and India.

They evangelized on a vast scale, planting colonies and converting natives as far as Japan. Nestorian states were formed, of which vague rumors, such as those of Prester John, trickled through to medieval Europe. For centuries Nestorians maintained themselves with varying fortunes throughout the boundless Asiatic continent. Of their spiritual or secular victories and defeats, their trials and persecutions, little is known, but apparently despite vast distances, the farflung bishoprics long remained in communication with the Catholicos, who assumed the title Patriarch of Babylon. The greater part of these Christian islands have long since disappeared, some crushed by the Islamic suffusion, others overwhelmed in the vast Mongolian upheaval, others suppressed by unifying Chinese rulers, others absorbed. On the Malabar Coast they survived the torments of the Portuguese Inquisition and ten thousand remain.

MONOPHYSITES

The Nestorians with their doctrine of the duality of Christ's nature may have been expelled, but the victorious pontiff, Cyril of Alexandria, pushed beyond the middle ground of the unconfused union of the two natures and asserted their absolute unity. He maintained that even while Christ seemed a helpless babe, He was actually God, omniscient, omnipotent, omnipresent. Cyril died in 444 and the abbot Eutyches of New Rome pressed these ideas further. He asserted that after the union of the two natures Christ had only one nature (that of the Holy Ghost) and that consequently His person was not like that of humans. A synod at New Rome excommunicated him, but he demanded a general convention. Dioscurus, Patriarch of Alexandria, supported him. The Emperor consequently convoked another council at Ephesus (449). The partisans of one nature were in the majority and set upon any advocate of two natures crying, "As he divides, so let him be divided!" and "Tear him asunder!" [1] The Patriarch of New Rome, leader of the Dyophysites, was so abused that he died a few days later.

Theodosius II accepted this tumultuous Monophysite victory, but Marcian did not. He convened the Fourth Ecumenical Council at Chalcedon in 451. This body condemned the Monophysites (as it condemned the Nestorians),· confirmed the decrees of the ecumenical councils of Nice, Constantinople, and Ephesus (431), and affirmed that Jesus was perfect in Godhood, perfect in Man-

[1] Adeney, *The Greek and Eastern Churches* (Edinburgh, 1908), p. 98.

hood, being truly God, truly Man, consubstantial with the Father in Godhood, consubstantial with humans in Manhood, in two natures without confusion, alteration, division, or separation.

Despite the canons of Chalcedon, many in the East, especially in Egypt and Syria, adhered to the doctrine of one nature as they clung to their indigenous tongues. It seemed as if the Council of Chalcedon had truncated the normal evolution of Eastern Christology, in which the divine increasingly dominates.

In Egypt popular resentment against the decisions of Chalcedon reached bitter extremes. The prelate sent to replace Dioscurus could only maintain himself behind an imperial guard of two thousand lances. Even these did not avail him after the death of Marcian in 457. He was butchered and his mangled remains were dragged through the streets. Cosmopolitan Alexandrians and wild desert monks passionately united to defend the divinity of Christ and their Monophysite Patriarch.

Eight years later a popular rising in Antioch swept another Monophysite into partriarchal power. Even in New Rome the Monophysites found a champion in the transient Emperor Basiliscus, who abrogated the decrees of Chalcedon (475–476). Disorder and bloodshed raged throughout the East as in the days of the Arian and Nestorian dissensions.

But the Monophysites' ideas evolved. They reached a point where they admitted that Christ had a composite personality and consequently both divine and human attributes, but they asserted the preponderance of the divine over the human. Seizing upon this concession, Zeno hoped to find a formula satisfying both Monophysites and Dyophysites in the Henotikon, a document signed by the bishops of the East and addressed to the clergy and people of Egypt for their approval and the signature of their Patriarch in 482. This instrument reaffirmed the decrees of the councils of Nice and New Rome and declared that Christ was Himself God Incarnate, consubstantial with the Father in Godhood, consubstantial with humans in Manhood, was Incarnate by the Holy Ghost of the Virgin Mary, Mother of God, was one Son, not two. The Henotikon, moreover, anathematized those who divided or confounded the natures, specifically Nestorius and Eutyches. It was generally approved except by a fanatical minority in Egypt and the Patriarch of Rome. A measure of peace returned to the Church.

While the great dogmatic wars were fought mainly in the Levant, the Occident was not devoid of controversies. In Africa at the beginning of the fifth century Donatists and Circumcellions still applied and accepted martyrdom with like pleasure. The Latin Church, supported by the government, was able to inflict the supreme sacrifice on them to such an extent that they dwindled rapidly until the Vandal conquest rescued them from extinction.

After the conquest of extensive areas of the Roman West by Arian Germans, Latin priests insensibly replaced Roman officials. The power of the Latin Church grew. As once imperial officials had looked to the Emperor in Rome for instructions, the clergy, especially in menaced areas, now turned to the Patriarch of Rome for aid. Basing its claim to supremacy on its foundation by Saint Peter rather than on its location in the quondam capital, the Roman see established ecclesiastical hegemony over the West.

The union of Church and State had reinforced episcopal authority and in the fifth century no vestige of early Christian democracy survived. Moreover, as the public life of the municipalities declined, the power of the bishops with their possession of the keys to heaven and their privilege of informing the Emperor of official or private oppression increased. Nevertheless, although priests often wore sober apparel, they were not yet separated from the laity by celibacy, special education, or distinctive garb.

As every city or parish had its bishop, so each province had a metropolitan (the bishop of the provincial metropolis). Above the metropolitan now stood the ecclesiastical exarch or primate, whose authority covered an imperial diocese. Superimposed on the dioceses were the patriarchates, whose spheres were defined about the middle of the fifth century.

1. The Patriarch of Rome, the highest ranking prelate, enjoyed ascendancy over the Nicene West, including part of the Dinaro-Balkan Peninsula. His competence was based on decrees of the Council of Sardica, Valentinian I, and Gratian, which granted him appellate jurisdiction. At first the title of pope (Greek, *pappas*, father) was used by any bishop. Gradually it came to be reserved for the patriarchs. Now it is commonly used exclusively for the Patriarch of Rome. In the East, however, it is popularly applied to any priest, much as priests in the West are called "father."

2. The Patriarch of New Rome had authority over Anatolia and part of the Balkan Peninsula.

3. The Patriarch of Alexandria held sway over Egypt and Cyrenaica.

4. The Patriarch of Antioch controlled Syria, Roman Mesopotamia, and Roman Arabia.

5. The Patriarch of Jerusalem had jurisdiction over Palestine.

6. The Archbishop Primate of Nicosia still heads the Church of Cyprus, whose apostolic origin and autonomy were recognized by the Council of Ephesus in 431.

Above him and the patriarchs towered the undefined power of the Emperor.

IV

The Lure of Hesperia

498–610

THE conclusion of the Isaurian hostilities in 498 did not bring peace. Saracens ravaged Syria, Nubians harried Upper Egypt, Libyan tribes were restive, Huns and Caucasians pillaged Anatolia, while Slavs and Bulgars raided the Balkan provinces. For defense against the Bulgars (who had come with the Huns and settled between the mouths of the Dnieper and the Danube) Anastasius constructed the Long Wall forty miles west of New Rome. This structure, of which traces remain, stretched forty-one miles from the Marmara to the Black Sea.

War had also broken out with Persia. Since the mid-fifth century the Persians had been occupied with the White Huns on their eastern confines. This Mongolian stem of strangely pale complexion had left the unprofitable vicinity of the Great Wall of China, crushed the kindred Kushans, and gradually established their dominion from the Indus to the Caspian. In 499 they helped the deposed Persian potentate Kavad regain the throne. Kavad subjected priesthood and nobility and thus strengthened the Sassanid state. He requested the Emperor to resume the gold subsidy "for the defense of the Caucasian passes." When it was not forthcoming he seized Theodosiopolis and Amida (502–503).

Anxious to take Constantia, he negotiated with the Jewish colony for its surrender. The conspiracy was discovered, and the indignant oppidans massacred the Jews. The disappointed King of Kings then attacked Edessa, a thorn in his devout Zarathustran side, for a legend was current that Jesus had by letter not only cured Abgar, the elderly Prince of Edessa, of gout but had in a postscript insured Edessa against capture by barbarians. The Brother of the Sun soon learned the value of this guaranty, which was inscribed on the city gates, and after an unsuccessful siege retired in enraged humiliation. Suddenly Huns burst through the Caucasus. Romans and Persians joined forces against the common menace.

Anastasius rigorously curtailed official corruption, introduced economies, reduced taxes, and accumulated a reserve. He upheld Zeno's Henotikon, which generally conciliated the Levantine Monophysites without repelling the Dyophysites. But it alienated the Latins and the inhabitants of New Rome. To enforce it he removed two patriarchs, quelled riots, at length in 511 named a Monophysite Patriarch, and withstood the acclamation of a rival emperor.

His religious course and economies also led to the revolt of Vitalian, the Count of the Federates stationed in Thrace (mostly Bulgars). He made himself master of the Balkan provinces, seized Galata on the Golden Horn, and menaced the capital with his fleet. The situation was so desperate that the Master General in the Presence preferred not to take the command. The Pretorian Prefect Marinus took charge. In a naval battle at the mouth of the Golden Horn in 515 the imperial navy for the first time employed a chemical compound that set the hostile ships afire. After this victory Marinus landed troops on the opposite shore of the Golden Horn. Vitalian fled.

The same year Ariadne died, and in 518 Anastasius breathed his last.

NIKA

Anastasius had created neither Caesar nor Augustus. The Senate consequently convened in the Great Hall of the Palace, while the guardsmen and the populace assembled in the Hippodrome. The High Chamberlain had entrusted Justin, Count of the Excubitors, with a large sum of money to secure the election of Theocritus. Instead, Justin procured his own elevation. He was crowned by the Patriarch in the Kathisma and acclaimed by guards and people in the Hippodrome.

Almost seventy, Justin had been an Illyrian swineherd. As a

*Mosaic of Justinian (reigned 527–565) with his suite in the
sixth-century church San Vitale in Ravenna. The Emperor holds a gold
offering for the completion of the church begun by the Ostrogoths.
The Patrician on his right is reputedly Belisarius; the second man to
his left is Maximian, Archbishop of Ravenna*

young man he had wandered to the capital and, recommended by
his handsome appearance, had joined the Excubitors. He had purchased and later married a barbarian captive, Lupicina, who now
became the Augusta Euphemia. He had adopted his nephew Petrus
Sabbatius, changing his name to Justinian and enrolling him in the
Candidates. After his uncle's accession Justinian, who was in his
mid-thirties, of medium height, with a round shaven face, a straight
nose, and curly hair, became successively Count of the Domestics,
Patrician, Master General in the Presence, Consul, Nobilissimus,
and Caesar.

Desiring to reunite the hesperian provinces to the Empire, Justinian persuaded his uncle, whom he succeeded in 527, to abandon
the Henotikon and rehabilitate the Council of Chalcedon. Thus,

the Latins were conciliated, while the Monophysites of the East were alienated. Nor was his wife, the Augusta Theodora, a quondam circus actress, a small, comely brunette with delicate features and large, dark eyes, and with great influence over him, able to convert him to Monophysitism.

Justin's administration had consumed the reserves of Anastasius and to elicit the sums required for his projects Justinian created John the Cappadocian Pretorian Prefect. John was an outstanding administrator and sought to strengthen the central authority, control the growing power of the great landowners, and increase the capacity of the subjects to pay taxes. He was, however, rapacious and unscrupulous and extracted taxes by base means. Moreover, Tribonian, the Quaestor of the Sacred Palace, freely sold justice. With such conduct apparently ignored by the Emperor, lower officials emulated it. While imperial fiscal voracity ruined many small provincial taxpayers, who streamed into New Rome, the inequitable administration of justice bred widespread distrust of the government. These grievances, however, were not the immediate cause of the riot in the Hippodrome in January 532.

In New Rome as in Old Rome circus drivers were popular heroes, and their admirers called themselves by the colors of their jackets. At first their partisans formed wealthy societies that provided for the maintenance of drivers, horses, and chariots. Soon they supplied grooms, guards, vestrymen, poets, singers, musicians, dancers, acrobats, buffoons, pantomimers, painters, and sculptors for the public divertissement. Only the Blues and Greens retained importance in New Rome and other large cities. They had crystallized into inimical brotherhoods, behind one or the other of which city populations ranged themselves. They formed both urban citizen guards (demes) and political parties, whose leaders were appointed by the government and through which public opinion could express itself. While both factions had mass support, it would seem that the Greens represented the poorer classes, the interests of trade and industry, and the Monophysites and that the Blues stood for the senatorial aristocracy, the great landowners, and the state church.[1] Even emperors were partisans. It was said that Justinian

[1] The composition of the circus factions is much discussed. See Dvornik in *Byzantina Metabyzantina*, 1, 1 (1946); Manojlovic in *Byzantion*, 11, 2 (1936); Ostrogorsky, *History of the Byzantine State* (New Brunswick, N.J., 1957), pp. 61–62.

Mosaic of the Empress Theodora (d. 547) with her suite in San Vitale, Ravenna

connived at the Blue's violences, and that any magistrate who dared condemn them risked his career. It would seem, on the contrary, that he sought to discipline both factions.

Indeed, when in 532 he refused to pardon two condemned men (a Blue and a Green), who had been rescued from the gallows by some monks, both factions united against him under the watchword *Nika* (conquer). They set fire to the city prison, the Chalke, the Senate House of the Augustaeum, Saint Sophia, the Baths of Zeuxippus, and the Portico of the Augustaeum. They demanded not only the release of the two men, but also the removal of the City Prefect, the Quaestor, and the Pretorian Prefect. Justinian yielded. But it was too late. The ruined peasants, who had joined the city masses as a result of his fiscal oppression, espoused the uprising. Senators, offended by his autocratic policy, abetted it. The Scholarians and the Excubitors refused to attack the rioters.

Justinian appealed to two generals, the young Illyrian Belisarius and the Gepid Mundus, who happened to be in the capital with their retainers, mostly Goths and Heruls, some fifteen hundred men. With this handful Belisarius fought an indecisive battle in the Augustaeum. The revolt raged on. The Pretorium, the Baths of Alexander, Saint Irene, and the finest quarters of the City were consumed in flames. Three days later Justinian appeared before the insurgents in the Kathisma and swore to comply with their wishes. He was insulted and withdrew precipitately. The crowd seized Hypatius, a nephew of Anastasius, and, despite his remonstrances, hailed him Emperor. Justinian decided to flee but was halted by Theodora, who said that she could not contemplate life without the purple.

Consequently, the eunuch Narses inserted himself into the turbulent multitude in the Hippodrome and spread gold, insinuations, and discord among the rebels. Suddenly, Belisarius at the head of his well-armed, disciplined retainers forced his way into the race course. Drawing his sword, he charged into the dense mass. Mundus, entering another gate with his Heruls, attacked the almost defenseless crowd from the rear. The malcontents were hemmed in by the marble walls of the arena, pressed helplessly together by their own numbers, and were an easy prey to the bristling steel of the stalwart barbarians. Night fell and the weary warriors continued to wield their weapons. When at length they lowered them thirty thousand dead, dying, or wounded lay on the famous race course. Hypatius and his brother were executed the next day. The Nika rebellion was at an end.

SAINT SOPHIA

Forty days later the charred rubble had been cleared away and a new Constantinople commenced to rise.

The early Christians had had little interest in the sometimes graceful, sometimes sensuous, sometimes imposing, but always free and natural Greco-Roman art. Beauty was often condemned as evil, art as the pastime of demons. But after the Christian Church had entered imperial favor, churches similar to Greco-Roman basilicae began to rise.

The translation of the capital from Rome to Byzantium was a

pregnant cultural event. What Athens had been to Hellenic culture, Alexandria to Hellenistic, Rome to Greco-Roman, New Rome became to Byzantine, heiress to them all and in a measure to Oriental cultures.

With the reestablishment of Persian power under the Sassanids in the third century Oriental art began to break through the Hellenic veneer that Alexander had spread over the East five centuries earlier. From Persia the reawakening culture expanded through Mesopotamia to Syria, Egypt, Armenia, and inner Anatolia. From the Caucasus to the upper Nile ancient motifs and forgotten ideas were reborn. Hellenistic artisans and architects of the Roman East came under their influence and the Romano-Hellenistic culture of the Empire was profoundly affected.

While Hellenic art had glorified the beauty of the human body and emotions, Oriental art sought to express the divine or depict a semi-divine despot. Hellenic suppleness stiffened under Oriental influence. While Greek architects had constructed buildings whose harmonious profiles and graceful proportions truthfully depicted the interior, Roman and Oriental builders constructed skeletons of brick, stone, and mortar and covered the surfaces, especially the interiors, with rich materials. Decorations were not subordinated to architectural plans but existed as separate entities.

The two centuries following the foundation of New Rome were a period of elimination, transformation, assimilation, and coordination. While elsewhere the Hellenic spirit was expiring, in New Rome and other imperial cities it was uniting Romano-Hellenistic with revived Persian, Syro-Mesopotamian, Armenian, Anatolian, and Egyptian elements and creating a new artistic era, whose salient Oriental characteristics are the monumental style, the polychrome decoration, and the dome, distinct from Roman domes in structure and purpose. Greek art was entering its last phase, united to luxurious Oriental techniques and tempered by the spirit of Christianity —Byzantinism.

As is usual in the transition of styles, the new spirit became apparent first in the decorative arts. Sculpture almost vanished, for most Christians of the fourth century still associated statues with Greek gods and believed them to be inhabited by demons. Moreover, while Hellenes saw the soul shining through the beauty of the body, Christians regarded nudity as sordid. Under Oriental influ-

Dante, Ravenna

Mosaic of beardless Christ the Redeemer in the apse of San Vitale, Ravenna

Preiss & Co., Munich

ences, however, Christian artists soon abandoned the indigent simplicity of the catacombs for the multicolored decorations of the
Levant. Stucco was replaced by precious materials, and sober Hellenic harmony yielded to vivid polychromy. Not satisfied with
only pavement mosaics, the artists of the Christian Empire spread
them over walls, apses, and cupolas. They found the youthful,
beardless Jesus too Apollonic and transformed Him into a solemn,
majestic, somewhat fierce Christ with a dark beard, joined eyebrows, a long nose, and tapering fingers—the Pantocrator or Master of the World. The Good Shepherd had yielded to the Oriental
potentate. Apostles, angels, and other personages evolved similarly
as the early symbolism, allegory, and Alexandrine motifs of church
frescos and mosaics yielded to impressive, serial, biblical, and mar-
tyric scenes, often pictured with poignant realism.

Soon Byzantine architects adopted new building methods and
ground plans. Christian basilicae were supplanted by domed rotun-
das; octagons; cruciform churches with five domes; or cruciform
churches with three apses, whose half-domes rested on a central
dome. Or a transformed basilica itself might be covered with a central dome resting, not on pillars, but on pendentives.

After the Nika rebellion the ruined parts of the Palace, the Senate House, the Porticos of the Augustaeum, Saint Irene, and the
Baths of Zeuxippus were rebuilt. The Church of the Holy Apostles, unstable because of earthquakes, was demolished and reconstructed in cruciform with five domes. A magnificent cistern,
whose domelets were supported by 212 columns, was built. But on
one building, above all, Justinian lavished the wealth of the Empire
—the Church of the Divine Wisdom, Saint Sophia. He entrusted
the task to two Anatolians, Anthemius of Tralles and Isidore of
Miletus, and laid the first stone.

Five years later he came to view the finished work. The exterior
of the golden-domed edifice is plain, repelling the world without to
amass beauties for the soul within. Justinian entered the genial creation that inaugurated the Byzantine artistic era. The mosaics of the
lofty dome glittered blue, gold, and silver. It was studded with stars
and had a colossal cross at the apex. Unlike Roman domes on a
round space, it rested lightly on pendentives over four wide arches,
supported by four massive piers at the angles of the nave. Over his
head was a semi-dome with two apses. In front of him was another

*Christ Pantokrator (Ruler of the World). Late-eleventh-century
mosaic in the central dome of the church at Daphni near Athens*

The sixth-century church San Vitale, Ravenna

semi-dome with three apses. Twenty years later the central dome was to collapse and to be reerected by Isidore's nephew, whose genius has preserved it for us. The side aisles are separated from the nave by two stories of arcaded columns, the upper floor reserved for women. Imposts have vanished, the Byzantine capitals bearing the full weight of the arches. Above the upper colonnade the expanse of the side arches are walled and studded with windows.

On the walls and the apses mosaics of fifty different hues scintillated. The backgrounds were dark blue and gold, the ornamentations and the figures multicolored. In these Byzantine mosaics lay the craft of ages. The grace of the ornament was Alexandrine. The noble lines of the draperies and the abstract expression of the faces were Hellenic. The large eyes, the grave miens, and a certain realism seemed Egyptian. The variegated colors of the vestments were Sassanian. Over it all forty deep windows at the base of the dome spread a soft light, blending the millions of cubes into an enchanting entity.

*Byzantine capital in
San Vitale, Ravenna*

Capitals and arches in the sixth-century church Saint Sophia in Istanbul

Below the mosaics are handsome marble slabs and two stories of the most beautiful, unfluted marble columns in the world—milk white from Proconnesus, clear green from Euboea, antique green from Laconia and Thessaly, red and white from Caria, white misted rose from Phrygia, porphyry from Upper Egypt, and golden yellow from Numidia. Lacelike sculptures of Syrian motifs caress the arcades, the diverse capitals, the moldings, and the friezes. The play of colors is continued on the pavement, where jaspers, alabasters, porphyrys, and serpentines mingle. In the center, surrounded by a silver enclosure, stood a domed ambo of precious marbles, encrusted with gems, gold, ivory, and silver. Beyond, a carved silver balustrade sheltered the golden altar, glittering with gems and enamels, and the patriarchal throne of gilded silver in the farther apse.

Overcome by the harmony, the profusion of wealth, the symmetrical proportions of the greatest church in Christendom, Justinian uttered, "Glory be to God, Who has thought me worthy to finish this work! Solomon, I have surpassed thee!" [2]

THE ARMY

Besides Anatolian, Thracian, and Illyrian Romans the army now included Goths, Gepids, Heruls, Vandals, Lombards, Persians, Armenians, Caucasians, Transoxian Iranians, Arabs, Moors, Slavs, Huns, and Nubians. These foreigners had introduced alien modes of combat. Roman javelins had yielded to Persian arrows and Slavic darts, the Roman maniple to the Germanic wedge. The chief military unit was now the numerus of 200–400 men, commanded by a tribune or a prepositus.

Numbering about 150,000 volunteers, the army was divided as follows:

1. The Allies (formerly Federates), who were led by their own chiefs and often joined the field army.

2. The Borderers, who guarded the frontiers and held land that they cultivated as their own. Such land passed to their sons subject to continued service.

3. The Stratiotai (reserve force), who came mostly from Illyria,

[2] Downey, *Constantinople* . . . (Norman, Okla., 1960), p. 113.

Thrace, and Anatolia and were the national troops, the bulwark against the fate that had overtaken the western provinces. Mainly infantry, they generally remained in their garrison cities. Justinian paid them so irregularly that, despite his injunctions, many of them engaged in other occupations beside their military duties. When they went into battle only the front ranks wore breastplates.

4. The Federates, who were now barbarian horsemen under Roman officers. Excellent fighters, they formed the nucleus of the armies of conquest. Since the stirrupped Gothic horse had trampled the helpless legions to death at Adrianople, cavalry had gradually become the fulcrum of the Roman army. Infantry was now regarded as inferior, and many battles were fought exclusively with mounted forces. From the Persians the Romans had adopted impregnable mail and armor and the extended use of archery. The Federate cataphract carried a sword, a lance, a shield, and a bow. Unlike the warriors of Antiquity, who were divided according to weapon, Justinian's campaigners were proficient in all arms. From a distance they could break the foes' ranks with a formidable flight of arrows and then sweep them from the field with an iron charge. While basically heavy horsemen, they could also fight on foot or serve as light cavalry. But they were undisciplined, disloyal, and interested mainly in rapine.

5. The mounted Bucellarians, who were generals' private retainers. They first appear toward the end of the fourth century. Mostly foreigners, they were as multiarmed as the Federates and were the elite of the field army. Wealthy officers sometimes equipped several thousand and, protected by such a force, were often insubordinate.

6. The palace guards (Domestics, Protectors, Scholarians, and Candidates), whose military value had declined since the emperors no longer took the field. They were rich young men, more decorative than martial.

7. The Excubitors, who formed a guard of greater military value.

VANDAL AFRICA

Justinian aimed to regain the West. A pretext for intervention in the Atlas provinces presented itself when the Vandal king of Africa was unseated by his cousin Gelimer. Justinian appointed Belisarius generalissimus and in addition to the few thousand Bucellarians gave him ten thousand infantrymen and six thousand horsemen. The expedition departed in ninety-two warships and five hundred transport vessels in June 533.

Belisarius, not yet thirty, was a tall, handsome Illyrian, hardy, courageous, and efficient. His wife Antonina is said to have been some fifteen years his senior and to have rendered him the most renowned cuckold in the Empire. She accompanied him, as did his legal adviser Procopius, who has given us a detailed account of his times.

It seems remarkable that Justinian should have considered some twenty thousand men sufficient to conquer the Vandals, who, though not numerous, enjoyed a high naval and military reputation. Nevertheless, their vigor appears to have abated after a century in Africa. Their horsemen, like other Germanic warriors, were probably poorly armored and wielded only spear and sword. Their Roman subjects detested them as heretics, while the Moors (Atlas Berbers) felt no loyalty toward them. Thus, Justinian was merely attacking a ruling class. Moreover, he inspired revolts in Sardinia and Tripolitania, and Gelimer sent five thousand men and the major part of his navy to Sardinia. Furthermore, the Ostrogoths of Italy were on bad terms with the Vandals and placed Sicilian harbors at Roman disposal.

On reaching Sicily, Belisarius learned that the Vandal fleet was still in Sardinia. He immediately crossed to Africa and landed 160 miles south of Carthage. Then, in constant view of his fleet he moved northward, restraining the troops from the customary pillage lest the inhabitants be alienated. After ten days the expedition arrived within sight of the Lake of Tunis. The cautious commander did not descend into the lowlands with his whole army, but, in conformity with ancient Roman custom, built a stockaded camp. Here he left his infantry and advanced with the cavalry to reconnoiter. He had reason to be wary, for at the tenth milestone from Carthage, Gelimer planned to converge on the invaders from three sides.

Gelimer's brother Ammatas, however, engaged the Roman van before the scheduled time and was slain. Coming from the south, Gelimer surprised the Romans and threw them back in confusion. At the tenth milestone he discovered his brother's corpse. Grief-stricken, his only thought was to bestow the last honors. While the

Vandals were thus occupied, Belisarius rallied his horsemen, led them back to the tenth milestone, and cut the foe to pieces. The survivors fled westward.

Toward evening of the next day the Romans reached Carthage. The inhabitants illumined the city and welcomed them as deliverers. Lest his warriors forget this commendable role during the night, Belisarius encamped outside the walls. On the morrow, while the fleet sailed into the Lake of Tunis, the troops were marched into the city in battle formation to avoid rapine. Moorish tribes offered submission.

Meanwhile, strengthened by the return of the Sardinian expedition, Gelimer had pitched his camp, including his warriors' wives, children, and property, at Tricamerum twenty miles west of Carthage. In mid-December Belisarius sallied forth, routed him, and took his camp. He was unable to keep his soldiers from rape and plunder, and Gelimer might have rallied his warriors and annihilated them. But he was not of the kidney to channel the flow of history. He was ultimately surrounded on a rocky crag. Refusing to capitulate, he requested from the Roman general a loaf of bread, a sponge, and a lyre, the first lest he forget its taste, the second to dry his tears, the third that he might compose a dirge on his misfortunes. After a few months of lamentations he surrendered. Tripolitania, Sardinia, Corsica, the Balearic Islands, Cherchel, and Ceuta also received Roman garrisons.

Belisarius was rewarded with the first triumph to be celebrated in New Rome and the first to be accorded a subject since the reign of Tiberius. The procession filed through the Hippodrome before the enthroned Emperor and his consort. First came the spoils, including the sacred golden vessels said to have adorned the Temple of Jerusalem in the time of Solomon. They had been taken to Rome by Titus, to Carthage by Gaiseric, and were now to be deposited in the Church of the Holy Sepulcher. Next came the scowling elite of the Vandal warriors, who were to form five imperial cavalry regiments. Then the purple-clad Vandal king approached with measured tread, uttering the solomonic phrase, "Vanity of vanities, all is vanity!" [3] This resignation notwithstanding, it was necessary to fell him into prostration. Finally Belisarius advanced, not in the traditional triumphal chariot, but on foot. He did not hesitate to fall

[3] Procopius, *History of the Wars*, trans. Dewing (London, 1916), II, 283.

down before their sacred majesties. He was awarded the Consulate for the following year, while the captive monarch was offered the Patriciate on condition that he abjure Arianism. He declined but accepted the more tangible gift of an Anatolian estate.

The Vandals remaining in Africa were dispossessed as heretics. Many fled to the mountains and mingled with the Moors. All trace of their centenary habitation of Africa vanished. Indeed, the only faint spoor of their peregrinations may be the name Andalusia, possibly a corruption of Vandalicia. Their kingdom was divided into seven provinces and became the Prefecture of Africa.

But many Moorish tribes remained unconquered. To subjugate them Solomon, an accidental eunuch, was entrusted with full civil and military powers (534). The westerly tribes, who held the greater part of Mauretania, had hardly submitted when the Roman mercenaries mutinied. They were overcome in 537 by the Patrician Germanus, a nephew of the Emperor. Moorish tribes watched the battle, aided the victors in the pursuit, and joined them in the plunder.

Two years later Solomon returned. Lavishly distributing titles, annual subsidies, and trinkets of sovereignty, he created a margin of Moorish client-princes, who served to check their desert kin. Moreover, on the southern confines of the Empire's reconquered territory he established a chain of walled villages, fortresses, and outposts. Behind these he prepared a line of fortified towns to shelter refugees. West of Cherchel the Roman reconquest amounted to only a few coastal cities. The westermost, Ceuta, whose only connection with the Empire was by sea, was rendered impregnable.

For a brief spell Solomon was able to impose peace. Then the Moors again revolted and slew him in battle (544). The situation was aggravated by harsh taxation and injudicious appointments. The latter were frequent, for Justinian provided for his own and his wife's relatives and favorites as well as for Antonina's numerous offspring. Africa was devastated and depopulated. Only after years of fighting did quiet return to the exhausted land.

Italy

OSTROGOTHIC ITALY

During the last years of Theodoric's long rule in Italy discord arose between him and the Senate. Moreover, Justin's oppression of Arians perturbed the Ostrogothic king. He sent the Pope to New Rome to indicate that unless it ceased he would retaliate against Catholics in Italy. The Pope secured the restitution of their churches to the Arians.

In 526 Theodoric died of dysentery. He had arranged for his eight-year-old grandson to succeed him under the regency of his widowed mother. Nine years later the young king was dead, his mother lay strangled on an island in Lake Bolsena, and her cousin Theodahad held the reins of power.

This afforded Justinian the figment for war. Mundus seized Dalmatia (535). Belisarius took Sicily, crossed to Reggio, and marched on Naples (536). Satisfied with Gothic rule, the Neapolitans refused generous terms of surrender. The influential Jewish colony viewed with especial horror the restoration of imperial authority with its concomitant religious persecution. Belisarius discovered that he could penetrate the city through an aqueduct. Wishing to avoid a sack, which would estrange the Italians, he assured the Neapolitans that the city was his and urged them to capitulate. His exhortations were spurned. That night his troops entered Naples. Carnage and spoliation commenced, the Huns ever in the van. The entire population might have been massacred had not Belisarius finally restored discipline.

The Ostrogoths elected Witigis king and did away with Theodahad. The new ruler found his kingdom threatened also by the Franks, whom Justinian had urged as Catholics to join the attack on the Arians. Witigis and his warriors moved north and bought peace with the Franks by the cession of Provence and two thousand pounds of gold. During his absence Rome opened her gates to Belisarius (December 536), who repaired the wall of Aurelian and filled the granaries.

Witigis returned, besieged the city, and cut the aqueducts. They were not repaired, and the antique art of bathing with all its adjuncts declined. Meanwhile, as the siege wore on, hunger began both within and without the walls. Gothic envoys, mentioning that the Goths had taken Italy from Odovacar at Zeno's behest, that they had always observed imperial laws, that they had respected the Romans' religion, and that they had reserved all civil posts for the Romans, urged Belisarius to withdraw and offered territorial cessions. It was of no avail, and the hungry Goths finally retired.

Reinforced, Belisarius left Rome to complete the conquest of Italy. In this campaign, devoted mostly to the reduction of cities and fortresses, he was continually hampered by his generals' insubordination, as when his order to relieve Milan, which had espoused the imperial cause, was ignored. Besieged by Ostrogoths, the famished city fell in 539. The war dragged on. Famine gripped Italy. Peasants died of starvation. Cannibalism occurred.

The Goths suffered from three impediments—their king's poor judgment; the lack of mounted archers, which rendered their horsemen deficient in long-range combat; and the absence of national feeling. Indeed, many Gothic garrisons delivered their forts and their services to the Empire. Thus, Belisarius gradually conquered most of Italy. Witigis retired to Ravenna. Here the Ostrogoths offered the Roman general the crown. Belisarius feigned pleasure, and the Goths opened the gates of Ravenna to him. All Gothic strongholds except Pavia and Verona admitted his troops, thinking that he was to rule Italy (540). Then he declared his loyalty to the Emperor. The prostitution of his honor had procured Italy for his imperial master. Yet even this aroused the suspicion of Justinian, who recalled him and refused him a triumph. His royal prisoner Witigis, however, was created Patrician and given an estate near the Persian border.

Justinian's apprehensions removed from Italy his most efficient general when he was needed to consolidate the gains of the war, conciliate the Goths, and win the Romans' loyalty. Italy was left in the hands of generals with equal powers, who did not cooperate. Officers, soldiers, tax-collectors, and landed magnates tryannized the Italians, who soon regretted the succor that they had given the reconquest.

The Goths rallied under Totila, defeated the Roman forces, and were welcomed by the weak and oppressed. In a social and economic revolution unprecedented in Italy Totila liberated serfs and slaves.[4] Moreover, his humane conduct of the war differed sharply from that of the Roman generals and his generous treatment of captured Naples in 543 contrasted with the imperial bloodbath seven years earlier. The greater part of Italy returned to Ostrogothic rule.

Belisarius was again sent to Italy, but with insufficient funds and forces. Thus, he could not prevent Totila from storming Rome (546). Not having enough men to garrison her and distrusting the citizens, the Gothic king removed the gates and demolished part of the walls. Then he abandoned her to clear southern Italy of the imperialists. Belisarius recaptured the Eternal City, restored the fortifications, and bearded the returning Goths. But after his recall in 548 Totila again entered the city (550). Four hundred Roman cavalrymen resisted two days in the Mausoleum of Hadrian, then accepted Totila's offer to serve in his army, for the imperial government owed them long-standing arrears.

---

[4] Stein, *Histoire du Bas-Empire* (Paris, 1949), II, 570–571.

Justinian rejected all Gothic peace overtures, and Totila carried the war into Sicily, occupied Sardinia and Corsica, and ravaged the shores of Greece. In despair the Emperor gave the supreme command to his Chamberlain, an old Armenian eunuch, Narses, who invaded Italy from the north with a large host of Romans, Heruls, Lombards, Gepids, Persians, Huns, and Slavs.

On a warm day in June 552, not far from the Sepulchers of the Gauls in the eastern Apennines, Narses faced the Ostrogothic king. Narses had the more numerous force and occupied a strongly defensive site, from which Totila vainly tried to draw him. During the morning the opposing armies were entertained by a single combat and by the equestrian feats that Totila in golden armor and with a purple-plumed helmet performed for their benefit. But nothing could lure Narses from his advantageous position. Finally Totila ordered his horsemen to sweep them out. The Gothic cavalry charged through a storm of arrows from the Roman flanks, which were facing inward. Decimated, they reached the Roman center of dismounted Lombards and Heruls behind breastworks but could not break it. Toward evening Narses commanded a general advance. The Gothic horse, weakened by losses and engulfed by Roman numbers, was pressed back into the Gothic foot, which was thrown into confusion. In the debacle Totila was transfixed by a Gepid spear. Narses butchered the captured Goths, advanced on thinly manned Rome, and took it by storm.

The Ostrogoths elected an unsurpassed warrior, Teïas, king and carried on the war. Treachery and misfortune pursued them. Their supplies were cut, and on an early autumn morning in 553 Teïas led his famished band through a damp, narrow valley near Mount Vesuvius against the breastworks that Narses had erected. They came on foot, for the nature of the ground and the Roman barriers rendered the use of horses futile. The Romans in overwhelming numbers rushed against the advancing Goths, in whose front rank strode their king. He became the target of Roman spears. Teïas caught them on his shield and slew his assailants with rapid thrusts of his deadly lance. Often, when his shield became heavy from the weapons clinging to it he called a bodyguard and with lightning dexterity discarded it for a new one. For hours the Gothic hero withstood the Roman mass, ever parrying and thrusting, steadfast, indefatigable, indomitable. The sun had traveled the third part of its course when Teïas, changing shields, exposed his breast for a brief instant. A javelin pierced his heart. So perished the last king of a dying nation.

The exulting Romans, thinking the war won, cut off his head and exposed it on a pole to both armies. But the Ostrogothic warriors fought on grimly until nightfall and at dawn, though suffering the gnawing pangs of thirst and hunger, again advanced to battle. All day the epic struggle raged, desperate, implacable, sanguinary. The shadows lengthened into dusk; the Goths remained unbroken. In their meridional eventide they fought and bled without hope or fear. The mountain night descended and the weary warriors returned to their camps, the Romans to eat and drink, the Goths to still in sleep the poignant pains of thirst, hunger, and wounds. But Narses, worried by his heavy losses, sent nocturnal emissaries to the Goths. Probably pledging unmolested withdrawal to their estates, the envoys induced them to abandon the useless conflict. A thousand Goths declined even this offer, broke through the Roman lines, and reached Gothic Pavia.

Indeed, the Goths still occupied many towns. Cumae, held by the brother of Teïas, yielded after a part of her bastions had been blown up by explosives placed in the Sibyl's cavern beneath.

Meanwhile, enticed by the enfeebled condition of the peninsula, Franks and Alamanni had burst into Italy. One group rambled plundering to Calabria, then, weakened by pestilence, retired booty-laden. The other body was joined by a number of Ostrogoths, who promised to make the Alamannic leader Butilin king if he defeated Narses. The opposing armies met near Capua in the autumn of 554. Narses had the greater force, but as at the battle of the Sepulchers, he maintained the defensive, placing his infantry in the center, his cavalry on the flanks. The unmounted Teutons, brandishing battle-axes and shouting thunderously, charged in a solid column against the Roman center, which gave ground. The Roman wings enveloped the barbarians and from a safe distance rained arrows on them. Then the Roman center moved forward. The barbarians were completely surrounded. Transfixed by darts from all sides, every issue of escape blocked, their compact mass shrank to a few small clusters of comrades-in-arms, who continued the battle with the frenzy of despair. Courage and brawn did not avail against the deadly Roman missiles. It is said that only five escaped the carnage.

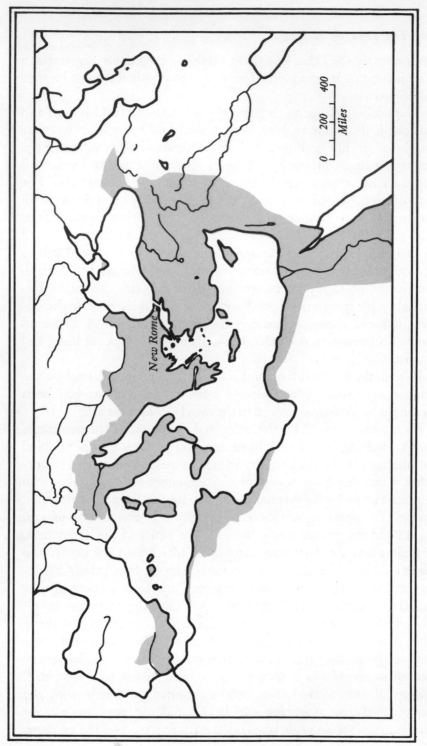

New Rome

The Empire About 560

In the Apennine fort, Conza, fifty miles east of Naples, the Goths held out until 555 when their commander was killed by the Romans during a parley. All Italy south of the Po was now in Roman hands. By 563 the transpadane provinces were reconquered. Thus, Ostrogothic rule came to an end and the thriving Italy of Theodoric returned to the Empire depopulated and economically ruined.

It may amaze that Justinian's armies could thus annihilate two nations before whom Romans had once trembled. There were many reasons. The Romans had progressed militarily, while the fighting qualities of the East Germans had probably deteriorated in the ease of the meridional environment. They were deficient in protective armor, used neither bow nor javelin, and lacked the unison of yore. Then they had charged in solid wedges of kinsmen bound to one another by ties of blood, alliance, and interest. Now, thinly spread over conquered lands, the links of consanguinity weakened, they had advanced into battle in groups of landowners. A ruling class facing a powerful, centralized empire, they had lacked the gold to keep an army in the field for a long period. Moreover, the East Germans were Arians, whom the Athanasian populations under their protection had regarded with abhorence. Nor had Justinian hesitated to inflame religious hatred. He had declared the purpose of the war to be the extermination of heretics. Moreover, the Roman inhabitants of Africa and Italy, though well treated by the Germans, had yearned for imperial rule. The widespread conception of a universal Roman Empire had even affected the Germanic kings. The Vandals had been independent of the Empire, but Theodoric had used the Emperor's image on his coins and had gladly accepted the Patriciate, as did most Germanic kings, who had not outgrown the idea that they were Roman Federates.

Like the Vandals, the Ostrogoths faded away as a national entity. Italy, like Africa, became a Pretorian Prefecture with thirteen civil provinces, while the military lined and fortified the southern foothills of the Alps. The once omnipotent Old Roman Senate, which had retained a measure of power under the Ostrogoths, vanished, for all the high officials who might compose it now resided in New Rome.

Justinian exacted from the war-weary country retroactive tax payments for his distant coffers. Totila had championed the poor and prostrate against the powerful and influential, had transformed serfs and slaves into free farmers, giving them land. Justinian reversed this course and reduced serfs and slaves to their previous status.[5] Moreover, the municipal autonomy existing under the Goths was largely destroyed. Industry, commerce, and the middle class declined. Italy was administered in the interests of the imperial officials, the imperial treasury, the imperial army. The Dark Age began.

VISIGOTHIC SPAIN AND DOMESTIC POLICY

The long and arduous Italian war had delayed the attack on Spain, but in 544 the Empire intervened in a Visigothic dynastic quarrel and with the aid of the Athanasian Hispano-Romans recovered the southern part of the Iberian Peninsula.

Not only were the populations of the recovered areas in the West hounded and ruined to provide the wherewithal for Justinian's plans, the entire Empire was impoverished. The Emperor seemed unable to judge the effort necessary to accomplish his ambitions. Thus he had not granted Belisarius the requisite men, gold, or authority for the rapid reconquest of the Apennine Peninsula. The result was the exhaustion of the Empire and the collapse of Italy. Moreover, although Justinian seemed ever without funds, he did not curtail his building activities. Instead, he reduced the army or withheld its pay. This false economy led to renewed invasions and the payment of imperial tribute on the one hand and to mutinies and the abuse of helpless subjects on the other. It has been said that Justinian shielded corrupt functionaries so long as they replenished his exchequer. Nevertheless, he and his Pretorian Prefect John the Cappadocian (reappointed soon after the Nika revolt and dismissed in 541 as a result of Theodora's enmity) made strenuous efforts to keep the revenue from bureaucrats' pockets.

They furthermore revised Diocletian's strict separation of civil and military authorities. In general vicars were suppressed and dioceses disappeared as administrative units. Officials tended to become directly responsible to the Emperor. In numerous cases two provinces were combined into one. Often civil and military power was

[5] Stein, *op. cit.*, II, 614.

united in the hands of the provincial governor, as in Cappadocia, which, except for the Emperor's extensive personal domains, was largely controlled by landed magnates, who with their armed bands could daunt imperial representatives. The Armenian provinces, which hitherto had lived under their own laws and customs, were romanized.

Justinian indubitably desired to rule well, but many of his reforms remained inoperative. To efface official corruption he abolished the sale of offices. To preclude the exploitation of the provinces by the governors he raised their salaries. Lest they be overawed by the landlords he increased their power and prestige. Yet, under the benign eye of a venal bureaucracy magnates maintained their own armies, prisons, and tax-collectors; terrorized the countryside; cut down any who opposed them; and illegally appropriated lands. Public authority declined. Judication was frequently purchased. Unpaid soldiers ran rampant and revenue officers raged mercilessly. Yet only a third of the returns reached the imperial treasury. Moreover, the revenue was diminishing, for much of the wealth had been taxed away. Brigandage, misery, anarchy, and revolt were rife.

As a measure of economy Justinian ceased conferring the Consulate on subjects in 541. This annual, duumviral office had replaced the regal authority a millennium earlier and had insensibly yielded power to the Senate and later to the emperors, who often adorned themselves with the ancient title. It became increasingly difficult to find persons able to expend the requisite two thousand pounds of gold for popular regalement, and often emperors were obliged to contribute. Hence, Justinian's measure. Later emperors assumed the Consulate upon their accession and dated from it.

LEGAL REFORM

Roman law, a vast epitomized conglomerate of Mediterranean customs and traditions, consisted of:

(a) statutes, which included the venerable Twelve Tables and the enactments of the kings, the early Republic, the Senate, and the emperors, all of which had been partially codified under Hadrian, Diocletian, and Theodosius II;

(b) jurisprudence, which embraced the works and opinions of the jurists of the second and third centuries, the Golden Age of Roman law.

Justinian appointed two commissions of jurists, both including the pagan Tribonian, later Quaestor. Their first task was to revise the Code of Theodosius II and add subsequent legislation. Contradictions were removed, archaic ordinances expurgated, superfluous preambles omitted, consolidations made, clarity and brevity fostered. The first edition of the Justinianic Code appeared in 529, the second five years later, amended to comprise new edicts. It contained 4652 laws, invalidated all previous legislation and codes, and simplified the tasks of magistrates and litigants.

The jurists' second performance was of equally great scope and utility. In the voluminous writings of the classical Roman jurists (of whom Gaius, Papinian, Ulpian, Paulus, and Modestinus were considered authoritative) conflicting opinions could be found. These conflicting citations rendered a judge's verdict difficult. Theodosius II had issued the Law of Citations, stipulating that the majority of quotations favorable to one side determine the decision and, if equally divided, that the opinion of Papinian be final. But the Law of Citations presupposed learning and libraries in imperial courts, which were often lacking. Hence, the jurists definitively adjudicated conflicting opinions and issued the Fifty Decisions.

After this trenchant labor the jurists reviewed the profuse material before them, eliminated repetition and contradiction, suppressed the unnecessary and the obsolete, and sorted, digested, and amended the legislation of thirteen centuries. In December 533 they published the Digest, comprising fifty books.

It is interesting to note that, though the Justinianic Code simplified the law of persons, the Digest still defined three classes:

1. Persons of Distinction, for whom the gravest penalty was usually deportation;

2. Persons of Humble Rank, including freedmen, who might be beheaded, sent to the mines, scourged, chained, banished, or receive an assortment of these punishments;

3. Slaves, who were generally certain of a flogging, possibly a little torture, and then, according to the merits of the case, crucifixion, cremation, or exposure to wild beasts.

Tribonian and two other jurists published the Institutes, a manual of civil law destined to be the official textbook for law students. To ensure the uniform and competent teaching of law Justinian abolished all law schools except those of New Rome and Beirut.

His final offering to imperial justice was the Novels, laws promulgated after the publication of the Code, which were collected and edited after his death. Beside transforming the cumbrous, contradictory, obsolete bulk of Roman law into an ordered, consistent, convenient, modern form, Justinian by his own enactments did much to simplify, equalize, and humanize its age-old principles. The influence of the Church is apparent in the severity with which heresy, divorce, seduction, homosexuality, legal incest, and extramarital coition were punished. Moreover, Christian emperors believed that they were mitigating the laws by frequently substituting mutilation for death. Nevertheless, the Code, the Fifty Decisions, the Digest, the Institutes, and the Novels are the foundation of much of the world's law.

PERSIA

In 531 Chosroes the Blessed succeeded his father, Kavad, and announced his accession to the Emperor. The intercourse between the Roman and Persian courts is the foundation of Occidental diplomacy. The sovereigns addressed each other as Brother and called their realms the two lights of the world. Roman statesmen greeted only the Persian and Ethiopian potentates as *Basileus*. Other kings had to be content with *rex*. The two monarchs concluded the so-called Endless Peace, providing for areas of preponderance in the Caucasus and Roman payment of a subsidy to Persia.

Chosroes made far-reaching fiscal, administrative, and military reforms and in 540 broke the Endless Peace. His pretext was a dispute between insignificant client Saracens. Possibly he thought to take advantage of Justinian's involvement in the Gothic war to extend his hegemony over the Armenians under Roman dominion.

It would seem that Armenia need not always have been the minion of great empires. The country is, in truth, cut by deep valleys connecting Anatolia with Iran, but it is protected by high mountains, bristling crags, impregnable forts, harsh winters, and a hardy, warlike people. United under a resolute leader, the Armenians might

have withstood Iranians and Romans. Such unity had existed before
the Cimmerian invasion of 710 B.C. when a powerful Khaldian
kingdom had maintained its independence. But Cimmerian chieftains carved out little mountain principalities and feudalism gnawed
at the vitals of the state. In 303 the Armenian king Tiridates established Christianity as the national religion, thus making Armenia the
first Christian state. The Persians began religious persecutions, and
the Armenians appealed to the Romans. Eventually, in 387, the
rival empires divided the unhappy country into zones of influence
(four-fifths for Persia, one-fifth for the Empire). The religious
bond with the Empire was weakened when the Armenian Church
rejected the decisions of the Council of Chalcedon of 451, which it
anathematized forty years later. And when Justinian tried to ro-
manize the Armenians under Roman control they solicited Persian
aid.

In the spring of 540 Chosroes crossed the Euphrates and advanced destroying and extorting toward the Orontes. Moving
down this fertile valley, he reached Antioch, demanded a thousand
pounds of gold as the price of his withdrawal, and was derided by
the populace. But when he bombarded the city from a rocky plateau on a level with the walls the garrison fled. The Persians seized
the deserted ramparts, cut down the half-armed demesmen in the
agora, and destroyed the city with its handsome marble edifices and
its colonnaded avenues, laid down with Hellenistic regularity over
eight centuries before.

After a bath in the Mediterranean the Brother of the Moon appeared before Apamea and expressed the pacific desire to preside at
the races. Upon learning that Justinian was a member of the Blue
circus faction, he professed himself a Green. After relieving the
city of its gold and silver he resumed his profitable extortions and
returned to Ctesiphon. Nearby he erected a Romano-Hellenistic
city on the plans of Antioch, embellished it with her spoils, and
peopled it with Antiochenes, on whom he conferred exceptional
privileges.

He devoted the following year to a campaign in Colchis. This
storied land, the prison of Prometheus and the home of the Golden
Fleece, lies at the eastern extremity of the Black Sea. It is bounded
on the north by the lofty peaks of the Caucasus, on the south by
Armenian mountains, and on the east by a range connecting the

Caucasus with the Armenian highlands. In contrast with the perpetual snows of the Caucasus and the harsh Armenian winds, sheltered Colchis enjoys a mild climate. Its river Phasis flows through magnificent forests, fertile orchards, and luxuriant subtropical vegetation. Apart from adjoining kin its inhabitants differ physically and linguistically from their neighbors. Though, like most Caucasian tribes, they have a Nordic sprinkling, they seem remotely related to the Egyptians. Herodotus believed them to be descendants of soldiers of the legendary Pharaoh Sesostris. Possibly Egyptian traders had settled there. Later, Greek colonies were planted. Ancient Persia, Pontus, and in 65 B.C. Rome successively extended a vague hegemony, but from the reign of Caesar to that of Justinian little is heard of Colchis. Possibly it fluctuated between Roman or Persian hegemony and independence. By the sixth century it had come to be known as Lazica after its ruling tribe.

Lazica was a Christian client-state of the Empire and with control of the Caucasian Passes was a valuable buffer. Relations were generally cordial. Lazic nobles visited New Rome and married Roman ladies. But when the Roman commander of the coastal fortress Petra imposed a monopoly on Lazic trade for his own profit the Lazi appealed to the Equal of the Stars. The latter, who appreciated the value of a country whence he could launch a fleet, gain supremacy of the Black Sea, ravage the Romans' coasts, and possibly attack their capital, hastened to succor them.

Felling trees to pass through primeval Iberian forests, Chosroes entered Lazica and advanced to the fortress of Petra. No one manned its walls. It seemed abandoned. The Great King sent a detachment with a battering beam to effect an entry. Suddenly the oaken gate opened and Roman soldiers scattered the surprised Iranians. Impaling the Persian officer in charge, the King of Kings attacked with vigor. The Roman commander was slain, a tower was demolished, and the garrison capitulated with the honors of war. After this success the Shahanshah hastened to defend Persian Mesopotamia but arrived after Belisarius' departure.

The warfare of 542 and 543 was hindered by the Great Plague, the greatest since the reign of Marcus Aurelius. Characterized by bubonic swellings, these pestilences were generally carried westward by fleas and rats from Babylonia or the Red Sea region, the links with the Far East.

In 544 Chosroes determined to efface the eyesore of the Magi, the city that a mere postscript of the Galilean had rendered impregnable—Edessa. To effect its downfall the Equal of Astral Bodies constructed near its walls a large, square mound of stones and tree trunks. Edessene sorties, archery, and offers of gold were of no avail; the structure rose ever higher. The Romans dug a tunnel reaching beneath it; enlarged the terminal; heaped into it wood smeared with sulphur, bitumen, and cedar oil; and ignited it. As soon as smoke issued from the mound, Edessenes discharged embers and burning arrows against it to mislead the Persians as to the smoke's origin. The structure collapsed in flames. Infuriated, Chosroes hurled his troops against the city of Christ. Three assaults were repulsed by the Edessenes, who, at length, gave the disappointed monarch five hundred pounds of gold to desist. The failure before Edessa led him to accept from Justinian two thousand pounds of gold and a five years' truce, exclusive of operations in Lazica.

Here the Christian Lazi had tired of the dominion of the Persians, who were attempting to convert them, and appealed to Justinian for aid. Roman troops were dispatched in 549 and eventually increased to fifty thousand men. But, though the Romans pushed the Iranians eastward, they could not evict them until a fifty-year peace treaty in 561 assigned Lazica to the Emperor. The rival empires also undertook not to proselytize on each other's territories, and the Romans agreed to annual payments "for the defense of the central Caucasian Passes."

COMMERCE

Gold was known to the Mediterranean World from remote times. It was mined or washed out of river beds in Egypt, Anatolia (where it made Croesus famous), Colchis (where Jason probably robbed the year's sheepskin-sifting, the Golden Fleece), Ophir (possibly in southern Arabia, whence Solomon drew his supply), Ethiopia, Macedonia, and in Roman times in Gaul, Spain, Dacia, Dalmatia, and the Rhineland. Originally used for ornamentation, it insensibly became money in the form of bars and was already coined in Egypt about 1700 B.C. The Phoenicians, the Greeks, and the Romans amassed stocks of it. While in the West mining declined after the barbarian invasions, in the East accumulated wealth, efficient exploitation of mines, and commerce made the Empire the greatest possessor of gold west of the Himalayas.

The Persian wars seriously interrupted imperial commerce with Farther Asia. Already in the second century, in order to throw off Parthian mercantile mediation, the Romans had annually dispatched a large fleet from the Red Sea to Ceylon, the emporium between East and West. Thither at stipulated seasons Chinese merchants brought silks, cloves, aloes (used mostly as a laxative), and sandalwood, while India sent spices, pepper, musk, aromatics, ivory, precious stones, pearls, sesame, cotton, and copper. In exchange the Romans offered glassware; enamelware; fine stuffs; embroideries; jewelry; objects of jade, coral, and amber; but mainly gold and silver.

In the third century Roman ships discontinued the voyages to Ceylon, and the Sassanid realm became the intermediary. Iranian vessels brought Oriental wares to the Tigro-Euphrates delta, whence those to be exported were transported mainly to Nisibis, which retained its importance as an entrepot between Persia and the Empire even after its cession to Persia in 363.[6] To shake off commercial dependence on Persia Justinian suggested to the ruler of Ethiopia and Yemen, who controlled the trade of the Red Sea and Central Africa with the Far East, that Ethiopian ships carry the Empire's commerce. But such was the influence of the Persian merchants in Ceylon that the project came to naught.

Persia also commanded the land route by which Chinese luxuries reached the Empire. Chinese caravans brought their merchandise to Samarcand and Bukhara, whence Persian merchants transferred them to Nisibis. Hoping to avoid this control, Justinian negotiated with the newly founded Turkish empire in Central Asia and for a time employed the ancient trade arteries from Lazica or the Sea of Azov to the Caspian and thence up the now desiccated western arm of the Oxus to the Transoxian oases.

Silk had been manufactured in China for over three thousand years, but the secret of its fabrication had been jealously guarded. About 550, however, two monks returned from China with hidden silkworm eggs and a knowledge of sericulture. As a result, silk-

---

[6] *Paulys Realencyclopädie,* 17, 1, 751–752.

worms were cultivated, mulberry orchards planted, and silk mills established at New Rome, Beirut, Tyre, and Antioch. The industry was declared a state monopoly and, though the finest silks were still drawn from China, a large part of the fabulous profits of the Occidental silk trade soon flowed into the imperial treasury.

As Persia was the commercial link between the Far East and the Empire, the Empire was the bond between Asia, Africa, and Europe. Syrian merchants carried westward silk and linen garments from Beirut and Tyre, purple from Palestinian Caesarea, pistachios from Damascus, strong wines from Gaza and Ascalon, furs from Cappadocia, papyrus from Egypt, and received in return oil, cattle, and clothing in Africa, oil, bacon, cloth, and mules in Spain, etc. From Ethiopia the Empire received incense, spices, papyrus, slaves, ivory, ebony, gold, gems, and ocher; from coastal Arabia incense, cassia, aloes, myrrh, and other perfumes. Lazica sent wheat, salt, wine, furs, leather, and slaves, while the tribes of the Black Sea steppe came to Cherson to barter skins, furs, and possibly amber against spices, jewelry, and rich materials.

SLAVS

Justinian's neglect of the Balkan Peninsula had disastrous consequences. Germans threatened from the northwest; Slavs and Huns from the northeast.

The most powerful of the Germanic tribes were the Lombards (Longobardi, because of the length of their beards) and the Gepids. About 500 the Lombards became Christians, being converted to Arianism, and annihilated the Heruls, who had settled in Noricum and Pannonia after the departure of the Ostrogoths. Of the survivors some returned to Scandinavia, some joined the Gepids, others served the Empire as Federates, but they vanished as a tribal entity. The Lombards took over Noricum and Pannonia and received from Justinian the status of Federates with ample subsidies. The Emperor encouraged warfare between them and the Gepids, who had occupied western Dacia after the battle of the Nedao in 454.

Along the lower Danube Slavs were coming into closer contact with the Empire. These Nordics had from time immemorial dwelt in the Pripet marshes and adjacent river basins. Not forming large communities and bearing only shields, darts, and poisoned arrows, they were easily conquered by such peoples as the Bastarnae, the Heruls, the Sarmatians, and later the Goths, who carried them southward as far as the Black Sea to till the soil. In contrast to the eruptive migrations of other Nordics, the unwarlike and rapidly multiplying Slavs spread imperceptibly, either as serfs, or if free, into thinly occupied lands. When the Goths yielded the Black Sea steppe to the Huns in 375 many Slavs were subjected by the newcomers. But in time Slavs learned to fight and invaded the Danube provinces.

Nor did Justinian's lavish diplomacy (gold, gifts, titles, intrigue, baptism, Roman brides, and education in New Rome) save the Balkan Peninsula. On the contrary, his subsidies probably encouraged invasion, and from the Black Sea to the Adriatic Huns and Slavs ravaged as far south as the Isthmus of Corinth. In 559 they broke through the Long Wall of Anastasius and insulted the majesty of the capital, protected only by decorative palatine guards. Belisarius, now sixty, gathered some veterans and peasants and put the invaders to flight. Soon after, Justinian deprived him of freedom and property but restored both in 563. Two years later the old warrior died.

Meanwhile, Justinian remained on the defensive. He rebuilt city walls, surrounded the Empire with powerful fortresses large enough to shelter refugees with their flocks, and linked this inner line with an outer chain of strongholds, which, in turn, was protected by a fringe of expensive barbarian clients.

RELIGIONS

In 529 Justinian opened the campaign against those pagans who, despite the destruction of their temples, the interdiction of household worship, the loss of civil rights, tortures, and massacres, still remained faithful to their gods. Justinian attacked first in New Rome and by public humiliations, imprisonment, starvation, torture, and carnage effaced her last pagans.

The same year he closed the Academy of Athens, where Neoplatonists taught law, medicine, and philology and misinterpreted

Plato and Aristotle. With the Academy and theaters closed, Athens became a provincial town. The Greco-Roman world was becoming Byzantine.

To suppress the remaining pagans Justinian sent military and missionaries throughout the Empire. In Anatolia alone seventy thousand are said to have been brutally baptized. Justinian closed the antique oasis shrine of Jupiter Ammon in the Egyptian Desert. He sent a military force to christianize the Temple of Isis on the Nile Island of Philae. He suppressed the School of Philosophers at Antioch and ancient sanctuaries in Palestine. He attacked the adoration of Astarte in Phoenicia, the sun worship around Baalbek, the moon cult in Mesopotamia. Above all, he tried with savage persecutions to extirpate the pagans in Greece. Yet some survived, and toward the end of the century pagans were again hounded and slaughtered. Paganism gradually expired, but the forcefully converted pagans brought their demigods, ceremonies, and processions into the Church.

Although Justinian called the Jews abominable men sitting in darkness,[7] he seems to have attacked them only spasmodically. But against the Samaritans, a sect that had separated from the main Jewish body before Christ, he proceeded so harshly that they revolted and were shattered by an imperial army. They have outlived persecutions and in 1966 still numbered six hundred.[8]

Justinian also persecuted heretics, especially in Syria and Anatolia, whose heretic islands (Arians, Nestorians, Montanists, Origenists, Manichaeans, and other Gnostics) may have been sedimentary, endogamous groups who for ages had resisted assimilation by invaders and now found in heresy protection against absorption. The Emperor attacked them fiercely, burning entire congregations in their churches.

With the more numerous Monophysites, however, the Equal of the Apostles negotiated, hoping to overcome their scruples by a slight recession from the Council of Chalcedon. Since they accused the imperial Church of Nestorian leanings, he tried to conciliate them by proscribing certain writings of three deceased theologians.

[7] Bury, *History of the Later Roman Empire* . . . *395–565* (London, 1923), II, 366.
[8] *Time*, April 1, 1966, p. 42.

He requested the approval of all patriarchs and bishops. The four eastern patriarchs acquiesced, but the Pope refused, fearing to derogate the Council of Chalcedon, which had absolved the three divines of heresy. He was summoned to New Rome and detained. To adjudicate the question Justinian convoked the Fifth Ecumenical Council at New Rome in 553. In compliance with his wishes it denounced the writings and persons of the incriminated theologians. Fourteen anathemas, directed chiefly against Nestorians, set forth the orthodox faith. The Pope was permitted to depart only after he had confirmed the Council's decrees. As a result, the bishops of Italy, Africa, and Illyria repudiated him.

To Justinian as to Constantine I the Church was part of the State. The emperors gave the canons of ecumenical councils the validity of imperial law and regarded priests as imperial officials. Indeed, bishops were responsible for the enforcement of laws pertaining to morals and for the defense of their flocks against unjust functionaries. Justinian even interfered with the conduct of monastic institutions, averring that the inmates' prayers were of great import to public welfare.

Some years after the Council of 553 Justinian took up a form of Monophysitism known as Aphthartodocetism (the doctrine of the incorruptibility and insensibility to human weaknesses of the earthly Body of Christ) and decided that the main Church adopt it, probably with the hope of establishing ecclesiastical unity. The greater part of the clergy resisted his edict, and he was about to commence coercion when death supervened (565).

MONASTICISM

In their early stages religions generally find chief expression in sacrifice and prayer. When these manifestations have developed into a spiritual system, asceticism often appears. Whether it be fasting, filth, vigils, silence, physical discomfort, self-impoverishment, sexual abstinence, or self-torture, asceticism is intended to purify the soul and thus attain a more intimate relationship with the Deity. This supposed communion or transfusion with the Almighty is mysticism. Asceticism and mysticism coordinated into a system of life is monasticism.

A thousand years before Christ monasticism was already part of the Brahmanic religion. Five hundred years later it was adopted by Buddhists. In Ptolemaic times it was practised by the worshipers of Serapis at Memphis, by the Jewish Therapeutae near Alexandria, and by the Jewish Essenes in Palestine.

Christian austerity developed simultaneously with sacrifice and prayer. It seemed recommended by the Savior, and Church Fathers indicated that, while the ascetic life was not expressly commanded by God, it would reap a special reward in Heaven. The conviction of the imminent Second Advent of Christ also turned early Christians from terrestrial to celestial concerns. But the Church, seeking universality, could not proceed too far toward austerity and expelled excessively ascetic sects.

Yet there were individuals who led austere lives but remained within the Church and society. About 250, however, in Egypt many ascetics became hermits on the outskirts of their communities. Soon they retreated to solitary abodes in the desert. Their numbers and their attempts to surpass one another in the acerbity of their rigors grew. They came to build their cells near one another and by 300 there were numerous eremitic settlements in the Nile Valley and the desert.

Early in the fourth century these agglomerations were organized into monasteries and the once independent anchorite sank into monastic subjection. To poverty and chastity he added a third vow—unthinking obedience, thus acknowledging the authority of the Church whose mundanity he had once deprecated. Regular religious offices were instituted in monasteries, but there remained a gulf of hostility between monks and secular priests.

Monks continued to struggle against demons as of old. But as monasteries gradually replaced hermitages, tales of heroic combats against overwhelming numbers of demons (in the most divers garbs) diminished. This subsidence was attributed to the fact that the early recluses had broken demonic power. The presence of brethren able to verify details may also have restrained the imagination of the fiercest demon fighters. Indeed, the war against demons was now carried on with discipline. Monks were instructed to conquer pride, anger, gluttony, dejection, vainglory, fornication, covetousness, and restless discontent largely by fasting and vigils. Nevertheless, excesses still occurred. An Egyptian monk once killed a gnat. He retired to the marshes, stripped himself naked, and invited the swarming insects to punish him. This they did so efficiently that when he emerged a half year later he resembled an elephant hide.

From Egypt monasticism spread throughout Christendom but did not entirely efface hermitry. Thirty miles east of Antioch Simeon took to pillars, his last being eighty feet high. Whn he died at seventy in 459 he had lived on a platform atop a column for thirty-six years. This feat earned him widespread veneration, the surname Stylites (from *stylos*, Greek for column), sainthood, and imitators as late as the sixteenth century.

In contrast to Semitic Syria, so fertile in exotic asperities, Anatolian Greeks resisted asceticism. About 340 a synod at Gangra anathematized those who propagated Egyptian monastic practices because they preached against marriage; refused the holy offices of married priests; set up their own conventicles; affected special garb; denounced riches; fasted on the day of the Lord; disparaged Christian hospitality; and induced married women to leave their husbands, cut off their hair, wear masculine dress, and adopt conventual life.

Soon there rose a man who transformed Christian monasticism— Basil of Cappadocian Caesarea, later known as Saint Basil the Great. He had studied literature and philosophy at Athens, examined asceticism, talked with hermits and monks in Egypt, Palestine, and Syria, and returned to Anatolia to live austerely. About 365 he entered the clergy and five years later was Metropolitan of Caesarea. Though his activities were limited to Cappadocia and Pontus, the rules that he elaborated for the monastery that he founded made him the father of Christian monasticism. Preferring cenobitic to solitary life, he expunged the schismatic tendencies of the ascetics and drew them under ecclesiastical control.

He wished monasteries to be near cities, that their example might edify the laity and, above all, that they might remain under the eye of the local bishop, lest they again break away from the Church. He insisted that monks engage in useful labor and circumscribed fasting, lest it impair spiritual and physical capabilities. Nevertheless, he enjoined a measure of fasting, as well as vigils, chastity, labor, and the limited use of tongue, eyes, and ears. He prescribed these practices not alone for monks but for all Christians, believing the goal of every Christian to be the emulation of the earthly Life of Christ insofar as his occupation permitted. By thus fusing the aims of monks and laymen he sought to draw them together. To reconcile monks with secular priests he associated the monastic life with the doctrines of redemption and grace, demanding ecclesiastical respect for those who sacrificed their existence to these dogmata and urging monks to revere the Church as the custodian of the tenets to which they devoted their lives.

Basil's monastic principles insensibly spread over Christendom, but a legal basis was needed to curb the turbulent monks. They often destroyed pagan temples, which might have been converted to other purposes. They agitated the masses and brought violence and bloodshed into religious disputes. They even stained the Council of Ephesus in 449 with blood. Consequently, the Council of Chalcedon in 451 subjected monasteries to the local bishops.

Justinian's legislation completed the mold of Eastern monasticism. Upon assuming the cowl, the individual surrendered all property and was forbidden to return to secular existence. The number of solitaries was restricted and they were obliged to sleep and eat within the monasteries. Local bishops were given a voice in the election of abbots and priors. Religious offices were to be performed only by ordained monks. Thus, by the sixth century Church and State had subdued and regulated the lives of the once wild monks.

AVARS

Justinian had accomplished much—legal reform and codification, Saint Sophia, farflung frontier fortifications, the reconquest of Africa, Italy, the western islands, and part of Spain. His reign had also witnessed invasions, devastation, and massacres in Syria, Anatolia, and the Balkan Peninsula, the impoverishment of his subjects, the debasement of the coin, the neglect of the army, the decline of official authority, and the persecution and estrangement of his Eastern subjects. He had wished to restore the West but had ruined it, while disregarding the interests of the East.[9] He had dreamed of

[9] Rubin, however, points out that while Justinian was undertaking aggressive wars in the West, he was also constructing great fortifications in the East. *Das Zeitalter Iustinians* (Berlin, 1960), I, 320.

restoring Latin grandeur, but the Empire was becoming steadily more hellenized. His ambitions had led him westward, but the danger lay in the north and the east. Theodora had died of cancer in 548 and Justinian breathed his last at eighty-three in 565.

His nephew, the Curopalates (a new rank below Caesar and Nobilissimus but above Patrician) succeeded him as Justin II. He struggled vainly to revive the exhausted Empire, terminated the lavish tributes to neighboring peoples, instituted economies, paid debts, and endeavored to curb the power of the great landowners. But he was unable to undo his uncle's disastrous neglect of that quarry of Roman manpower, the Balkan Peninsula.

The mare-milk drinking Avars reached the Black Sea steppe in 558, defeated Bulgars and Antae (probably Slavs dominated by Altaians), moved northwestward, crumpled Slavs and their vestigial German masters, and established themselves in Bohemia. They united with the Lombards to crush the Gepids in Transylvania and pitched their central camp in the fertile Danube-Theiss basin, excellent pasture for mounted nomads (567). Then they pushed the Lombards from their lands. This event was doubly unfortunate for the Empire. It led to the Lombard invasion of Italy and exposed blighted Balkania to Avars to devastate and Slavs to populate.

The Avar conquests revealed that there were almost no more Germans east of the Elbe. After they had migrated southward and westward Slavs had filtered into the abandoned lands. The expulsion of the Lombards from Pannonia cleared all Europe east of the Alps of Germans. Baian, the Khagan of the Avars, was able to construct a vast Avaro-Slavic state between the Baltic and the Danube, the Alps and the Black Sea, settling great numbers of Slavs along his western borders as a barrier against the Germans.

LOMBARDS

In extirpating the Ostrogoths Justinian had destroyed the natural defenders of Italy, and when in 568 the Lombards invaded the exhausted land they encountered little resistance. The thirty-five Roman dukes in the north acted as if they were feudal lords and there was little concerted action. The Lombards were equally divided. Their numbers were small and their king, when they had one, had little power over the chiefs. They were not versed in siege warfare, nor did they build a large navy. Thus they were unable to conquer the entire peninsula.

Even so, barely a decade after Justinian's reconquest of Italy, the Empire retained only the Dalmatian coastline; Istria; Venetia; Ravenna with a strip of the Adriatic; Genoa with Liguria; five cities and their territories between Ravenna and Rome, which came to be known as the Pentapolis; Rome with a band along the Tyrrhenian; Naples and environs, the southern peninsulas; and Sicily.

The Lombard dukes vaguely acknowledged a king, who resided at Pavia. His authority was precarious and the Lombard duchies of Spoleto and Benevento were practically independent. Moreover, Lombard landlords assumed military, financial, and judicial authority on their domains. Public functions were thus localized and the landholder stood between his tenants and the duke or king.

Although the landholders were nominally the king's tenants and vassals, inasmuch as they held land from him in compensation for their military service, actually he lost control of the land with its inhabitants and generally also of the landholder. He could not tax his vassals, for Germanic warriors regarded taxation as an infringement on their liberties. Herein lay the weakness of the feudal state. The Empire, though reduced in size, weakened by invasion, official corruption, and military insubordination, remained a great power because of her ability to tax. She could maintain her army, navy, and civil service on a permanent basis and concentrate her strength, while the feudal states of the West, not distinguishing between property and sovereignty, had so distributed their power that they were capable of only spasmodic efforts.

In the Empire the preservation of direct taxation by the central government discouraged feudalization. Moreover, her money-economy with its consequent division of labor permitted her to feed a denser population. In the Germanic kingdoms, however, the Roman bureaucracy was destroyed, while the great landowners remained or were replaced by conquering Germans. The great estate became the basic unit of the economic and social order. Direct taxation disappeared and barter supplanted the money economy. The feudal king sustained his phantom state with the proceeds of his own domains, while he paid his warriors with allocations of land. When he had no more to confer he sought it by war, either against his own vassals or a neighbor. He was thus obliged periodically to reconquer his realm. His authority rested on his presence and the force under his immediate command. He could not afford to fortify frontiers, maintain a large professional army, or build a navy. Thus, the Lombards could not unite the Apennine Peninsula, and thirteen centuries were to elapse before it was unified.

The Lombard conquest and the chronic state of war led to the fusion of civil and military authority in remnant Roman Italy, whose governor bore the military title of Exarch but was popularly called the Patrician because he always received that dignity. His authority was similar to that of the Ostrogothic kings. His tribunes acquired estates and became landlords, while the great landowners became hereditary tribunes. The inhabitants were bound to the soil or their vocations and forced to serve their tribunician lords in war. Thus, Roman Italy came to be dominated by a feudalistic landed-military-official aristocracy. In Africa the authority of civil officials also tended to yield to that of the Exarch.

CHAOS

Meanwhile, in the East Avaro-Slavs had occupied the Balkan Peninsula, the Persians were despoiling Mesopotamia and Syria, mercenaries were rioting. The mental health of Justin II broke. He adopted Tiberius, the tall, handsome, Thracian Count of the Ex cubitors, created him Caesar with regent powers in 574, Augustus in 578, and then expired. Four years later, as the popular Tiberius II, the first Greek-speaking Emperor, lay dying of dysentery, he conferred his daughter and the Empire on the forty-three-year-old, Cappadocian Count of the Excubitors Maurice.

The Antonine adoptive system seemed to relive. Maurice confronted Visigothic hostilities in Spain, a Moorish war in Africa, the Lombards in Italy, the Persians in the East, Avars devastating Balkania to the extremities of Greece and the walls of the capital, and Slavs appropriating the land. But for these farflung campaigns he lacked men and money. Old quarries of manpower had vanished. The Germanic tribes had moved westward and shaped their own kingdoms. The Thraco-Illyrians had been obliterated, absorbed, or driven into the mountains by invasion. The Slavs, who replaced

Enlarged gold coin of Maurice (reigned 582–602)

them, were still too wild. The Hunnic tribes were subject to the Avars.

For the manpower of Armenia Maurice continued the war with Persia, which had begun in 572. Though Chosroes the Blessed, who had entertained Roman arms for a half century, died in 579, the war dragged on until 590, when a rebellion expelled Chosroes II. He appealed to Maurice, who replaced him on the throne and received in return a tract of Mesopotamia and the major portion of Persarmenia (591). It seemed the culmination of the efforts of Tiberius and Maurice to transform Persia into a permanent partner against swarming Barbaria.

Maurice now dispatched his army against the Avars and Slavs and after lengthy hostilities drove many over the Danube. But when in 602 he commanded the troops to winter north of that river they mutinied, acclaimed a noncommissioned officer, Phocas, Exarch, and marched on New Rome, where Maurice was unpopular because of his reforms and economies. The circus factions united against him, and he fled to Chalcedon but was captured. Phocas was crowned by the Patriarch outside the walls and entered the City in a chariot drawn by four white steeds.

He immolated the five sons of Maurice in their father's presence, then murdered the resigned parent, exposed their six heads to insult and putrefaction, and later beheaded the Empress and her three daughters. These outrages inaugurated a reign of terror, directed especially against aristocrats, Monophysites, and the Greens. Yet in Rome a column, described as the last monument of Antiquity, was erected to Phocas in the Forum.

His reign has been called the greatest catastrophe of the Empire since the loss of the West.[10] While he was performing ingeniously cruel homicides or endeavoring to baptize Jews by force, Persians were approaching the Bosporus, Avars and Slavs the Long Wall. Fiscal corruption, religious persecution, and invasion weakened the bonds of a common civilization. Preroman nationalities came to the surface under separate religious banners. Blues and Greens wrangled. Plague, famine, and riots rocked a state on the verge of dissolution. In this dark hour the Exarch of Africa fitted out an expedition and placed his son Heraclius in command. When in 610 his fleet cast anchor in the Marmara, New Rome opened her gates. Senate, Patriarch, and people acclaimed Heraclius Emperor and Phocas was dispatched.

[10] Theiss, *Die griechischen Kaiser* (Hamburg, 1959), p. 327.

V

The Heracliads

610–716

BORN in Cappadocia about 575, possibly of an Armenian father, Heraclius was blond, bearded, strongly built, of medium height, mentally and physically accomplished, studious, religious, eloquent. He faced an apparently hopeless situation. The Roman Orient lay at the mercy of the Persians. Balkania was in the hands of Avaro-Slavs. Roman Spain was succumbing to Visigothic reconquest (probably completed in 629). Many provincials, notably Syrians, Egyptians, and Armenians, had long since been estranged by religious persecution or excessive taxation and had recovered a greater consciousness of their preroman nationality. They offered little resistance to the Persians. Even the Pindic Greeks hated a government that burdened them with taxes but seemed passive while the Slavs drove them from their lands. Thus, the Pindic Greeks now dwelt mainly in fortified towns, while Slavs occupied the countryside.

The central government's authority appeared to have vanished. The provinces defended and governed themselves. The imperial administration seemed in disorder, the treasury empty, the army diminished and demoralized. Justinian's grinding exactions had enfeebled the peasants, whose fields were seized by great landlords or rapacious officials, who together constituted a powerful aristocracy and restricted the Emperor's freedom of action. The parasitic populace of the capital still clamored for bread, games, and largesses. The Church still insisted on the persecution of heretics. An innumerable host of aulic attendants still expected their emoluments.

PERSIANS AND AVARS

The Persians swept from victory to victory. When Heraclius sent envoys of peace Chosroes II murdered them. In 614, aided by persecuted Jews, the Persians stormed Jerusalem. The carnage lasted three days and fifty-seven thousand inhabitants are said to have been butchered. The wood of the True Cross, the most precious relic in Christendom, fell into Zarathustran hands. Three centuries earlier Helena, the canonized mother of Constantine I, had excavated it on Mount Calvary, sent part to her son, and deposited the remainder in the Church of the Resurrection in Jerusalem. The adjective "True" is used because she is said to have discovered three crosses and that of the Savior revealed itself by a miracle.

Soon the invincible Iranians occupied Egypt and Cyrenaica. As alienated Nestorians had facilitated their conquest of Syria, estranged Monophysites aided that of Egypt.[1] By 615 the Persians were at Chalcedon, but their attempt to cross to Europe was beaten back.

Yet, at New Rome Heraclius was hampered by an independent aristocracy and a populace whose sustenance since the loss of Egypt

Enlarged coins of Heraclius (reigned 610–641) and the Persian King of Kings Chosroes II (reigned 590–628) surrounded by his celestial kin

[1] Jones, *op. cit.*, II; 1034–1035, however, states that only Jews were actively hostile to the Empire.

From Fritz Krischen, *"Die Landmauer von Konstantinopel,"*
Archäologisches Institut des Deutschen Reiches, Vol. 6

Reconstruction of the Golden Gate

had become a heavy drain on the resources of the reduced Empire.
He resolved to transplant the capital to Carthage, whence, un-
fettered by a wilful nobility, an incubic populace, and a palatial
household, he could recover the lost imperial lands. A tremor ran
through New Rome. The Patriarch Sergius adjured the monarch
not to abandon the City and loaned him Church treasure. The populace sacrificed the dole. Emperor, Church, and people united to defend their freedom, save the Empire, redeem the Holy Land, and
retrieve the True Cross.

Heraclius arranged to discuss peace with the Avar Khagan at
Marmaran Heraclea, in whose hippodrome the barbarians were to
be lavishly entertained (619). But as he was riding in stately procession toward Heraclea, he became aware of stealthy movements
of the Avar cavalry. The barbarians were cutting off his retreat.
He cast aside his imperial cloak, doffed his diadem, girded it on his
arm, wheeled about with his brilliant retinue, and began a mad ride
toward New Rome. Mile after mile the Avar horsemen pursued the
imperial riders, who galloped through the Golden Gate with barely
a moment to spare. Despite this perfidy the Emperor finally bought
peace and was free to attack the Persians.

In 622, clad as a penitent and bearing an image of the Virgin said
not to have been made by human hands, Heraclius descended to the
marble Marmaran port of the Bucoleon, where the fleet bearing the
new army awaited him. He boarded the imperial dromon and gave

the signal to weigh anchor. As the galleys moved slowly away, fervent prayers rose from New Rome's churches. The first of the crusades had begun.

At Nicomedia the Emperor was joined by scattered veterans, peasant-soldiers whom he had established in Anatolia, and dispossessed Romans from all parts of the mutilated realm. He apparently rounded Anatolia and encamped near sheltered Issus, the site of Alexander's victory over the Persians almost a millennium earlier. Here exercises, maneuvers, vibrant addresses, inspired sermons, and promises of land grants in the regions to be reconquered from the Zarathustrans occupied the days, and the confused multitude became an ardent, disciplined army. With it Heraclius marched, maneuvered, retreated, and drew the Persians into the Antitaurus, where their cavalry could not deploy. Here, at the head of his host, his boots wet with blood, he drove them into the surrounding ravines and cut them down (January 623). Cistauric Anatolia was cleared of the foe. The victorious Emperor returned to his capital, now freed from the hated proximity of the Persians, but again menaced by the Avars beyond the Long Wall.

To his appeal to Chosroes for peace negotiations he received a reply in which the Equal of the Stars referred to himself as the beloved of the gods and the master of the world and to Heraclius as his vile and insensate slave, wrote contemptuously of Jesus' inability to help the Empire, and offered pardon if Heraclius surrendered himself to him.

Conscious of the propagandistic value of the King of Kings' message, Heraclius published it and rejoined his army, which had wintered in Pontus (March 623). He marched eastward through deep Armenian valleys, enrolling many Armenians. Turning south, he invaded the fertile tableland of Atropatene, the Zarathustran Holy Land. The Christian soldiers visited the calamities of war on this fruitful area and their religious indignation on Zarathustran altars and temples. In the morning dew of a scorched summer they reached Urmia, reputed birthplace of Zarathustra, extinguished the perpetual flame, and reduced the town to ashes. Jerusalem was avenged.

As they approached Ganzaca, seat of a royal treasure, Chosroes II fled at the head of forty thousand men. The vast hoard, containing the legendary spoil of Croesus, fell to the Romans, who razed the

Photograph by Wim Swaan in David Talbot Rice,
Constantinople

*The Golden Gate today. This view shows the massive marble Golden
Gate, which formed part of the Inner Wall, behind the Outer Wall
with its small foregate*

Temple of the Sun, wherein stood a statue of the Shahanshah, surrounded by his kin—the sun, the moon, and the stars, occasionally
enlivened by artificial rain and thunder.

The troops wanted to push on to Ctesiphon, but Heraclius preferred to winter in Albania, where he could strengthen his army
with Caucasian recruits. The matter was referred to God. Three
days the army fasted. On the fourth the Emperor opened the Bible,
apparently at random, and read a verse, which unmistakably commanded him to retire to the Cyrus. He liberated fifty thousand captives. This move conciliated the Medes and increased their hatred of
Chosroes, who continued to reject peace.

When Heraclius emerged from winter quarters in 624 three Persian hosts converged on him. The Roman hero marched, counter-
marched, and retreated, ever clinging to the Armenian highlands,
where the Persian cavalry was of little use. Finally two Persian

armies cornered him near the Araxes. In the dead of night he extricated his force and took up a hidden position on a wooded hillock. The Persians pursued precipitately. Suddenly the Romans attacked and shattered them. With lightning rapidity Heraclius assailed and scattered the third Iranian contingent. Wearied by defeat and futile marches, the Persians retired to winter in fortified cities south of the Araxes.

On a cold December dawn the Emperor and his small force scaled the walls of a town on Lake Van, where the foremost Persian general, Shahr Baraz, and his troops were wintering. The surprised Persians groped frantically for their arms, but compact Roman detachments, sword in hand, were upon them. Shahr Baraz jumped half-clothed into the saddle and with a few officers galloped out of the doomed city. The sun rose on a desperate sight. The surviving Persians, half-naked satraps and officers, their wives and children in nightgowns, soldiers, and townspeople, entrenched on flat roofs, were desperately hurling everything within reach on the mailed Romans below. The houses were set afire, and the last defenders died in the flames. The Romans established their winter quarters in the town.

During the winter at Lake Van, Heraclius decided to carry the campaign of 625 westward. Surmounting the snow-capped Armenian mountains in the early spring, he recovered Martyropolis, traversed the Tigris, and at Amida rested his army, laden with spoil and captives. He then moved to the Euphrates, on whose west bank Shahr Baraz awaited him. With that genius for eluding even the most experienced generals Heraclius forded the river north of Samosata and entered Cilicia.

Again he faced Shahr Baraz, encamped on the opposite bank of the Sarus. Emboldened by their victories and anxious to prove their devotion to their Emperor, the Roman troops rushed impetuously across the bridge and assaulted the Persian camp. The foe simulated retreat. The Romans followed. The hidden Persian flanks closed, pressing the Romans back over the bridge in disorder. Emerging from his tent, Heraclius saw his troops in headlong flight. With possibly the life of the Empire at stake, he seized his sword and dashed through his fleeing army to the bridge. The Persian warrior leading the pursuit dealt him a crushing blow. The Emperor supported it on his shield, thrust before the Iranian had withdrawn his arm, and sent him hurtling into the torrent. The Romans rallied to his side and cleared the bridge. Heraclius, wounded, spattered with blood, his armor bent and riddled, led them in closed ranks through a hail of weapons against the Persian camp. Easily recognized by his purple buskins, he was violently attacked but fought until twilight terminated the battle. The next day Shahr Baraz retreated, and Heraclius led his men into Pontic winter quarters.

Chosroes II may have gnashed his teeth. For two decades he had thought his armies invincible. The utter destruction of the Roman Empire had seemed within his grasp. Then Heraclius had sallied forth with his devoted band, cut down the most renowned Persian regiments, outwitted the most famous Persian generals, driven the Brother of the Moon himself into humiliating flight, devastated his realm, razed his palaces, seized his treasures, profaned and destroyed his sanctuaries.

Yet the Equal of the Stars rejected a peace restoring the former frontiers. Making a supreme effort to retrieve his lost prestige, appease the enraged magi, and crush the hated Christian realm forever, he mustered all available able-bodied men and concerted with the Avars for a joint attack on New Rome.

Thus, in the summer of 626 Shahr Baraz at the head of 50,000 men occupied Chalcedon, while the Avar Khagan with a motley horde of 80,000 forced the Long Wall and encamped outside the city ramparts. When imperial ambassadors strove to bribe the Khagan he contemptuously told them not to presume to tempt the future master of the City and offered to allow the inhabitants to depart, each with an undergarment and a shirt. These scornful words were followed by a general assault supported by a variety of formidable siege implements.

But the Emperor had entrusted the defense of the City to the image of the Virgin not made by hands and to several thousand carefully instructed veterans. While the fleetless Iranians in Chalcedon remained inactive, the Khagan's warriors were repulsed at New Rome's land wall with heavy losses. Moreover, his rude fleet on the upper Golden Horn was sunk by imperial galleys. At length his men refused to attack and the haughty Khagan withdrew beyond the Danube. Thereafter Avar power declined, just as Hunnic dominance had collapsed after a brief spell of glory, for, whatever their martial talents, the Ural-Altaic peoples had, because of their nomadic life and the vast extent of their sparsely populated original homes, not become state builders.

Heraclius had not sought to prevent the Persians from marching on Chalcedon. Nor had he thrown himself and his army into the capital. Instead, he had preserved his dreaded mobility and had trisected his army. A select corps defended New Rome. Another contingent under his brother Theodore defeated a Persian army in Pontus. Such was Chosroes' fury at this discomfiture that he insulted and lashed his defeated general's corpse.

With the remainder of his troops Heraclius marched eastward and negotiated with the Khazars. It is unknown when this probably Turkish people reached the lands between the Caspian and the Black Sea. The rays of history first fall on them in the sixth century as part of a great Turkish empire. They soon seceded and became natural foes of the Persians, who prevented their expansion across the Caucasus. Now Heraclius met their Khagan and possibly betrothed his daughter to him. In any event, the Khagan loaned him forty thousand warriors. Thus reinforced, Heraclius again ravaged Media and went into winter quarters in enemy territory, losing his Khazar auxiliaries upon the Khagan's untimely death.

In the spring of 627 Heraclius devastated Media and Assyria. Yet the King of Kings still refused peace. He assembled a last army, to whose general he intimated with sinister significance that he was to conquer or perish. The opposing hosts met near the ruins of Nineveh on a December dawn of 627. Heraclius on his famous battle horse charged at the head of his troops. A Persian general rode against him. The Emperor swung his sword with a powerful backhand stroke and stretched him headless on the ground. A second Iranian general met a similar fate. A third galloped up. His spear pierced the imperial lip, but the next moment he too lay lifeless on the field. The engagement became general and raged for hours. At length, Heraclius espied the Persian commander in golden armor, broke through his guards, and killed him with one sword stroke. Finally, the leaderless Iranian host broke.

Marching south, Heraclius traversed the salt lands between the Zagros range and the Tigris. Through this mournful region rivers carry rich alluvia, which overflow and form oases called Paradises. In the Paradise where over a thousand years earlier Xenophon and ten thousand Greeks had rested and hunted the Roman army spent

Christmas. Then they moved on Dastagerd. Chosroes had fled, and the garrison surrendered. Heraclius seized the huge royal treasure, burned the fire temple and the fugitive potentate's palace, but spared the inhabitants (January 628). The Roman soldiers regaled themselves on the roes, gazelles, onagers, ostriches, peacocks, pheasants, swans, and lions of the royal park and hunting preserves. Meanwhile, satraps deposed Chosroes, who was soon put to death.

With wise moderation Heraclius made peace with the new monarch, demanding only the return of all Roman prisoners and territory (628). Of the "two lights of the world" one was almost extinguished, while the Roman Empire, after an almost total eclipse, seemed to shine with renewed brilliance. The fame of her Emperor reached the uttermost points of Europe and deep into the vastness of Asia.

TRIUMPH

New Rome impatiently awaited Heraclius' return. On the appointed day he passed in triumph through the Golden Gate. Standing beside gold and laurel crosses in a triumphal chariot drawn by four elephants, the diadem on his brow, the purple mantle on his shoulders, the scepter in his hand, Heraclius moved slowly through his thankful capital, preceded by the Wood of the True Cross, the standards of Crassus, Valerian, and Julian, and over three hundred Sassanian ensigns. Around him on magnificent mounts rode his guards and officers in golden armor. Behind him came Senators and other dignitaries. The houses of the triumphal avenue were covered with precious draperies. On the balconies the flames of thousands of candles flickered palely in the sunlight. The air was thick with myrrh and incense and the avenue was dense with people frantically acclaiming the incomparable hero, who combined the qualities of Moses and Alexander. Poets longed for the genius of Homer to sing his deeds. Finding no parallel in Jewish or Christian history, they harked back to the dim demigods of Antiquity.

But the Emperor's reverend attitude recalled that thanks were due, not to him, but to Jesus, Who had given them victory. The inhabitants' hearts went out to him, for they no longer saw the handsome young man who had come to them eighteen years earlier. The weight and cares of the Empire, the fatigues and hardships of six successive campaigns, the emotions and wounds of many battles had whitened his hair, bent his shoulders, lined and scarred his face, broken his health.

The triumphal cortege reached Saint Sophia amid acclamations, "Long live our greatest, most pious, ever victorious Basileus, the Equal of the Apostles, the Earthly Representative of God!" [2] Bearing the Wood, the Emperor greeted the Patriarch who had once adjured him not to abandon the capital. As he entered the sacred precincts, the people intoned the victory hymn believed to be the same that Moses and the children of Israel had sung coming out of the land of bondage. Heraclius prostrated himself at the altar, offered God the triumph, and deposited the Holy Wood, an act that Christian churches still celebrate. Never had a Roman general penetrated so far east. Since Caesar no Roman had fought with such uniform success. Reaching back to a distant era when the genius of Hannibal had threatened the existence of the Republic, the Senate hailed him a new Scipio.

In the spring of 630 Heraclius and the Empress Martina, his niece and second wife, set out to restore the Wood of the True Cross to Jerusalem. Entering the Holy City clad as a pilgrim but surrounded by the resplendent armor and plumes of his entourage, he reverently replaced the beloved Wood in the Church of the Holy Sepulcher. The Patriarch of Jerusalem verified that the seal that Helena had affixed to its silver case was intact, that no heathen hand had touched it.

MONOTHELETISM

The crusade was over, and Heraclius endeavored to support the shaken Persian empire, the civilized rampart against the shifting barbarians of the plains. But he had pressing domestic problems. Syrians and Egyptians, alienated by religious persecution, had gladly accepted Persian rule. Indeed, in those areas where the Hel-

---

[2] Pernice, *L'Imperatore Eraclio* (Florence, 1905), p. 178.

lenistic veneer was disappearing, heretics were in a majority, Nestorians in Mesopotamia and Monophysites in Syria and Egypt, while Armenians also had their own form of Christianity.

In an effort to conciliate the Monophysites and bind them to the artificial structure of the Empire by ties of a common faith, Heraclius and the Patriarch Sergius offered the monoenergetic doctrine. The councils had decreed that Christ had a divine and a human nature but had not determined the singularity or the duality of His activity or His will. Essentially the Monophysites believed Christ to have one nature. Hence, regarding His nature or natures no compromise was possible, but Heraclius hoped to unite Monophysites and Dyophysites on the common ground of one activity. The patriarchs of New Rome, Alexandria, and Antioch agreed. The Pope, however, insisted that Christ had two activities but one will. The Levantine patriarchs consented and Monoenergetic became Monothelete. After centuries of discord the Church seemed about to be reunited under the dogma of one will.

But Sophronius, a former monk, now Patriarch of Jerusalem, refused to compromise with the Monophysites and rallied the likeminded. The Church and the peoples of the Empire were again torn asunder. The attempt to unify the Church had failed.

THE THEME SYSTEM

It had long been the Empire's practice to grant hereditary land to border soldiers on condition of military service. Moreover, in menaced districts Justinian had given civil authority to commanding generals.

In the midst of the Persian War Heraclius took advantage of its destruction of many great Anatolian estates to combine the ancient institution of settled borderers with that of military governors and to extend his reorganization, the theme system, from the frontiers inland. He thus organized Anatolia into themes. A theme was a regiment commanded by a strategos (general). Imperceptibly the word came also to denote the province where the theme was stationed.

Heraclius installed staunch soldiers in Anatolian and Armenian themes and made inalienable, tax-free grants of land to them on

condition of hereditary military service. Many peasants also assumed military obligations in return for such small-holdings. These
soldier-farmers and farmer-soldiers received modest pay, their main
remuneration being the land-grants. The effects of the system were
revolutionary. It fostered the rise of free farmers, restored agriculture, provided national soldiers with an interest in the defense and
survival of the Empire, established an efficient military defense, relieved the treasury, reduced the number of officials, and partially
accounts for the astonishing reversal of fortune in the Persian War.
It was Heraclius' greatest gift to the future survival of the Empire.
Later emperors were to build on his theme system, and as long as it
endured the Empire was secure.[3]

SLAVS

Since the defeat before New Rome in 626 central Avar power
had declined. Masses of Slavs, some in disconnected bands, others
under Altaic leaders, fled from their dominion into the Balkan Peninsula. Thus, Slovenes, Serbs, and Croats entered Illyria. The Slavs
sought, not spoils, but homes. As their northern brothers had qui-
etly taken much of the land vacated by Germans, the southern
Slavs flooded the Balkan Peninsula, depopulated by centuries of invasion.

They assimilated the Slavs already there as well as Illyrians.
Many romanized Thraco-Illyrians, however, withdrew into the
mountains. To this day, though spread from the Bug to the Gulf of
Corinth and from the Adriatic to the Black Sea, they have obsti-
nately clung to their customs, their Latin speech, and their name,
for, though the Slavs call them Vlachs, they proudly style themselves Rumans.

Other romanized Thraco-Illyrians fled to Dalmatian cities,
promontories, and islands. In 639 the inhabitants of Salona retreated
to the defensible Palace of Diocletian. In 656 the citizens of the
antique Greek colony, Epidaurus, retired to a tenable cape, Ragusa,
now Dubrovnik. Others established themselves at Cattaro (Kotor).

[3] For different views regarding the establishment of the first themes see
Baynes in *English Historical Review* of July 1952 and Pertusi in *Aevum* of
April 1954.

Zara held out. These Dalmatian Romans were bound to the Empire by the presence of a strategos at Zara, the payment of tribute, and the contribution of ships and sailors for Adriatic service.

Unlatinized Illyrians receded into inaccessible mountains to rejoin remote kinsmen, the Albanians, and to this day retain their ancient speech, the only survivor of the once widespread Illyrian tongue.

Unable to prevent the slavonization of the Balkan Peninsula and appreciating the value of settled masses between the Empire and the Avar realm, Heraclius recognized the Slavs as Federates and, hoping for a closer bond, undertook their conversion to Christianity. Nevertheless, the Empire had little control over them.

The Slavic occupation of the Balkan Peninsula drove a wedge between the Greek East and the Latin West and enhanced the alienation that was developing from their increasing linguistic and cultural differences. This estrangement was to subvert Christian unity and expose a large part of Christendom to Turkish conquest. Its effects are perhaps still symbolized by the Iron Curtain of the twentieth century.[4]

ARAB EXPLOSION

On the caravan road stretching northward from Yemen in a barren hollow fifty miles from the Red Sea is the holy town of Mecca, the mart of the Bedouins (Arabic, desert dwellers). Within her walls is Arabia's most sacred shrine, the Kaaba (cube). It contained the images of Arabian and other gods and a stone said to have been white when it reposed in heaven, but to have been darkened on earth by votaries' kisses. Meccan merchants exploited the Arabs' religious veneration for their town, encouraged pilgrimages to the Kaaba, and arranged fairs to coincide with them.

About 570 Mohammed was born in Mecca. Orphaned at an early age, he grew to be a sturdy, handsome, large-headed, strong-bearded camel driver, ultimately a merchant. He married a wealthy widow and devoted himself to theological meditations. At forty he

---

[4] See Randa in *Der Donauraum,* 3, 3 (1958) and Ostrogorsky in *Dumbarton Oaks Papers,* 13 (1959).

began to proselytize. His first convert was his wife, whom he ele-vated to the rank of one of the four perfect women of humanity (the other three being the wife of the biblical Pharaoh, the Virgin Mary, and his first daughter, Fatima). He entered into converse with the Archangel Gabriel, who transmitted to him the contents of an eternal book.

In Mecca the agitation of his converts disturbed the order and tolerance necessary for Meccan prosperity. Unpopular, even men-aced, they secretly departed on a Friday of 622. This is the first year of the Mohammedan era, which employs the lunar year of 354 days. As a result, the Moslem religious calendar is unrelated to the seasons.

Mohammed and his little group migrated to Yathrib, an oasis set-tlement about 250 miles north of Mecca. In recognition of its friendly reception Mohammed later changed its name to Medina (City of the Prophet). From here he and his companions plundered caravans and oases with such success that even Bedouin tribes, gen-erally contemptuous of townsmen, joined him. Perhaps in order to partake of the spoils these men of the desert accepted Islam (sub-mission). Mohammed's fortunes and religion prospered. In 630 he took possession of Mecca amid general acclaim and destroyed the objects of worship in the Kaaba with the exception of the sacred stone, which, he averred, had been given to Abraham by the Arch-angel Gabriel.

Two years later the Prophet died, leaving to his adherents the results of twenty years of discourse with the Archangel Gabriel—the Koran (Book), the basis of Islam. Mohammed recognized Jesus, Moses, and Abraham as his precursors and considered it his especial mission to restore the pristine purity of Allah's revelations to them, which had been distorted by Jews and Christians.

Islam is in many respects similar to Judaism and Christianity, with which the Prophet had frequent contacts. Allah is the only God. Man was created to obey Him and His Prophet, to have un-thinking faith in both, to fear divine punishment, and to enjoy the good things that Allah put into the world for him. While the Hell of the Moslems (those who submit) resembles the Judeo-Christian Hell, the Moslem Paradise offers perpetual youth, silken tents, soft cushions, delicious fruits, cool gardens, and graceful, dark-eyed girls. Death in the service of the Prophet secures immediate entrance to this blissful abode.

Making no distinction between temporal and spiritual matters, Mohammed legislated, as circumstances demanded, on the most varied subjects—testaments, slavery, marriage, commerce, dress, the use of the right hand for greeting and eating, the left for unclean purposes, etc. Wine, pork, gambling, and more than four wives (except for the Prophet) were forbidden. Love, peace, repentance, good deeds, and forgiveness were advocated.

Upon Mohammed's death in 632 his faithful companion Abu Bekr, the father of his favorite wife Aisha, was elected Khalif (successor) of the Moslem community. He faced a difficult situation. Bedouin tribes refused the obligatory alms and new prophets, animated by Mohammed's success, arose among them. But Abu Bekr's profitable foray against the Roman Empire and the overthrow of would-be prophets demonstrated the excellence of Islam to the dissident tribesmen. Central Arabia and Yemen became definitively Mohammedan. Success was soon to convert the entire peninsula. Before his death in 634 Abu Bekr designated the austere Omar as his successor. Since raids, the Bedouins' chief interest, against coreligionaries were prohibited, an attack on the rich empires in the north seemed indicated.

The Arabs invaded Palestine and Syria and defeated the local Roman forces. Heraclius, who was in Emesa, dispatched an army against the invaders in Judaea, while another contingent held off the main Arab force on the Yarmuk. Apparently his intention was to crush the intruders in Judaea, take Akaba, and thus sever the supply lines of the Arabs on the Yarmuk. But when the latter learned that the Romans were advancing against their brethren in Judaea they moved rapidly southward, crossed the Moab Mountains, rejoined their comrades in Judaea, and in July 634 helped rout the Romans at Ajnadain.

Possibly this victory deflected the Arabs' thoughts from plunder to conquest. In any event their main army returned to the Yarmuk, overran the Roman position in September 634, and a year later took Damascus, apparently with the help of its Monophysite bishop. The Arabs advanced to Emesa and Hama, and Heraclius withdrew to Antioch. To the south only Jerusalem, Caesarea, Tyre, Sidon, Beirut, and Tripoli held out.

Undaunted, the Emperor reconstituted an army. But, prostrated by disease, he did not take personal command, although the sight of the aging hero in battle armor might have fired the soldiers and silenced the bickering generals. On the advance of this new Roman force in the spring of 636 the Arabs retreated to the south bank of the Yarmuk, where they could receive reinforcements from the desert, withdraw to it if necessary, possibly even lure the Romans into it. The Romans, however, merely reoccupied the north bank of the river. Months passed. While in the Roman camp insubordination led to fighting between regiments, the reinforced Arabs gradually outflanked and encircled them. In August they converged and annihilated them.[5]

Syria and Palestine were doomed. Antioch and other cities fell to the invaders, some valiantly defended, others easily yielded, still others betrayed. In general, the Semites readily submitted to distant kinsmen, who brought religious freedom, and the Greek or hellenized inhabitants grimly resisted.

Probably in 637 the Patriarch Sophronius of Jerusalem realized that the Holy City could not hold out. He consequently informed the besiegers that he was prepared to capitulate, but only to Omar himself. The pious Khalif came, not as the head of an expanding empire, but as a simple pilgrim, clad in a shabby cloak, mounted on a camel, carrying a bag of dates, a sack of wheat, a goatskin of water, and a wooden bowl. Squatting on the earth, he dictated to the Patriarch mild conditions of surrender. Church bells were no longer to be rung, crosses were not to adorn the church roofs, proselytism among Moslems was not to take place, Jews were to have equal rights with Christians. Then, accompanied by Sophronius, Omar took over the city. Wishing to visit the Church of the Holy Sepulcher, he deferred to the Patriarch's suggestion that he doff his filthy fleece for a more becoming robe. He viewed the ruins of the Temple of Solomon and commanded the erection of a sanctuary over the rock on which it was believed that Abraham had prepared to sacrifice Isaac, Jacob had rested his head, and from which Mohammed had ascended to heaven.

While proud Caesarea held out until betrayed (640?), the invin-

---

[5] The author is indebted to Glubb, *The Great Arab Conquests* (Englewood Cliffs, N.J., 1963) for the reconstruction of the military operations leading to the second battle of the Yarmuk.

cible Arabs swept forward to the Taurus and the Armenian foothills (639). Soon they were to subject the Armenians, who had rejected the Christological modifications of the Council of Chalcedon and had also been estranged by Roman religious persecution.

Heraclius had spent six years in Syria and Palestine, endeavoring to conciliate the Semitic population by civil and financial reforms and theological compromise. But a religious settlement had been thwarted by the Patriarch of Jerusalem. Thus, Semitic disaffection facilitated the Arab conquest. Suffering from dropsy and tormented by the loss of the Holy Land, Heraclius returned to New Rome with the True Cross, once the object of his greatest glory, now the companion of his misfortunes (637). The stricken Emperor rode slowly down the triumphal avenue, where nine years earlier he had received an unparalleled ovation, while the Patriarch, sobbing a mournful litany, solemnly bore the Wood to Saint Sophia.

Meanwhile, the Arabs pursued their victorious course. After the battle of the Yarmuk Omar strengthened his forces on the lower Euphrates and in a four-day battle at Kadesia wiped out the Persian army (637?). The oppressed Babylonian peasants greeted their Semitic cousins as deliverers. Ctesiphon with its tremendous treasure fell. Thereafter the Saracens (tent dwellers) confronted, not a friendly Semitic population, but Iranians, who barred the entrance to the Iranian tableland at Nihawand. They were crushed in a titanic combat (642?). Even then they fought over every foot and only the next year did the Arabs reach Isfahan. And not until 650 did they break the obstinate resistance of Persepolis and Persia proper.

Pushing into Khorasan, the Arabs drove Yazdagird III to the Oxus, where he lost his last soldiers in battle with the Turks. Almost alone, between the conquerors of the present and the future, the young King of Misfortunes was assassinated in a mill in the lowlands south of the Oxus, the last shred of his empire (651). Except for a narrow tract on the southern rim of the Caspian, which maintained itself a century longer, the expanse covered by the Persian empire returned to Semitic rule after a lapse of twelve hundred years. As the centuries passed the Iranians gradually accepted Islam. Today there remain only twenty thousand Zarathustrans in Iran and a hundred twenty thousand in India (the Parsees), who still proudly count their years from the reign of Yazdagird III, the last king on whom reposed the divine glory of Ahuramazda.

After the fall of Persia Armenia sought the protection of the Emperor, who named an Armenian Curopalates as civil head of the country. But when the imperial Church attempted to ingest the Armenian Church the Armenian lords accepted religiously tolerant Arab hegemony (653). The Arabs shrewdly allowed feudalism to subsist and levied heavy tribute. The Armenian peasants, oppressed by native lords and Arab conquerors, sank ever lower. The bonds between Armenian feudal families were not political but linguistic, traditional, and, above all, religious. Common action was possible only through the Church and its head, the Catholicos. But the Church was at the mercy of the lords and could not impose unity. Fearing imperial assimilation, it preferred the suzerainty of the Moslems, who were too different to absorb the Armenians. Only when the khalifs became harsh did Armenia call upon the Empire.

What were the causes of the extraordinary victories of tribes theretofore regarded with contempt by Roman and Persian generals? Were the Arab horsemen so irresistible, their arms so formidable? On the contrary, at this time Arabian horses were rare and expensive. Those who owned them rode on camels and only mounted their steeds on the battlefield. Others rode on asses. The desert warriors were armed with straight sabers, lances, javelins, and bows. Some wore coats of mail or breastplates, helmets, and occasionally shields. Many fought on foot. Was it religious fervor? At this early stage, probably not. There may have been many ardent Mohammedans, but they were mostly townsmen, for Islam, like early Christianity, was essentially an urban religion. The hardy Bedouins fought for Allah as the Jews had contended for Yaweh, the Romans for Christ, the Persians for the purity of fire, but as with Jewish, Roman, and Persian soldiers, their chief interest was probably spoil and license. Islam, offering plunder to the warriors who lived and dark-eyed virgins to those who fell, was merely the means of uniting them. The reasons for their successes may perhaps be found elsewhere. For centuries powerful empires on Arabian confines had prevented great migrations. Their numbers now exceeded the resources of the dry peninsula and invested them with the irresistible force of a hungry nation hurled against surfeited civilizations. Islam gave them unity, efficient and dedicated leaders, and the immediate goal of conquering the kindred natives of Palestine, Syria, and Babylonia, whose loyalty to the distracted Roman and Persian empires had lapsed.

Why had it lapsed? Throughout the Levant the official, cultural, religious, and commercial medium was Greek, but the Egyptian autochthons clung to their ancient Hamitic tongue, while in Palestine, Syria, and part of Mesopotamia the indigenes employed Semitic Aramaic dialects. But these linguistic divisions need not have alienated Egyptians and Syrians. There were probably three main reasons for their estrangement. They performed no military service and were often despoiled by imperial troops. They were subjected to excessive taxation. And, above all, they were persecuted because of their Christological doctrines. The Jews were also hounded and formed a hostile community. Thus, Jews, Syrians, and Egyptians welcomed first the Persians and then the Saracens as liberators.

Moreover, until the invasion had been well under way, the imperial government, used to petty Arab raids, had not realized that a greater and more united expansion than the German migrations of earlier centuries was in progress. Nor did imperial officials at first suspect that a world religion had been born. They thought that they confronted some form of Arianism. Furthermore, not only was the Empire exhausted by twenty-six years of war with Persia, but the recent repayment of the war debt to the Church had necessitated higher taxes and a reduction of the army.

The Arab conquests were made on simple principles. The conquered peoples were offered the choice of Islam, tribute, or the sword. If they refused Islam they were allowed to retain their lands, laws, and customs and were subjected to a tribute that was generally less heavy than Roman taxes. Stunned by the rapidity of the conquest, the religious tolerance, and the fiscal moderation, many Romans unreservedly submitted to Arab rule.

Strong in their own union and in the discord of their weakened opponents, the Arabs swept on. In 640 they took Pelusium, the key to Egypt, defeated the Romans at Heliopolis and Memphis, and beleaguered Babylon.

Heraclius, though almost helpless from dropsy, was equipping an armament to save Egypt, the granary of the Empire, when death overtook him in February 641. Amid a sorrowing populace, the hero of a hundred battles was laid to rest in a white onyx coffin in the Church of the Holy Apostles.

Heraclius left the Empire jointly to the ailing son of his first nuptials, Constantine III, who died of consumption after a few months, and young Heracleon, the eldest son of his niece and second wife, Martina, who thus became regent. She and her offspring were unpopular because her marriage to her uncle was viewed as incestuous. Taking advantage of her unpopularity, certain nobles accused her of poisoning Constantine. With the assent of the Senate, always active when the imperium was in weak hands, they forced their way into the Sacred Palace, cut out Martina's tongue, and amputated young Heracleon's nose, causing his death. Constantine's elder son Constans II, aged eleven, became Basileus and after the murder of the overly ambitious chief conspirator against Martina, was advised by the Senate, mostly wealthy officials and great landowners (641).

The dynastic crisis and the minority hampered resistance to the Moslems. Not only was the armament that Heraclius had prepared to relieve Egypt not dispatched; troops were recalled from Egypt. Babylon fell and the invaders reached Alexandria with over a million inhabitants, four thousand palaces, four thousand baths, and four hundred theaters. Located on a land tongue, protected by the sea and Lake Mareotis, the city of the Ptolemies seemed impregnable. But her garrison was depleted and her inhabitants were disheartened by the apparent indifference of the central government. She surrendered in 642, was briefly recaptured by a Roman naval expedition three years later, and then retaken by the Arabs. New Rome's granary was lost. The Arabs spread over Cyrenaica, Tripolitania, and Nubia. Yet Nubia remained Christian until the fourteenth century. At Ethiopia the Moslem tide receded. This ancient state, judaized according to tradition by the son of Solomon and the Queen of Sheba, had been christianized about 300. It now remained an isolated Christian island in a swelling Moslem sea and insensibly lost contact with the outer world.

In 644 Omar was assassinated by an enslaved Persian and the Meccan merchant aristocrats elected Mohammed's aged son-in-law Othman Commander of the Faithful. Omar had distrusted the sea and forbidden the construction of a fleet, but Othman permitted Syrian and Egyptian shipyards to resume work.

Thus about 649 Muawia, governor of Syria, was able to send an armada against Cyprus. Racially, culturally, strategically, and commercially a link between three continents, Cyprus had been annexed to the Empire in 58 B.C. Although it had prospered, it lost its strategic importance in an exclusively Roman sea. Now, however, it could be used as a base for assaults on Syria, and the Arabs soon established a garrison on the island. For over three centuries Cyprus was to alternate between imperial and khalifal dominion or to be occupied by the two powers simultaneously and generally to be taxed by both.

Muawia also took Rhodes, but it was reconquered by the Romans eight years later. During his brief possession of the island the fallen existence of a wonder of Antiquity, the Colossus of Rhodes, came to an end. Colossus was a hundred-foot bronze sungod cast from the spoils of an abortive Antigonid attack in 304 B.C. Twelve years were consumed in its construction and erection. It was overturned by an earthquake in 224 B.C. and for nine centuries its shattered body excited the curiosity of travelers. The Arabs sold the bronze fragments to an Edessene Jew, who shipped them to the mainland, loaded them on a thousand camels, and sold them at an appreciable profit.

The Arabs had begun their expansion as plunderers but, welcomed by Semites and Hamites, became conquerors and created a vast empire. Had they confined themselves to the conquest of Semites, they might still form a compact state from the Armenian foothills to the Arabian Sea. But fortune favored their arms and they carved out a vast heterogeneous domain. Still in the patriarchal stage, they little knew how to administer an extensive realm. Consequently, they provided chiefly for the collection and distribution of tribute and left to their subjects a large measure of autonomy. They were not bent on destruction, but on preservation, in order to ensure the regular flow of tribute into the coffers of Medina, the capital of the Khalifate. While there were frequent massacres, they also took many cities by capitulation without pillage or carnage. From their new subjects they exacted only tribute. Nevertheless, considering themselves an aristocracy, the Arabs at first avoided fraternization, and it was not until after Omar's death that they acquired land in conquered regions.

Early Islam seemed to acquire the Hellenistic aspect that had mantled the East since Alexander. But as the Semitic and other Oriental elements in the Khalifate broke through the Hellenic layer, the political, religious, and racial gap between the Arabian and the Roman empires was widened by cultural and conventional differences.

Many conquered Romans accepted Islam. Some preferred the unity and tolerance of early Islam to Christian controversy and intolerance. Others, weak and poor, contrasted the equity of Moslem law to Roman law, which imposed harsher punishments on the poor, the weak, and the enslaved than on the wealthy, the strong, and the free. Others magarized for social advantage.

TRUNCATED EMPIRE

In one decade the Roman Empire had sunk from the paramount power west of the Great Wall of China to a largely Greek-speaking realm with Latins in Africa and parts of Italy and unassimilated Slavs in the Balkan Peninsula. The Hellenic element in southern Italy and Sicily had been strengthened by Greeks driven from their Pindic homeland by Slavs after 580 and probably by other Greek-speaking Romans fleeing the Persian and Arab conquests.[6] Nevertheless, the marrow of the Empire was Anatolia, which Heraclius had converted into a bristling barrier. But even it might not have availed against the Moslem onslaught had not the Anatolians been bound to the capital by identical theological convictions. Thus, while Islam spread to the oceans, it could not shatter the Tauric frontier. Had the guardians of those confines faltered New Rome could not have held out and Europe might have become Mohammedan.

The adult Constans II was imbued with two ardent aims—to recover the ravished provinces and to halt the endless theological disputes that had played so important a part in their loss. His offensive against Syria frustrated, he determined to crush the rising Moslem sea power. He closed with the Moslem fleet off the Lycian

[6] For the survival of Greek in Magna Graecia from ancient times see Parlangèli in *Akten des XI . . . Byzantinistenkongresses* (Munich, 1960) and for its reinforcement in the Middle Ages Charanis in *American Historical Review*, 52, 1 (1946).

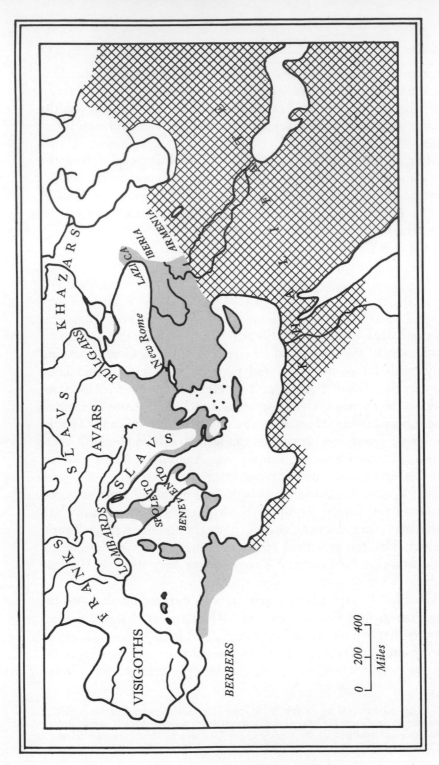

SLAVS

KHAZARS

BULGARS

AVARS

IBERIA

LAZICA

ARMENIA

New Rome

SLAVS

FRANKS

LOMBARDS

SPOLETO

BENEVENTO

VISIGOTHS

BERBERS

0   200   400

Miles

The Empire About 650

coast in 655 but was discomfited and had to abandon his flagship in disguise.

His effort to unite Monotheletes and Dyotheletes in the face of expanding Islam was also fruitless. In 648 he had issued a model of faith, the *Type*, which treated the One or Two Wills as Heraclius had treated the One or Two Energies, and forbade further discussion. But the Dyotheletes viewed this neutral edict with the same abhorrence with which they regarded Monotheletism. In his struggle to impose unity Constans banished the Pope and executed the Dyotheletes' presumptive candidate for the throne, his brother Theodosius.

Having defeated and transplanted Balkan Slavs to Anatolia and having lost Armenia to the Moslems, Constans left his hostile capital to fortify the Roman West (662). He stopped at thriving Athens (for Helladic cities had been revigorated by the influx of Greeks from the interior, now largely in Slavic hands), proceeded to Tarento, failed to subdue the Lombard Duke of Benevento, and visited Rome. He settled at Syracuse, fortified Sicily against the incursions of Moslems (which had begun in 652), and waged inconclusive war against them in Africa. Back in Syracuse, he was preparing to rub himself with Gallic soap in the Baths of Daphne when an attendant struck him on the head with a silver soap container. The Emperor sank into his bath and drowned (668).

It was perhaps upon him rather than upon his son and successor Constantine IV that the epithet "Bearded" (*Pogonatos*) had been bestowed.[7] However that might be, though Roman respect for office had long restrained the custom of nicknaming sovereigns instituted with Caligula (Little Boot), Greek banter left few emperors without a sobriquet.

The Greek tongue had gradually supplanted Latin in the Empire.[8] The process was accelerated by the slavonization of Illyria, which until about 550 had been the prime source of Latin-speaking soldiers. Those latinized Illyrians who clung to the Dalmatian strand were termed Romans (the Latin word), while elsewhere Ro-

---

[7] See Brook in *Byzantinische Zeitschrift*, 17 (1908).

[8] Charanis points out that the use of Greek by Roman officials was already common in the early Empire and was not a break in the continuity of the Roman tradition. *Bucknell Review* (May 1963).

man subjects were called Romaians (the Greek for Roman). Imperial Greek retained many Latinisms. Military commands were still Latin, and it was to be minted on certain imperial coins several centuries longer, lest its disuse seem a renunciation of lost provinces. Much official Latin had already been imbibed into Greek. While the Emperor acquired the Hellenic titles *Basileus, Autocrator, Despot,* and *Sebastos,* and while *Consul* yielded to *Hypatos, Prefect* to *Exarch,* etc., yet the Empress remained *Augusta,* a barbarian king, *rex. Barbarian,* incidentally, was applied to any foreign nation in both languages.

While *Romaic* was employed for the speech and subjects of the Empire, *Hellene* now designated an impious or unchristian person, *Helladic* signified an inhabitant of the Pindic Peninsula, and *pagan* (Latin for rural) stood for secular as opposed to sacred. The Empire was not called *Greek* except by rivals, who resented the universal implications of *Roman.* But so intimate was the relationship that *Greek* and *Roman* became practically synonymous.

The Greek language of the Empire may be trisected:

1. the simplified, popular Romaic dialects, which had absorbed Oriental and Latin expressions and differed according to district;

2. the idiom of the educated, which had also simplified ancient Greek and assimilated Latinisms;

3. the conventional written medium called Hellenic, the descendant of Hellenistic Greek.

Byzantines were as passionately concerned with theology as the classical Greeks had been with politics. But possibly other reasons led thematic troops to march on New Rome and demand that the young Emperor crown his two brothers in order that the Heavenly Trinity be reflected by an earthly one. Constantine IV lauded their piety, invited the leaders into the capital, executed them, and amputated his brothers' noses.

In due course he confronted a khalifal assault. In 656 the oligarchy of Meccan merchants had been terminated by the assassination of the Khalif Othman. Ali, kinsman of the Prophet and widower of his daughter Fatima, was elected Khalif, defeated Mohammad's favorite wife Aisha, and made Kufa near the Euphrates his capital. Medina slipped back to the quiet of a provincial, albeit sacred town. But Muawia, governor of Syria, owner and self-styled avenger of the bloody shirt of his kinsman Othman, uprose. He became sole Khalif after the murder of Ali in 661 with Damascus as his capital.

Having gained possession of strategic Aegean points as well as Cyzicus, he sent an armada against New Rome, the bulwark of Christendom and the gateway to Europe (674). If it fell, Europe lay at his mercy. The rival navies joined issue in the Marmara. The imperial fleet spat forth Greek Fire. Its composition, a jealously guarded secret, was a liquid compound, which special syphon ships projected against enemy vessels. When it struck it burst into flames that water could not quench. Several years the Moslems assailed the Great City and then departed in silent rage. A storm off Pamphylia dashed their ships on the rocks and a Roman squadron obliterated the survivors. The chastened Khalif purchased peace at the annual price of three thousand pieces of gold, fifty slaves, and fifty thoroughbred horses. All Europe rejoiced and sent gifts to Constantine IV, the guardian of Europe, the defender of the faith, the supreme sovereign of Christendom.

The paramount potentate was less fortunate in hostilities with the Bulgars. This mixed Ural-Altaic people had swept westward in the wake of the cognate Huns. Settled in the Black Sea steppe, they had regained independence after the disruption of the Hunnic empire in 454 and lost it a century later to the Avars. Soon after, shaking off the Avar yoke, a large group had moved northeastward and founded Great Bulgary on the banks of the Kama and the middle Volga. Others, pressed by the Khazars (who dwelt between the Caspian and the Sea of Azov), forged into Bessarabia. In 679 they traversed the Danube and constrained Constantine IV to pay tribute and cede them land between the Danube and the Balkan range, peopled mostly by disunited Slavs.

Upon the conclusion of peace Constantine IV convoked the Sixth Ecumenical Council at New Rome to resolve the Monothelete controversy (680). After a year's deliberations, including a miscarried miracle when a monk tried to revive a corpse by whispering mystic formulae, the assembly concluded that the Monothelete dogma diminished Christ's humanity and was heretical. It decreed that He had two natural wills and two natural activities without division, alteration, separation, or confusion. Thus, the Christological controversy was finally closed. Most of the Monophysites had been torn from the Empire and Monotheletism was no longer needed to placate them. Yet, though Jesus was doctrinally still human, in Byzantine hearts He seems to have become ever more divine, remote, and omnipotent. The Virgin and the saints insensibly assumed His mediatory function.

The Council also discussed chronology. Early Greek calendars were as numerous as the statelets. Each city reckoned according to the reign of her king or the incumbency of her chief magistrate. After 776 B.C., however, time came to be computed by the Olympiads. The Romans also calculated dates from the tenure of rulers or magistrates and created an era, counting from the legendary foundation of Rome in 753 B.C. Later, Romans often recorded from Caesar's calendar reform in 46 B.C. Many nations or cities of the Empire continued to number from some regional or municipal event. Christians numerated from the birth of Abraham, putatively 2016 B.C., or from the creation of the world, supposedly in 5508 B.C. It was this method that the Council adopted in 691. Others preferred to date from the birth of Christ, which they placed a few years too late. Charlemagne was to embrace this system.

END OF THE HERACLIADS

Having provided for external security and internal peace, Constantine IV died of dysentery at thirty-three, leaving the Empire to his sixteen-year-old son Justinian II (685).

This dynast soon entered negotiations with the Khalif. The Khalifate was no longer the elective empire of the Meccan merchants but the hereditary realm of Muawia's descendants, the Umaiads. After the murder of Othman in 656 the disunity of the Arab empire had become apparent, for the Arabs had not accepted Mohammed's theory of equality. Pride of birth or station, contempt, rivalry, and hatred cleft townsman from Bedouin, town from town, tribe from tribe, north from south, early convert from later proselyte, Arab of conquered Iraq from Arab of conquered Syria, and, above all, Arab from alien. While the jealousies of the dry peninsula raged in the uttermost extremities of the Khalifate, sectaries formed to dispute the succession of the Umaiads. Thus weakened, the Khalif agreed not only to share the revenues of Cyprus, Armenia, and Iberia with the Emperor but made both financial and territorial concessions to him in order to enlist his collaboration in the removal of the troublesome Mardaites (Syriac for rebels) from the Khalifate (688 or 689).

The Mardaites were staunch Monotheletes who had fled from imperial persecution to the wooded Lebanese mountains, with whose Monophysite denizens they had coalesced. They defied Moslem efforts to dislodge them and offered asylum to Christian fugitives. Justinian enrolled twelve thousand and disseminated them in Anatolia, Thrace, and Hellas. But many Mardaites distrusted him and clung to Lebanon. From them the Maronites, affiliated with the Catholic Church since 1736, are believed to be descended.

The spirited young sovereign refused the tribute to the Bulgars, took the field, and returned with possibly sixty thousand Slavs, whom he settled on the southern Marmaran shore, depopulated since the Arab occupation of Cyzicus. From them he formed an auxiliary corps. He effected several such human transplantations, moving Cypriotes to a new city near Cyzicus and resettling Anatolians.

This policy may have been motivated by the conflict between the Emperor and the aristocracy, that is, the Senate, for the great Anatolian landowners or archons operated politically through their members in the Senate and militarily through their officers in the army. Justinian II endeavored to weaken them by incarcerations, confiscations, executions, and vast human displacements to remove Anatolians loyal to them and introduce outlanders directly dependent on him.

He also rejected the Khalif's annual payment because it was in the new khalital coinage bearing Koranic verselets and not in the customary municipal Syrian coin with the Emperor's effigy. Though protesting his desire for peace, the Khalif accepted the challenge of the infidel who insulted the Word of Allah. Placing the recent treaty on a lance in token of his innocence, he advanced into the Empire and in 691 encountered the Emperor, most of whose imported Slavic troops deserted. Put to flight, Justinian is said to have butchered the loyal Slavs and their families upon reaching the Marmara, while the Khalif retook the recently ceded Armenian provinces.

Justinian II was also unfortunate in New Rome. He released Leontius, an Isaurian magnate and the prime general of the realm, from a three-year confinement. During the night Leontius liberated other imprisoned magnates and veterans. Joining forces with the Patriarch and the Blues, they dragged Justinian to the Hippodrome, where, as day dawned, his nose and tongue were slit and he was banished to antique Cherson (695).

Already before the time of Herodotus, Greek Black Sea cities had controlled the mouths of the rivers that brought wheat, furs, gold, and amber from Scythia. Though in constant contact with Scythic savages, sword-worshipers, life-sacrificers, blood-drinkers, arrow-poisoners, and flea-eaters, these hardy traders had retained the elements of Hellenic civilization, went into battle chanting Homeric verses, delighted in oratorical eloquence, cultivated mind and body, and erected beautiful public edifices. Most of these cities eventually succumbed to barbarians. But on the Crimean Peninsula stood Cherson, founded by Bithynian Dorians five centuries before Christ. Isolated in swarming Barbaria, this lonely survival of the Hellenic civic spirit, though long under Roman hegemony, still upheld its archaic municipal administration. Empires fell and fierce Asiatic hordes rushed madly westward, but Cherson continued through the centuries to thrive on the export of salt fish, hides, cattle, oil, corn, and wine.

With Justinian II in this mild exile, Leontius faced war in the Caucasus and Arab aggression in Anatolia and Africa. In 681 the Arabs had swept across North Africa to the Atlantic. But Moors (Berbers) and Romans had driven them back to Cyrenaica, even forcing them to evacuate sacred Kairawan, which they had founded in 670 and which is hallowed because three hairs of Mohammed's beard repose in a mosque outside its walls.

In 697 the Arabs took Carthage. The Roman navy moved against the quondam Punic metropolis, broke through the chain at the entrance of the port, and redeemed the city. But when a large Moslem armament arrived the Romans hastily departed. Control of the western Mediterranean was lost. Fearing punishment, the officers draped the purple on the Drungary Aspimar. Aspimar changed his Germanic name to Tiberius III and moved on New Rome, which was opened to him by the Greens and partially looted by his men. Leontius' nose was slit, his head tonsured, and he was immured in a monastery (698).

Tiberius III successfully continued the exhausting khalifal war.

Indeed, while Islam was girdling the world, it could not conquer Anatolia, where it was frustrated by the flexible thematic system and an indomitable, militarized Christian population. Tiberius strengthened the Pamphylian coast with settlements of Mardaites, restored Cypriotes to Cyprus, induced the Khalif to return his Cypriote captives, established a Mardaite garrison on the island, and took the offensive against the Khalifate.

Meanwhile, Justinian had fled to the Khazars. Honored by his presence, the Khagan gave him his sister in marriage and a home in the former Greek city of Phanagoria. Roman ambassadors offered a generous reward for the imperial fugitive, alive or otherwise, and the Khagan determined to do away with him. Informed of these designs by his wife, Justinian strangled the assassins and escaped to the Bulgars. He won over the Sublime Khan, marched with him on New Rome at the head of a large Bulgaro-Slavic host, penetrated the city through an unguarded aqueduct, and bestowed on the Khan the Caesarate and an abundance of gold (705).

Justinian wreaked vengeance on those instrumental in his over-throw or not sanguine about his return. Leontius and Tiberius III were led through the streets in fetters and hurled on the dais in the Kathisma. Here the enthroned Heracliad placed an imperial foot on each of their napes, which were later to feel the more conclusive weight of the executioner's blade. The Emperor blinded the Patriarch and indiscriminately butchered bureaucrats, officers, and soldiers. His excessive executions so weakened the army that Tiberius' gains against the Moslems were lost. Those Ravennese who had expressed pleasure at his removal in 695 were bound and placed in a ship, which was ignited. Prominent Chersonites were drowned or roasted on spits. Not satisfied with the number of victims, Justinian sent a force to Cherson with minute instructions for further slaughter. But the expedition united with the Chersonites and proclaimed the Armenian Bardanes Emperor Philippicus. New Rome opened her gates to the new Isapostol and the last of the Heracliads was killed (711).

The Bulgars reached the city walls, the Moslems crossed the Taurus, and a conspiracy of Anatolian themes cost Philippicus throne and sight (713). Before the military conspirators could elect their candidate the bureaucrats in the Senate, supported by the circus factions, arranged the coronation of Artemius, secretary of the dethroned Emperor. He assumed the name Anastasius II and dispatched a force to Phoenicia, where the Arabs were felling cypresses to prepare another armada against the Christian capital. At Rhodes, however, Anatolian troops murdered the commander of the fleet, seized a tax-collector named Theodosius at Adramyttium, imposed the imperial insignia on him, and invested the capital, which was betrayed and plundered (715). Anastasius II entered a Salonican monastery.

The Anatolian magnates again held the Empire, but it seemed impossible to reconcile their own with imperial interests. When they elected a candidate he could either rule on their behalf, thus feudalizing and enfeebling the Empire, or he could seek to break their power. During the impotent reign of Theodosius III administration declined, military discipline decayed, Moslems and Bulgaro-Slavs neared the capital. As a century before, the Empire seemed on the verge of dissolution.

Hopes were soon fixed on Leo, Strategos of the Anatolic theme. Born about 680 in Isauria or Syria and exported to Thrace with his parents by Justinian II, Leo had presented that monarch with a flock of sheep when he was advancing on New Rome with the Bulgars in 705. Justinian had given him a dangerous mission in the Caucasus, whence after many adventures he returned in 713. Anastasius II created him Strategos of the Anatolic theme, the most powerful military post in the Empire. Leo, who had not participated in the revolt against Anastasius, now advanced to Nicomedia, where he routed the magnates' army (716). Theodosius III retired to a monastery at Ephesus.

VI

The Iconoclasts

717–867

I N March 717 Leo III, on whose bearded visage were marked
strength, humor, shrewdness, and determination, rode through
the Golden Gate. Five months later New Rome was besieged by
the Arabs.

The Khalifate had attained the pinnacle of power. Its confines
reached the Caucasus, the Chinese border, the Indus, the Atlantic.
Its expansion into northwest Africa had driven many latinized or
hellenized town dwellers to migrate to Sicily, Italy, or Spain, but
most of the Berbers had after titanic struggles accepted Islam. Some
Berbers adopted Arabic. Others retained their antediluvian dialects.
Their conversion to Islam had probably been motivated largely by
the prospect of booty. To appease them the Khalifate was pushed
into further conquests.

Thus in 711 the Berber Tarik crossed the Strait of Hercules
with an Arabo-Berber host. The cliff in whose shadow he landed
became Gebel Tarik (Mount Tarik), which has developed into Gibraltar. In the Iberian Peninsula Visigoths and Romans had fused
after most of the former had adopted the Nicene creed in 589.
Nevertheless, it was domestic dissension in the Visigothic kingdom
that precipitated the Moslem invasion.

Not far from Lake Janda the Gothic King Roderick met the Moslems and their Spanish allies. For days the battle raged, then part of
his army deserted to Tarik. Two years later he is believed to have
made his last stand near Salamanca. His warriors withdrew slowly
northward and at the Cantabrian range halted the Moslem ad-

From H. G. Goodacre, A Handbook of the Coinage of the Byzantine Empire; *the coin is in the British Museum*

Enlarged gold solidus of Leo III (reigned 717–741)

vance. They interbred with Iberians, and centuries later their progeny issued forth to reconquer their ancestral land.

Meanwhile, the Moslem victors sequestered a fifth of the land, eased the lot of the serfs, and terminated religious persecutions. Left in the possession of their lands and relieved of feudal and ecclesiastical oppression, many Christians abandoned the Trinity for Allah.

In the Levant the Umaiad Khalif needed only to crush the residual Empire and Europe would be within his grasp. Eighty thousand Moslems assailed New Rome's land walls, while eighteen hundred ships moved against her (717). The assault failed. A bitter winter followed, and many of the besieging Moslems perished.

Suddenly, in the dead of a spring night Roman sentinels on the marine walls heard coming over the waters the joyous shout, "Long live the Emperor!" The splash of oars became audible. Romans from Egypt in the Khalif's naval service were returning to the Empire. Thus reinforced, Leo attacked and further weakened the khalifal fleet. Then he trapped a fresh Moslem army near Nicomedia. Famine broke out among the besiegers, who reputedly ate the flesh of their dead comrades. Pestilence struck. The Bulgars attacked. At length the survivors withdrew (718). The bastion on the Bosporus had again saved Europe. The remnant of the Moslem land force reached Syria, but the fleet was shattered by a tempest in the Aegean and then annihilated by the Roman navy.

About this time Leo III crushed a usurper in Sicily as well as the quondam Emperor Anastasius II, who had left his cell in Salonica and marched on New Rome with a Bulgarian host. But the City remained faithful to Leo, and the Bulgars turned the former sovereign over to him for decapitation.

REFORM

In the provinces Justinian's Latin legal labors had been superseded by translations, local usage, ecclesiastical canons, and the opinions of judges, who were frequently corrupt.

To ensure justice and adjust law to Christian custom a committee studied Justinian's law books, later decrees, Leo's enactments, and modern practice and issued the *Ecloga* (Selection). It infused the spirit of medieval Christianity into Justinian's law and supplemented the reasonings of Roman jurists with biblical revelation.

The *Ecloga* also enunciated the duties of the Emperor, the Patriarch, the City Prefect, etc. The Emperor should have orthodox theological views and uphold the dictates of the Holy Scripture, the ecumenical councils, and Roman legislation. He should serve his subjects, preserve the Empire, recover lost provinces, and make new conquests, for the concept that the Empire should rule the world was as fresh as in the days of Caesar.

As the Emperor provided for the physical well-being of the Empire, the Patriarch should care for her spiritual health, and harmony between the two was essential.

The City Prefect ranked above the strategoi. In the capital and for a hundred miles beyond the land walls his authority was second to the Emperor's. He was civil judge, head of the gilds, and controller of the exchange and of meat prices. He was responsible for public order and could expel undesirables.

The Quaestor of the Sacred Palace now supervised strangers in the City. He inquired whence they came and why. If they sought judication he expedited it in order to hasten their departure, for provincials were allowed to sojourn in New Rome only for important reasons. Indeed, since the Nika revolt of 532 the capital had excluded idlers. The Quaestor expelled vagrants and gave work to the unemployed at municipal tasks, as in state bakeries, for the government still furnished bread and games.

The *Ecloga* abolished differential punishments. All men except slaves were now equal before the law and the emancipation of slaves was simplified.

The personal law of the *Ecloga* was steeped in ecclesiastical precepts. While Justinian's Code permitted concubinage, the *Ecloga* forbade it, declaring that a concubine was a wife. Prescribing harsh punishments for fornication, it deprived illegitimate children of the rights theretofore accorded them. While Justinian had forbidden the marriage of a Christian to a Jew, the *Ecloga* also prohibited wedlock with a heretic or a seventh cousin. The Roman principle that marriage is freely contracted and hence can be dissolved by mutual agreement yielded to the Christian dogma that man and wife are one flesh. Divorce was possible only if the wife committed adultery, if the husband were impotent, if either endangered the other's life by calumniation, or if either were a leper. Moreover, the *Ecloga* upset exclusive paternal power and vouchsafed equal rights to both parents.

Leo III also abolished the system whereby plaintiffs paid the judge. Instead, the state defrayed the judiciary expenses. And he liberated municipal councilors from fiscal responsibility for their district.

There were furthermore military, maritime, and agricultural codes, promulgated either by the Heracliads or the Isaurians.

The Military Code enumerated severe penalties for flight, disobedience, mutiny, adultery, etc.

The Maritime Code (also called the Rhodian Law, for Rhodes had once been the commercial focus of the Levant) tabulated ancient Mediterranean laws. It minimized commercial risks by fixing liability for losses through storm or piracy among shipowners, freightowners, and passengers, thus fostering the development of the merchant marine.

The Agricultural Code reveals a transformation in the condition of the peasantry. The Romans found serfdom in the Hellenistic East and among Germanic tribes, who had imposed it on Celts. Diocletian universalized it to keep the land productive and taxable. Serfs and their progeny were attached to the land, could not marry free women or enter the army, and paid rent and poll taxes. Great estates came to dominate the countryside. But when after Justinian I the enfeebled Empire confronted Slavs, Avars, Persians, and Arabs, many serfs fled, or were enrolled in the army, or were abducted. If they returned it was difficult to impose their former bondage. Moreover, the wide gaps torn out of the agricultural population by war were filled with Slavs, Armenians, and Mardaites, who would have nothing of serfdom. Taking advantage of this situation, Heraclius and his dynasty established the thematic system, which fostered the rise of free farmers. While great estates with slaves and serfs remained, the prime characteristic of the postheraclian Empire's husbandry is the free farmers, the fiscal and military foundation of her power. It is with them, their villages (which bore collective tax liability), and the protection of their property that the Agricultural Code or Farmer's Law was concerned. On the foundation of a growing free peasantry and a controlled aristocracy the Empire continued to grow strong.

The former Strategos of the Anatolic theme did not neglect the military establishment. Under the stress of foreign invasion the imperial administration had gradually been militarized and provinces had been transformed into themes such as Anatolikon, Armeniakon, Thrakesion, Opsikion, and the naval Cibyraiot. Leo III reduced their size, lest an ambitious strategos be tempted by his puissance. Within their themes the strategoi enjoyed full civil, military, and judicial, but not fiscal authority. As strategoi Leo selected, not local landowners, but loyal and efficient officers and administrators. Moreover, by moving troops from their native themes he sought to transform provincial loyalty into national patriotism.

ICONOCLASM

Leo turned his reforming eyes to the Church. Priests had foregone private business and now devoted themselves exclusively to the Church. In the fifth century they had commenced wearing dark clothing. In the sixth they had been forbidden to wear their hair long and the tonsure had commenced. In the seventh marriage after ordination had been forbidden and bishops were required to be celibate.

Images had been abhorred by early Christians as proscribed by God and as works of the devil. Sculptors and painters joining the Church had to renounce their vocation. But with the mass conversion of pagans in the fourth century Christian iconography began. Soon processions were arranged to honor relics or icons of Christ, the Virgin, saints, and martyrs or to combat misfortunes. Hymns were dedicated to them. Solemn oaths were sworn on them. Miracles were expected of them, in particular of those said not to have been made by human hands but to have fallen from Heaven. Possessing many of these hallowed likenesses, and precious, if often dubious relics, the clergy, especially monks, encouraged their veneration.

Leo III and other iconoclasts believed images of the divine to be impossible and those of the holy debasing and held their veneration to be contrary to biblical and apostolic commands. They thought that iconodulia might lead the Church into heresy by dividing the human and the divine within Christ and that it had angered God, thus bringing misfortune on the Empire. Leo did not attack Christian doctrine but Christian practices.[1] Indeed, he tried to force the remnants of the inconoclastic Montanists in Phrygia to return to the main Church. They preferred to burn to death in their churches.

In general the European parts of the Empire were iconodulic in contrast to central and southern Anatolia, where iconoclasts were numerous. In 726 one of Leo's officers removing a public image of Christ in New Rome was killed by a group of women. Soon fervently iconodulic Hellas and the Cyclades proclaimed an emperor and dispatched an armada against New Rome, only to succumb to marine fire (727).

The Patriarch refused to cooperate in the destruction of icons, was deposed, and succeeded by his syncellus (the Emperor's representative at the patriarchal court). The new Patriarch sanctioned Leo's iconoclastic course.

In the West imperial officers attempting to abolish images were murdered. The Pope, supported by the now Nicene King of the Lombards, defied the Emperor, who transferred Sicily, southern Italy, and the western part of the Balkan Peninsula from his jurisdiction to that of the Patriarch of New Rome.

Leo's assault on iconodulia was not carried out in an atmosphere of external peace. In 726 unshod Arabian horses and camels again began to trot over the Tauric passes. At length, in 740 Leo met a khalifal host at Acroïnon and in an epic struggle wiped it out. A year later he died at the age of sixty, probably of dysentery, and was succeeded by his son Constantine.

[1] Jenkins (*Byzantium . . . 610–1071*, New York, 1966, pp. 80–83) stresses the Monophysite, Jewish, and Moslem antecedents of Iconoclasm.

CONSTANTINE V

Now twenty-two, Constantine V was gay, brilliant, and fond of horses. Associated in the imperium at the age of two, he had married the daughter of the Khazar Khagan, traditional friend of the Emperor and foe of the Khalif.

A year after his accession Constantine was encamped in Anatolia, awaiting his brother-in-law, the Curopalates Artavasdus, for a campaign against the Khalifate. Twenty-four years earlier Artavasdus had helped his father seize the throne and had been rewarded with the hand of the Emperor's daughter and the presumptive succession. Suddenly Artavasdus attacked. Taken off guard, Constantine fled to his faithful Anatolics at Amorium.

Artavasdus assumed the imperium, announced Constantine's death, affirmed his iconodulic orthodoxy, entered the capital, and created his elder son Nicephorus Co-Emperor. He was supported by the Opsikian and Armeniac troops, the Armenian auxiliaries, and the iconodulic European themes, while Constantine was sustained by the iconoclastic Anatolic, Thrakesian, and Cibyraiot themes.

In May 743 Constantine discomfited Artavasdus at Sardis, in August routed his younger son at Modrina, and in November retook New Rome by a sudden assault. Artavasdus and his sons were exposed in the Hippodrome in chains and blinded, and in 746 Constantine launched the delayed offensive against the Khalifate. He pushed the Roman frontier eastward, resettled Christians from the Khalifate in Thrace, and destroyed the khalifal fleet.

Constantine continued his father's effort to transform local into national patriotism, using men from various themes in his campaigns and frontier forts. He continued the mass transplantations of Justinian II, not only to absorb the Slavs and combat local allegiance, but also to scatter iconoclasts among iconodules. His resettlements were accelerated by a plague (744–746) similar to those in the reigns of Marcus Aurelius and Justinian I. He refilled New Rome with iconodules from the European provinces, apparently hoping to influence the newcomers personally. He subjugated the turbulent Slavs of Macedonia and Thessaly, moved many to Opsikion, and pro-

This former Church of Saint Theodosia in Istanbul was probably built before 900 and named after the woman who in 726 overturned the ladder of the officer removing the image of Christ from the entrance to the Great Palace on orders of the iconoclastic Emperor Leo III. When the Turks burst into the city in 1453, they found the church adorned with roses. Possibly because of this it was called Gül Jami (Rose Mosque) when it was transformed into a Moslem sanctuary over a century later. According to legend, the last Roman Emperor, Constantine XI (reigned 1448–1453), is interred in one of its piers

vided for their hellenization. He also settled Slavic refugees from the Bulgars in Anatolia.

In the interim the abolition of images had gained adherents, notably among the educated, the military, and the secular clergy. Constantine gradually eliminated icons from the capital and from those Anatolian regions where the population was favorably disposed.

But iconoclasm was fanatically opposed by monks, the multitude under their influence, especially women, and part of the secular clergy. Their opposition convinced the Emperor that the weight of a council was required to suppress iconodulia. Carefully chosen divines from all parts of the Empire assembled in the Palace of Hieria near Chalcedon in 754. After seven months of deliberation they declared images to be the work of Satan and demons. Administering the usual fulminations, they decreed that images be removed from churches, that no more be manufactured or venerated, and that transgressors be punished by imperial authorities as heretics.

With their many institutions, immense wealth, extensive lands, and powerful hold over the people, monks formed a state within a state. Most of them and many others defied the Council's decrees, and in 765 Constantine decided to break their opposition, resorting to exile, corporal punishment, derision in the Hippodrome, forcible marriage, executions, and confiscation of monastic properties. By 770 iconodulia seemed crushed in New Rome and Anatolia. But many monks and laymen fled with their images. Possibly fifty thousand settled in southern Italy and strengthened the Hellenic element there. Indeed, a Greek vernacular still lingers in remote mountain hamlets of Italy's extremities. In contrast to Latin-speaking imperial Italy, which, influenced by popes and Germanic kings, was slipping away from the Empire, Greek-speaking Italy remained steadfastly imperial.

Meanwhile, the Bulgars, who had united and disciplined countless Slavs and created a compact state from the Carpathians to the Balkans, were eager to reach the Aegean and crossed the Balkans in 756. Threatened with the loss of the European provinces, Constantine took the field. After seven years of warfare he confronted the Bulgar Khan at Anchialus. An entire day the opposing hosts writhed in battle. As night fell, the blood-spattered Roman cavalry

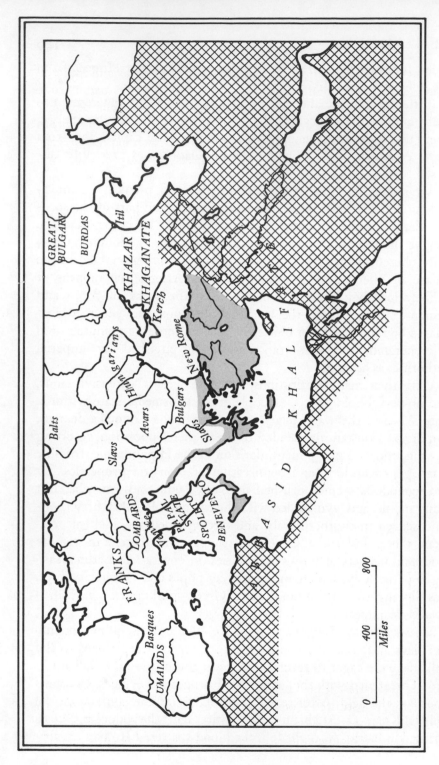

The Empire About 770

broke through the serried but flagging Bulgarian ranks and inflicted heavy carnage. Soon after, the Emperor, still in battle armor, rode into New Rome at the head of his victorious troops. The next day the booty was displayed in the Hippodrome, while the circus factions avenged the ravages of Thrace and Macedonia on the captives. The Bulgars' southward thrust had been halted.

In 773, however, Constantine was informed by spies that they were again preparing to invade the Empire. He annihilated them at Lithosoria (the Blue Stones). Returning from another punitive campaign against them in 775, the Emperor, now fifty-seven, was consumed by a fever caused by leg ulcers. His worried veterans bore him to Selymbria in a litter and placed him on a ship to carry him to New Rome. They had seen their companion of a score of campaigns for the last time. Constantine V died on the way and was interred in the Church of the Holy Apostles.

ICONODULIC REACTION

Constantine's son Leo IV succeeded to the throne and died in 780.

His ten-year-old son and colleague Constantine VI assumed the supreme dignity, while his Athenian mother Irene became regent. She had apparently reluctantly renounced iconodulia upon her marriage to Leo IV in 768. A conspiracy was spun around the eldest of the five surviving sons of the third nuptials of Constantine V, but the plot was uncovered and the five were tonsured (780). The following year the Strategos of Sicily revolted in their name but was suppressed.

Irene permitted iconodulia and in 786 convened a council in the Church of the Holy Apostles to condemn iconoclasm and officially restore iconodulia. But veteran guardsmen dispersed the assemblage. They were removed from the City on the pretext of an expedition against the Khalifate, disarmed, and disbanded. Another council was convoked, not in New Rome, where there were numerous iconoclasts, but in Nice. It pronounced the customary anathemas, reinstituted iconodulia, indicated that veneration was to be directed, not to the icon, but to the personages depicted, and in this context proclaimed cures and miracles possible (787).

After the annulment of the engagement of Constantine VI to Charlemagne's daughter Irene obliged her son to marry a Paphlagonian maiden, Maria (788). Two years later she demanded from the army an oath that he not rule during her lifetime. The thematic troops refused, declared their loyalty to the grandson of Constantine V, and deposed the woman to whose incompetence they attributed their discomfitures (790).

But Constantine VI also met defeat. He fled from the Bulgars, and many veteran officers fell or were captured (792). Four years later he avenged himself when in reply to the Sublime Khan's demand for increased tribute he forwarded him a napkin containing horse dung.

Before the reverse in Bulgaria the Emperor had restored the imperium to his mother. The Armeniac troops had refused to recognize her. After the campaign the young dynast blinded their strategos, put their leaders to death, tattooed "Armeniac Conspirator" on the faces of a thousand, and led them to New Rome in chains. Suspecting his five uncles, who were living obscurely in a monastery, he blinded the eldest and amputated the tongues of the other four.

In 795 he divorced Maria and married Theodote amid popular murmuring. In the autumn of 796, while he and his mother were taking hot iron and sulphur baths at Prusa, tidings arrived that Theodote had given birth to a son (destined to die in infancy). Constantine VI hastened to New Rome. During his absence Irene bribed his officers to arrange for the failure of his spring campaign against the Khalifate in order further to discredit him.

Then, in the summer of 797 her assassins fell upon him, but he escaped to Anatolia. Her minions in his suite dragged him back to the Great Palace during the night. He was taken to his natal Purple Chamber, whose creation was attributed to Constantine I. Soon the executioner appeared. He had been instructed by Irene not merely to hold hot metal near her son's eyes or simply to perforate them, but to tear them out, thus causing blood poisoning and death. The gory deed was done, but the last of the Isaurians is believed to have survived in darkness.

Irene now assumed the title of Emperor, not Empress, for legal female rule would violate imperial tradition. She blinded her four brothers-in-law, whose tongues had been severed by her son, brought confusion into the imperial finances, paid tribute to Moslems and Bulgars, and ceded Istria to the Franks.

FRANKS

Despite dynastic divisions the Franks had continued to expand. During the seventh century the Merovingian dynasties seemed to decay. Their palace mayors grasped the actual power and created subdynasties. A scion of the most powerful of these, Charles Martel, repulsed a plundering Moslem force at Tours in 732 and was hailed the savior of Christian Europe. His son Pepin consigned the last Merovingian to a monastery and assumed the regal title (751).

In Italy during the eighth century little help against Lombard attacks on imperial possessions came from New Rome, grappling with Moslems and Bulgars. As a result, the authority of the almost penniless imperial Duke of Rome yielded to that of the wealthy Successor of Saint Peter, who provided for the defense of the city. When the Lombards finally took Ravenna in 751 the Empire's position in Italy was shattered. The Exarch of Ravenna and the Duke of Rome disappeared, and the Emperor appointed the Pope to replace the latter. But the Lombards threatened Rome itself.

Receiving no assistance from New Rome, the Pope appealed to the Franks, sanctioned Pepin's dethronement of the last Merovingian, and anointed him King of the Franks and Patrician of the Romans. In return, Pepin crossed the Alps, relieved Rome, and took from the Lombards Ravenna and the Pentapolis (Rimini, Pesaro, Fano, Sinigaglia, Ancona, and an inland area), which he delivered to the Pope, who accepted them, not for the Emperor, but for himself (756). Papal agents replaced imperial officials, much as local bodies had supplanted imperial functionaries elsewhere in the West, while still acknowledging the Emperor as sovereign.

In 774 the Frankish King Charlemagne crushed the Lombard kingdom and assumed its crown. Another Germanic state founded on the ruins of the Roman West had come to grief. The Lombard tongue lingered on for three centuries and the name still clings to northern Italy. Meanwhile, the Lombard Duke of Spoleto acknowledged the Pope as his formal lord, while the Duke of Benevento made an equally intangible submission to Charlemagne.

Charlemagne made it clear that he was overlord in Italy, and the Pope ceased dating by the Emperor's regnal years to reckon by those of the Patriciate of Charlemagne. Rome and the Ravennese (which in memory of New Rome's rule was called Romagna until the nineteenth century) broke their last political ties with the Empire. Lombardy and Corsica became the Kingdom of Italy under Charlemagne's son Pepin (781).

Charlemagne advanced in other directions, establishing the Frankish border on the southern foothills of the Pyrenees, annexing Bavaria, and for a quarter century warring against the heathen Saxon tribes. He finally prevailed and amid streams of blood imposed on them the religion of love. The Frankish realm reached the Elbe and commenced extending its dominion over the Slavs beyond (799).

In the plains encompassing the Styrian Alps and the Theiss the Avars dwelt in nine circular enclosures, whence they ruled a diminished domain. Their Slavic serfs, the Slovenes, welcomed the Franks, who took the Khagan's Ring, thirty-eight miles in circumference, with the fabulous loot of two centuries. The Khagan submitted to Charlemagne and then to Christ (796) and the once formidable Avars soon vanish from history. (But on the northern slopes of the Caucasus, the Lesghian Avars, left behind when the horde swept westward, still hunt and herd as of yore.) The western Slavs acknowledged the suzerainty of Charlemagne, who was now supreme as far east as the Oder, the Theiss, and the Drina.

While he was worshiping at Saint Peter's in Rome in 800 the Pope placed a crown on his head. The prepared congregation acclaimed him Emperor. Whatever the Pope's intention may have been, the idea of two Roman empires did not yet exist, and Charlemagne apparently hoped to transform his new dignity into reality by proposing matrimony to the elderly Augusta Irene.

But in New Rome in 802 military and bureaucratic leaders deposed her. Nicephorus, an efficient finance minister, was proclaimed Emperor and crowned by the Patriarch. Irene was banished and soon died. After naval hostilities against the Empire in the Adriatic Charlemagne withdrew his claim to Venetia and the coastal towns of Istria and Dalmatia. Consequently, in 812 the Empire recognized his dignity *Emperor*, reserving the title *Emperor of the Romans* for the sovereign in New Rome.

From H. G. Goodacre, A Handbook of the Coinage of the
Byzantine Empire; *the coin is in the British Museum*

*Enlarged gold solidus with Nicephorus I (reigned 802–811) on obverse
and his beardless son Stauricius (reigned 811) on reverse*

NICEPHORUS I

Nicephorus, an Anatolian of possibly Arabian descent, reformed
the neglected finances and strengthened the theme system of military small-holdings. In the Peloponnese and elsewhere in the Balkan
Peninsula he began to subjugate the Slavs and sought to hellenize
them by settling military, Greek-speaking subjects among them.
The gradual spread of the thematic system in the European
provinces would seem to indicate that a measure of imperial control
was being extended over them.

Nicephorus accepted the restoration of images but reapplied taxation of religious institutions, was tolerant toward iconoclasts, and
insisted on imperial control of the Church. He encountered much
monastic opposition, notably of the monks of Studion within the
walls near the Golden Gate. They denied the Emperor's right to
undo ecclesiastical enactments. Nicephorus consequently dispersed
them, including their abbot Theodore, a leading iconodule.

In Byzantine monastic evolution Theodore was the direct successor of Basil and Justinian I. The former propagated the monastic
ideal; the latter codified it; Theodore systematized it. Like Benedict
in the West three centuries earlier, Theodore gave Byzantine monasticism minute regulations, which insensibly became the monastic
standard of the East. Providing for the monks' manual and intellectual labors and specifically dividing monastic activities, the Studite
system established a complete hierarchy. Among other rules it excluded female animals and pretty youths from monasteries.

Nicephorus turned his attention to the Khalifate, which had

changed greatly since the early eighth century when, master from the Atlantic to the Himalayas, the Commander of the Faithful had sent his warriors against New Rome. Since the reign of Ali (656–661) Islam had three main sects, which disagreed on the succession to the Khalifate:

1. the Sunnites, who considered the khalifal office elective but restricted to Mohammed's Meccan tribe. The Umaiad khalifs were naturally Sunnites.

2. the Shiites, who esteemed Ali (kinsman of the Prophet and husband of his daughter Fatima) and his descendants alone entitled to the office. The Shiites (Iranians, Iraki, and Arabs) themselves were divided on which of Ali's scions was the rightful khalif and on social and doctrinal principles.

3. the Kharijites, who maintained that any believer was eligible for the high incumbency.

The Umaiads were rocked by dynastic and Arab tribal strife in Syria and by Shiite and Kharijite risings in Iran, Iraq, and Arabia. Finally the Shiites elected Khalif, not an Alid, but a scion of the Prophet's uncle Abbas and drove the Umaiad Khalif into Egypt, where in 750 he fell with his last troops.

The patriarchal Sunnite Umaiads were replaced by the absolute Sunnite Abbasids, who headed what came to be a largely Iranian empire. Administrative posts slipped from Arab aristocrats, as such, to cosmopolitan officials, whose authority was based, not on Arabian lineage, but on the Khalif's will. The army no longer necessarily included Bedouin contingents but was recruited indiscriminately. The seat of the Khalifate passed to an ancient Sumerian settlement on the Tigris, thirty miles from Ctesiphon's ruins—Bagdad. Inhabited by Nestorians, this hamlet, many of whose bricks bore the imprint of Nebuchadnezzar, was supplanted by a circular city of three concentric walls of sundried bricks (766). Favorably located amid fertile Babylonian gardens, a focal point of great land and water trade routes, Bagdad became a center of commerce, learning, science, wealth, and religion, comparable only to New Rome. Thus, the Khalifate was now Arabic only in religion, dynasty, and in a measure in language (having replaced Persian and Greek as the official medium about 690 and remaining for centuries the cultural organ).

Loosely joined, it contrasted singularly with the compact Roman

state. The provinces enjoyed autonomy, while the central government collected the ground tax and provided for irrigation and the
combined postal and intelligence system. The khalifal army included Iranians, Arabs, Egyptians, Berbers, Negroes, and soon
Turks. Cut into regiments of one thousand men under a kaid, ten
regiments were generally commanded by an emir, who thus corresponded to the Roman strategos. But in the decentralized Khalifate
the emir's actual power was far greater. Many were virtually independent. Others founded states, though retaining the title of emir.

An Umaiad had escaped the slaughter of his family and established an independent emirate in Spain (756). The emir of Kairawan owed only nominal allegiance to the Khalif. The Berbers to
the west also formed states of their own.

In 803 Nicephorus wrote the famous Khalif Harun that the fal-
tering female Irene had submitted to tribute, the double of which
she ought to have extracted from him, and demanded that Harun
restore the fruits of his injustice or abide by the decision of the
sword. Soon after, the Moslems passed through the Cilician Gates.
This pass was seventy miles long, but the actual Gates were a
narrow corridor of a hundred yards between perpendicular cliffs.
The passage could be held by a few men, although no such feat
is recorded. At the northern exit stood Mount Lulon, the key to
the pass. Possession of its fortress passed back and forth between
Romans and Moslems. Hindered by a revolt in Anatolia, Nicephorus did not take the field until 804. He was wounded and lost two
grim battles. As a result, he wrote to Harun that the Prophet had
taught that Christians be regarded as brothers, that the Creator disapproved of unjust bloodshed, that all men have to answer to Him
for their acts, and that in a spirit of amity he was disposed to grant
his wishes. The Empire resumed the payment of tribute.

The Emperor then devoted his attention to the menacing Bulgars. These regnant Altaians were steadily being slavized and only
their name still bespeaks their Mongoloid origin. As they spread
southward, they moved their headquarters to the southern Dobrudja.
Here they erected Pliska, a fortified camp with the palace of the
Sublime Khan. His realm now covered the ancient provinces of
Dacia and Moesia and was encircled by a ditch and a mound, whose
traces may still be discerned.

In 808 the ambitious Khan Krum invaded Macedonia, defeated a

Roman army, and captured the soldiers' pay, eleven hundred pounds of gold. The following year he cunningly seized Sofia, butchered its garrison, and wrecked the town. Nicephorus, who had been hampered by mutiny at Adrianople, finally crossed the Balkans and plundered Pliska. He also transported thousands of Romans to menaced Macedonia to keep the unassimilated Slavs in check.

In 811 he again traversed the Balkans and looted Pliska. The Bulgars fled into the Balkans. Returning southward, the Romans were in a narrow defile when suddenly they faced a heavy timber barrier. Nicephorus gazed at the precipitous heights on either side, then looked back. Here too, the enemy had blocked the pass. He was trapped. With somber premonitions of death the Roman soldiers encamped. Attack was useless, escape impossible. Two days passed. Then just before dawn the Bulgars fell upon the sleeping Romans. Unable to form, the Emperor and almost all his men were cut down. For over four centuries no such single disaster had overtaken Roman arms, no emperor had fallen in battle. Krum exposed the Emperor's head on a lance for a few days, then lined the skull with silver and used it in drinking orgies with his shaven-headed boliads. Thus the Isapostol's cranium gave the Empire the needed respite. His son, the Co-Emperor Stauracius; his son-in-law, the Curopalates Michael Rangabé; and a few others had escaped in the confusion. But Stauracius' spine had been wounded and he was slowly dying. Consequently, the military, the Senate, and the Patriarch created Michael Emperor of the Romans (October 811). Stauracius assumed monastic garb and died three months later.

LEO V

Michael Rangabé was a Thracian with curly black hair and beard, superstitious, and easily swayed by monks and his wife Procopia. He squandered Nicephorus' reserve, revoked his ecclesiastical enactments, persecuted Paulicians (evangelical Christians in Anatolia without an organized priesthood and believing in two independent principles), and recalled exiles. Among them was Leo, a short Armenian officer with a bristling beard, who had risen from the ranks and been degraded, scourged, and banished by Nicephorus for neglect of duty. He now became Patrician and Strategos of the Anatolics.

Meanwhile, Krum was spreading terror in Macedonia and Thrace. Michael assembled Anatolian themes despite their grumbling at having to fight in Europe. Near Adrianople the two monarchs spent a fortnight observing each other (June 813). Krum hesitated because Slavs and Bulgars were inferior to Romans in open field. Michael had no apparent reason for wavering. At length, the commander of the Thracians and Macedonians sent word to the Emperor that he was attacking and routed the foe. But the Anatolics on the other wing broke into flight and were followed by the other Anatolian troops. The European regiments held off Krum until their general fell.

Instigated by Leo, the Anatolics had feigned cowardice in order to discredit the reign by defeat. Michael returned to New Rome, leaving Leo in charge of the army. Leo was proclaimed Emperor by his troops, welcomed by the Senate, and crowned by the Patriarch at Saint Sophia. Michael took the cowl and fled to an adjacent sanctuary with his wife and children. Leo V rendered their sons ineligible for the throne by emasculation and separated the family. Procopia was immured in a convent in the City, while Michael spent his remaining thirty years on a rocky Princes' islet within view of his former capital.

Six days after Leo's accession Krum appeared before the ramparts of the capital and entertained the Romans with a foot bath in the Marmara, human and animal sacrifices, martial displays, and his pompous and solitary procession through a double row of admiring concubines. After these exhibitions he requested the Emperor to deliver to him a number of virgins and to permit him to plunge his lance into the Golden Gate. When this proposal was rejected he deprived the Romans of the sight of his person. But he soon discovered that to take New Rome was beyond his powers and acceded to Leo's suggestion that they meet unarmed on the right bank of the Golden Horn just outside the walls. Krum came with his brother-in-law, the latter's son, and his treasurer. Leo arrived on the imperial barge soon after. They had commenced converse when a member of the Emperor's entourage signaled to three hidden men to fall upon the redoubtable Bulgar. His comrades shielded him while he leaped on his steed. An arrow struck him, but he clung to his horse and reached his camp alone.

His wrath knew no bounds. He desolated the suburbs, took starving Adrianople, and sent its inhabitants to settle in his trans-danubian provinces, where they were permitted to elect their own governor. Krum's frequent transfer of Romans to his realm is evidence of his desire for a permanent state as well as the amenities and technical advantages of Byzantine civilization.

In the late autumn of 813 Leo encamped near Mesembria in the vicinity of the Bulgar bivouac. During the night he slipped out of camp with a select body of troops and remained hidden behind a contiguous hill all day. The rumor that he had fled spread to the foe. Intending to deal with the leaderless Roman host on the morrow, the Bulgars slept soundly. Leo with his detachment and the contingent left in camp converged on the sleeping Bulgars in the dead of night and wiped them out. He then raided Bulgaria and indulged in large massacres. The Bulgars invaded the Empire the next year and carried off many inhabitants. The hostilities ended abruptly when Krum burst a blood vessel in 814.

His son Omurtag concluded with Leo a solemn thirty-year peace, whose validity was certified by reciprocal oaths. The Emperor swore upon a sword, dead dogs, and other objects according to Bulgar rites, while the Bulgars deposed on the Bible. The treaty fixed a boundary running west from Develtus. Along this line the Bulgars were permitted to draw a ditch, an earthen rampart, and a wooden palisade—the Great Fence, whose contour is still visible.

With peace in the north and only border hostilities with the Khalifate, the Emperor attacked iconodulia. Among medieval Romans there were probably few unreligious persons. Leo V, who had spent his life in the largely iconoclastic Anatolian army, apparently attributed imperial misfortunes to the restoration of images in 787. Possibly he also feared the monks' crescent power and wealth, for emperors and subjects sought to amass heavenly treasures by building and endowing monasteries. The wealth, the reputations of a few ascetics, and the possession of sacred relics and icons gave the monks a hold over the Church, the populace, and the women of the court. Indeed, under Michael they had directed imperial policy. In 815 a synod declared that the public welfare depended on orthodoxy, condemned the manufacture and veneration of icons as traditionally unwarranted, and annulled the decrees of 787. But while Leo III had taken the iconodules unaware, Leo V encountered organized opposition and theological arguments.

The iconodules asserted that God Himself had used effigies when He made His Son in His Own Image and when, being invisible, He had used a likeness of Himself to appear to Adam, Abraham, and Moses; that the unseen angels made a similar use of images when revealing themselves to humans; and that Christ had mentioned Caesar's bust on a coin. They also argued that the New Testament did not forbid images. In this connection they pointed out that the Trinity was not mentioned in the Bible. They adduced the utility of images, their miracles, their education of the illiterate, their illustrative value for the literate, and their defensive avail against evil demons, who feared them because they contained the strength of the depicted. They alleged that representations were to the original as the shadow to the body and led the votary from the visible to the invisible. The iconodules further affirmed that hatred of images emanated from the devil and demons because they portrayed their defeat; that those who gainsaid Chirst's Image denied His Incarnation and were Arians or Monophysites; and that those who loathed pictures because of their material implied that God created evil.

Before Christmas 820 Michael, a comrade-in-arms of Leo, Patrician, and Domestic of the Excubitors, was found guilty of conspiracy and condemned to die by fire immediately. But the Empress Theodosia implored her husband not to execute the sentence before the celebration of the Nativity. The Basileus consented to delay the execution, but with vague presentiments, for he said to his wife that while she had released his soul from sin, it was perhaps at the cost of his life. Michael's fellow conspirators concealed themselves in the Palace Chapel of Saint Stephen, where soon after daybreak, as Leo V was singing the matins with the choristers, they sprang upon him. Seizing a candelabrum from the altar, the Emperor warded off their blades until his improvised weapon was shattered. "One and a half," so called because of his gigantic stature, brought his sword down on the shoulder of the defenseless Emperor with such force that his right arm and the clutched remnant of the candelabrum were completely severed from the body. The head followed.

MICHAEL II

The murderers rushed to Michael's cell and dragged him, still fettered, to the throne to receive the homage of the imperial dignitaries. Toward noon the chains were removed and Michael II was crowned by the Patriarch in Saint Sophia. Born in Amorium, the capital of the Anatolic theme, of half-hellenized Phrygian stock, he had started life as a groom and, like Leo, had risen from the ranks. Uneducated, superstitious, and boorish, he soon became the butt of the City's wits. He exposed Leo's maimed corpse in the Hippodrome, emasculated his four sons, and exiled them and Theodosia to the Princes' Islands. He created his adolescent son Theophilus Augustus and, in accordance with a custom dating from the eighth century, sent agents throughout the Empire to find him a wife. Maidens conforming to certain standards of beauty, of a specified height, and with definite head and foot measurements were assembled in the Great Palace and presented to the prince for selection.

But Michael had other cares. During Leo's last months Thomas, a lame, white-haired, romanized Slavic officer, had assumed the purple and the name of Constantine in Asia and had declared himself the champion of the poor and the iconodules. Many Anatolian regiments joined his standard. Thomas displayed his strength in Syria and made a treaty with the Khalif Mamun, who recognized him as Emperor of the Romans. Thomas reciprocated with a subsidy and was crowned by the Patriarch of Antioch, a subject of the Khalif. He reentered the Empire with eighty thousand Romans, Anatolian Slavs, Persians, Armenians, Caucasians (some said to be ten feet tall), Arabs, Turks, Magyars or Inner Bulgars, Negroes, Crimean Goths, and Vandals (mentioned for the last time in history). Iconodules, Paulicians, and the Aegean fleet adhered to him. Crossing to Thrace, he rallied the Slavs and besieged the capital (December 821). But the Bulgars fell on him from the rear and discomfited him near Heraclea. Then Michael attacked, and Thomas' demoralized troops capitulated. Thomas fled to Arcadiopolis, where his last soldiers finally delivered him to the Emperor (October 823). Michael placed his foot on the neck of the fallen potentate of the provinces and with cruel delight imparted his fate to him—amputation of hands and feet, exposure on an ass, and transfixion on a stake.

As a result of the rebellion and the ensuing heavy taxation, many small farmers, especially in Anatolia, were forced to transfer their lands to neighboring great landowners or monastic institutions.

About 828 Moslem sectaries from Andalusia seized Crete. Using the stone of dead Knossos, they built a new capital, which they surrounded with a deep moat (whence the island was named Chandax, which became Candia). Mostly young and single, they merged with the natives. Their fleet ravaged the Aegean and disrupted imperial commerce. Unable to dislodge the intruders, the Empire revived her navy, neglected since the decline of the khalifal fleet after the accession of the Abbasids.

Soon after the execution of Thomas, the widowed Emperor had married the daughter of Constantine VI, a nun, whom the Patriarch released from her vows. The monks, however, who loathed the Emperor because he had forbidden public iconodulia and public discussion thereof, vented much indignation. Curiously, Michael was shocked when informed that Euphemius, a naval officer in Sicily, had also wed a nun. He commanded the removal of the impious officer's nose. To preserve his physiognomy and his wife Euphemius appropriated the scepter and Sicily. Driven out, he appealed to the Tunisian Emir and in 827 returned to the fertile island with Moslems, who had raided it since about 650 and made several efforts to conquer it. Euphemius was soon murdered and the Moslems began a long contest for its possession.

THEOPHILUS

Michael II died of kidney disease in 829 and his cultured and accomplished son Theophilus took over the state. To remove the stain on the accession of his dynasty he decapitated the assassins of Leo V in the Hippodrome. His attention was soon attracted to the Khalifate, which, though in the throes of dynastic and sectarian strife, still carried on a desultory holy war against the Empire. It was now dominated by Iranians. Yet Iranian votaries, the Khurramites, under invincible mahdis (guides) did not recognize the Khalif and held an extensive area in the northern part of the Khalifate. Babak, the third Mahdi, who had allegedly slain over two hundred fifty thousand khalifal warriors, sent the Emperor contingents

From Spyridon Lampros, Portraits of Byzantine Emperors;
the fifteenth-century manuscript miniature from which
it was taken is in the Biblioteca Estense, Modena

Theophilus (reigned 829–842) and Michael III (reigned 842–867)

to serve against the Khalif. With these hardy allies Theophilus met
the Khalif Mamun, who had passed through the Cilician Gates. In
the ensuing battle Theophilus was pressed back into the ranks of his
Khurramites, who discussed selling him to Mamun. The Domestic
Manuel, a recalled exile who had served the Khalif against them,
understood them, seized the bridle of the Emperor's horse, and cut
a path through them.

Mamun died in 833. His successor concentrated his forces against
Babak and after stupendous efforts brought him to bay. Babak
offered to become Christian. Anxious to convert so valuable an ally,
Theophilus crossed the Taurus, destroyed Zapetra, put the male
inhabitants to the sword, sent the women and children into captiv-

ity, extracted Roman captives and tribute from Melitene, traversed the Euphrates, burned Arsamosata, and celebrated a pompous triumph (837). He appeared on the race course in the uniform of the Blues. Driving a white chariot, he won the victor's crown and was hailed an incomparable champion.

But while he was receiving the plaudits of the populace, his ally Babak met his end. The Khalif was free to attack the Empire. He inscribed on his banners the object of his campaign—Amorium, the thriving native city of the imperial dynasty. On a fertile plain near Dazimon (now Tokat) Theophilus confronted the invaders. The Roman line gave way. Only Theophilus and Manuel with two thousand horse held their ground. They were surrounded, but a sudden shower wet the bows of the Moslems, who brought up catapults and bombarded them with rocks. Thereupon the valiant band broke through the enemy lines to safety.

The Moslems took Ankara, stormed Amorium, butchered the inhabitants, and, as was their wont, withdrew from Roman soil at the end of the campaign (838). They took forty-two Christians to the new seat of the Khalifate, Samarra, where the Khalif is alleged to have spent seven years trying to convert them. Finally, given the choice between Islam or death, they unhesitatingly chose the latter. They are the last recorded martyrs of the Orthodox Church.

Roman successes dampened the Khalif's martial ardor and a truce was arranged (841). Regarding the exchange of captives he wrote Theophilus that since God esteemed Moslems more than Christians, he would return two Christians for each Moslem and thus eclipse him in everything.

Indeed, in poetry, science, letters, philosophy, and the assimilation of Hellenistic, Persian, Hindu, and Jewish culture, Bagdad and Samarra rivaled or surpassed New Rome. Possibly as a result, Theophilus proceeded to new constructions in the Great Palace. Apart from the deserted Bucoleon of Theodosius II on the Marmara, the Great Palace at this time comprised Constantine's buildings (which probably resembled Diocletian's Romano-Oriental palace in Split) and the domed, apsed, octagonal Golden Hall of Justin II, which was in the gardens sloping to the Marmara.

Between it and Constantine's structures Theophilus erected a series of pavilions with mosaics of fauna and flora in Neo-Hellenistic, iconoclastic style. Among the pavilions was a new throne room

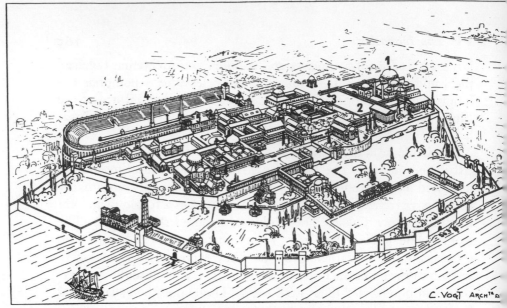

From Berthold Rubin, Das Zeitalter Iustinians; *drawn by C. Vogt in 1934*

Reconstruction of the Great Palace and environs as they may have appeared in the tenth century: 1. Saint Sophia; 2. Augustaeum; 3. Chalke Gate; 4. Hippodrome; 5. Kathisma (Imperial Box)

with gilded dome, multicolored marble walls, and three shell-like apses. From it a silver portal opened into a colonnaded crescent-shaped hall, the Sigma, also with gilded dome and multicolored marble. This hall faced a marble court, where on festive occasions spiced wine filled the fountain. Not far off were the Emperor's summer sleeping pavilion, the Hall of the Pearl (in whose main room eight rose-tinted columns supported a pearly cupola), and a villa for Theophilus' daughters, from which flowed a stairway of white Carian marble.

In the throne room of the Golden Hall Theophilus installed golden lions, griffins, and a golden plane tree with birds on its branches. When an ambassador entered the Emperor's presence the lions roared, the birds chirped, and a golden organ sounded.

In forbidding the manufacture of images in the capital Theophilus clashed with the monks who sold and extolled them. But the struggle over images was limited to New Rome.

In January 842 Theophilus was attacked by dysentery. Sensing death, he took two measures to secure the throne for his infant son. He decapitated the most likely candidate for the diadem, the popular general Theophobus, King of the Khurramites within the Empire, and appointed regents to assist the Paphlagonian Empress Theodora, notably her favorite, the chief minister Theoctistus.

EARLY YEARS OF MICHAEL III

The restoration of images was ardently desired by the Empress, the greater part of the clergy, the monks, and the populace. The dissenting regent Manuel and the Patriarch were ousted, a council was convened, the decrees of 787 were reaffirmed, and the most eminent iconoclasts of the ninth century, with the exception of the late Emperor, were anathematized. On the first Sunday of Lent 843 the triumph of iconodulia was celebrated by a solemn procession, headed by the Empress Theodora, the young Emperor, and the new Patriarch. The day is still a festival of the Orthodox Church, which venerates Theodora as a saint.

Iconoclasm was gradually to expire, while the Incarnation became the central dogma of Eastern Christianity. Proof of it was seen in images, since, it was indicated, if Christ had not been human He could not have been delineated.

Although the Khalifate was weakened by internecine strife, there were aggressive Moslems in Crete and Sicily and Bulgars in Macedonia. Yet Theoctistus continued Theophilus' persecution of the Paulicians, who in a broad mountain belt from the Mediterranean to the Black Sea formed a solid bulwark against Islam. An imperial army advanced against the hated heretics and was enthusiastically reported to have butchered a hundred thousand. Thus, the flank of the Empire was exposed. The surviving Paulicians fled to the Emir of Melitene, who settled them around Tephrike, whence they could harry the state that had deprived them of their homes, tortured them, and slaughtered their kin.

Meanwhile, in Greece, Peloponnesian Slavs continued to raid the towns of the residual Greeks. Thracian and Macedonian troops reduced them to obedience. They were gradually christianized and hellenized. But the process was slow, and in the tenth century the Greek countryside was still largely Slavonic. Yet insensibly they ceased to live apart and became Greeks. Only on the inaccessible slopes of the Taygetos did they preserve their tribal organization until the fifteenth century, when they vanished as Slavs. The Slavic faculty of absorption had yielded to that of the Aegeans.

In 855 Theodora and Theoctistus were alarmed by the affection of Michael III, now sixteen, for Eudocia Ingerina, the beautiful daughter of the imperial treasurer, whose influence they feared. They convoked the fairest females of the Empire to the Great Palace and obliged the unhappy lover to select a wife. He chose another Eudocia.[2] Embittered, yet powerless in the hands of his mother and Theoctistus, Michael turned to Bardas, his brilliant and cultured maternal uncle. Theoctistus was dispatched in 855, and two years later when the Empress sought to regain power she was tonsured.

Michael III sought his companions among actors, charioteers, athletes, and comedians. One of his cronies was known as The Pig. One day Michael sent a message to his mother that the Patriarch was at the Palace and would be glad to give her his benediction. The pious Empress hastened to the Golden Hall, where she believed that she saw the pontiff, his face partly covered by sacred vestments, seated beside the Emperor, apparently lost in holy reflections. She reverently knelt at his feet and besought him not to forget her in his prayers. What was not her deferent astonishment when the venerable prelate arose, performed a sprightly jig, turned his back, and emitted into her face a detonating accumulation of intestinal gas. Her stupefaction changed to devout dudgeon when The Pig threw back his hood and declared that she could not deny that even in this he had tried to do her honor.

Michael III left the government in the efficient hands of his uncle Bardas, whom he created Curopalates and later Caesar. (Since Theodosius I, the Caesarate had been reserved for younger sons, relatives, and possible successors, while the Emperor's son and heir became Augustus.) Bardas' first cares were for the Tauric frontier, where the Emir of Melitene and the Paulicians were harassing the imperial confines. Bardas and Michael penetrated enemy territory and besieged Arsamosata. Within the city was the brilliant Paulician leader Karbeas, a former Roman officer, who had gone over to the evangelical sect upon learning that his father had been cru-

[2] Adontz believes that Michael met Eudocia Ingerina only after his marriage. See "La portée historique de l'oraison funèbre de Basile I par son fils Léon VI le Sage" in *Byzantion*, 8, 2 (1933).

cified by the Romans for refusing to abjure his religious convictions. Suddenly the city gates opened. Karbeas charged out at the head of a small band of Paulicians and Moslems, routed the Roman army, and took the imperial camp with many officers, although Bardas and Michael escaped (859). The Emir of Melitene and Karbeas now invaded the Empire. Then in 863 Bardas' brother Petronas trapped and killed the Emir near the Halys.

The khalifs were weakening. Not trusting Arabs, Iranians, or Iraki, the Abbasids had engaged Turkish guards. The Turks were a rough lot and their excesses caused continual disorders in Bagdad. To avoid riots the Khalif Mutasim had moved to a small place called Samarra sixty miles northwest of Bagdad (836). But thus isolated, the khalifs were in the power of their guards, who made and unmade them. Khalifal authority declined and many emirs became practically independent. Revolts and internecine wars between emirs, sects, and races rocked the disintegrating Khalifate.

PHOTIUS

Apparently the Patriarch Ignatius, cowled and castrated son of Michael I, was involved in the conspiracy of 857 to restore the Empress-Mother to power. He represented the intransigent faction of monks, churchmen, and laymen who might be called zealots and opposed Bardas' moderate party. At the request of the new regime he abdicated, was deported, and was declared deposed by a synod. Possibly fearing to deepen the gulf between zealots and moderates if they chose his successor from one or the other group, the assembled churchmen elected a layman, the imperial First Secretary Photius. The most learned man of the age, Photius surpassed his contemporaries in knowledge of the ancients and in purity and beauty of speech. He was as versed in theology, philology, and philosophy as in law, medicine, and the natural sciences. His home was a center for classicists and scientists. Laic and theological education hardly differed, and in six consecutive days he was tonsured and ordained lector, subdeacon, deacon, priest, and bishop.

He dispatched the customary inthronistic letters to his four patriarchal colleagues. Pope Nicholas I withheld his recognition pending a report of his legates on the circumstances of Ignatius' abdication and Photius' elevation. He also requested the return of Illyricum, Calabria, and Sicily to papal jurisdiction. It has been suggested that he interjected this matter with the hope that the Emperor might make some concession in exchange for recognition of Photius. However that might be, in New Rome the Emperor and the Patriarch opposed reopening the question of the patriarchal succession, since Ignatius' retirement had been in conformity with canonical rules, since he had been deposed by a synod in order to manifest that he had ceased to be Patriarch, and since his successor had been elected in accordance with the laws of the Eastern Church. Nevertheless, yielding to the urgings of the papal legates, they agreed to place it on the agenda of the impending council on condition that the legates give a final verdict without the delay of reference to the Pope. The legates apparently felt that this was so important a concession to the Papacy, whose primacy was thus freely acknowledged, that it warranted their exceeding their instructions and passing judgment themselves. The Council of 861 opened and they ratified Ignatius' deposition.

Three developments, however, prevented ecclesiastical peace. First, Ignatius retracted his resignation. Second, the Pope repudiated his legates and convoked a synod in 863, which excommunicated Photius and declared him stripped of his patriarchal dignity and Ignatius restored to it. Third, the Pope supplanted the Patriarch as spiritual overlord of Bulgaria (866). Papal missionaries in Bulgaria attacked the customs of the Eastern Church. In the crisis Photius convoked a council. Pope Nicholas was condemned for interference in the affairs of another see. Moreover, countering the assaults of the papal missionaries in Bulgaria, the Council anathematized as heretical certain practices and doctrines that they were teaching the Bulgars, notably the addition to the creed of the words "and from the Son" (*filioque*).

First added to the creed elaborated at Nice and Chalcedon by a council in Toledo in 589, these words had been adopted by other Latin churches. They declare the Holy Ghost to proceed from Father and Son, while the Eastern Church, adhering to the traditional creed, believes the Holy Ghost to proceed from the Father through the Son. Nevertheless, the Council of 867 did not attack the Latin Church as a whole or the primacy of Rome.

This fact and Nicholas' acceptance as orthodox of Photius' professed faith in the procession of the Holy Ghost from the Father alone were ignored, forgotten, concealed, or distorted. Indeed, Nicholas' letter to the Archbishop of Reims left the impression that Photius had attacked the whole Western Church. Thus, in the West the clash over Bulgaria attained a false significance that was for ages to poison relations between East and West and profoundly to affect the course of history.

Over a thousand years passed. Then a Roman Catholic priest, Francis Dvornik, in one of the great achievements of modern research (*The Photian Schism*, 1948) cut through the errors, mistranslations, and fabrications of centuries to reconstruct the course of events and to reveal Photius, not as the bitter foe of Christian unity, but as a great, generous, and forgiving Patriarch, who urged that each Church tolerate the different practices of the other.

THE NORTH

Extensive missionary enterprises among the non-Christian peoples of Europe were undertaken during Photius' incumbency.

Bulgars, Moravia

Since the thirty-year peace of 815 imperial relations with the Bulgars had been pacific, although in 836 about thirty thousand Romans settled beyond the Danube by Krum decided to return to the Empire. They defeated the obstructing Bulgars, beat off plundering Hungarians, and pushed on to the Black Sea, where an imperial fleet awaited them. At New Rome the Emperor welcomed them and sent them home.

In 862 Bardas was alarmed by reports of Frankish-Bulgarian negotiations for the conversion of the Bulgars to Latin Christianity. While the Bulgarian army was north of the Carpathians, Michael III invaded Bulgaria by land and sea and concluded a treaty without a battle. Bulgaria obtained a strip of uninhabited imperial territory along the Balkans and accepted New Rome's ecclesiastical supremacy. Khan Boris was baptized Michael, and Orthodox clergy streamed into Bulgaria. But Boris-Michael was dissatisfied with ecclesiastical dependence on New Rome and took advantage of a domestic crisis in the Empire in 866 to transfer allegiance to the Pope, who offered better conditions.

In 884 Orthodox missionaries were also to be driven from distant Moravia by Franks.

Balkan Slavs

In the Balkan Peninsula the efforts of Orthodox missionaries, notably of the Salonican brothers Methodius and Constantine-Cyril, known as the Apostles of the Slavs, were more enduring. Cyril gave the Slavs their own script (disguised Greek letters still used by Serbs, Bulgars, and Russians). Thus were formed national churches, which preserved the identity and unity of their communicants during centuries of foreign dominion.

Russians

The Russians (Rus, Germanic for sea-rover) were North Germanic warrior-merchants of eastern Scandinavia, who established themselves on the waterways of western Russia in the ninth century, extended their sway over Slavs and others, and monopolized the trade of northeastern Europe with Itil, New Rome, and Bagdad.[3] Against meridional luxuries (gold, wine, silks, fruits, etc.) they traded corn, furs, Slavs, swords, honey, swan down, seal teeth, Baltic amber, and Bulgarian leather. Their annual trading parties were military expeditions, for the western trade route to the Dnieper mouth led through the territory of the marauding Hungarians, while the eastern artery to the Volga delta passed through the haunts of the predatory Patzinaks. From the Dnieper mouth some Russian ships proceeded to Varna and Mesembria, while others voyaged to Cherson and to Khazar Phanagoria. From here Jewish merchants shipped their wares on to Itil, Trebizond, and Bagdad. Those Russians who floated down the Volga to Itil often sailed out on the Caspian to Moslem ports, even occasionally debarking to continue on to Bagdad by camel. The imperial authorities at Cherson exacted 10 per cent on merchandise for Khazaria, while the

---

[3] For a different and novel account of the rise of the early Russians see Vernadsky, *The Origins of Russia* (New York, 1959).

Khazars levied a similar duty on goods passing through Itil to the Khalifate.

The Russians easily turned from barter to piracy. In 860, while Bardas and the Emperor were fighting Paulicians and Moslems and the greater part of the navy was off Sicily, they entered the Bosporus in two hundred vessels, plundered the wealthy suburbs on its banks and the Princes' Islands, and attacked the Great City. The inhabitants placed their hopes in a garment of the Virgin, believed to have been discovered in her church at Blachernae during the Avar siege in the seventh century. The precious relic led a procession around the walls and inspired the defenders. Bardas and Michael returned by forced marches. The Black Sea fleet moved toward the Bosporus. The Russians were trapped. Some captured Russians accepted baptism and entered the imperial navy. They were the first Varangians (Norsemen or Scandinavians) to serve the Empire. Soon Photius dispatched missionaries to convert the Russians.

Khazars

Khazaria lay between the Caspian and the Dnieper. Its wooden capital Itil on the Volga delta was the winter abode of the Khagan, who in summer erected a camp in the plains. He had come to be regarded as sacred and led a secluded life with no share in civil or military affairs, which were in the hands of the Beg (viceroy). When misfortunes visited the Khazar realm, however, the people demanded that the Beg slay the Khagan, whom they believed to be in divine disfavor. Or, after a reign of a stipulated number of years the Khagan was dispatched because his time had elapsed. In the 860's[4] a khagan or beg decided that Khazar prestige would be enhanced by the adoption of an established Mediterranean religion. In order not to place himself in spiritual dependence on either the Emperor or the Khalif he adopted Judaism. The ruling and wealthy classes followed suit.

The Khazar realm included a Gothic vestige in the Crimea; Bosporus (Kerch), an ancient Greek colony; the Inner Bulgars be-

---

[4] See Vernadsky in *Byzantion*, 25, American Series, I (1940–1941), and *Cambridge Medieval History* (1966), IV, I, 492–493.

tween the Dnieper and the Sea of Azov; the Hungarians between the Don and the Dnieper north of the Bulgars; the Burdas (probably Turks) around the middle Volga; and numberless Slavs. Relations with the Empire were generally friendly, for both states faced the Khalifate, the Bulgars, and now, Russians. To Khazaria Photius also sent missionaries.

Alans

Pressed against the Black Sea between the northern slopes of the Caucasus and the Kuban, the pastoral Alans, the only identified remnant of the once widespread Sarmatians, still led an independent existence. It is said that their houses were so close that if a cock crowed he was answered by all the others in the realm. Their kings probably became Christian during the ninth century and received from the Emperor the title of Exusiocrator, but, like the Khazars, the people continued their ancestral religious practices. Wedged in the Khazar flank, the Alans were valuable allies of the Empire, for they controlled the main entrance to the Caucasus, the Alan Gates.

Steppe Movements

About 860 the Cumans pushed the flea-eating, linguistically related Turkish Patzinaks westward across the Volga. The Patzinaks in turn drove the Hungarians over the Dnieper. Seizing Bulgarian lands between the Dnieper and Pruth, the Hungarians were joined by rebellious Khazar clans, the Kabars.

Cherson

Cherson, last of the Greek city-states and northernmost outpost of the Empire, was transformed into the Theme of the Klimata by Theophilus, although she seems to have retained a measure of autonomy. The steppe tribes no longer assailed her, for they realized her value as a mart where they could exchange wax, furs, and leather for silks, linens, muslins, purple, spices, and rugs imitating panther skins.

CULTURAL TRENDS (IV–IX CENTURIES)

As Athens had yielded to Alexandria after Egypto-Orientalism had fused with Hellenism, so Alexandria was supplanted by New Rome after Christianity had blended with Romano-Hellenisticism. For three centuries after the foundation of New Rome the Romano-Hellenistic genius struggled and fused with the Oriental-Christian spirit and, as the union of Hellenic with Egypto-Oriental had formed the Hellenistic, the mating of Romano-Hellenistic with Oriental-Christian formed the Byzantine.

Dogmatic Christianity restricted Byzantine scholars, who could attain originality only in theology, history, and sacred poetry. Thus, during the three centuries of Christiano-Hellenistic fusion (330–650) theology gradually replaced philosophy; philology remained stationary; while poetry, history, rhetoric, and epistolography flourished and evolved. Though the Greek language adapted itself to the changing world with new and foreign words, scholars did not wander very far from the Attic model. Thus, while churchmen united Hellenistic rhetoric with Syrian imagery, scholars still employed the archaic idiom of Homer and Herodotus.

In the fourth century poetry, which for over a thousand years had been governed by the classical law of quantity, received a new metric principle—the accent, as in the speech of the time. Hymns were accentuated and rimed while secular verse struggled to retain the antique quantitative rule, only to be gradually altered by the accent of Middle Greek.

The fourth century likewise marked the beginning of the Byzantine theological era. The classically educated churchmen of the fourth and fifth centuries—Eusebius of Caesarea, Athanasius, Basil, Gregory Nazianus, Gregory of Nyssa, John Chrysostom, Cyril of Alexandria—became the unquestioned authorities for future theological endeavors, whether in dogma, polemics, exegesis, ecclesiastical history, asceticism, mysticism, clerical eloquence, hagiography, or catenae.

Byzantine historians continued the labors of Herodotus and Thucydides chronologically, technically, and linguistically, faithfully composing histories in classical Greek throughout all vicissitudes. Often the historians were contemporaries or active statesmen, yet they generally strove to be objective, citing documents, consulting eye-witnesses, quoting foreign writers, and inserting geographical and ethnographical accounts. There were also popular chroniclers, who wrote for the less educated in the vulgate, which with passing time differed ever more from Attic Greek.

Three, centuries of cultural struggle left Christianism dominant and seems to have been followed by two centuries of relative unproductivity (650–850), though the eighth century may have been more prolific than is realized, for iconoclastic works were largely destroyed. But, unlike the West, the Empire had no Dark Age, no break in the classical tradition. There was little distinction between lay and cleric education, and in the ninth century three laymen occupied the patriarchal throne. The higher learning of the laity in large part prevented the Byzantines from becoming as dependent on the Church as Western Europeans.

The restoration of images in 843 marked the end of Byzantine theological evolution, for the Church repelled any further Greek philosophy. Instead, Hellenisticism burst into secular bloom. Hellenic philosophy and science revived. The University of Theodosius II was reestablished in the Golden Hall with chairs of grammar, rhetoric, dialectic, music, philology, philosophy, medicine, mathematics, and astronomy. The professors were paid by the government and instruction was gratuitous. The reborn knowledge of Antiquity was soon put to practical use despite the violent opposition of many monks, who attributed the new scientific proficiency to the complicity of the devil and sought to crush free thought and artistic urges.

In art and architecture the Byzantine style flowered in the reign of Justinian I and spread throughout the Mediterranean World. During the misfortunes of the seventh century building declined within the embattled Empire, yet such was the genius and fecundity of Byzantine architects, the multiple variations of their domes, and the solidity of their structures that they were employed even by the nationalistic Sassanids and later by khalifs. The Dome of the Rock erected in Jerusalem in 690 and the Great Mosque of Damascus are Byzantine creations and were decorated by Byzantine artists.

The West also employed Byzantine architects and imported the works of Byzantine artists and craftsmen, including large numbers of luxuriant, lacelike capitals.

What statuary had been to the ancient Greeks, mosaics were to the Byzantines. Clear and harmonious mosaics of calm, symmetrically placed figures covered many walls. Like the sculptor, the mosaicist sought to make his persons stand out in relief. But while the sculptor obtained this effect through the play of light and shadow, the mosaicist created it by placing the figures against a uniform background. In modest buildings mural paintings evince an Oriental realism, while in manuscripts miniatures cling to the graceful Alexandrian tradition in the frames, though the figures tend toward Oriental rigidity. (It was in Ptolemaic Alexandria that the illumination of manuscripts began.)

In the eighth century iconoclasm swept away many traditional Christian impediments and brought a partial return to realism and the Hellenistic traditions of Alexandria. Instead of religious scenes, mosaics and mural paintings now depicted landscapes, fauna, flora, hunts, horse races, contemporary history, etc. Alexandrine picturesqueness replaced Oriental monumentality, though adopting Oriental and Moslem motifs.

After the eighth century Byzantine art flowed in two definite currents, only vaguely visible in preceding centuries. One was Hellenistic, harmonious, elegant, and decorative; the other was Oriental, monastic, popular, and otherworldly. It was the first current that bestowed the artistic splendor on the delicate creations that Byzantine artists spread throughout the world—mosaics; paintings; illuminated manuscripts; ivory, gold, or silver carvings; enamels; fabrics; ceramics; glass; and jewelry.

Since the Arab explosion there had been a steady Armenian and Syrian immigration into Anatolia as the Hellenic population receded coastward. The hardy Armenians were quickly romanized and soon became preeminent in the Empire. Theodora, Manuel, Bardas, and Photius were of Armenian blood.

Such was the age of Bardas and Photius—many Slavs, Syrians, and Armenians assimilated; possibly a quarter of the army Armenian;[5] the Moslems checked; missionaries ranging far and wide; the Empire administered with a large measure of justice and efficiency;

[5] Charanis, *The Armenians in the Byzantine Empire* (Lisbon, 1963), p. 21, describes the Empire of the ninth and tenth centuries as Greco-Armenian, Greek for her civilization and Armenian for the element that directed her destinies and provided many of her defenders (p. 57).

the Church in the hands of a brilliant scholar; art and letters flourishing; the multinational army coordinated; the navy reviving; investment increasing; and the economy thriving.

BASIL

Among Michael's cronies was Basil, who was probably born near Adrianople about 812, the son of Armeno-Slavic Thracian peasants.[6] Known as the Macedonian, he wandered to the Great City as a young man. Of towering build with thick, curly hair framing a large but illiterate head and an energetic visage, he became the groom of a wealthy courtier. Accompanying his master to the Peloponnese, he met a mature widow of great fortune, who lavished wealth on his stalwart person. Yet Basil remained in his master's service until he attracted the Emperor's attention about 856 by throwing an invincible Bulgarian wrestler. Michael III enrolled him in his guard, later made him Grand Chamberlain (a post usually occupied by a eunuch) and in 862 Patrician, and caused him to divorce his wife in order to become the passive husband of his mistress Eudocia Ingerina. Desiring to replace the Caesar Bardas, Basil concocted a series of perjuries and intrigues to poison the mind of the Emperor, who finally decided to do away with his powerful uncle on the impending expedition against Crete.

The expeditionary force was encamped near the mouth of the Meander on a warm April morning of 866. The Caesar Bardas, clad in a peach-colored cloak and followed by his elegant retinue, rode to the Emperor's tent to recommend embarkation. He entered the tent alone and engaged the Emperor in converse. Suddenly Basil and his fellow assassins rushed at him with drawn swords and cut him to pieces. The attack on Crete was deferred, and Michael returned to murmuring New Rome, adopted Basil, and created him Co-Emperor.

On a tempestuous September night of 867 in the Palace of Saint Mamas on the left bank of the Golden Horn Michael III sank into his bed in alcoholic torpor. The attendant Patrician observed that the door's bolts had been dislocated but was unable to rouse the

---

[6] For the problem of Basil's descent, birth, and youth see Adontz, "L'âge et l'origine de l'empereur Basile I" in *Byzantion*, 8, 2 (1933).

Emperor. Basil and his fellow murderers broke in, hurled the Patrician and the Grand Chamberlain to the floor, hacked the Emperor to death, rowed across the stormy Golden Horn, and took possession of the Great Palace. The capital awoke to find Basil sole Basileus.

VII

The Early Macedonians

867–963

ABOUT fifty-five and energetic, Basil assailed the legislation of the iconoclastic emperors, seeking to return to Justinian's principles. He issued a manual establishing those laws and customs that were still in force and those that were obsolete. Like the *Ecloga*, it was soon translated into Slavic and was used by Serbs, Bulgarians, and Russians. Moreover, he and his successor published two large collections of laws. These legal labors revived and modernized Justinian's work but perforce retained much of the *Ecloga*. This monumental achievement outlived the Empire and influenced Slavic law.

The assassination of Bardas had weakened the moderate party, and in murdering Michael, Basil may have acted in concert with the zealots. However that might be, he based his power on their support, secured Photius' resignation, reinstalled Ignatius as Patriarch, and convoked a council (869–870). It was attended by the legates of Pope Hadrian II, who demanded that the Eastern prelates condemn Photius as a condition of admission to the conclave. So shocked were the Eastern divines by this demand to prejudge Photius that only twelve attended the first sitting. Indeed, Basil and Ignatius were reproached for subjecting the Eastern Church to Rome. But Basil insisted that a hearing be given Photius, who denied the legates' right to judge him. He and many of his clerical adherents were nonetheless excommunicated and banished.

Yet at this time Photius' missionary and possibly diplomatic activities achieved a signal success. Dissatisfied with the Pope's refusal to name either of his candidates Archbishop of Bulgaria, Boris-

Michael sent an embassy to the Council to ascertain to which patriarchate Bulgaria belonged. Overriding the papal legates' protests, representatives of the other patriarchs determined that Bulgaria belonged to the New Roman see. Giving the Bulgarian Church a certain autonomy, Ignatius consecrated an archbishop and ten bishops for Bulgaria.[1]

Basil and Ignatius continued the missionary policy of Bardas and Photius, rechristianized or converted Dalmatian, Peloponnesian, and other Slavs in the Balkan Peninsula, pursued the conversion of Russians, even proselytized in the Khalifate. They formed native clergies and endeavored to convert foreign prisoners or hostages, while Roman captives abroad also spread the gospel. Foes were thus often transformed into friends. Indeed, the Roman government viewed missionary labors as a prime diplomatic action. Thus, in the efforts to reunite Armenia to the Empire the emperors continually essayed to bring the Armenian Church into Orthodox communion. But the Armenian Church, the oldest state church in Christendom, was too closely identified with the nation itself. The persecution of heretics and the attempts to assimilate Jews by forcible conversion were equally futile.

In the Peloponnese Basil was more fortunate. Centuries before, Laconians had fled from the Spartan yoke to the Maïna Mountains of the sea-beaten promontory of Taenarum. Here they still dwell and speak an antique Laconian dialect. Fortifying the passes of the inaccessible peninsula, they became bandits or pirates and ages later repelled the swarming Slavs. But in their rocky recesses the Maïnotes still worshiped the ancient gods. The Emperor took the necessary military measures and the Maïnotes were baptized.

Meanwhile, with a large part of the clergy loyal to Photius and many Photian churchmen excommunicated and exiled, Ignatius found it difficult to exercise his patriarchal duties. The Emperor realized that his own position was weakened by the schism that the Council of 869–870 had deepened. Moreover, since the moderates had more widespread support than the zealots and since his chief concern was to retain the throne, he took steps to conciliate the moderates, recalled Photius (probably in 873), gave him quarters in the Palace, and entrusted his children's education to him.

[1] Dvornik, *The Photian Schism*, Ch. 5.

Apparently in 876 Photius and Ignatius arranged for a council to revoke the decrees that had excommunicated the moderates. They also seem to have agreed that Photius would resume the patriarchate upon Ignatius' demise, which occurred in 877. Thus, when the papal legates arrived for the Council they found Photius again in office. It met in 879–880 and with the concurrence of Pope John VIII annulled all papal and conciliar condemnations of Photius. Peace was thus restored between the Greek and Latin churches and was not again broken during Photius' incumbency. In the East, however, a few zealots persevered in their opposition despite Photius' conciliatory attitude.[2]

THE TAURIC FRONTIER

On the Tauric frontier the Moslems held the watershed and defiles that led into Anatolia. They could thus easily invade the Empire and prevent retaliation. A few miles east of Roman Sebastea, Caesarea, Tyana, and Heraclea Moslem forts at the western ends of the mountain passes were a perpetual menace. Under these difficult conditions the Roman defense was so organized that as soon as the Moslems were espied moving through the passes (usually in spring and summer, when fodder was plentiful), a beacon on the nearest height transmitted the message to New Rome by intermediary hill fires. But the settled Borderers did not wait for orders from the capital. The civilians were concentrated in forts and the military gathered according to plan. Infantry hastened to the passes, while horse archers with darkened equipment harried the invaders, delaying them until the arrival of thematic troops. Often the Moslems were trapped returning with their spoil.

Both sides of the Tauric range had been depopulated by war and the massacre and transplantation of heretics. On the Moslem side were sects or races that had suffered from Christian persecutions— Slavs, Armenians, and Paulicians. The last were settled around Tephrike and frequently raided the Empire. Their military successes made them rich and independent and aroused Moslem jealousy. Consequently, when in 871 Basil took the field against them

[2] *op. cit.*, Chs. 6–8.

the Emir of Melitene left them to their fate. But the Paulicians routed the Emperor and swept on to Ankara. Later, a Roman general destroyed Tephrike and crushed the valorous sect in a nocturnal battle.

Master of the road from Sebastea to Tephrike, Basil was free to rectify the Tauric frontier. The time was propitious. The Empire was at peace with her northern neighbors, while the khalifs were at the mercy of their Turkish guards and sat helpless in Samarra while their realm disintegrated into practically independent emirates. Indeed, such was the weakness of the khalifs that from 869 to 883 Negro slaves impuniously ravaged Basra and the Tigro-Euphrates delta.

The Roman forces advanced against the Emir of Melitene, who without his Paulician allies lost Zapetra, Samosata, and the defiles through which he had been wont to invade the Empire. Basil joined his victorious army, attacked Melitene, was defeated, and returned to New Rome in triumph.

Despite this reverse, he carried on the war methodically, attacking the passes in Moslem hands. In 877 he took the forts that controlled the Cilician defiles and during the next five years occupied the roads from the Halys basin to upper Cilicia. Though he did not take Tarsus, Melitene, or Germanicea, though he did not capture all the Tauric passes and only partially seized others, he seized the keys of the range. The Romans could now penetrate Cilicia and Mesopotamia at will, while Moslem inroads were hampered.

Different were Basil's relations with the circle of principalities around Mount Ararat known as Armenia. Since the seventh century the country had languished under Moslem dominion, firmly based on Armenian disunity. To collect the tribute (for which an army was required) the Khalif appointed an Armenian magnate Prince of Princes. (Affecting an inexistent authority over Armenian affairs, emperors often conferred a similar title.) One family, the Bagratids, gradually came to occupy this post hereditarily. They had formerly claimed descent from an Armenian god, but when the nation changed religions, discovered an ancestor among the remote forebears of the Virgin. Despite this lineage, they faithfully served the Moslems. In 885 and 887 a Bagratid was granted the regal title by Khalif and Emperor, both anxious to win Armenian support in the border war.

LEO VI

The spouse of Basil's youth had borne him four daughters, whom Basil sent to a convent, and about 860 a son, Constantine. After Basil had become the passive husband of Michael's mistress Eudocia Ingerina, she gave birth to Leo (866), whom Basil dedicated to the cowl upon Michael's death. But after he had draped the Augustan purple on Constantine, for appearances he did the same to Leo, certain that Constantine would succeed to the throne. Constantine, however, died in 879. Sensing that his progeny was doomed to dynastic extinction, Basil declared the eight-year-old son of his second nuptials, Alexander, Co-Emperor. But he realized that Alexander could not supersede Leo. Longing to do away with Leo, he accused him of conspiracy, threw him into a narrow prison (881), and wanted to blind him, but was restrained by the murmurings of the people and the remonstrances of Photius and the court. Bowing to public opinion, he freed Leo.

Broken, aged, and haunted by the thought that his sins had brought about the death of his son, Basil devoted himself to hunting. It is said that in August 886 he cornered a stag near Rhegium, that the animal pushed its antlers under his belt, lifted him from the saddle, and carried him sixteen miles before an attendant managed to free him. Upon regaining consciousness Basil is said to have commanded the decapitation of his rescuer. Nine days later he exhaled his soul. Possibly this fabulous account hides his assassination. However that might be, hardly had his remains been interred than the body of Michael III was brought from Chrysopolis and with solemn pomp also placed in the Church of the Holy Apostles. It would seem that Leo VI was thus disowning the murderer of his father and demonstrating that the Amorian dynasty again reigned.[3]

Tonsured almost before he had hair, Co-Emperor at four, subject to Basil's brutal whims, forcibly married, stripped of the purple, incarcerated, and threatened with the removal of his sight at a tender age, Leo VI was now twenty, delicate, interested in letters, and inclined to orate.

[3] Adontz in "La portée historique de l'oraison funèbre de Basile I par son fils Léon VI le Sage" (*Byzantion* 8, 2, 1933) and Vogt in "La jeunesse de Léon VI le Sage" (*Revue historique*, 174, 3, 1934) declare Leo the son of Basil.

*Mosaic in Saint Sophia in Istanbul showing Christ investing an
emperor, who is probably Leo VI (886–912), with Holy
Wisdom. On the Gospel in Christ's Hand are the words "Peace be with
you! I am the Light of the World"*

Desiring to elevate his brother, the Syncellus Stephen, to the Patriarchate, Leo obtained Photius' abdication. Photius was nonetheless tried for seeking to overthrow Leo and, though acquitted, sent into exile, where he died in 892.

Leo thereby altered the mode of patriarchal election. Theretofore, a synod had elected the Patriarch, the Senate had concurred, and the Emperor had confirmed him. Now the metropolitans had only the power of recommendation. The Emperor appointed one of their three nominees or his own choice, generally the Syncellus, whose knowledge of the Emperor's wishes and whose experience in the patriarchal chancellery prepared him for the high office.

Leo VI also abolished the Senate's theoretic right to legislate. This was a mere formality, for the Emperor had long since been accepted as the Vicar of God, in whom all power resided. Beside him there were only the army and the bureaucracy, which were in principle his instruments, and the Church, whose protector he was.

Leo abandoned the practice whereby the Emperor became Consul in the first year of his reign. Thus ended the long career of the Consulate, which had succeeded the royal power fourteen centuries before.

Early in Leo's reign the Moslems inflicted a number of defeats on the imperial forces in Cilicia, but the rise of a Shiite sect, the Karmathians, soon occupied the shadow-khalifs, who could send no help to the fighting emirs on the Roman borders. Toward 900 the Romans again pushed forward, annexed the land between the Amanus range and the Euphrates, retook Theodosiopolis, and advanced the frontier to the upper Araxes.

GOVERNMENT

Leo reorganized court dignities, which were named after offices that had lost their original significance, such as Patrician and Magister. Members of the imperial family could become Basileopator (as Leo's father-in-law), Curopalates, Nobilissimus, and Caesar.

The system of central government remained essentially the same as in the days of Constantine I, but the ministers' functions were less extensive and their number was consequently greater. Sixty officials now headed the central administrative departments.

Most of the duties of the defunct Master of the Offices were divided among the Prepositus of Petitions, the Logothete of the Course (minister of the postal system and of domestic and foreign affairs), and the First Secretary (head of the imperial correspondence and archives).

The functions of the former counts of the Sacred Largesses and of the Private Estates were now fulfilled by the Sacellarius, a general controller, who received the net revenue from other ministers and placed it into the central treasury; the Logothete General, who collected the taxes; the Great Curator, who managed the crown estates; the Chartulary of the Sacellium, in charge of the revenues of the crown lands; the Logothete of the Herds, who administered the Anatolian pastures, where horses and mules were reared for the army; the Count of the Stable, who directed the imperial stables, the breeding of horses, and their retirement when old or ill; the Military Logothete, who handled the military treasury; the Chartulary of the Wardrobe, who was master of the mint and of public factories.

Entry into the bureaucracy, except into the highest posts, was emptorial. As the highroad to honor, riches, and power, many wealthy provincial families purchased admittance, while most professional officials acquired lands as the best form of investment. Thus, landed and administrative aristocrats merged and tended to oppress small farmers, both as proprietors ambitious to enlarge their estates and as officials anxious to redeem the price of their office. Their cupidity and oppression of the free husbandmen were the frequent concern of the emperors.

In the themes Leo VI with few exceptions abolished municipal autonomy. Prefectures, dioceses, pretorian prefects, and master generals had long since vanished. Lest the general and governor of the theme, the strategos, who was directly responsible to the Emperor, gain too much local power, he and his relatives were forbidden to marry inhabitants of the theme, acquire property therein, or accept presents during his incumbency. After its expiration he was obliged to remain in the theme fifty days in case anyone desired to bring charges. Moreover, the thematic Metropolitan could inform the Emperor of any malfeasance.

Leo removed some of the impediments to the acquisition of authority and property by the wealthy and powerful, thus encouraging their feudalizing tendencies.[4]

ARMY

The army of the ninth and tenth centuries comprised probably 120,000 men and was perhaps the most efficient force in the world. Beside natives, Mardaites, and Paulicians, it included Armenians, Caucasians, Khazars, Patzinaks, Varangians, Hungarians, Bulgars,

[4] *Cambridge Medieval History* (1966), IV, I, 141–142.

Slavs, and Arabs. Byzantine civilization, regular pay, good treatment, excellent weapons, privileges, efficient officers, victories, regi-
mental traditions, and the instillation of religious enthusiasm assimilated these heterogeneous elements into a national army that for
centuries baffled powerful states and fierce barbarians. Unfortu-
nately the native troops were often exclusively loyal to their local
leader, while the foreigners were frequently unruly.

Apart from the Emperor's personal bodyguards (Hetairia, Silentiaries, Vestitors, Mandators, Candidates, Strators, and Spatha-
rians), the army was divided into Tagmata and Themata.

The tagmatic troops, whose regiments numbered between 1500
and 4000, were stationed in New Rome, Bithynia, Thrace, and
Macedonia and included the four privileged cavalry regiments:

1. the Scholarians, whose commander, the Domestic,[5] was commander-in-chief of the army and head of the Blues, who were offi-
cered by counts and lower-ranking domestics, were mustered from
the aristocracy, and formed an elegant parade regiment;

2. the Excubitors, whose commanding domestic was head of the
Greens;

3. the Watch, which furnished the Emperor's campaign sentinels;

4. the Hikanati, who guarded the Emperor in palace or camp.

In a wider sense the Tagmata embraced also:

1. the numeri, infantrymen who defended the capital;

2. the infantry under the Count of the Walls, who guarded the
capital's bulwarks;

3. the Optimati, formerly elite Gothic warriors, now mostly infantry stationed around Nicomedia, where they tended to the bag-
gage of the other tagmatic regiments in case of war;

4. the capital fleet under a drungary.

The thematic troops defended the provinces. A theme counted
between four thousand and ten thousand men and was divided into
two or three turms (brigades, but, like themes, also districts). Com-

---

[5] The Domestic of the Schools is first mentioned as commander-in-chief
in the eighth century. In the tenth century the command was divided between a Domestic of the Schools for Asia and another for Europe. About
1100 a Grand Domestic was created with authority over the two Domestics
of the Schools. In the thirteenth century the title Domestic of the Schools
became purely ornamental. See Guilland in *Revue des études byzantines,* 6
(1948).

manded by a turmarch, the turm had five drungi (battalions), commanded by drungaries. A drungus contained five banda under counts, the immediate superiors of the lower officers, kentarchs, and dekarchs. The numbers of these units varied, but there were probably about fifteen hundred men in the average drungus and about three hundred in the bandon.

The greater part of the thematic troops were heavy and light cavalry (cataphracts and trapezites). Special troops, *deputates*, cared for the wounded, while *cantators*, following antique Hellenic custom, stimulated the soldiers with orations.

The eastern themes enjoyed precedence over naval and western themes. Their strategoi were remunerated by the central government, while the commanders of western and of most naval themes raised their pay locally. Smaller circumscriptions, kleisurarchies, were severed from themes in frontier districts, generally with a mountain pass requiring immediate defense by settled Borderers.

NAVY

The removal of the khalifal capital from Syria in 750 and the consequent decline of khalifal naval power in the Mediterranean led the Empire to neglect her navy. Thus, about 828 Spanish Moslems were able to seize Crete, while African Moslems gained a foothold in Sicily.

Cretan and Syrian sea raiders despoiled, massacred, or enslaved the inhabitants of Aegean cities. On a summer day in 904 a fleet of Cretan, Syrian, and Egyptian ships, commanded by a Roman renegade, Leo of Tripolis, suddenly appeared off Salonica, the second city of the Empire. The Moslems debarked, ineffectually assailed the land walls, and withdrew to their ships. The next day their fleet suddenly spewed forth Greek Fire, grenades, stones, and arrows and drove the demesmen from the low harbor wall. The Moslems scaled it and after an indiscriminate massacre collected enormous riches. They abducted many Salonicans. Some died of thirst, hunger, or suffocation before they reached Crete, where the Syrian and Egyptian participants received their share of the booty and of the twenty-two thousand Christians, mostly young and salable. They were sold at Damascus and at Fostat and taken to Arabia,

Ethiopia, and beyond. Many of those who remained in Crete, a great slave emporium, were bought by former Christians and resold to friends in the Empire.

After this catastrophe Leo VI rebuilt the navy. The tagmatic fleet in capital waters was employed for extensive campaigns and thematic squadrons policed the coasts. Varangians joined the tagmatic fleet, while Romans in maritime themes received hereditary fiefs for naval service. In keeping with Roman tradition, however, naval personnel received lower emoluments, fiefs, and honors than the military.

Triremes, as in Antiquity, were still the chief warships, though they were now called dromons and sometimes also had sails. The large ones were manned by two hundred thirty rowers and seventy marines, were equipped with war engines on the turrets and bronze syphons for Greek Fire, and were swift and powerful. Though the secret of Greek Fire had been betrayed, the reorganized Roman navy was more efficient than Moslem fleets. Although it was discomfited by Leo of Tripolis off Chios in 912, thanks to its watchful thematic squadrons, the Empire became relatively immune to Moslem raiders, who impuniously ravaged feudalized, fleetless western Christendom.

PROVINCES

The Asiatic themes or kleisurarchies included *Anatolikon* in central Anatolia, whose strategos was the ranking thematic officer and had an annual salary of forty pounds of gold; *Armeniakon* on the Black Sea; *Thrakesion* on the Aegean with offspring of Slavs imported by Justinian II; *Opsikion* (from Obsequentes, a guard regiment of Marcus Aurelius) on the Marmara; *Bucellarion* with commissary troops on the Black Sea; *Cappadocia; Chaldia* on the Black Sea; *Colonea; Charsianon; Mesopotamia; Seleucia;* the mountainous *Lykandos;* the important naval *Cibyraiot* on the southern Anatolian coast; the naval *Samos* covering Anatolian coasts and adjacent islands; the *Aegean* protecting the islands, the Dardanelles, and the western Marmara.

The eastern European themes included the *Klimata* (Cherson, which informed New Rome of nomadic movements in the

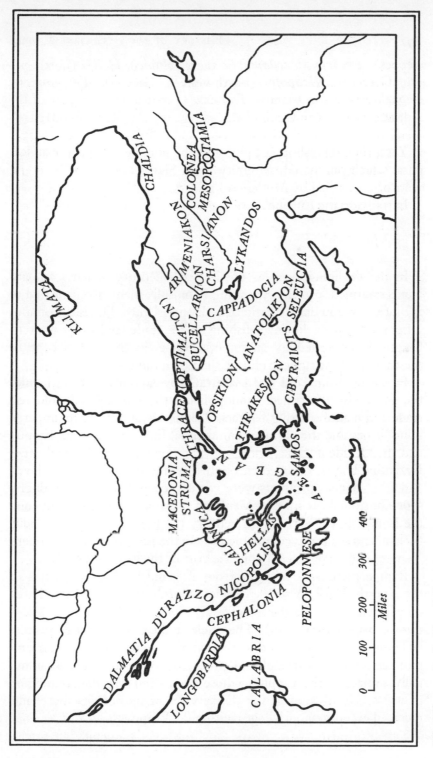

The Themes in the Tenth Century

steppes); *Thrace; Macedonia; Struma; Salonica; Hellas* (northeastern Greece); *Nicopolis* (northwestern Greece); *Peloponnese; Cephalonia* (Ionian Islands); *Durazzo* (a strip at the entrance of the Adriatic, where a few cities held out against the Slavic flood); *Dalmatia* (coastal towns of Latin speech and religion with the strategos at Zara, the archbishop at Split, and the commercial center at Ragusa, which purchased immunity from Slavic raids by tribute and were often assailed by Moslem sea raiders).

In transadriatic Europe there were:

Venetia

In the declining decades of the sixth century when Lombard bands swarmed into the Apennine Peninsula, many Romans fled to the safety of alluvial Adriatic strands and islands. The islet communities tended to bicker over fishing rights, trade, and other matters. Originally governed by an imperial duke, in the eighth century they acquired the right to choose their own duke (doge).

Protected from land and sea attack by lagoons and mudbanks, the silt duchy flourished, monopolizing the regional salt and fish trade and manufacturing baskets. Taking advantage of its imperial bond, it became the cardinal commercial link between the Empire and the Occident. Silks, wines, purple, linens, peacocks, and other Byzantine luxuries flowed through it, while metals, woods, slaves, and other ponent products were carried to the Empire. The duchy soon controlled the marshy Venetian Plain between the Brenta and the Isonzo. In the early ninth century the Franks attacked Venetia by land and sea but were unable to take the islets of Rialto (modern Venice) and recognized Venetia as part of the Empire (812).

Rialtan merchants brought from Alexandria alleged remains of the Apostle Mark. A small, wooden church was erected beside the ducal palace to house them and Saint Mark supplanted Saint Theodore as patron saint (828). The duchy built a large fleet to protect its commerce. Its navy and its mercantile connection with the Empire rendered it powerful and prosperous, but it remained nominally subject to the Empire, whose commerce was the foundation of its wealth. Moreover, for the services of its fleet its merchants received exceptional privileges within the Empire.

Sicily

In 827 Moslems from Tunisia began a long struggle for Sicily. They took Palermo in 831 and in 843 captured Messina with Neapolitan assistance. When in 859 impregnable Enna was betrayed into their hands the Empire's position in the island was shattered. Later, the Moslems made a land and sea assault on Syracuse, for sixteen centuries the western fount of Hellenic culture. Despite famine and pestilence, the Syracusans resisted nine months, eating leather and ground bones. Under heavy bombardment a tower and part of the wall collapsed into the sea (878). The Berbers rushed forward. Five days the torn and fleshless Christian warriors held up the Moslem torrent. Then it poured into the city over their lifeless bodies. The inhabitants were massacred or enslaved; much wealth, including a million gold pieces, was captured; and the city was razed. Thus died the antique rival of Athens, Alexandria, Carthage, and Rome. Only in a few mountain strongholds did the Romans hold out.

Calabria, Apulia, Longobardia

Since ancient times the heel of Italy had been known as Calabria, the toe as Bruttium. In the seventh century the two were united as the Duchy of Calabria and the name Bruttium fell into disuse until revived in the twentieth century. About 668 the Beneventine Lombards conquered most of the heel and the name Calabria became exclusively associated with the mountainous toe. In 758 the Romans regained the greater part of the heel, which received the ancient name of the district on its northern border, Apulia.

About 840, Moslems commenced raiding southern Italy. Favored by alliance with Naples, the feudal anarchy of the Beneventine principality, and the amity of Lombard lords and Campanian cities, they established themselves at Tarento, Bari, Benevento, and in Calabria. When their ravages reached Rome in 846 Christian Italy called upon the Franks for aid. Charlemagne's vast realm had just been trisected by his grandsons. One received Germany, another Gaul, and a third obtained land between the two as well as the kingdom of Italy. It was to the last that the appeal went.

The Franks drove the Moslems from the city of Benevento but went no farther (847). Then, while the wrangling Lombards split into three states (Benevento, Salerno, and Capua), the Moslems created the Sultanate of Bari under the nominal suzerainty of the Khalif of Bagdad. In the years that followed the Sultan's bands ravaged the imperial peninsulas, the Lombard principalities, the Campanian cities, and the Adriatic coastline, and repulsed two Frankish armies. After reducing the Lombards the Franks finally took Bari from the Moslems (871) and expelled them from Campania.

In 876 the Apulian Lombards acknowledged the Basileus' suzerainty and opened Bari's gates to his officers. The Empire thus regained control of the Adriatic. Alarmed at growing Roman power, Benevento, Salerno, and Capua made peace with the Moslems, who were established on the Garigliano, at Agropoli, and at Sepino. From these bases they destroyed the monasteries on Monte Cassino, marauded to the Tiber, and laid Rome under tribute. The imperial navy defeated the fleet of the Emir of Kairawan, while a powerful Roman army swept the Moslems from Tarento (880). Five years later an eminent Roman general, Nicephorus Phocas, expelled the remaining Moslems from Calabria and conquered the Lombards dwelling between the toe and the heel. Thus, the toe (Calabria), the heel (Apulia), and Longobardia as far north as the spur were bound together under Roman rule, while Salerno, Spoleto, Naples, Capua, and, after a brief war, Benevento became imperial vassal states.

In 915 the Strategos of Longobardia rallied imperial Italy, the Pope, Capua-Benevento, Salerno, Spoleto, Naples, and Gaeta and wiped out the last Moslem stronghold in Italy, a fortified colony on the Garigliano. Imperial prestige on the peninsula reached heights not known since the reign of Constans II. All Italy south of Terracina on the Tyrrhenian and Termoli on the Adriatic acknowledged imperial rule or suzerainty. But the additional imperial troops were recalled for service elsewhere, and already in 918 Sicilian Moslems sacked Reggio and imposed tribute.

Naples

After the fall of the Exarchate in 751 Naples imperceptibly shuffled off imperial rule. The office of her duke became hereditary, and the Greek tongue gradually fell into disuse except in educated circles, where it lingered for centuries. Industry and commerce throve. In order to withstand the Beneventine Lombards Naples became an ally of the Moslems.

(It is perhaps interesting to note how a duke came to be ranked above a count. Since the early Empire the count [*comes*, companion of the Emperor] had been a member of the Emperor's staff or governor of an important province. The duke [*dux*, leader], first mentioned under Hadrian, was a commander of frontier troops and inferior to the count in rank and office. Employed in distant parts of the later Empire, such as Italy, and drawing their salaries from customs receipts, the dukes became relatively independent during the centuries when the Empire was locked in combat with Persians, Avars, Arabs, and Bulgars. Consequently, Occidentals came to regard a duke as a semi-autonomous ruler.)

Amalfi

This Greco-Latin city-state, ruled by an occasionally hereditary prefect, also had good relations with the Moslems.

Gaeta

The most Greek of the Campanian cities, Gaeta's head, the Hypatos (Greek for Consul), became hereditary about 870.

Corsica, Sardinia, Malta, Balearic Islands

The embattled Empire of the seventh and eighth centuries was unable to provide adequately for the defense of her islands in the western Mediterranean. Already in the seventh century *Corsica* slipped from imperial control into a lawlessness that rendered its bandits notorious until the twentieth century. Adjacent *Sardinia* was also left to defend itself against Moslem raids and by the ninth century was independent of the Empire. *Malta* fell to the Moslems in 870 and the already practically independent *Balearic Islands* in 903.

COMMERCE AND INDUSTRY

The loss of Egypt and Syria, terminals of the sea and land routes from the Far East, had shaken the imperial economy. Although the diminished Empire had as far as possible adopted the commerce and industries of her lost provinces, the Arab expansion and the intermittent Romano-khalifal warfare seriously impeded commerce.

During intervals of peace, however, the Empire and the Khalifate traded and Byzantines could still wear Chinese silks and enjoy the other imported luxuries that their complex civilization required. Some Far Eastern merchandise reached the Empire through Cherson, but in the main the Khalifate was the intermediary. The Empire exported Far Eastern wares only in small quantities and then usually to Russia or Bulgaria. Her merchants no longer maintained counters in the West as had her Syrian subjects before the Arab conquest. Instead (while Scandinavia and the Northeast drew Byzantine manufactures from the markets of Novgorod), Italians came east in search of Byzantine and Moslem merchandise. Thus, Venice, Trani, Bari, Brindisi, Salerno, Amalfi, Naples, and Gaeta grew rich as purveyors to East and West.

Industry in New Rome was monopolized or controlled. State monopoly was rooted in the old Roman policy of supplying the capital masses with grain and bread, to which Constantine I probably added other foods. To feed the capital the provinces paid part of their taxes in produce. Justinian I not only declared silk manufacture a state monopoly but also forbade his subjects to purchase grain directly from the peasants. Imperial fiscal agents collected it in lieu of taxes and resold it at a profit to themselves and the government.

According to ancient Mediterranean custom the City's industries were organized into gilds under the supervision of the City Prefect, who determined the most favorable time and place for the acquisition of raw materials as well as their purchase and selling prices. The head of a gild divided the merchandise among the members, who were allowed to market only a certain quantity in a defined quarter of the City. Thus, on the main arteries only shops of goldsmiths, silversmiths, jewelers, etc. were permitted, while perfumers were located in the vicinity of the Palace. Merchants were protected against unfair competition. Noisy advertising and hawking were prohibited. Shortages, superabundance, and depressions were minimized, while the consumer was protected against speculators and assured of reliable quality and measure at fixed prices. Middlemen were forbidden. As in ancient Egypt and Athens, foreign traders could not deal with one another but only with local merchants. A high standard of honesty was maintained. Contracts were registered in churches and foreigners were assured of ethical treatment and good merchandise. Foreigners' wares were also priced by the Prefect, who assigned their place and period of sale. The main purpose of this gild system, which probably existed in all imperial cities, was apparently to ensure government control of trade and industry in the interest of the state and the consumer.

Despite the government's economic control, there are indications that as the political activity of the circus factions declined, that of gildsmen increased, that they had paramilitary formations, that they came to act as organs of public opinion, and that, notably in the eleventh century, they took part in the overthrow of emperors.[6]

While the Empire profited from her situation as intermediary between East and West and grew rich on commerce and industry, agriculture remained preponderant. Indeed, the very control that the government exercised over commerce and industry probably deflected investment of capital from them to land. Thus, while on the one hand the feudalizing tendencies of great landowners were strengthened, on the other the Empire's industrial and commercial expansion and the growth of a strong middle class were impeded. Such developments could only weaken a centralized state.

LEO, ALEXANDER, AND ZOË

Leo VI became enamored of Zoë at an early age, but Basil married him to Theophano (882). He may have chosen her because her delicate health seemed to preclude parturition. Thus, Leo would remain without issue and Basil's progeny would inherit the diadem. Despite his marriage, Leo continued to see Zoë. His wife com-

---

[6] See Vryonis in *Dumbarton Oaks Papers*, 17 (1963).

plained to Basil, who seized Leo by the hair, hurled him to the ground, delivered a number of heartfelt kicks, and married Zoë to another. Theophano turned ascetic and died in 897. She was sainted after miracles at her tomb were reported.

Despite the murmurings of the pious, Leo married the widowed Zoë, who died in 899. Although third nuptials were condemned by the Church, public opinion, and himself, Leo married a third time (900). But his wife and their infant died in childbirth. Leo became interested in another Zoë, a lady of dark-eyed charm, and asked the Patriarch Nicholas Mysticus to legalize their union. The suggestion shocked, pained, and incensed the prelate. In 905 a son was born to Zoë in the Purple Chamber. Leo urged the Patriarch to baptize and thereby legitimize the child. The Patriarch consented on condition that the Emperor renounce his mistress. The child was baptized Constantine at Saint Sophia. Three days later the Emperor renounced his mistress, that is, he wed her and created her Augusta. The outraged Patriarch defrocked the priest who had sanctified the wedlock and forbade the sovereign entry to Saint Sophia. The Emperor obtained papal dispensation and banished Nicholas, while a synod revoked the interdiction and elected the Syncellus Patriarch. Again the clergy was divided, and a number of Nicholas' partisans were exiled or imprisoned.

Leo VI died in 912. His half-brother, the Co-Emperor Alexander, became the senior colleague of Constantine VII, the young son of Leo and Zoë. The feud born on that stormy September night when Basil murdered Michael III had been intensified by Basil's mistreatment of Leo and had tacitly persisted between Leo and Alexander. Now, after years of impotence, Alexander finally held his father's scepter. He expelled Zoë from the Palace, dismissed many of Leo's officials and officers, deposed his Patriarch, reinstalled Nicholas, and died suddenly in 913. Nicholas headed the regency until 914 when Zoë returned and ejected him from the Palace but not from the Patriarchate.

Meanwhile, the powerful Emir of Azerbaijan and other Moslem potentates, together with Armenian henchmen, were overrunning Armenia and threatening to subject it to direct Moslem rule. The Romans crushed a Moslem force and reestablished the imperial ally in western Armenia (915). Peace was made and captives were exchanged.

Zoë was free to deal with the Bulgars. But in the ensuing campaign the Drungary of the Fleets, Romanus Lecapenus, an Armenian peasant's son, conducted himself in a manner that seemed treasonable and was partly responsible for the disastrous defeat of the Domestic Leo Phocas in 917. Zoë would have blinded Lecapenus, but military reverses had shaken her own position. She sought Phocas' active support, and it was rumored that she planned to marry him.

Alarmed, the young Emperor's suite appealed to Lecapenus. A maze of intrigue followed, and Phocas' troops were won over to the boy-Emperor, for dynastic loyalty was crystallizing in the Empire. Phocas was blinded (at which Lecapenus expressed indignation), seated backward on an ass, and exposed in the Hippodrome (919). Zoë was relegated to a convent. Her courtiers and those of the Emperor were expelled from the Palace. Lecapenus' daughter Helena was wed to Constantine VII, now thirteen, and Lecapenus became successively Magister, Basileopator, and Caesar.

ROMANUS LECAPENUS

Shortly after obtaining the Caesarate, Romanus Lecapenus, who was now about fifty, informed the Senate that while he prized its authorization to wear the purple buskins, he found imperial feet with a plebeian head ridiculous and asked it either to take back his purple footgear or grant him the diadem. It was placed on his head by Constantine VII and the Patriarch Nicholas (919). The new Emperor created his wife Augusta and his son Christopher Co-Emperor.

He convoked a council to reunite the Church after the schism caused by Leo's fourth marriage. Concord was easily reached by the condemnation of fourth nuptials. This was agreeable to Lecapenus, since it lowered the standing of his young associate, and to Nicholas, since it vindicated his position. In June 920 the imperial Church solemnly celebrated its reunion, and Constantine heard his legitimacy tolerated exceptionally, while fourth and third marriages were likened to garbage.

Lecapenus consolidated his dynastic position. He and his eldest son Christopher, who died in 931, ranked above Constantine VII.

Two other sons became Co-Emperors, but since they seemed irresponsible, Lecapenus granted Constantine VII precedence over them. He placed friends and partisans into high office. John Curcuas, a faithful Armenian friend and an intrepid officer, was appointed Domestic in 923. After the death of Nicholas in 925 his loyal friend Theophanes became the most important member of his council. In 933 Lecapenus' youngest son, the Syncellus Theophylact, became Patriarch. Thus, without struggle the Church passed under imperial control. The young pontiff maintained two thousand horses and reputedly considered his mares' confinements more important than the sacraments. Finding the latter dull, he introduced some pantomime.

Lecapenus also entrusted important posts to eunuchs, who, because they were ineligible for the imperium, were thought to be devoid of ambition. Nevertheless, castration was not considered stigmatic, as in the West. Indeed, thanks to eunuchs in powerful positions, the emperors could ward off the feudalization of the administration. In general Lecapenus opened office to talent and selected honest officials.

Since Basil's reign many free husbandmen and peasant communities with elected magistrates, who rendered justice and collected taxes, had sunk into serfdom or disappeared. Even military fiefs were being absorbed. The army was suffering. The land was unpeopling. Vast tracts were accumulating in the hands of churches, monasteries, landowner-officials, and landed generals. Lecapenus recognized the peril of this trend and legislated against it. Stressing that he did so not of hatred for the strong but of love for the poor and concern for the common safety, he declared that since the Empire depended on her free farmers for taxes, recruits, and most of the necessities of life, her welfare would be subverted unless existing abuses were abolished. Possibly bearing in mind that many churches, monasteries, and landed magnates used their influence to obtain tax exemptions, he indicated that the extension of their power would cause irreparable harm. He decreed that military small-holdings alienated during the previous thirty years be returned without compensation to their original owners, that magnates might acquire land from small proprietors only if related to them, and that for ten years after its transfer the property might be redeemed by relatives or neighbors. When a severe winter, poor harvests, and famine led many peasants illegally to sell their lands to magnates for trifling sums, Lecapenus authorized them to redeem them at the same price. He also decreed that whoever became a monk might give only the price of his land, not the land itself, to the monastery.

It is difficult to know to what extent Lecapenus' legislation on behalf of free cultivators and military small-holders was enforced because the interested official-landlord class often sought to frustrate it rather than enforce it. Moreover, frequently the peasant himself would transfer his land to a neighboring magnate in order to obtain protection from oppressive taxation or the extortions of tax-collectors.

SIMEON

From Develtus on the Black Sea the Bulgarian border with the Empire passed north of Adrianople and Salonica, reached southeastward to include northern Epirus, and ran northward to Serbia along the eastern borders of the themes Nicopolis and Durazzo.

In 889 Boris-Michael, Bulgaria's first Christian king and first national saint, withdrew to a monastery. When his son Vladimir and the boliads attempted to restore their ancestral religion he returned, placed his younger son Simeon on the throne, and imposed Christianity. Simeon had studied in New Rome and ardently desired to raise his country's culture. Greek religious writings were translated into Slavonic and an encyclopedia of Byzantine knowledge was compiled. Great Preslav became an echo of New Rome. But when in 894 Bulgarian trade counters were transferred from New Rome to Salonica and duties increased, Simeon made war on the Empire.

Imperial diplomats instigated the Hungarians, who still dwelt between the Dnieper and the Danube, to invade Bulgaria. Caught between the disciplined imperial army and the wild steppe horde, Simeon called upon the ferocious Patzinaks. The Hungarians were in turn trapped between Simeon's crafty generalship and the irresistible Patzinaks and were forced out of their lands.

A tribal chief, Arpad, led them over the Carpathians in 896 and attacked the peoples of the plain beyond, part of which belonged to the Bulgars. A decade later Slavonic Moravia had ceased to exist. Slavs, Bulgars, Rumans, the vestige of Attila's Huns, and the last

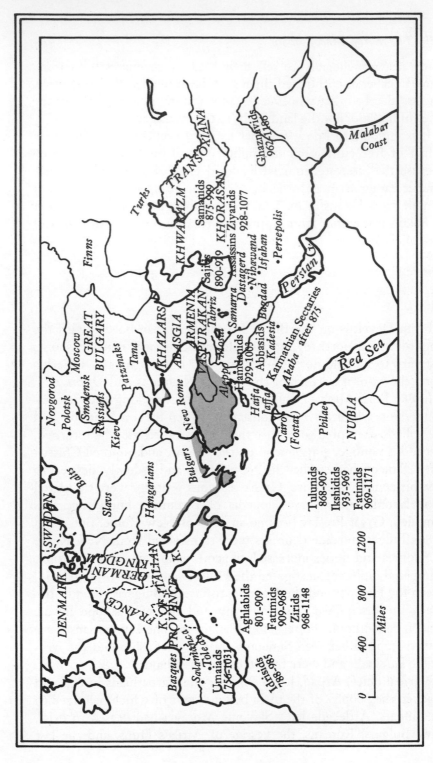

The Empire About 920 And The Dynasties That Governed Islam In The Tenth Century

Malabar
Coast

Ghaznavids
962-1186

Turks

TRANSOXIANA
KHWARAZM
Samanids
875-999
KHORASAN
Assassins Ziyarids
890-919 928-1077
Nihawand
•Dastagerd •Isfahan •Persepolis
Samarra

Sajids
Tabriz
•Mosul
Hamdanids
929-1003
Abbasids
Kadesia
Karmathian Sectaries
after 875

ARMENIA
VASPURAKAN
ABASGIA
KHAZARS

Baghdad

Persian G

Red Sea

Aleppo

Haifa
Jaffa
Cairo
(Fostat)
Philae
NUBIA

Akaba

Finns

GREAT
BULGARY
Moscow
Novgorod
•Polotsk
•Smolensk
Patzinaks
Russians
Tana
Kiev

New Rome

Bulgars

Baltic
SWEDEN
Slavs
Hungarians

DENMARK
GERMAN
KINGDOM
K. OF ITALIAN K.
FRANCE
PROVENCE K.

Basques
Salamanca•
•Toledo
Umaiads
756-1031
Idrisids
788-985

Aghlabids
801-909
Fatimids
909-968
Zirids
968-1148

Tulunids
868-905
Ikshidids
935-969
Fatimids
969-1171

0   400   800   1200

Miles

Avars submitted to Hungarian dominion. The vast Slavic mass between the Baltic and the Adriatic was split asunder and the possibility of a panslavic union covering half of Europe ceased to trouble Roman statesmen.

Meanwhile, Simeon had lost his remaining transdanubian territory to the Patzinaks, who were thus supreme from the Don to the Danube. But he defeated the Empire and received commercial satisfaction and tribute.

When Alexander became Emperor in 912 he refused to pay this subsidy. Simeon marched on New Rome, where the Patriarch Nicholas had become regent. In order to induce him to withdraw, Nicholas apparently bestowed on him the title of Emperor and agreed that the young Constantine VII should marry his daughter. As imperial father-in-law and possibly regent he might make himself master of the Empire. Perhaps because of this accord Zoë was able to overthrow Nicholas in 914. Simeon again made war and exterminated an imperial army under the Domestic Leo Phocas near Anchialus in 917. A half century later the bones of the fallen still whitened the tragic field.

When Lecapenus became father-in-law of Constantine VII in 919 Simeon demanded his deposition. He ravaged Macedonia and Thrace but could not pierce New Rome's ramparts. Lecapenus remained mostly on the defensive, but incited Serbs, Hungarians, Patzinaks, Russians, even Alans against Simeon. The ambitious Bulgar exhausted his state in a fruitless attempt to conquer the Empire, whose diplomacy baffled him.

Finally, he requested an interview with the Emperor. A pier, partitioned by a fence to separate the monarchs, was constructed in the Golden Horn beyond the walls. In late 924 Lecapenus, bearing the Cloak of the Virgin of Blachernae, met Simeon. In measured words he reproached the Bulgar for his unchristian conduct and discoursed on the transience of life and the final reckoning. Simeon consented to a subsidized truce.

But to assuage his unstilled ambition he adopted the title Caesar (Czar) of the Bulgars and Emperor (Autocrator) of the Romans, which the Pope confirmed. Simeon, moreover, freed Bulgaria of New Rome's ecclesiastical suzerainty and renamed the Bulgarian Archbishop Patriarch of Preslav. After these titular triumphs he subdued the Serbs, but when he attacked the Croats his army was annihilated. He died in 927, and Bulgaria was soon invaded by Croats, Hungarians, and Patzinaks.

His son Peter married Lecapenus' granddaughter and received the annual subsidy as an allowance for his consort. His imperial title was confirmed and his ambassadors were consequently granted precedence over all others at New Rome. The title and autonomy of the Bulgarian Patriarch were recognized. Berea was ceded to the Bulgars; Develtus and Anchialus were returned to the Empire. Bulgaria became practically an imperial client-state, for Simeon's prostrating reign had exposed her to the fierce nomads of the steppes and had accentuated the hatred between her hellenized court and clergy, her Bulgar boliads, and her Slavic peasantry.

DIPLOMACY

To prevent incursions of wild steppe tribes Roman statesmen had for centuries employed gifts, trade, intrigue, dignities, and conversions. By the success with which it upheld imperial pretensions and the craft with which it nugated and tamed fierce Eurasian hordes, Byzantine diplomacy has probably not been surpassed. The prestige of antiquity and civilization was exploited to the utmost. The loss of any part of the Empire was not officially acknowledged, and Constantine VII still wrote of the Emperor as master of the seas as far as the Columns of Hercules. The names of lost provinces were preserved. Hope was not lost that they would one day be recovered, for it was believed that only in the Empire, the noble flower of the universe, could liberty, happiness, and salvation be found. To leave her was to depart from civilization.

When barbarian ambassadors arrived at the imperial borders a powerful guard of honor escorted them to the capital. At the Capital of Civilization, the Navel of the Earth, trained diplomats received, entertained, and watched them, lest they purchase arms or discover the secrets of Roman power. If they were neighboring barbarians they were shown, not the wealth of the City, not the beauty and elegance of the women, but the physiques of the imperial guards, the size and strength of the ramparts. If they were from a distant country, their attention was directed to the desirability of friendship with the center of wealth, silk, purple, and religion. Imperial missives usually lauded the barbarian recipients as heroic, conquering, renowned, etc. When imperial envoys were abroad they always admired the sights, however primitive.

The Emperor, the Kosmokrator, was the father of foreign rulers, on whom he bestowed Roman titles. As their spiritual father, he sought to unite them to him in religious unity. State and Church collaborated to convert barbarians, instilled into their minds the superiority of Christianity, and often transformed fierce enemy tribes into Christian nations looking to holy New Rome for guidance. For centuries the Empire had held barbarians at bay by force when necessary, diplomacy when possible, and conversion when feasible until they wore themselves out in futile fighting or accepted Byzantine civilization.

But hardly had they been tamed when fresh hordes were flung into the steppes by the Central Asiatic whirlpool. Fierce and fearless, they inspired terror in the hearts of their half-civilized kinsmen and pushed them westward. Yet, no matter how barbarous or faithless, they were soon entangled in the meshes of Byzantine diplomacy. Under no emperor were the relations with the barbarian nations adjusted with greater skill than under Lecapenus.

KHAZARS AND PATZINAKS

Between the Sea of Azov and the Caspian the Khazars no longer killed their sacred faineant khagans on the occurrence of public misfortunes. They enjoyed religious freedom, and in order to provide impartial justice Jews, Moslems, Christians, and heathens shared the judiciary. The ruling classes were still Jewish, and Jewish missionaries proselytized from the Urals to the Carpathians. Though reduced in power, the Khazars dominated the Moslem-Christian Burdas to the north and formed a buffer against new Asiatic tribes moving west. For over three centuries their relations with the Empire had been friendly.

West of the Khazar realm from the Don to the Danube on the stoneless, windswept steppe, hot in summer, cold in winter, now stretched the felt tents of the bearded, malodorous, blood-drinking, carrion-eating Patzinaks, the most savage nomads of the steppes. Like other Turks, they were divided into tribes, one of whose chieftains was chosen to lead them in time of war. Always ahorse, they carried only a lance and made swift but concentrated charges. If their foe stood firm they dispersed so rapidly that it was impossible to engage them, but if the enemy broke they held together and ruthlessly rode them down.

It was the especial merit of Roman diplomacy to maintain amicable intercourse with these powerful barbarians, the terror of the neighboring Khazars, Russians, Bulgars, and Hungarians. Indeed, it was the potent Patzinak alliance that generally enabled Lecapenus to preserve peace.

RUSSIANS

Along river basins north of the Patzinaks the Russians had created a vast commercial confederacy of Slavic, Finnish, and Turkish tribes under the overlordship of the Great Prince of Kiev. From fortified wooden trading posts, such as Kiev, Smolensk, Polotsk, and Novgorod, they collected tribute at the head of armed contingents.

Of enormous size, the Russians were the prime foot soldiers of Barbaria. They wore heavy iron helmets and complete coats of mail and carried huge shields reaching to the ground. If they were obliged to turn their backs on the foe they hooked these shields on their shoulders and presented an impenetrable wall. They carried spears, double-edged swords, and battle-axes. Their tactics differed from those of the mounted Altaic bowmen, whose strength lay in their mobility. The Russians advanced into battle in an iron wedge, much as their West German cousins of Tacitus' day. While fighting they roared themselves into a fury to obliviate wounds and fatigue. They believed that if a warrior died under the blows of an enemy he became his slave in the nether life. Consequently, when salvation was impossible they plunged their own swords into their vitals.

A trade treaty with the Empire permitted Russian merchants to enter New Rome for a limited period under guard and defrayed the cost of their sojourn. In 912 the Romans found it necessary to supplement the treaty with reciprocal clauses regarding punishments for theft and murder.

In 941 the Russians secretly prepared a naval expedition against New Rome and bribed the Patzinaks to let them pass through their land unhindered. The surprise was almost complete. The imperial navy was in the Aegean when word of the Russians' departure reached the City. In the Golden Horn lay only fifteen water-logged galleys. These Lecapenus hastily made seaworthy and placed under the command of his faithful Theophanes. When the Russian armada appeared at the northern mouth of the Bosporus, Theophanes attacked with Greek Fire. Terrified, the Russians plied hastily eastward.

They landed on the Bithynian coast and spread horror over the countryside. It is recounted that they crucified or impaled their captives or used them as targets. Into the heads of priests and monks they hammered nails. Local troops and an army under the Domestic John Curcuas converged on them. They sought to flee. But the sea was now guarded by Theophanes with the imperial navy. It could not attack the light Russian vessels in the shallow coastal bays but could prevent their reaching deep water.

On a dark night the Russians attempted to cross the Bosporus to Thrace. But Theophanes was upon them, sprinkling their ships with Greek Fire. Then naptha-grenades; heavy rocks; metal projectiles; poisonous vapor-bombs; pots of burning oil; and containers of venomous serpents, scorpions, and other vicious creatures crashed down on them. Their ships were destroyed. The desperate Northmen sought refuge from the burning tongues of Greek Fire in the swift Bosporan current, but it followed, burning regardless of water, engulfing them in a fluid hell as they sank under the weight of their armor. Few escaped.

Theophanes returned to the capital with the banner of the Virgin fluttering from his flagship and became Grand Chamberlain (since the reign of Michael III the most weighty court post). Then in the presence of foreign envoys the Russian captives were beheaded in the Hippodrome as a warning to barbarian nations to prefer the Empire's amity. The Russians seem to have understood and in 944 concluded a new trade treaty with the Empire.

HUNGARIANS, SERBS, AND CROATS

The Hungarians twice raged over helpless Bulgaria and entered Thrace (934 and 943). Western Europe suffered bitterly from their incursions. Hungarian tribes spread in different directions, uniting only when necessary to crush an enemy concentration. But generally their light, disciplined, well-armed horsemen made surprise attacks and disappeared before the enemy could converge. The Danube, the Alps, the Venetian lagoons, and the Pyrenees ceased to be barriers. They raided as far south as Campania, as far west as the Khalifate of Cordoba, and tales spread of their atrocities, the human blood they drank, the babes they ate.

In mountainous, inaccessible Illyria dwelt Southern Slavs. Of these the Serbs formed semi-feudal agricultural statelets west of Bulgaria. Their turbulent lords, the zupans, now elected a grand zupan, generally from the same family. Since the reign of Heraclius the Serbs had been nominal vassals of the Empire, who gave them their civilization and to whom they were united by the bonds of religion and hatred of the Bulgars, who sought to subject them. After the Bulgarian Simeon had treacherously captured their Grand Zupan and scattered the inhabitants in the 920's he annexed the country. Soon after Simeon's death in 927 the Grand Zupan escaped. With Roman aid he rallied his fugitive people, threw off Bulgarian rule, and returned to imperial allegiance.

Northwest of the Serbs lived the Croats, whose confines reached the Drave and Istria. This largely Slavic people was also ruled by feudal zupans (or bans) under a grand zupan, who in 914[7] assumed the royal title. They had alternately fallen under vague Roman, Frankish, and Bulgarian dominion and now had to contend with the fierce Hungarians. After the decline of Frankish power they had established a stronger and more compact state than the Serbs. They are said to have had an army of 60,000 horse and 100,000 foot. Their adherence to Latin Christianity tended to separate them from other Slavs.

OFFENSIVE AGAINST ISLAM

Debarrassed of the Bulgars, Lecapenus took the offensive against Islam. After the destruction of Leo of Tripolis' fleet off Lemnos, the Domestic John Curcuas in 926 attacked the Moslem emirs on

[7] Guldescu, *History of Medieval Croatia* (The Hague, 1964), p. 114.

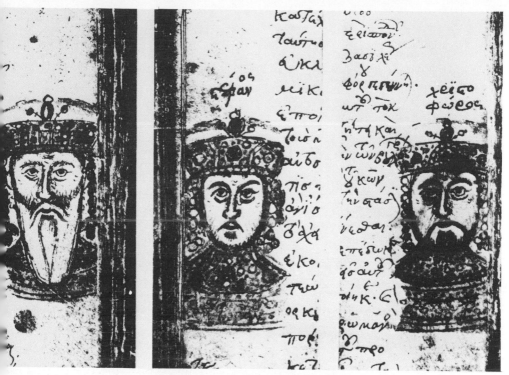

Romanus Lecapenus (reigned 919–944) and his sons Stephen and Christopher

the Tauric border. Eighteen years later the Roman frontier had been pushed to the Tigris, Melitene had been annexed, Samosata and the region of Lake Van had acknowledged Roman suzerainty, and Moslem hegemony in Armenia was at an end. Curcuas had breathed a new spirit into the army and was hailed a second Trajan.

Then in 944 he swept conquering to the walls of Edessa and announced that if the Edessenes turned over to him the towel with which Veronica had reputedly dried the Face of Jesus and which still bore the imprint of His Features he would spare the city and release two hundred Moslem prisoners. Despite a riot of the Edessene Christians, the holy relic was delivered to him. On its triumphal journey to the capital it is said to have performed a series of miracles. In New Rome it was humbly received by Emperor, Patriarch, and the highest dignitaries. Curcuas' glory echoed throughout Christendom.

This former convent church of Myrelaion (myrrh oil) in Istanbul was restored in the tenth century and reveals a revived interest in exterior design. It was transformed into the mosque Bodrum in 1574 and a minaret was added

Lecapenus had already announced that Constantine VII was to succeed him. Thus, his sons Stephen and Constantine knew that if their father died on the throne the imperium would escape them. Consequently, in December 944, during the midday hours when the Great Palace was closed, they seized their aged and ailing father, rowed him to Prote (the nearest of the Princes' Islands), and tonsured him. They had only to seize Constantine VII. But rumor of their doings had spread through the City. Crowds gathered before the Palace and demanded to see Constantine. The brothers dared not beard public opinion. They had unseated their father only to cede seniority to their brother-in-law.

Forty days later they were sent to join their father. On Prote's stony strand he expressed appreciation that their Majesties deigned to visit him, lauded the filial love that had impelled them to come,

From H. G. Goodacre, A Handbook of the Coinage of the Byzantine Empire; *the coin is in the British Museum*

Enlarged gold solidus of Constantine VII Porphyrogenitus (reigned 912–959)

and assured them that everything was prepared for their reception —ice-cold water, delicious beans, and fresh vegetables. But they did not long remain the butt of their father's humor. Stephen was ultimately sent to Lesbos, where in 963 he was poisoned by order of the regent Empress Theophano. Constantine was exiled to Samothrace, where he was killed attempting to escape in 948. His son was castrated. Christopher's son was tonsured.

Lecapenus, meanwhile, was content to end his days in pious penitence. He convoked the holiest monks of the Empire to Prote to hear his confession and witness his humiliation. Before three hundred members of the ascetic elite he read from a book a detailed list of his sins and asked forgiveness for them while the monks chanted the Kyrie Eleison. A neophyte then publicly insulted and scourged him. The sin-book was sent to a holy man on Bithynian Olympus, who fasted and prayed over it so effectively that the list disappeared. Lecapenus had obtained divine absolution and could die in peace. Only a plot by his faithful Theophanes and his son, the Patriarch, to restore him to the throne disturbed his last days. In June 948 he died and was buried with his purified sin-book.[8]

CONSTANTINE VII AND BYZANTINE CIVILIZATION

Constantine VII was now forty (945). He was scholarly, artistic, religious, timid, and gentle, but subject to sudden rages. Known as

[8] The writer is indebted to Runciman's work on the reign of Lecapenus.

the Porphyrogenitus (born in the purple), he had spent his life in the Palace. He left the reins of government largely in the hands of his wife (Lecapenus' daughter, the Augusta Helena) and of Basil, Lecapenus' castrated bastard, whom he created Patrician and Grand Chamberlain.[9]

In the higher civil posts Lecapenus' appointees were replaced by the Purple-Born's partisans. Corruption and inefficiency crept in and the administration returned to mediocrity. The army was turned over to the Phocas family. Bardas Phocas, brother of Lecapenus' blinded rival, became Domestic and his three sons received thematic commands. Despite the changes in personnel, Lecapenus' general policies, in particular his efforts to protect free peasants and military small-holders from powerful neighbors, were continued.

Although Constantine VII never approached a battlefield, he celebrated triumphs. On such occasions rulers or important captives were forced to prostrate themselves before him in the Augustaeum to the slow strophes of the hymn that the children of Israel were said to have chanted on emerging from Egypt. The prisoner's head would be placed under the Basileus' purple-shod foot and the nape of his neck under the point of the imperial lance. Later, in the Hippodrome, the triumphal procession filed past him. At a given signal the captives fell in the dust before him and their standards were hurled to the ground, while the circus factions intoned his praises. After this humiliation the captives were permitted to watch the games, received no ill-treatment, and awaited the day of their exchange.

After granting audiences to ambassadors the Porphyrogenitus enjoyed conversing with them in a less formal ambiance to glean information of their countries. This was not possible at the audience, at which the Emperor sat on a golden throne in a hemicycle

---

[9] Already in the first century Domitian had forbidden castration. Justinian I decreed that perpetrators thereof be subjected to the same operation, sent to the mines, and forfeit their property, while the victimized slave was to be manumitted. Yet the practice persisted. Apparently even noble families occasionally emasculated a son in order to ensure his advancement in the imperial service, for the emperors had greater confidence in eunuchs than in the bearded. Leo VI even reduced the penalties for castration to a fine and ten years' exile for the instigator and whipping, tonsure, deprivation of property, and ten years' banishment for the operator. There was contradiction in the emperors' efforts to eradicate the practice and the large number of eunuchs in the Great Palace. The palatine eunuchs were, however, mostly of Abasgian origin. See Guilland in *Revue des études byzantines*, 1 (1943).

of dignitaries and did not condescend to speak directly to foreigners. Indeed, while envoys, flanked by eunuchs, were prostrating themselves before him, his throne was rapidly elevated and his costume changed. Thus, when they raised their eyes they beheld the Emperor high above them in different robes.

The Porphyrogenitus was a gourmet. He preferred resinous wines from Nice, Chios, or Naupactus. At imperial banquets he would give delicacies of his to guests who sat on the side of the table cloth, which covered only half the width of the table. The repast usually began with cold meats and sausages, strongly seasoned with oil, garlic, and onions, and was followed by roasts and warm dishes. Fat kid was a choice roast and was prepared with onions, leeks, garlic, and an oil dressing or sauce of fetid roe. Finger bowls were presented before the dessert, which consisted of cakes, fruits, sweetmeats, and honey tarts. During the meal the Demarch of the Blues and some of his men entertained with a grave hymn and a Pyrrhic dance, an ancient Greek ceremony. After the meal a fierce dance known as the Goths of Alaric was performed. Then came acrobats and jugglers.

In the field, the imperial commissary always took along rice, lentils, various beans, almonds, pistachios, bacon, fat, cheese, salt fish, caviar, kids, sheep, milk cows, and wine. Fowl and fresh vegetables were usually obtained on the road.

The populace had tripe, cheese, and often wine for breakfast. At lunch meat soup, fish stew, and a ragout were washed down by a resinous wine. Tuna and mackerel were popular fishes. Both white and brown bread were eaten. The larder might contain wheat, whey, honey, celery, leeks, lettuce, endives, spinach, mountain spinach, turnips, eggplants, artichokes, cabbages, cauliflower, beets, water cress, mushrooms, lentils, chick peas, mutton, bacon, olive oil, linseed oil, vinegar, almonds, pomegranates, walnuts, fir cones, hemp seeds, raisins, garum, pepper, salt, caraway seeds, cumin, spikenard, mush, saffron, etc.

A father of the eleventh century advised his son that if a friend came to town to visit him, he should lodge him outside his home, lest he try to flirt with his womenfolk, falsely boast of having seduced his wife, or criticize his way of living. The father also counseled his son to avoid physicians, who might make him worse in order to treat him longer. He urged him not to overeat, even to fast

occasionally, avoid herb decotions, drink absinthe for his health, eat
rhubarb for liver disorders, bleed himself in February, May, and
September, and in wartime not to insult the foe from the walls.

Unlike Western Europeans, Byzantine men wore their hair long
and dressed in robes. Nobles, accompanied by eunuchs and retainers, traversed the city on horseback or in chariots encrusted with
gold and silver and drawn by four horses. Costly silks, furs, pur-
ples, linens, and jewelry could safely be worn.

In the narrow streets the dwellings of the poor were constructed
of wood, since there was no other cheap building material near
New Rome. Nevertheless, they were superior to those of the prosperous in the West. Burghers' houses were of two or three stories,
for space in the Great City was limited. The façades had geometric
designs of rose-colored brick, brick alternating with stone, or brick
partly encrusted with marble or faïence and generally had arched
windows. Ornamental bands of brick or marble marked the stories.
A portico often preceded the façade, while loggias and balconies
extended from upper floors, thus covering and darkening the usually narrow streets. Exterior doors were of iron. Within, they were
of wood. The stairways were also of wood, the floors of brick or
marble. The long reception room was vaulted and often rose to the
roof. In clement weather the family lived in shaded inner courts.

Theology was the main subject of discussion, for to the typical
Byzantine the Deity seemed very close and spoke to them through
frequent omens and theological subtleties. Monasteries were not
gloomy, specialized centers, but havens of peace for all.

Despite continual warfare, Byzantines never lost their interest in
letters and Antiquity, although free, dynamic Hellenic thought had
long since been fettered and infiltrated by Oriental-Christianism.

The secular revival of Hellenic knowledge inaugurated by Bardas and Photius had engendered an encyclopedic era of research,
recuperation, and recapitulation. While Hellenic philosophy and
ancient geography were misinterpreted or suppressed to suit
Christian teachings, in other subjects there were vast compilations,
reaching back fifteen centuries, and the wisdom of ages was applied
to daily problems. Participating in this inventorial activity, the
Purple-Born wrote important works on history, statecraft, and foreign peoples. Compendia of war science, administration, diplomacy,
ceremonies, foreign nations, agriculture, medicine, and an anthol-

ogy of pagan and Christian poems were also published during his reign.

Byzantine architecture blossomed into variegated refinements and subtle divisions and combinations of thrusts. In general churches became smaller; the cruciform plan began to predominate, though often with a square exterior; and the interiors became more spacious. The drum between the supporting arches and the dome was now built polygonally, higher, and was pierced with slim columned windows. At the same time the dome was reduced, thus giving the edifices a lighter, more slender appearance. Moreover, with the reduction in the size of the domes their number was increased. The exterior brick surfaces were enlivened with geometric designs of brick or brick and stone or were partially encrusted with tiling, sculptured slabs, or multicolored marble, thus forming friezes or enhancing apertures supported by slender columnets.

There were regional differences. Helladic edifices show a stronger Oriental, especially Armenian, influence than those of the capital. Yet, while builders in Constantinople liked blind arcades and softened angles, the Helladics preferred flat surfaces and sharp angles. Venice retained old Byzantine forms long after they had been abandoned in the capital.

Since the iconoclastic movement lay and religious art had flowed in two streams, the former essentially inspired by the Hellenistic era, the latter sprung from the dogmatic creative impulse of the eighth century. But the flowering of profane art in the ninth and tenth centuries profoundly affected religious art, which came to accept Hellenistic models, rustic scenes, allegoric figures, serene facial beauty, and draperies disclosing the lines of the body.

While secular mosaics roamed freely over various subjects, ecclesiastical mosaics had in the ninth century become the symbolic expression of orthodox dogma. Each subject was assigned a definite place from the Pantocrator in the center of the cupola to Judas in the vestibule. Although inherently Oriental with inverted perspective, the models were ninth century Byzantines, who became traditional. Though fettered by dogmatic rules, the majestic attitudes and draperies of the figures reveal a deep sense of design and color.

Mural paintings had also become either worldly or dogmatic. The same evolution is discernible in manuscript miniatures. They were either Alexandrıne, arabesque, and elegant with flourishing fauna and flora mingling with geometric and architectural motifs or monastic, dogmatic, and traditional, eliminating anything of classical inspiration or individual fancy. Precious silks and other fabrics of delicate tints, embroidered with powerful colors, often with gold and silver, customarily retained Sassanian decorative motifs, exotic flora, real or fantastic animals symmetrically confronting each other, or religious and historical subjects. Byzantine sculptors, working in bronze, gold, silver, ivory, cameo, and steatite, were partly inspired by the Hellenic and created noble masterpieces.

Enameling had come to the Empire from the Sassanian realm. Progress in chemistry permitted the Byzantines to widen the range of colors. Thus, in the ninth and tenth centuries beautiful polychrome enamels of sky blue, turquoise, violet, purple, and flesh tints on golden or electron frames, crowns, icons, crosses, chalices, jewelry, reliquaries, etc. spread over the world.

The brilliance of refined Byzantine art radiated over Eurasia, and from the Urals to Gibraltar craftsmen avidly sought Byzantine creations for instruction and inspiration.[10]

DIGENIS AKRITAS

In the somber valleys and rugged defiles of the sanguinary Tauric frontier the war against the Moslems went on. Generations of Christian warriors fought and bled. Whoever may have been the prototype of the hero of the popular epic, *Digenis Akritas* of the mid-tenth century,[11] the name *Digenis* indicated that he was of two races, *Akritas* that he was a guardian of the frontier.

In a raid on imperial territory the Emir Musur carried off a strategos' daughter, fell in love, and became Christian in order to marry her. Of this union was born Digenis, who grew to be a youth with blond locks, large eyes, white skin, black eyebrows, broad chest, and handsome proportions. A proficient hunter and warrior, he was well educated and could sing, play the lyre, and appreciate the

---

[10] The writer is indebted to Rambaud's work on the reign of Constantine VII.

[11] *Cambridge Medieval History* (1967), IV, 2, p. 260.

beauties of art and nature. In early youth he distinguished himself against deer, bears, and lions and joined border bandits with whom he demonstrated his peerless prowess and valiance.

Soon his thoughts turned to more tender deeds. The frontier strategos' daughter Eudocia was of marvelous beauty. Her hair was blond, her eyebrows black, her face like rose-tinted snow. Many men had tried to abduct her, only to meet misfortune. She was carefully guarded in the women's quarters in a beautiful chamber covered with mosaics. Digenis with his lyre came to her window to sing of his pristine passion. Eudocia fell in love. At length they eloped, weeping with joy. Before galloping off with his bride, Digenis stopped at the castle gate to ask his father-in-law's blessing and to suggest that he thank God for giving him such a son-in-law. The strategos, his sons, and suite overtook the couple. Digenis unhorsed the strategos' guards and again requested his blessing. The strategos gave it and offered Digenis a resplendent wedding and a huge dowry, including vast estates and hundreds of servants. Digenis thought it safer to lead his bride to his parents' home, where the wedding festivities lasted three months.

Then he turned to eradicating banditry and defending the frontier, camping with his wife amid fragrant flowers and in cool forests. He committed an occasional infidelity, once with a Moslem maid, another time with a descendant of Amazons whom Alexander had brought from India fourteen centuries before. But he deeply regretted these indiscretions and desired to do penance, for he was a devout Christian, ardently venerated the saints, and often spent entire nights praying and singing hymns. In war he was compassionate toward a defeated foe and considerate toward the weaker sex. Having brought peace to his district, Digenis retired to a palace of fabulous luxury on the Euphrates, whose interior was decorated with gold, pearls, precious stones, and mosaics of Biblical, Homeric, and Macedonian history.

Digenis refused the Basileus' invitation to the Great City and respectfully suggested that if the Emperor wished to see him he come to the banks of the Euphrates with a small escort. When the sovereign came Digenis offered advice regarding the governance of the realm and urged him to provide for indigent soldiers. These independent frontier fighters affected none of the subservience of courtiers.

At thirty-three Digenis fell mortally ill. Before dying he told his wife of his eternal love and of his pain that his death should cause her sorrow. He urged her not to mourn too much and to remarry. But Eudocia died with him.

THE HOLY WAR

The reconquest of the lost lands of the Empire went slowly and was accompanied by many defeats, for the Moslems had long since organized, trained, and disciplined their mercenary armies on the Roman model. The Romans no longer faced a khalif, but hardy, independent emirs, since the actual authority of the Abbasid Khalifate was limited to the area of Bagdad, to which the khalifs had returned from Samarra in 892. So low was Islam's reputation that when the Iranian Samanids took over eastern Iran in 903 they sought their ancestry, not among early Moslem heroes, but among the Sassanids and replaced Arabic with Persian as the literary language. In 945 another Iranian family, the Buyids, rulers of western Iran, drove the Turks, who had dominated the Sunnite khalifs for a century, from Iraq and, though Shiites, took over their protection. Effective khalifal authority was at an end.

A year earlier Ali, Shiite and scion of the Hamdanid family that controlled a large part of Mesopotamia, had seized Aleppo from the Turkish Ikshidids, who ruled Egypt and Syria. Making it his capital, he waged unceasing holy war against the Empire and was hailed the Sword of the Khalifate. To his banner rallied devout Moslems of the Levant.

In 950 at the head of 35,000 men Ali penetrated to within seven days' march of New Rome, burning churches and monasteries and massacring those Christians whom he could not abduct. He discomfited the veteran Domestic Bardas Phocas and captured 120 patricians. As he was recrossing the Taurus with his captives and booty-laden camels, Bardas ambushed him in a defile. Rocks rained on his horsemen, who quickly butchered the important captives before they fell under the Roman onslaught. Ali himself broke through the Roman lines. Closely pursued, he reached a cliff, goaded his horse, and plunged into the depth. The horse landed on its feet.

The Romans invaded his realm. In 953 they ravaged the country-side of Antioch and Aleppo. Ali battered them near Germanicea, took away their booty, and captured the Domestic's son Constantine. When he died in prison six years later Ali sent sympathy to his father and delivered the corpse to Aleppine Christians. Meanwhile, in 955 Nicephorus Phocas had replaced his aged and scarred father as Domestic. His troops cut down Ali's best horsemen and overran his territory.

CRETE

Lecapenus' son Theophylact, a striking exception in the devout patriarchal roster, still scandalized the pious with his originality, life of pleasure, and hippomania until a stallion threw and killed him in 956. The Purple-Born thought to atone for his impiety by appointing as his successor an austere, castrated monk from Prote, Polyeuctes, who soon attacked the Emperor for having tolerated him.

Constantine and Helena had five daughters and a son, Romanus, born in 939 and created Co-Emperor in 945. Not appreciating the treatises that his father wrote for him or his father's scholarly circle, Romanus devoted himself to sports and associated with athletes, comedians, effeminate courtiers, and prostitutes. At an early age he became enamored of a publican's daughter, a girl of rare beauty, whose name was changed to Theophano and whom he married in 956. A son was born to them and named Basil. It was said that Theophano was as ambitious and unscrupulous as she was beautiful and seductive and that she and Romanus mixed poison in his father's food. However that might be, Constantine, who was fifty-four, fell ill and sought relief on the slopes of Bithynian Mount Olympus. The monks on the holy mount could not cure him and he descended to the ancient health resort Prusa, which Hannibal had advised Prusias, King of Bithynia, to found. The waters were of no avail and Constantine VII returned to New Rome to die (959).

Romanus II was twenty, Theophano eighteen. They tonsured his five sisters and immured them in separate convents. The disconsolate mother died. The staff of Constantine VII yielded to his son's favorites. The eunuch Joseph Bringas, Patrician, Grand Prepositus, and Drungary of the Fleets, became Grand Chamberlain. With the government in his efficient hands Romanus could retire to the country and his pleasures.

Bringas decided to make another effort to tear Crete from the Moslems, who since 828 had rendered the Aegean unsafe. Five imperial expeditions against the island had failed. Again the elite of the tagmatic and thematic troops was selected. The command was given to the Domestic Nicephorus Phocas, popular with the soldiers and the masses. Now forty-eight, he had short legs under a powerful, slightly corpulent torso surmounted by a large head. He had long black hair, an extremely dark complexion, thick eyebrows, dark, pensive eyes, an arched nose, and a short graying beard. Since the deaths of his wife and son this man of austere and mystic tendencies had sought solace in religion. He frequented monks, ate no meat, slept on the floor, and took an oath of chastity. But he was also an eloquent orator and a gifted general.

In early summer 960 the armament was ready. Multitudes had assembled in churches and on the maritime walls. At the marble port of the Palace in sumptuous array were the Emperor, the Patriarch, and the highest dignitaries. Suddenly the crowds grew silent. The Patriarch blessed the fleet and the Emperor gave the signal for departure. The vividly painted galleys, banners and pennants flying, prows gleaming, the warriors' armor and weapons glittering, slowly began to move. A roar came from the City and echoed back from the masses on the Asiatic shore. Drums rolled, cymbals clashed, trumpets sounded, the strange instruments of Altaic mercenaries beat. The war songs of the barbarian troops, the regulated acclamations of the factions, the hymns of the pious, the canticles of the monks flowed over the blue waters. From the City's churches, convents, monasteries, and sanctuaries rose hymns to the victory-giving Virgin and prayers to innumerable saints.

Joined by thematic contingents on the way, the Christian fleet soon appeared off the Cretan coast. On the beach a Moslem host waited, its white robes and polished weapons glistening in the sunlight. From the towers of the dromons Roman archers and war engines drove the Moslems to the heights above. The dromons were steered to the beach. Suddenly their sides opened, planks fell into place, and the astonished Moslems saw heavy Roman cavalry ride out of the ships. Each division was accompanied by a bishop with a numerous staff and a large, beautiful cross bearing a fragment of the True Cross.

Russian infantrymen charged up the hill under a cloud of Moslem arrows, which fell harmlessly on their roof of shields. Their spears bristling, they plunged into the dense mass of naked black men, white-robed Bedouins, mailed warriors, and wild, shouting dervishes, while imperial archers plied the Moslems from the flanks. Raucous Arab drums beat feverishly, cymbals clashed franticly. It was in vain. The Moslems began to fall back. Then the iron Roman cataphracts rode into them and wreaked frightful carnage. The survivors broke and fled.

Nicephorus Phocas ordered the fleet to surround the island to prevent the arrival of Moslems from Cilicia, Syria, Egypt, Africa, or Spain, who theretofore had generally frustrated Roman reconquest.

Meanwhile, the Roman army marched inland. The steppe mercenaries had never seen such laden fruit trees and, despite the efforts of the commander of the van, dispersed to quench their thirst and satiate their palates with unknown delights. Moslems fell upon them and almost wiped them out. Phocas nevertheless continued the advance on Chandax, maintaining iron discipline, crushing Moslem opposition, devastating the countryside. Many inhabitants, whose forebears had been Christians, greeted the imperial troops as deliverers.

At length the army arrived in view of Chandax, built of the stones of Knossus, where the legendary Daedalus was believed to have built a labyrinth on an Egyptian model and mastered the science of flight and where the mythical Minotaur succumbed to Theseus. The Roman troops gazed in dismay at the wide, deep moat and the formidable walls, on which two chariots abreast could be driven. On the land side the city was protected by an enormous, perpendicular rock and on the north by the sea, although the harbor had long since filled up. Capture by assault appeared impossible. Starvation seemed the only course. While their ships blockaded the city, the Romans drew around it a large ditch and a stone wall, whose ends reached the sea at either side. Behind this line they built their palisaded camp. Separate detachments covered the island, took towns and forts, crushed Moslem bands, and gathered food. Desperate sallies from Chandax and relief expeditions of Asiatic and

African Moslems were beaten off. Summer and autumn passed. Finally forty thousand Moslems from the interior and Africa marched against the Roman camp. Their attack was to coincide with a sortie from the city. The Christians would be surrounded and annihilated. Informed of the plan, Phocas moved secretly and on a moonlit night his mailed horsemen converged on the camp of the sleeping relief army. It was too late for the Moslems to form and through the long, bright night the iron Roman warriors cut them down as they rallied in small groups.

On the morrow, the day of the projected sortie from Chandax, a horrible sight greeted the inhabitants. Outside the walls on rows of long pikes in battle formation were impaled the heads of the victims of the night. Soon Roman catapults commenced raining heads and corpses into the unhappy city. Many belonged to cherished kin. Women shrieked and tore out their hair. Men groaned and plucked out their beards. A ghastly gloom settled over the starving city, whose plight was soon aggravated by winter and incessant rains.

But the besiegers were also suffering. Hostilities, a dry summer, and a locust plague had ruined the Anatolian harvest. There was a food shortage in New Rome and shipments to Crete were delayed. Rations ran short and the men commenced to murmur. Apparently only Phocas' ardent and eloquent words prevented mutiny. Meanwhile in the capital Bringas intimidated the hoarders and profiteers and dispatched provisions. To distract his men Phocas built an elegant Byzantine church, which was dedicated to the Virgin.

In the interim starving Chandax was becoming desperate. The aged but energetic Emir determined to make a secret mass attack on the Roman camp. The Roman intelligence service informed Phocas of the project. Suddenly the gates of Chandax flew open. Fifteen hundred horse and thirty-six thousand foot, all in mail, penetrated the Roman lines. The Romans retreated. The Moslems followed, fell into an ambush, broke through, fell into another and another. The survivors of the first three sought to flee forward and fell into a fourth. One doughty Moslem rider reached Phocas, who pierced him with his lance. Obeying their leader's mighty voice, the Roman forces closed in. A massacre followed. The survivors fled. The wizened old Emir on the city walls ordered the gates to be closed on them. The cruel command was disobeyed. The Candiotes had lost enough on that sad day.

Winter passed, but the suffering Moslems held out, bombarded day and night by arrows, stones, fire, iron hooks, and hot oil, never free from the sound of exploding grenades and the crash of rock against the walls. They fervently hoped that a succoring squadron might break through the Roman fleet. Bearing this in mind, Phocas commanded an assault against a part of the wall that the Roman catapults had macerated. The trumpets sounded, the drums rolled, the barbarian instruments beat, the hymn of the Victorious Virgin rose, and the Romans dashed forward under a roof of shields, pushing captives before them. On a tower a madly gesticulating Saracen sorceress invoked the power of Allah and hurled vile imprecations at the attackers. Lest the accursed pig-eaters fail to grasp her meaning, she tore off her clothes, turned her back, and in scrawny nakedness demonstrated her low opinion of them. An accurate archer put a facetious end to her obscenities. Meanwhile, the suffering, fleshless defenders beat off the assailants.

A larger breach was required. Roman artillery continued to batter the weakened spot. In March 961 there was a solemn matutinal ceremony in the Roman camp. Phocas, ahorse in sumptuous armor and surrounded by his military and ecclesiastical staff, addressed the army. He pointed to white clouds. There, he said, the Mother of God on a radiant throne was blessing her faithful Christian soldiers. About her on white steeds were warrior saints, Demetrius, young Proconsul of Achaia, who had enjoyed a martyr's death in Salonica in 306; George, the blond Syrian youth in a shining breastplate; and two Theodores. Also present was the Archangel Michael, commander of the celestial hosts, with wings of blinding whiteness, an elegant bejeweled robe, and a flaming sword. Raising his arms heavenward, Phocas called upon them all and upon Christ Pantocrator to cast down the ramparts of Chandax as once the walls of Jericho had fallen. To those who were about to die in the war against the Agarenes, sons of bitches, deniers of the True Word, sectaries of a false prophet, and eaters of tainted camel flesh, he promised martyr palms, to those who survived, booty, donatives, and a magnificent triumph. As he spoke, priests went through the ranks conferring absolution, giving communion, and displaying the wood of the True Cross, pieces of saints' bones, and a hundred other sacred relics.

After the ceremony the assault began. Ballistae, catapults, and arbalists hurled rocks against the weakened part of the wall and cleared it with a shower of arrows and stones. Two towers were rolled forward. Their pyrotechnicians kept the Moslems at bay with hand grenades and Greek Fire, while a huge iron-capped battering ram thudded steadily against the wall and sappers, who had crossed the moat, dug a tunnel, filled it with combustibles, and set them afire. The Roman sappers, the battering ram squad, and the rolling towers retreated precipitately. The flames rapidly consumed the dry supporting joist and two towers of the wall collapsed into the moat.

The troops plunged into the city and butchered everyone they encountered. Emaciated Moslem warriors rallied in narrow streets to fight to the bitter end. Phocas galloped into the city and calmed his frenzied soldiers. The slaughter stopped. The Moslems surrendered. The aged, bent, bald, but still fiery Emir, his family, the chiefs, the youngest and strongest men, the most beautiful women, and the most representative part of the booty were set aside for the triumph. The rest of the population and the loot of 134 years were turned over to the Roman combatants. Delirious with joy, they acclaimed their beloved general the Victorious. The inhabitants were set up for sale. Slave dealers were at hand, for in the Middle Ages they followed armies. For men from whom the flush of youth had passed there was little demand. Many were put to the sword, dying in the bitter knowledge that their wives and children were doomed to slavery. It is said that the Roman campaign in Crete extirpated two hundred thousand Moslems and that an equal number, mostly women and children, was sold into servitude. The Aegean population was liberated from the incubus of Cretan raids; commerce could again move freely; and the imperial navy had regained an outpost of major strategic importance.

Phocas accorded his soldiers a few days to enjoy the fruits of victory. Then the slaves were put to work. The walls of Chandax were demolished and its moat was filled. A powerful Roman fort was built on an adjacent height. The rest of the island submitted. Mosques, pulpits, and Korans were destroyed. Crete became a theme and was reconverted to Christianity.

Messengers brought the glad tidings to New Rome, and a nocturnal thanksgiving was solemnly celebrated at Saint Sophia. Phocas was immediately recalled, lest his soldiers raise him to the purple. He was not accorded the triumph in which the victor stood in a chariot drawn by four white horses, but an ovation on foot. In the triumphal defile marched the aged Emir and his family, proud in adversity. He was granted a villa in the suburbs and given a generous allowance. A dignity might even have been conferred on him, but he refused to abjure his faith. His son, however, accepted his conquerors' religion, entered the guards, distinguished himself, and died a dozen years later fighting gallantly for his adopted country. His descendants were absorbed into the nation. Indeed, except for the triumphal humiliation imposed on the conquered, which apparently the prestige of the Empire required, New Rome was ever prepared to receive her foes to her bosom. If they acceptd Christianity high honors were open to them.

CILICIA

While Phocas had been conquering Crete, the Sword of the Khalifate at the head of thirty thousand horsemen had invaded Anatolia. After weeks of rapine he took the road homeward. In November 960 the Moslems reached the Taurus, driving herds and captives before them. Ali was well pleased. He rode beside the long files of his elegantly equipped horsemen and booty-laden camels, put his mare through a series of fancy steps, hurled his lance into the air and caught it at full gallop. The column entered the pass. Soon he would be in his wondrous palace at Aleppo. Poets would sing of his glorious deeds. His wives would marvel.

Suddenly Roman trumpets sounded. An avalanche of rocks and tree trunks rolled down from both sides of the defile and spread havoc among his men. Then with a roar the troops of Leo Phocas, the brother of Nicephorus, fell upon the elite of Islam. The Hamdanid resisted furiously. It was hopeless. His army was doomed. His mare was killed under him. His equerry, a former Christian, gave him his mount and fell the next instant. He broke through the Roman lines and galloped furiously out of the defile. He reached Aleppo with three hundred horsemen, all that was left of an army that had been the pride of Islam. The rest lay in the wild Tauric pass or were to be sold on the slave mart of New Rome.

In strong, efficient hands the Roman army was, if not invincible,

at least indestructible. With it Nicephorus Phocas could now crush
Ali, the bulwark of Levantine Islam, open the road to Jerusalem
and Bagdad, and restore the East to Christ and Empire. That was
the mighty mystic's goal. His first step must be the conquest of
Cilicia. While elsewhere the Roman frontier had moved eastward
since the reign of Basil, the Moslems clung tenaciously to Cilicia,
where the Taurus still separated Islam and Christendom. Cilicia was
powerfully protected against north and west by high peaks, dense
forests, inaccessible defiles, and impregnable forts. Even if these ob-
stacles were surmounted, the conqueror would still face an armed,
warlike Moslem peasantry and martial emirs at Tarsus, Anazarbus,
and Adana with strong forces, watchtowers, redoubts, fortified villages, and stubborn walled towns.

In 962 Phocas forced the Taurus; conquered and garrisoned
about sixty forts and towns; took powerful Anazarbus with an
enormous booty, including 40,000 lances and 40,000 coats of mail;
and laid waste the countryside, cutting down fruit trees, for it was
necessary to starve out the Moslem population before repeopling
the area with Christians. To protect his acquisitions from the south
Phocas seized the passes of the Amanus, the mountain chain that
shields Cilicia on the east and south.

The road to Syria lay open. Phocas circumvented the forces that
the Sword of the Khalifate sent against him and soon beheld the
gleaming cupolas and minarets of Aleppo, flashing white amid the
verdure of the surrounding oasis. The former Berea, Aleppo was
possibly founded by the Hittites. It was famed for its Emir's en-
trancing palace, its inhabitants' elegance, the splendors of Moslem
art in full bloom, and the excellence of its pistachios.

His best troops erring in the Syrian hills, Ali gathered his guards,
Aleppine townsmen, and Syrian peasants and attempted to defend
an adjacent stream. But the Moslems could not beard the Roman
regulars, and when John Tzimisces, who had swum across the river
several miles upstream with a select cavalry troop, fell on their
flank, they broke. The helpless Aleppine foot was slaughtered. The
Emir's kinsmen and highest officials fell. Many of those who
reached Aleppo were crushed to death at the Jewish Gate. Ali was
cut off from the city. Hotly pursued, he galloped eastward and vanished in the desert.

While the poetic Emir was lamenting his fate in a caravansary, the Romans were ravishing his beautiful palace in the gardened Aleppine suburbs. Arabian stallions and mares, eight hundred horses, two thousand mules, two thousand camels, six thousand coats of mail, three hundred loads of marvelous linens, three hundred of sumptuous silks, gold and silver plates, a hundred of ornate weapons, artillery, and a huge booty in coin fell into the hands of the Romans, who set fire to the Moslem masterpiece.

Abetted by sedition within Aleppo, Phocas' army scaled its walls on a December dawn of 962 and amid rivers of blood cut down its defenders and inhabitants. Some found safety in the citadel. Of the rest only ten thousand were spared—the comeliest females and children. The boys were destined to become, as usual, members of the Watch, the Excubitors, and the Hikanati. No such spoil as that of Aleppo had been taken since the reign of Heraclius. The Romans wrecked the greater part of the city and recrossed the Amanus.

BRINGAS

The army had not yet reached Caesarea when the demise of Romanus II in March 963 was announced. It is said that this athletic young man died at twenty-four from the excesses of debauchery. It was also rumored that his consort Theophano had poisoned him.

However that might be, Theophano was now twenty-two and the mother of four children (two Emperors, Basil II and Constantine VIII, and two daughters). Though she was officially regent, the reins of government lay in the hands of the Grand Chamberlain Bringas. So jealous of his power was this haughty and energetic eunuch that when Phocas had disbanded his army and hastened to the capital to see the Empress he proposed to blind him. But he dared not, for the populace would not brook it. Thus, despite his opposition, Phocas entered New Rome in triumph, carrying with him from Aleppo what were reputedly the tatters of the robe of Saint John the Baptist. But Bringas feared his popularity, position, wealth, and relationship to the Empress and determined to apprehend him. Phocas sought sanctuary in Saint Sophia. Patriarch and populace guarded him against the eunuch's minions, while Theophano convoked the Senate, ever a factor in times of regencies or weak rulers. Phocas was acclaimed, his position as Domestic was confirmed, and he was granted a measure of supervision over the government's actions. The powerful Domestic rejoined his army.

Bringas wrote to the man who in military reputation and popularity stood second to Phocas, John Tzimisces, Strategos of the Anatolics. He offered to name him Domestic and to give the command of the European forces to his kinsman Romanus Curcuas, the son of Lecapenus' famous Domestic, if they would dispose of Phocas. Bringas even indicated to Tzimisces that his new post would be a stepping-stone to the purple. Tzimisces and Curcuas went to the tent where Phocas lay ill and urged him to overthrow Bringas.

On an extensive plain outside Cappadocian Caesarea the forces of the East were drawn up at dawn in July 963. When the first rays of the rising sun glittered on the polished helmets and lances of the world's foremost army John Tzimisces and other officers in parade armor proceeded to the Domestic's tent. When he appeared they unsheathed their swords, pointed them skyward, acclaimed him Emperor of the Romans, and raised him on a large shield. The entire army echoed, "Long live Nicephorus Augustus! Long live the invincible Emperor! May God protect him! On to the City!" [12]

Phocas affected the customary reluctance. It was of no avail. His officers shod him with the purple buskins. But he refused the diadem and thus gave symbolic proof that he was not usurping the prior rights of the two young Porphyrogeniti. He harangued and inflamed the army, received the Metropolitan's blessing at the cathedral of Caesarea, created Tzimisces Magister and Domestic, charged him with the war against the Moslems, and marched on New Rome.

Bringas relied on the Macedonian troops to hold the capital and withdrew all craft from the Asiatic shore. Thus, Nicephorus II was unable to cross with his army. Meanwhile, Bringas ordered the arrest of his relatives and partisans. The former Domestic Bardas Phocas, now over eighty, and his son Leo sought refuge in Saint Sophia. When Bringas' soldiers attempted to seize them the capital populace uprose. They found a leader when the gigantic and majestic figure of Basil the Bastard appeared in the Augustaeum at the head of his three thousand armed slaves and servants. This castrated

---

12 Schlumberger, . . . *Nicéphore Phocas* (Paris, 1890), p. 282.

personage, whom Bringas had supplanted as Grand Chamberlain, led the masses and massacred Bringas' arrogant Macedonians. Even after they had crushed resistance and driven Bringas to Saint Sophia they sacked his residence and those of his adherents. Then, still led by Basil, they seized the fleet and crossed the Bosporus to welcome their new Emperor, while Leo Phocas took possession of the City.[13]

---

[13] The last three sections are based largely on Schlumberger's work on Nicephorus Phocas.

VIII

Fighting Emperors

963–1025

A SOLDIER-Emperor had again reached the throne. As Lecapenus had allowed Constantine VII to live undisturbed but powerless beside him, now Nicephorus II harbored the little Porphyrogeniti, who also soon yielded precedence to their mighty Co-Emperor.

Nicephorus inaugurated his reign with mildness. Bringas was exiled to his native Paphlagonia and lived peacefully, if ruefully, until 971. Basil again became Grand Chamberlain; the Emperor's war-scarred father Bardas, Caesar; his brother Leo, Curopalates and European Domestic; while Theophano became the wife of the ascetic cinquantenarian monarch. Incensed at the second nuptials, the Patriarch Polyeuctes for a time refused communion to the Emperor.

After the conquest of Chandax, Phocas had from his share of the booty given a hundred pounds of gold to his spiritual father Athanasius to construct a monastery on Mount Athos, where he had intended, as soon as his duties permitted, to spend his remaining days. It is uncertain when religious recluses first settled on this striking promontory. By the ninth century it already had some monasteries, which suffered from Moslem raids. The reconquest of Crete brought security to Athos, and in 963 Athanasius began to build the laura that Phocas so ardently desired. Soon monks from other countries also founded lauras. Successive emperors accorded the Holy Mount privileges and it became a veritable autonomous republic, tax-free and exempt from patriarchal authority. No human or animal female is permitted within its bounds and to this day it remains the petrified relic of a past age.

IN XPO DEO FIDVS
REX ET TIRAINVS
GRECORVM·NICHI
FORVS PHOCAS DO
MESTICVS STVDI
ORVM:~

From Spyridon Lampros, Portraits of Byzantine Emperors; *the*
manuscript miniature from which it was taken is in the Library
San Marco, Venice

Nicephorus II Phocas (reigned 963–969)

Despite his asceticism and his predilection for monastic society, Nicephorus did not ignore the harm that excessive monasticism did to state and society. For centuries emperors, empresses, pontiffs, and the wealthy had sought earthly retreats and heavenly rewards by endowing convents and monasteries. As a result, the Empire was dotted with monastic establishments, which deprived the peasants of land, the army of manpower, the state of revenue, and often the land of cultivation. It has been estimated that by the tenth century a third of the usable land was again in the hands of pious institutions, as it had been before iconoclasm.[1] Nicephorus forbade the construction of such institutions, the enlargement of old ones, and their acquisition of any property at the expense of the poor. He admonished cenobites to think more of heavenly than of worldly possessions and not to dwell in cities or on the most fertile lands, but to retire to the wastes, as early Christian celibates had.

Nicephorus also viewed with concern the Greeks' aversion to military life. To reawaken the military spirit of this important element of the population he requested the clergy to honor as martyrs all Christian soldiers who fell in holy war against the infidels. The proposal was rejected by the Patriarch.

SICILY

In Sicily Roman rule was still quivering. In 926 after seven months' siege Taormina had again fallen into Moslem hands. Alone Rametta remained free. In this impregnable mountain fortress hardy Christians had for a century repelled fierce Moslem onslaughts and offered refuge to coreligionaries.

Hardly had Nicephorus become Emperor when news reached him that the Moslems were besieging Rametta in force. In 964 a Roman fleet with over forty thousand men under the command of the pious eunuch Nicetas departed to reconquer Sicily with its many fervent Christians. Although the African Fatimid Khalif sent Berber effectives to strengthen the Sicilian Moslems, the Romans took Messina, Termini, Taormina, Leontini, and Syracuse.

From Messina the dashing Patrician Manuel, bastard cousin of

---

[1] See Charanis' pithy article in *Dumbarton Oaks Papers*, 4 (1948).

the Emperor, rode with a handsome cavalry corps to the relief of Rametta. At dawn in October 965 he and his cataphracts advanced through a narrow pass toward the steep-walled amphitheatric recess in whose center on a rocky eminence starving Rametta still defied the Moslems. The Moslem commander Hassan left a contingent in his camp to cope with a possible sortie from Rametta, occupied the defiles through which the Roman flanks were advancing, and with an elite troop blocked the pass through which Manuel was coursing.

Realizing that succor was coming, the Ramettans sallied forth, but enfeebled by starvation, were driven back. Nor could the Roman wings break through the lateral defiles. In the main pass the Roman cataphracts engaged the unmounted Moslems in bitter battle. From its steep sides Manuel's light artillery bombarded them with stones and arrows. At length they began to break. Hassan intoned an ancient hymn. Inspired by the solemn grandeur of the venerable strophes echoing against the mountain walls, his warriors stopped fleeing and joined their voices to his. Hassan raised his saber and led a headlong charge. The Romans broke. Manuel and his patricians tried desperately to rally them. It was of no avail. Followed by his staff, Manuel charged into the dense Moslem mass, hewing about fiercely with his sword. His faithful officers were soon lost in a sea of white robes, clashing shields, thrusting lances. One by one they fell. Manuel's armor was impermeable. He fought on. His mount was hamstrung. Rider and steed came to the ground and perished under a hundred blows. A moment later his faithful equerry, who had struggled heroically at his side, was also brought down.

A storm broke and torrents gushed down the mountain sides. The fleeing Roman horsemen plunged into muddy ravines and almost as many met death in the haste of flight as at the hands of the Berbers. Ten thousand Romans yielded the ghost.

Moslem reinforcements advanced from Palermo and swept the Roman forces from the reoccupied cities of the east coast. Rametta held out until January 965, when the Moslems scaled the walls. The famished survivors fought to the death. So ended the age-old bond between the Greeks and the land of Persephone and twelve centuries of Roman rule.

As the survivors of the Roman expedition were sadly embarking from Reggio, a large Moslem fleet beset them with grappling hooks. All day between Scylla and Charybdis Moslem and Christian struggled from galley to galley on decks slippery with blood. When the sun set the great Roman armament was no more. But the sanguinary waters of the strait flowed into peaceful channels, for Nicephorus II wished to be free to efface the Emirate of Aleppo and reconquer the Holy Land, now in the hands of the Ikshidids of Egypt, while the Fatimid Khalif coveted Egypt. Moreover, the dominions of both seemed threatened by the vast German realm that stretched from the Baltic to the Tiber.

ITALY

The disunited German tribes remaining east of the Rhine after the great migrations had been conquered by Charlemagne. In the trifold partition of his realm in 843 one of his grandsons obtained the territory east of the Rhine and north of the Alps. Thus was formed the German kingdom. Over a century later the German King Otto crossed the Alps, declared himself King of Italy, and in 962 was crowned Emperor by the Pope. The similar coronation of Charlemagne in 800 had not changed his relation to his subjects and the title had fallen into disuse with the disruption of the Frankish realm. Otto's title, however, implied the union of Italy and Germany and came to connote overlord of vassals. For centuries it was to lure German suzerains to sanguinary efforts to control Italy. Meanwhile, Otto desired that part of the Apennine Peninsula under the dominion of New Rome.

Although Calabria had been strengthened by fugitive Christians from Sicily, was proud of its Greek heritage, and was faithful to New Rome, Roman Italy was harassed by frequent risings of Lombard subjects, revolts of the Lombard vassals (the princes of Capua-Benevento and of Salerno), and devastating incursions of Sicilian and Slavic corsairs, who sacked cities, slaughtered or abducted the inhabitants, or imposed tribute. These problems vanished only when the Empire maintained strong land and sea forces in Italy.

Such was not the case in 967 when Otto marched south. Capua-Benevento and Salerno accepted his overlordship. To complete the conquest of Italy Otto requested for his son and heir the hand of a porphyrogenita with the two Italian themes as her dowry. Not waiting for a reply, he invaded the theme of Longobardia and laid siege to Bari (968). But Nicephorus had reorganized, recolonized, and refortified Roman Italy, and Otto spent a futile month before Bari's ramparts. Salerno returned to Roman suzerainty, and Otto's ambitious plans slipped into useless hostilities.

ANTIOCH

One of Nicephorus' first acts on assuming the purple was to send the Domestic John Tzimisces to Cilicia, where the indefatigable Sword of the Khalifate was attacking the recent Roman reconquests. A bitter struggle followed. On one occasion Tzimisces ambushed fifteen thousand Moslems. The survivors abandoned their mounts and sought refuge on the summit of a steep hill. Surrounded, they refused to capitulate and for two days repulsed all Roman attacks. At length Tzimisces led his troops up the hillside through a hail of arrows and stones and killed the fiercely fighting Moslems to the last man.

In 965 Roman forces retook Cyprus, whose rule the Empire had since 688 shared with the Moslems. Thus the Cilician coast was secured from Moslem attack, while the reconquest of Syria was facilitated. Nicephorus fortified the island and elevated it to a theme. After three centuries of economic decay it again became a prosperous imperial emporium.

In Cilicia Moslem power was concentrated in the strongly fortified cities of Mopsuestia and Tarsus, both under semi-independent, aggressive emirs. Wealthy, maritime Mopsuestia with a population of two hundred thousand lay inland on both sides fo the Pyramus. The Emperor bombarded it with stones, grenades, burning oil, and inflamed javelins. Espying a weak spot in the wall near the river, he had his sappers undermine it at night. At dawn they set fire to combustiles and the supports that they had set up. Rampart and tower collapsed, and to the strains of the Pathfinding Virgin Roman officers led their columns into the breach. Massacre and rapine followed. The young were enslaved. The survivors of the garrison and their families were sent off to populate the Empire, to defend its frontiers, and to be romanized (965).

Nicephorus advanced against Tarsus, which his brother, the Curopalates, had already invested. The birthplace of Saint Paul, Tarsus is situated among fecund orchards on both banks of the Cydnus, navigable up to this point. A deep moat and a double row of formidable walls shielded the opulent city. The Emperor commanded that two banners be placed before its ramparts, one to symbolize the land of the Romans, the other, the land of Islam. Heralds invited all those who loved justice, impartiality, sanctity of property, family life, children, good roads, just laws, and kind treatment to rally around the first and those who upheld adultery, oppressive legislation, violence, extortion, and the confiscation of property to assemble around the second. It is not recorded that the latter drew any partisans.

Suffering from famine and disease, Tarsus offered to submit. The Emir, the Kadi, the chief sheiks, and the city's elders in white robes prostrated their shaven heads in the dust before the invincible Equal of the Apostles and kissed his knees. After distributing a requisite number of kicks he courteously invited them to sit at his table and hear his conditions of peace. They included the surrender of the city and the evacuation of its Moslem inhabitants, who were to be escorted to Aleppine confines. The Moslems had no choice but to accept (965).

Thereupon the Romans proceeded with the traditional ritual and converted the Grand Mosque into a stable for the cavalry. The conquest of Cilicia was complete. The progeny of Christians driven into the mountains generations before descended into the fertile fields. Moslems who clung to their lands more than to their faith accepted the Trinity. Many Armenians replaced those Moslems who departed. Reconstruction began. The famine caused by the Roman destruction of crops subsided.

In 967 the once redoutable Sword of the Khalifate, weakened by defeat and loss of land, shaken by revolt, crushed by gout, paralysis, retention of urine, and aged by the fatigues of war, expired at fifty-two in his beloved Aleppo.

A year later Nicephorus again devastated Syria, recovered the reputed head of Saint John the Forerunner at ancient Emesa, crossed the Lebanon range, distributed Roman garrisons at strategic points, and led his booty-laden troops north with a hundred thousand of the flower of Moslem youth of both sexes, leaving the Aleppine Emirate in a state of disintegration with officials and towns revolting. Islam was aghast.

Before returning to his capital the Emperor invested Antioch and left in command his bastard and castrated nephew, the Patrician Peter Phocas. Famine and the continual alarms of the siege gradually wore down the defenders' vigilance, while Antiochene Christians informed the Romans of their moves. Following such intelligence, the Patrician Michael Burtzes, who commanded a fort overlooking the city, scaled its walls with three hundred picked men in nocturnal silence. His attempt to capture a populous and well-garrisoned city with such a small force seemed the more foolhardy because at that moment Peter Phocas was marching on Aleppo. Nevertheless, Burtzes and his three hundred warriors killed the guards of the nearest tower, took a second tower, and filtered into the city. But the alarm had been given and the city was soon in arms. Oppressed by overwhelming weight, the rash Roman detachments reformed, retreated, and entrenched themselves on the part of the wall that they had captured. Three days and three nights the gallant group held out between their two towers, desperately fighting off the Moslem mass, the target of Moslem artillery, hand grenades, and burning arrows.

Suddenly Peter Phocas appeared on the luxuriant Orontine plain. Ladders were placed on the Roman part of the wall and Roman troops flowed up. They took tower after tower and hacked down a gate to let in the bulk of their army. Moslem dominion of Antioch went down amid blood and fire (October 969). The great mosque was converted into a pigsty. Ten thousand of the handsomest youth of both sexes were sent to the capital for the slave marts, the guards, or palatine service. The Moslem survivors were exiled and the city was repopulated with Christians, refortified, and strongly garrisoned.

Peter Phocas resumed the road to Aleppo and took it by storm. Only the citadel held out. The Emir became a Roman vassal and submitted to tribute, a head tax, customs duties, and tax exemption for Christians. Thus, while western Syria with Antioch was annexed to the Empire, the area around Aleppo acknowledged Roman suzerainty.

A tremor ran through Islam. Roman arms had never been so uniformly victorious against Moslems. With Cilicia and the Taurus firmly in Roman hands the road to Levantine reconquest was open.

BULGARIA

Though for almost forty years Bulgaria had kept the peace, it had not been forgotten that she could rapidly concentrate her full military strength against New Rome, as Simeon had earlier in the century. Now, weakened by the Bogomil heresy, the disaffection of her anti-Roman boliads, and the inroads of Patzinaks, Hungarians, and Serbs, Nicephorus II proposed to conquer her. Hence, when the Bulgarian Caesar's envoys came to New Rome for the yearly subsidy of almost four decades' standing the Isapostol insulted and scourged them. He took the field, seized Bulgarian frontier forts, then inexplicably returned to New Rome.

But he did not renounce his plan. He would use northern neighbors to disrupt the kingdom, then perhaps complete the conquest in a single campaign. With this in mind he dispatched a gold-laden Chersonite to the court of the Great Prince of Kiev, Sviatoslav (son of Olga, who had come to New Rome in 957, been warmly entertained by the imperial family and baptized by the Patriarch). This half-wild Russian, who, continuing his father's assaults against Khazaria, had all but extinguished that hated commercial rival, was easily persuaded to attack affluent Bulgaria.

Consequently, in August 968 Sviatoslav and his Russian giants crossed the Danube and with their Odinic fury, thunderous war chant, and heavy swords put the Bulgarian host to flight. All northern Bulgaria fell into their hands. These wild Northmen, whose very wounds seemed to delight them, spread over the terrorized countryside, slaughtering for pure pleasure, impaling and crucifying captives, employing them as targets, or driving nails into their heads. In 969 Sviatoslav departed to expel the Patzinaks from his own land but announced his imminent return, for he seemed bent on conquest. From Bulgaria he hoped to fulfill the dream of Russian rulers—the capture of fabulous Tzarigrad, the queen city on the Bosporus.

Nicephorus moved to avert the danger. He made peace with the

Bulgarian Tsar, who sent two princesses to New Rome to be affianced to the young Emperors. In July 969 Sviatoslav reappeared with sixty thousand warriors, annihilated the Bulgarian army, took Great Preslav, and captured the young Tsar Boris. Bulgarian resistance ended. Sviatoslav prepared to traverse the Balkans to cross swords with the mightiest monarch of the age.

TZIMISCES

Nicephorus became unpopular because, in order to finance his reconquests, he had increased taxes and requisitions and suppressed the customary donations to senators, pious institutions, and the capital masses. Moreover, at his bidding a synod decreed that no bishop be appointed without his consent. Thus, he could nominate his supporters and control their revenues. These measures were insufficient to cover the cost of his reconquests. He consequently depreciated the currency, paid governmental debts with debased coin, but accepted payments only in unadulterated specie. Prices and indignation rose.

By these measures Nicephorus antagonized every social class except the army. He was assailed by a mob while returning to the Palace from a religious procession (967). He remained calm and mildly suppressed the disorders. Nevertheless, he erected a high, thick, crenelated wall with towers around the Great Palace and transformed the deserted Palace of Bucoleon into a fortified castle, which became his favorite residence.

The death of his father, the aged Caesar Bardas, depressed him and he slipped more and more into mystic austerity. Theophano was disappointed in a husband who was in the field for long periods and when at home did not sleep in the imperial bed but on a panther skin, wrapped in a coarse but saintly hair shirt. She found consolation in the company of the elegant Domestic John Tzimisces.

This grandnephew of Lecapenus' famous Armenian Domestic Curcuas was now about forty-five. Though short, he was well built, strong, agile, and handsome. He had red hair and beard, blue eyes, a light complexion, and a finely shaped nose. He excelled in sports and in battle plunged fearlessly into Moslem ranks, wielding his sword with deadly dexterity. He was dashing, generous, patient, and the idol of his soldiers. Unlike the Emperor, to whom he was bound by maternal kinship and comradeship-in-arms, he enjoyed the company of women and the pleasures of the table.

Whether because of his relationship with Theophano or of some insubordination, Tzimisces was removed as Domestic and banished to his estates. Chagrined at his departure, Theophano persuaded her husband to permit him to return to his house at Chalcedon. The lovers then determined to do away with the Basileus. Accomplices were found in his entourage, for his dislike of courtiers was resented.

In December 969 the conspirators slipped into the Augusta's quarters disguised as women. Night fell. The Emperor retired to the imperial bedchamber in the castle of Bucoleon. Fearing that he might bolt the door and frustrate their plans, the Empress told him that she was going to see the Bulgarian princesses, who had recently arrived at the Palace, that she would return immediately, that he need not lock the door. The Basileus continued reading the Holy Script, but at length, fatigued by the labors of the day, fell asleep.

Without, a tempest raged and snow commenced to fall. Toward eleven o'clock Tzimisces' boat loomed through the storm. Hoisted to Theophano's quarters, he joined the other assassins. Theophano led them to the imperial bedchamber, where they found the Emperor sleeping on the floor and kicked him. As he started up, a sword was brought down on his head and almost cut his face in two. The pious potentate called upon the Mother of God and collapsed. The conspirators hurled their grievances into his bloody visage. Tzimisces kicked him brutally, spat insults into his face, tore out his beard. A sword-handle broke his jaw and teeth. He preserved a devout dignity. Another sword blow fractured his skull and, as his guards approached, a saber tore through his heart. The guards reached the Bucoleon. A window of the castle was opened. Between smoking torches the mutilated head of Nicephorus II was held up by its long black hair. The barbarians of the guard halted in bereft indecision. There was no heir to protect, nothing to save.

Tzimisces hastened to the Golden Hall, donned the purple buskins and other symbols of sovereignty, seated himself on the throne, and was acclaimed. His first care was to confer with the castrated bastard Basil, a man of vigor, courage, shrewdness, and experience. Appointed Grand Chamberlain by Constantine VII, he had in 958 defeated the Moslems in an obstinate battle and had celebrated a triumph in the Hippodrome. A year later he had been driven from office by Romanus II. But in 963 he had overthrown Bringas and delivered the City to Nicephorus II, who had appointed him Grand Chamberlain and bestowed on him the title President of the Senate. Under Nicephorus he had functioned more as counselor than as executive. Consequently, he had not attempted to thwart the conspiracy. Tzimisces confirmed him in his high office and generally followed his political advice. Thanks to him there was neither disorder nor bloodshed. Before sunrise officers and officials especially attached to Nicephorus were dismissed. The late Emperor's brother Leo and his two sons were exiled, but Leo's emasculated bastard Peter Phocas, the conqueror of Antioch, was retained, since his physique precluded the imperium.

However smoothly Basil had organized the change of regime, Tzimisces realized that his claim to the diadem was invalid until he had been crowned by the Patriarch. But Polyeuctes refused to consecrate him until the guilty had been punished, the woman who had plotted the murder had been driven from the Sacred Palace, and Tzimisces had devoted his personal fortune to relieve the starving peasants of Thrace and improve the leper hospital at Chrysopolis. Tzimisces distributed his fortune, swore that he had not touched a hair on Phocas' head, subjected two of his least influential accomplices to torture and death, and banished Theophano.

Twenty-nine, beautiful, avid for power, and longing for the handsome widower whom she had expected to marry, Theophano was cut to the deepest recesses of her heart. She, who had believed herself bound to Tzimisces in love and crime, was shipped off to the Isle of Prote. Here, from a naked cell and in the rude costume of a nun, the wretched woman could see the Palace where she had once reigned and plotted the deaths of possibly three emperors. She escaped, sought sanctuary in Saint Sophia, and was granted her wish to see Tzimisces. Imprecating him and Basil, she attacked the Grand Chamberlain physically. She was wrenched away and immured in a convent in the wildest part of the Armeniac theme.

Meanwhile, a fortnight after the murder of Nicephorus II John Tzimisces, having fulfilled the Patriarch's conditions, was anointed and crowned in Saint Sophia. The new Emperor remitted taxes, distributed largesses, and doled out wheat to allay the scarcity.

SVIATOSLAV

In March 970 Sviatoslav left prostrate Bulgaria and traversed the still snow-draped Balkans with a formidable host of Russians, Finns, Slavs, Patzinaks, Hungarians, and Bulgarians. The secular fears of Roman diplomats were realized—a vast barbarian union, a veritable tidal wave, was rolling toward New Rome. The barbarians took Bulgarian Philippopolis amid streams of blood and impaled the survivors in rows facing their homes. The cities of Macedonia submitted to the northern conqueror. In the crisis New Roman poets called upon the murdered hero to rise from his sarcophagus in the Church of the Holy Apostles.

But the ivory scepter of Caesar was grasped by a man, who, however false and unscrupulous, was a renowned general. Calling his troops from Asia, he formed an elite corps, the Immortals, so called because after every battle the ranks were to be refilled with the best soldiers in the army. Meanwhile, he sent the vanguard to entertain the arms of Sviatoslav with orders to remain on the defensive. In command he placed the Magister Bardas Sclerus. Second in command was the famous eunuch Peter Phocas, who recently had cut down an indomitable Hungarian raider in single combat. With this small force, possibly twelve thousand men, Sclerus advanced to Adrianople but withdrew upon the approach of the Russian horde. The barbarian vanguard followed. The Romans took to flight. The barbarians broke in pursuit. Then suddenly near Arcadiopolis the Roman cavalry converged and exterminated the Russian van, mostly Patzinaks.

Though with inferior numbers, Sclerus now moved against the main Russian force. Glittering in elegant armor and on excellent mounts, the Roman horsemen advanced with ease and precision, their lances lowered. In front rode their officers, led by Sclerus, a peerless warrior whose beautiful armor bore evidence of the high civilization he represented.

The Russians were flanked by light Bulgarian and Hungarian horsemen. In the center behind enormous shields strode the Russian giants, iron from head to foot, with deadly two-handed swords, huge double-edged battle-axes, and long, powerful lances. As of old, when in glacial Scandinavia their ancestral gods had contended with primeval giants, they fought on foot. In Bulgaria, however, some of their leaders had learned to fight mounted.

One of these galloped against Sclerus and brought his huge sword down on the Magister's head. The helmet of the imperial arsenals supported the blow and Sclerus struck, splitting the Russian's helmet and head. Another Varangian rode up to avenge his death, but before he had reached the Magister his still beardless brother, the Patrician Constantine Sclerus, had dispatched him.

The Romans easily dispersed the light Bulgarian and Hungarian cavalry on the enemy flanks and closed with the Russians, natural warriors, contemptuous of death, of gigantic stature, imbued with Odinic frenzy, and avid for the wealth and mysteries of Tzarigrad. The epic clash had lasted for hours when suddenly the boreal roar was drowned by the Christian war hymn, the roll of drums, the sound of trumpets. Imperial troops, hidden in the woods, fell on the Russian flanks. Wearied by the titanic struggle and the superior Roman tactics and seeing themselves hemmed in on three sides, the Russians began to flee. One of their leaders, in shining armor and on horseback, rallied them. Sclerus struck him down. Thereupon the warriors of Odin took to headlong flight. But their long, powerful legs were no match for the swift Anatolian steeds and the Roman cavalry cut them down without mercy. The vision of Tzarigrad faded into Valhalla. Sviatoslav grimly recrossed the Balkans.

Tzimisces was preparing to drive him from Danubian Bulgaria when news reached him that Bardas Phocas, son of the Curopalates Leo and nephew of the late Emperor, had assumed the imperium at Cappadocian Caesarea and gained the allegiance of Anatolian troops, who still cherished the memory of Nicephorus the Victorious. The campaign against the Russians was deferred. Bardas Sclerus moved against the pretender, won over the dissident regiments, and captured Phocas, who was tonsured and exiled to the island of Chios.

Later, during Tzimisces' absence in Bulgaria, Leo Phocas tried to seize power but was foiled and blinded by Basil. Worried by the sentiment for the Phocas family, Tzimisces had already sought to solidify his dynastic position by marrying one of Constantine VII's five daughters, whom Romanus and Theophano had entombed in a convent twelve years earlier—Theodora. She was no longer in the first flush of youth, but was chaste, modest, born in the purple, and the aunt of Tzimisces' young colleagues.

In the spring of 971 the Autocrator left the Great City to crush the Russians in Bulgaria, while the fleet moved toward the Danube to sever their retreat. The Romans passed the perilous Balkans unhindered, for it was Holy Week and the Russians did not believe that they would undertake hostilities. Soon the Roman van beheld Great Preslav and the Russian host encamped outside its walls. Trumpets, horns, cymbals, and drums called to battle, and the Roman army hurtled across the fertile plain against the Northmen, who hastily formed their customary wedge. A furious fray followed. At the height of the battle Tzimisces ordered the Immortals to charge into the barbarian left flank. With lowered lances this brilliant troop rode into the heaving boreal giants and cracked the huge wedge. The Russian center was uncovered and gave ground. The right flank faltered. Soon the Russians broke into precipitate flight toward Great Preslav. The Immortals cut off their retreat and bestrewed the lush field with their cadavers. Only nightfall ended the carnage.

In the morning Basil arrived with artillery. Under a barrage concentrated on the defenders of part of Preslav's walls Roman troops set ladders in place and, holding their shields over their heads, climbed through a rain of projectiles. A youth from the Anatolic theme reached the top, beheaded a son of the Dnieper with a stroke of his sword, and held off the Russians while his companions mounted the wall. The Russians fled down to the streets, where they were massacred in the approving presence of the Bulgars whom they had so recently oppressed. A remnant sought refuge in the fortified wooden palace. After unsuccessful attempts to take it the Emperor commanded that it be set afire. The flames spread rapidly and consumed many of the Russians. Others were killed as they jumped from the walls. A few thousand came out and massed in front of the palace. Bardas Sclerus attacked them, and only a handful escaped through smoke and night to Sviatoslav at Silistria.

Finding the dethroned Tsar in Preslav, Tzimisces shrewdly recognized him as ruler of Bulgaria. Bulgarian auxiliaries began to desert Sviatoslav. Infuriated, he beheaded three hundred Bulgarian boliads in his service. Later, on a swampy, undulating plain twelve miles from Silistria he drew up his remaining Russians behind a wall of huge shields and bristling spears. On the flanks were Patzinak and Bulgarian horsemen. The Romans, heavy infantry in the center, cataphracts on the wings, engaged them. All day the battle raged. Toward sunset the Emperor hurled his last reserves, heavy horsemen, against the stubborn Nordic wedge. It broke, and as night fell, Sviatoslav and the survivors fled to Silistria.

The Roman troops rendered thanks to the Megalomartyr Saint George. On the morrow they erected a vast camp on a plateau, dug a ditch, and threw up a mound around it. On the top of the mound they placed shields and lances to form an impenetrable wall. The Emperor was still completing the encirclement of the city when the Roman fleet appeared on the Danube and cut the Russians from home. Spring slipped into summer. Futile sorties, continual bombardment, famine, and disease reduced the Russian numbers. Many dreamt of flight or capitulation.

Only Sviatoslav's fiery eloquence swept them into a final encounter. As the summer sun was shedding its last rays, the pitiful debris of the once formidable array marched out of Silistria to conquer or die. Behind the enormous shields no longer trod the fierce, fearless conquerors of yesteryear, but emaciated specters. In desperate fury they hurled themselves against the invincible Romans. The Roman line bent, and the Emperor threw himself into the melee to restore it. During a lull he challenged Sviatoslav to decide the issue by personal combat. The Great Prince declined. Anemas, son of the last Emir of Crete and a popular officer of the Immortals, rode against Sviatoslav and knocked him from his horse with a powerful sword stroke on the nape. But his blade had not penetrated. Anemas was soon overwhelmed by Russians. So died a former foe of the Empire, who had come to love the mother of nations. Dismayed by his death, the Romans fell back. Again the Emperor led the charge and this time broke the Russian wedge. The sons of the North scattered. But Sclerus had cut off their retreat. From all sides imperial forces closed in. One by one the arctic titans fell. Darkness descended, but the carnage continued methodically and skilfully. Sviatoslav and a vestige escaped to Silistria and passed the night in tears and maledictions.

His pride and ambition humbled, he begged for peace, food, the Empire's amity, the privilege of trading with her, and the honor of an interview with her sovereign. Rarely did the Empire spurn a vanquished foe. Sviatoslav bound himself not to return to the Balkan Peninsula, not to attack Cherson, and to aid the Empire if attacked. Thereupon the Romans distributed food, and on the southern bank of the Danube the two erstwhile enemies met. The Emperor, in embossed, inlaid, damascened, even enameled golden armor, trotted toward the river bank on a charger covered with gold, pearls, gems, cameos, and silks. He was attended by officers and dignitaries in rich and sparkling raiment. The Great Prince of Kiev approached by water, rowing with his last fighters. From his shaven head there sprouted at each temple a lock of hair in sign of his rank, from his upper lip drooped a long mustache, from one ear hung a ring embellished with a ruby and two pearls. He was clad in white and was distinguishable from his warriors by the cleanness of his robe. He seemed fierce and somber and had some Slavic traits, for the Russians like the Bulgars were being slavonized. Upon seeing the Autocrator he arose. After a few words the two adversaries parted.

Sviatoslav led back the chastened survivors of the host that was to have seized Tzarigrad. The bones of possibly forty thousand of their fellows and the myth of Russian invincibility remained behind. The peoples of the steppe, who two years earlier had quailed before them, now regarded them with contempt. To reach Kiev Sviatoslav and his weary, wounded fellows had to traverse the land of the Patzinaks. But though the Patzinaks had been his allies when he overran Bulgaria and presumed to march against New Rome, they were now hostile and had returned to the Roman orbit. He besought Roman intercession for safe passage. Possibly fearing that the vanquished Varangian thirsted for revenge, the Basileus may not have pressed the plea for peaceful passage or even have encouraged the Patzinaks to reject it.

However that might be, Sviatoslav and his weakened, wounded men were forced to fight their way through hostile tribesmen. Winter fell and they built a camp of the rocks that encumber the Dnieper below the rapids. Here they spent the long, sad winter, hoping for help from Kiev. Again they suffered the pangs of hunger, yet those who strayed too far from the snowbound encampment fell a prey to roaming Patzinaks. When spring returned they broke camp but were soon trapped by the Patzinaks. Sviatoslav and his last companions fell (973). Only a few of the carefree warriors who had plunged into Bulgaria six years earlier reached Kiev to recount the long agony.

Tzimisces annexed Bulgaria. Thus, a buffer-state was suppressed, and the Patzinaks became the immediate neighbors of the Empire. The Emperor returned to the God-Guarded City in triumph. In the triumphal chariot, adorned with the Bulgarian trappings of sovereignty, stood, not the Emperor, but the Bulgarian icon of the Virgin.

Boris, the young Bulgarian monarch, marched in the triumph and on the Augustaeum divested himself of the diadem, tunic, and buskins that Lecapenus had accorded his father. Then he was elevated to the rank of Magister. The Bulgarian Patriarch was deposed and Bulgaria reentered the see of the Patriarch of New Rome. The conquered land received Roman strategoi, Roman garrisons, and Paulician settlers.[2]

FATIMIDS

In North Africa the Shiite Fatimids, who claimed descent from the Prophet's daughter, replaced the Sunnite Aghlabids in 909 and entered into rivalry with the Abbasid Khalifate for the spiritual and temporal command of the faithful. Fatimid rule spread to Sicily and the Atlantic. In 969 the Fatimids took Egypt and Syria from the Sunnite Ikshidids. Northwestern Africa (the Maghreb) fell to another dynasty, which, however, acknowledged Fatimid suzerainty. In 971 Fatimid forces advanced to besiege Antioch, where they found a captain worthy of their metal—Michael Burtzes, now Duke of Antioch. Five months they beleaguered the city, then abruptly withdrew, for in their rear the Shiite Karmathians, partisans of the dispossessed Ikshidids, had defeated the Fatimid governor of Syria. They rolled the Fatimids back to Egypt and were only stemmed beneath the walls of Cairo.

Tzimisces invaded the tottering Abbasid Khalifate, blighted

[2] Many historians believe that by 969 a West Bulgarian state had taken shape beside Danubian Bulgaria and that this western state was not conquered by Tzimisces. This writer accepts the viewpoint of Anastasijevic that no such state existed and that all Bulgaria submitted to Tzimisces. *Recueil Uspenskij*, I (1930).

many Mesopotamian groves, sacked numerous cities, slew many Moslems, and concluded that the growing Fatimid Khalifate, which was already retrieving Syria, was a greater threat to the Empire.

In June 974 the Fatimids reentered Damascus. Later, they drove the Romans from Tripoli and Beirut. To counter their advance Tzimisces ascended the Orontes Valley with a strong force in the spring of 975. He accepted the submission of Emesa, stormed Baalbek, and crossed the Antilebanon.

As the Emperor, glittering in golden armor, and his brilliant staff were riding through the palm groves and verdant gardens that encompass Damascus, the city portals were suddenly flung open. At the head of white-robed dignitaries rode the Turkish Emir Aftekin, nominal Fatimid vassal. When they reached the Emperor they dismounted, prostrated themselves, and kissed the dust in front of their new master. Tzimisces asked them to remount, graciously commanded his new vassal to give an equestrian demonstration, and was so impressed that he courteously asked for his horse, lance, and sword. The Emperor lavished gifts on the Emir, converted him to Christianity, and accepted the tribute offered.

After a further exchange of amenities and a pleasant sojourn in the Syrian capital Tzimisces advanced to the Sea of Galilee. In this sacred land evoking memories of Christ the Christian soldiers, who yearned to retake the Holy Sepulcher, avoided violence as much as possible. Tiberias, Nazareth, and Caesarea yielded to them.

Meanwhile, Fatimid troops had fled to the coastal cities, where, reinforced by the Egyptian fleet, they menaced Roman communications. With heavy hearts the Christians turned away from the road to the Holy City and marched homeward. They retook Beirut, once the site of a Roman law school; accepted the submission of Sidon, already in 1500 B.C. the greatest city of Phoenicia with counters dotted over the Mediterranean and Black Seas; and stormed Byblos. (It was possibly from aged Byblos, already in contact with Egypt three thousand years before Christ, that the alphabet spread westward. The city became the main emporium of papyrus. Consequently, the Greeks called papyrus *byblos*. Later the word came to mean book, finally the Holy Scripture.)

Continuing northward, the Romans crushed Fatimid resistance, wrecked towns and forts, abducted the inhabitants, and reverently carried with them the holiest relics of the crusade—the supposed sandals of Jesus, hair of Saint John the Baptist, and a picture of the Crucifixion, from which blood was said to flow when a Jew imitated the centurion who had pierced the Savior's side. The Anointed of God installed Roman governors and garrisons to prepare the reconquered places for reincorporation into the Empire, while the Orthodox clergy recommenced the persecution of Monophysites.

The Christian army recrossed the Taurus and wound its way through Anatolia, whose roads and valleys no longer resounded to unshod hoofs and the raucous shouts of Moslem marauders. Suddenly the Emperor was assailed by rigidity, torpor, and a burning fever. Pustules covered his shoulders. Blood flowed from his eyes. Had the scorned woman who gnawed her life away in a shadowy Armeniac convent or Basil, possibly facing dismissal because of inordinate acquisition of public lands, contrived to poison him? Or had he contracted typhus? Whatever the cause, he realized that his life had almost run its course. He ordered the completion of his tomb in the Oratory of the Savior of the Chalke and returned to New Rome. After distribution of his personal property, a lengthy confession, and a torrent of tears over his sins, the popular John I expired in January 976 at the age of fifty-one. Alone among the successors of Constantine he was buried within the Palace walls.

BARDAS SCLERUS

The wedlock of Tzimisces and Theodora had been without issue, and this modest Porphyrogenita now disappears from history, either in the sheltered Palace gyneceum or in a convent. Supremacy reverted to the sons of Romanus II—Basil II and Constantine VIII. Basil was eighteen, his brother two years younger. In the shadow of their mighty associates these titular Emperors had led lives of ease and pleasure and were unprepared to rule. The reins of government remained in the hands of their granduncle Basil.

This masterful eunuch, the son of Lecapenus and a Slavic captive, who had held important posts for over thirty years, permitted Theophano to return. The woman who had been accused of the murder of four emperors was no longer the dazzling creature of yore. Six years of ulcerating hate and remorse in the somber solitude of a mountain convent had left their mark and she sank into the recesses of the gyneceum.

But there was in the Empire another figure, whose fame, power, and wealth alarmed the Grand Chamberlain. This was the Domestic Bardas Sclerus, the hero of a hundred battles. He was deprived of his high post and given the command of the frontier duchy of Mesopotamia. But the idol of the army could not be so easily brushed aside. When he reached his duchy he declared himself the associate of the two young Emperors (976). Soldiers flocked to his standard, and he marched on the Great City. Basil sent the illustrious eunuch, the Domestic Peter Phocas, against him. Two years later Peter and many of the most redoubtable fighters of the realm had fallen. Bleeding from the wounds of war and a prey to famine and wolves, Anatolia lay at Sclerus' feet.

In desperation Basil sent to the verdant isle of Chios, where dwelt a banished monk, Bardas Phocas. A great general under his uncle Nicephorus II, he had declared himself Emperor after his uncle's death, only to surrender to Sclerus in a wild Tauric retreat and to be sent into tonsured exile.

He was now brought to New Rome and into Basil's presence. After abjuring imperial aspirations he was created Domestic and assured that neither the Grand Chamberlain nor the young Emperors would take any important step without consulting him. But to oppose the Anatolian potentate he had only the debris of two years' warfare. He crossed Anatolia in disguise and joined the loyal forces at Caesarea. Here, in his native Cappadocia the glory of his name, the power of his family, and the wealth of the capital brought recruits to his banner. He reconstituted the loyal forces, confronted Sclerus near Amorium, was wounded and defeated, withdrew eastward, and was again routed. In the spring of 979, reinforced by an auxiliary corps from the Curopalates of Iberia, he met Sclerus near the Halys. Again his troops gave way.

In despair Phocas galloped out between the armies. Realizing that he desired single combat, Sclerus rode out to accept the challenge. The two armies stood breathless before the heroic scene. A member of the former imperial family risking his life for the eunuch's government; the ruler of Anatolia accepting a duel with the issue already decided in his favor. They charged against each other. Sclerus' blade missed, and Phocas' mace crashed down on his head.

Bleeding profusely, he fell to the ground. His riderless Arabian steed, covered with its master's blood, dashed through his army's ranks. Thinking their Emperor dead, his soldiers broke into flight.

Sclerus regained consciousness amid the tumult of his fleeing army. His sense of martial honor had perhaps cost him the Empire. With a few faithful companions he rode from the scene of battle. Ever pursued, he galloped day and night through the realm he had just lost. He crossed the Euphrates and at Moslem Mayyafarikin, the former Martyropolis, sent to Bagdad to request asylum from the Buyid Sultan and the Abbasid Khalif. As a result, he and three hundred devoted veterans found refuge and relaxation from the dust and wounds of four years' fighting in a luxurious Bagdad palace on an islet in the Tigris. Nor could Basil's offers tear from the Khalif these martial guests.

The civil war left the Empire with a weakened army, prostrate provinces, and a depleted treasury. But with the government in Basil's firm hands and the army under Bardas Phocas' able command she was able to preserve her recent Asiatic reconquests. Indeed, except for occasional fighting over Aleppo, which balanced successfully between the Empire and the Fatimids, or border trouble when some mahdi roused desert tribes to holy war, relations with the Fatimids were peaceful, notably after 1000.

In New Rome the nominal ruler, Basil II, was changing from a carefree, sensual spendthrift to a sober, frugal ascetic and was growing restive under the lofty tutelage of his granduncle Basil. Though the old man to whom he owed his throne had served the Empire forty years, Basil II banished him (985). Now about twenty-seven, he rigidly excluded his brother Constantine VIII from imperial authority. While the latter seemed content to continue a life of pleasure, Basil II became hard, coarse, haughty, secretive, irascible, austere, and suspicious. He remained unmarried. Possibly a physical misfortune had abruptly deflected his ebullient vitality from personal gratification to public service.

However that might be, he was determined to curb the magnates' power. Whether he or Tzimisces rescinded the law of Nicephorus II forbidding the extension of pious institutions is uncertain. Basil II, however, did legislate to protect the property of free farmers and villages from absorption. He decreed that all property acquired from the poor by the powerful since the edict of his great-grandfather Lecapenus in 922 be restored without compensation and without regard to the length of time held (996). He took stringent measures to repossess public properties illegally in private hands. He also transferred the tax liability of delinquent peasant communities to the magnates, thus saving small cultivators from ruin and flight, assuring the state a secure source for defaulted revenue, and weakening the magnates, whose crescent power threatened the Empire with feudalization.

Suddenly, early in 987 a thunderclap reverberated throughout the Empire. After seven years Bardas Sclerus and his companions had left Bagdad, fought their way through Mesopotamian bandits, and crossed the Euphrates. Sclerus entered Melitene amid the acclamations of the hardy and mixed frontier folk. This indomitable warrior and loyal comrade fired their hearts more than the Porphyrogenitus. He resumed the purple and marched on New Rome at the head of a motley band of adventurers, welcomed by overtaxed Anatolians and the Church, which feared the omnipotence of a hereditary monarch but could impose conditions on a newcomer.

Basil was aghast. Only Bardas Phocas was capable of withstanding the illustrious exile of Bagdad, but he had recently been dismissed. As nine years before in a dark hour his granduncle had turned to Phocas, Basil II now reinstated him with instructions to drive out Sclerus. Instead, Phocas resumed the imperium and rallied the Anatolian army to his standard. Of the three Emperors, Phocas stood for the army, Sclerus was in a measure the champion of the Church, and Basil II was the proponent of imperial omnipotence.

Sclerus and Phocas, who had overthrown each other in 971 and 979, met near the upper Pyramus and agreed to share the imperium and unite their forces. But Phocas treacherously imprisoned his gallant associate in the same Tauric fortress where he had surrendered to him in 971. Soon Anatolia accepted his authority.

Basil II still held the God-Guarded City, an insuperable obstacle to so many claimants of the diadem. But his only troops were his guards and the vestige of the European army. In dismay, he called upon the Great Prince of Russia, Vladimir, son of Sviatoslav. Understanding Basil's difficult position, the barbarian imposed exorbitant terms for six thousand picked Russian warriors. Thus strengthened, Basil secretly crossed the Bosporus and at dawn overwhelmed Phocas' troops at Chrysopolis (988). He impaled, hanged, and cru-

cified many of the officers who had fought for the Empire in nox-
ious Danubian swamps, burning Syrian sands, and wild Tauric ravines.

In April 989 the opposing armies met near Abydus. Espying Basil
II and Constantine VIII trotting along the front of the European
forces, Phocas galloped out from the ranks to duel for the Empire.
But Basil II was not a Bardas Sclerus. He clutched an icon of the
Virgin said not to have been made by human hands and ordered his
archers to discharge at the approaching warrior. Phocas rode on
through a hail of arrows. Of a sudden he reined in, trotted off to an
eminence, dismounted, reclined, and died, either from poison or a
heart attack. Shaken by his death, his troops fled. Basil's soldiers
pursued, butchered, captured. The two hereditary Emperors returned to the capital in triumph behind Phocas' impaled head. Captured officers, bound on asses and facing the animals' hind quarters,
were exposed to the insults and blows of the populace, and put to
death in the Hippodrome.

But Sclerus had meanwhile regained his liberty. Veterans, fugitives from Basil's brutality, and men who acknowledged no hereditary right to the purple rallied to their beloved Basileus, whose intrepid spirit overcame adversity, captivity, age. But, lacking a large
army, he avoided pitched battles and waged petty warfare. For a
space he ruled a phantom realm of ever changing borders in the
heart of Anatolia, a haven to all who fled from the tyranny of the
dynast. The overwhelming forces of New Rome could neither
crush the fearless captain and his resolute band nor wean his loyal
followers from their allegiance. They preferred liberty and hard-
ship under Bardas to wealth and ease under Basil.

At length Basil offered peace to his indomitable adversary.
Stricken with years, losing his sight from cataracts, and concerned
for the future of his faithful fellows, Sclerus wrung from the hard
monarch the most generous terms that any rival for the imperium
had ever obtained. His adherents were to retain the dignities and
properties that he had bestowed on them and to return in peace to
their homes. Sclerus himself was to exchange the title of Basileus for
that of Curopalates, recover his confiscated estates, and obtain the
Armeniac theme as fief. His brother Constantine, his son Romanus,
and the son of Bardas Phocas were to receive lands, titles, honors,
offices.

When the articles of peace had been signed Sclerus, clad in the imperial purple for the last time, reviewed his devoted band in battle array. Recalling their fallen comrades, their victories and defeats, their common joys and sorrows, he bade a moving farewell to the unshaken brothers of his glories and his misfortunes.

Constantine VIII escorted the famous pretender to an imperial domain on the Asiatic bank of the Bosporus. Here in an impressive outdoor setting the enthroned Basil II, vigorous and in the prime of life, awaited the old lion. Meanwhile, Sclerus' cataracts had crystallized. Thus, when Basil saw approaching an aged man with the uncertain gait of the blind he expressed amazement to his court dignitaries that this should be the man who had made them all tremble. But his attention was suddenly drawn to the purple buskins that Sclerus still wore. Shocked by the impiety, he averted his gaze and refused to receive him until they had been removed. Upon the fulfilment of this final formality, however, the Emperor rose to greet him, invited him to table, shared his goblet with him, conferred the title of Curopalates on him, and discussed with him the causes, motives, and events of their two conflicts.

The conciliation seemed complete, yet Basil feared the effects of Sclerus' magnetic personality in the land of his devoted partisans and transferred him to an estate in the lower Maritza Valley. Here the kindly old man survived two years, esteemed by all who knew him and was twice visited by Basil. He is said to have died in March 991. Five days later his brother Constantine, unshaken companion of his adversity, followed the once mighty monarch of the provinces to the grave.

ANNE AND VLADIMIR

After the victory at Abydus Basil II hesitated to fulfill the most humiliating promise to the Great Prince of Kiev—the marriage of his sister Anne to the rude Russian. Indignant at the delay, Vladimir severed the water supply of antique Cherson and forced it to capitulate. The fall of Cherson, New Rome's link with the steppes, home of steppe diplomats, mart of north and south, and the boreal eye of the Empire that warned of the movements of the steppe tribes, induced Basil to acquit himself of his obligation. But before stooping to send his sister to the uncouth Varangian he insisted that Vladimir accept baptism and restore Cherson to the Empire.

Anne was now twenty-eight and had spent her life amid the splendors and refinements of the Great Palace. She was horrified to learn that she had been betrothed to a bloodthirsty heathen. But the reasons of state were inexorable. In 989 the unhappy little princess embarked for Cherson, sobbing plaintively as the gleaming domes and shaded terraces of the Great Palace slipped from view. No longer could she watch the dolphins playing in the limpid blue waters of the Marmara or the doves fluttering around the golden dome of Saint Sophia. No more would she listen to the nightingales singing in the Palace gardens or view the rich pageantry of Court and Church. She was abandoning the gentle life of luxury, the City of refreshing baths and fountains, the center of civilization, for the rude and filthy huts of Barbaria. But a great mission was imposed on the disconsolate Porphyrogenita.

Upon her arrival at Cherson, accompanied by a pompous suite and, above all, a numerous clergy, Vladimir was baptized and united to her in wedlock. He restored Cherson to the Empire and departed with his bride for Kiev. Here he destroyed the idols to which he had recently sacrificed human lives. Moreover, he intimated to the populace that whoever did not appear on the banks of the holy Dnieper on the morrow to receive baptism would incur his savage displeasure. From Kiev he disseminated the gospel in an equally forceful manner throughout his vague dominions, which from the Volkhov Dnieper river route had spread eastward to the confluence of the Oka and the Volga, westward to the Niemen and the Pruth. In 991 the first Metropolitan left New Rome for Kiev and, as Vladimir grew milder under the influence of his wife and her religion, churches were built, priests were established, and schools were founded. Byzantine civilization commenced to shape the life of the Russo-Slavic nation. Russia came to be the religious, cultural, and commercial tie between new Rome and the North as far as Iceland.

The six thousand Russian mercenaries remained in the Empire and formed the famous Varangian infantry guard, outstanding for strength, courage, and loyalty. Northmen from Scandinavia, Iceland, and later from England were also admitted to the guard or enrolled in the regular Varangian regiments created during the previous century.

In 1016 the Russians crushed Khazaria, ancient ally of the Empire. Only a small canton in the Crimea called Khazaria survived until 1441. Basil seemed pleased to see this Jewish state dissolve under the blows of the Orthodox Russians. Yet the fall of Khazaria removed a bulwark that had stemmed the wild tribes of Central Asia.

BULGAROKTONOS

Tzimisces' demise and Sclerus' assumption of the imperium in 976 incited the newly conquered Bulgars to expel most of the Roman garrisons and ultimately to acknowledge Samuel as Tsar. The heart of his Bulgaria was in the wild, mountainous region of ancient Macedonia around limpid Lakes Ochrida and Prespa. He and his Roman-hating boliads based their power on the allegiance of the Slavic tribes of the Ochridan area, rugged mountains, impregnable forts, and the religious toleration that gained them the support of the powerful Bogomils.

In 986 Samuel held large parts of the themes Thrace, Macedonia, Struma, Salonica, and Hellas and was marching toward the Isthmus of Corinth to subject the Peloponnese. Abruptly he gave the signal to retreat. Basil II had overthrown the Grand Chamberlain. Without informing the Domestic Bardas Phocas, as stipulated eight years earlier, he had assembled the European troops and ascended the broad Maritza Valley. Stationing a rear guard in Philippopolis, he crossed Trajan's Pass, traversed the Danube-Aegean watershed, and descended into the fertile bed of the vanished lake where lay Sofia. With the Maritza Valley and Trajan's Pass in his hands, he lacked only Sofia to sever Danubian Bulgaria from the rest of the realm.

Samuel hastened to the scene. He dared not engage the compact Roman army in the open but occupied adjacent heights and by harassing tactics forced Basil to raise the siege and retreat. As the Romans were winding their way up the long, wooded Pass of Trajan, the Bulgars fell upon them from both sides. Havoc followed. Roman cavalry beat off the foe, but gradually succumbed to the avalanche of missiles. Deprived of his horsemen, the Emperor was in peril. Armenian infantrymen took him into their midst and fought their way upward. At length the battered remnant reached Philippopolis.

With rage in his heart Basil descended into the open Maritza Valley, dotted with tumuli of shadowy races of the past. The catastrophe had apparently been due to wilful neglect of higher officers, who resented the sudden intrusion of the theretofore dormant dynast. Basil dismissed the Domestic Bardas Phocas. Then Bardas Sclerus returned and civil war ensued.

Only after its conclusion could Basil return to the bleeding Bulgarian border. The Roman frontier defenses had been overrun by Samuel. Once powerful forts were now rubble and once populous communities haunts of wild beasts. What remained to the Empire in Thrace and Macedonia lay open to Bulgar incursions. Armenian military settlers, estranged by religious persecution, and alienated Roman magnates had accepted the rule of Samuel, who now controlled two thirds of the Balkan Peninsula from the Adriatic to the Black Sea, from the Danube to the Spercheus, and seemed destined to expand farther.

Basil took the offensive in 991 and fought fiercely for four years. Called away to prevent the Fatimids from taking Aleppo, his absence encouraged Samuel again to plunder as far as the Isthmus of Corinth. Returning booty-laden, he reached the swollen Spercheus (997). On the yonder bank was a Roman army under Nicephorus Uranus. The overflowing river seemed impassable and the Tsar pitched his camp with unconcern. The Romans, however, forded the river during the night and at dawn fell upon his unsuspecting camp. Hardly a man escaped. Samuel and his son, both wounded, remained hidden all day under a heap of Bulgarian corpses. At night they crept from their deathly lair, and, suffering cruelly from their wounds, fled over the Pindic passes to Bulgarian Epirus. Uranus returned to New Rome with twelve thousand Bulgarian warriors, who were destined to fight for their conquerors on other fronts. The battle of the Spercheus was decisive. By eliminating the flower of Samuel's forces it destroyed his offensive power and prevented the further, possibly the complete slavonization of Greece.

In 1001 Basil resumed personal command of the war with the Bulgars, whose annihilation he regarded as his foremost task. In four bitter years of desperate fighting he tore back the lost parts of the European themes, Danubian Bulgaria, and the passes leading over the Rhodope into the Bulgarian rump. He carried fire and sword into the isolated valleys of the Struma, the Morava, and the Vardar. He blotted out the new armies that the determined Tsar mustered. Slowly but surely he drew a ring of iron around the shrunken Bulgarian realm. Closing in, he occupied Vodena, dominating the ancient Via Egnatia between Salonica and Durazzo, Vidin on the Danube, Skoplje on the Vardar, and in 1005 Durazzo on the Adriatic.

His strength broken and his realm restricted to the Ochrida region, Samuel continued the hopeless struggle in a labyrinth of mountain ranges, dark defiles, impenetrable forests, and natural strongholds, fighting every step, building barricades across ravines, digging trenches across passes, staging ambushes. But the Roman war machine moved inexorably forward under an Emperor who campaigned regardless of season and never allowed the order of battle to be broken, even in pursuit of a fleeing enemy.

In a desperate effort to save his diminished state Samuel in 1014 built a powerful barricade across a defile in the Struma Valley and beat off the Isapostol's troops. But an imperial officer led a select corps around the pass, turned the Bulgarian flank, and fell upon them from above. Terrified by the sudden attack, the Bulgars broke. The main Roman force penetrated the barrier and commenced a terrible massacre. Samuel's son hastily helped his aging father into the saddle and they galloped off together, abandoning their hopelessly enveloped warriors. Fourteen thousand prisoners are said to have remained in Roman hands.

The war had lasted thirty-eight years, and Basil determined on a measure whose ghastly horror was designed to crush the Bulgarian will to fight. The fettered Bulgars were led before Roman executioners and one by one their eyes were gouged out. Every hundredth man was left with a single eye to lead his comrades back to their master at Prilep. The eyeless multitude stumbled into Samuel's presence. The sight of their gory sockets, distorted features, and uncertain gait overcame even the hardened old Tsar, who fell dying at their feet. The hapless men faltered to their homes, bringing to hamlets and hidden dales the horrendous message of the inflexible Vicar of God. The Bulgars' resistance slackened.

From Spyridon Lampros, Portraits of Byzantine Emperors; *the manuscript from which it was taken is in the Library San Marco, Venice*

Psalter miniature of Basil II (reigned 976–1025). Christ holds a heavenly crown over him; the Archangel Gabriel crowns him; the Archangel Michael arms him; warrior saints, including Theodore, Demetrius, and George, surround him; diminutive courtiers prostrate themselves before him

But nationalists rallied them. Basil pushed into the heart of Ochridan Bulgaria. Masses of Bulgar captives were sent to strengthen the Empire's Asiatic frontiers. Armenians and Georgians were planted in vacant Bulgarian lands. Bulgaria shrank to the wild highlands around Castoria and Lakes Ochrida and Prespa. This last lair soon felt the heavy tread of the Roman monarch. Ochrida fell in 1016. Although over half of the Bulgar nation was no more, the struggle dragged on two more years. In 1018 after forty-two years of warfare the first boliads submitted. Basil distributed titles. The submissions became general. The Patriarch yielded. The widow of the last Tsar with the surviving members of the royal family surrendered. Basil received her kindly and conferred a dignity on her. Of more interest to the soldiers was the royal treasure, which was distributed among them. Relieved of the Bulgar menace, Serbs and Croats came to do homage to the mighty monarch.

Basil divided the conquered country into themes, encouraged his soldiers to settle there, and erected forts. He based his dominion on the goodwill of the boliads and the Church. He showered the boliads with titles and privileges. While he reduced the Patriarch of Ochrida to an autocephalous archbishop, he gave him jurisdiction over the extensive Slavic area of the late Bulgarian state. Although appointed by the Emperor, the Bulgarian pontiff was thus independent of the Patriarch of New Rome. Moreover, Basil accorded the Bulgarians a large measure of autonomy and permitted them to pay their taxes in kind instead of in gold.

Leaving Ochrida, Basil marched southward with his veterans. When they reached the Spercheus they saw the whitened bones of the Bulgars who had fallen twenty-three years earlier at the beginning of their long national agony. At broadened Thermopylae they found an enormous wall, which the Strategos of Hellas had built to prevent further Bulgarian invasion. When Leonidas and his stouthearted band had held the pass in 480 B.C. it was a narrow track between a steep cliff and the Malian Gulf. But the sea insensibly retreated and the pass grew wider. In Basil's time the sea had probably receded about two miles. Today it is three miles from the historic cliff.

The victorious army continued on through Thebes, the capital of the theme of Hellas, to Athens, now a quiet provincial town. It was not the remains of her golden age that attracted the Equal of the Apostles to the city of Pallas, but his devout desire to render thanks to the Virgin of the Parthenon. After this pious act Basil embarked at Piraeus to return to his capital in triumph (1019). The man who thirty-three years before had undertaken to crush the Bulgar menace had grown old at the task. As the iron old Emperor, past sixty and gray-bearded but still erect and vigorous, stood in the triumphal chariot, the demesmen hailed him Bulgaroktonos (Bulgar-Butcher).

The reconquest of the Balkan Peninsula had rendered his capital less dependent on the feudalizing Anatolian nobility. From the sunny Adriatic to the somber Black Sea, from the Save and the Danube to the southernmost extremities of the Peloponnese all was Roman. Roman power included northern Syria and Phoenicia and reached the distant Cyrus and Tigris. The road seemed open to further reconquest. But the men who fought for the Empire were not all her own sons who could spread her civilization and assimilate alien peoples. The Roman conquests were made by motley armies of different nationalities, who could win battles but not absorb their foes.

ARMENIA

To consolidate Roman control over the Armenian-Caucasian area, the Bulgar-Butcher led an army eastward in 1021. Encountering bitter cold, he went into winter quarters at Trebizond, ancient capital of the kings of Pontus. Lodged against a slope of terraced gardens and vineyards on the Black Sea, this city was watered by a thousand streams of crystalline water. Industrially and commercially prosperous, it was famed for wines; salt fish; multicolored silks, linens, and woolens; and an international mart, where New Roman luxuries, Balkan staples, Russian skins, Caucasian honey, Chinese silks, Indian spices and perfumes, gems from Ceylon, and golden brocades from Bagdad and Cairo could be acquired.

In the east the Seljuk Turks threatened the Armenian statelets with submersion. As a result, Basil was able to conclude with the Bagratid King of Kings (who directly controlled only the Ani-Ararat area) a treaty whereby his kingdom was to pass to the Empire upon his death and his heir was to be compensated with land within the Empire. Also under Seljuk pressure the King of Vaspurakan, who claimed descent from Sennacherib and whose domain reached from Lake Van to beyond the Araxes, transferred it to the Empire and was created Patrician, Duke of Mesopotamia, and hereditary Strategos of the Sebastean theme. In 1022 the new strategos entered his fief with many of his subjects, while Nicephorus Comnenus assumed command in the former kingdom and soon enlarged it at the expense of neighboring emirs.

During Basil's sojourn in the east, Anatolic troops draped the purple on Nicephorus Phocas, son of Bardas Phocas and grandnephew of Nicephorus II. From all over Anatolia, especially from Cappadocia, even from Basil's personal command veterans streamed to the scion of the glorious Phocas family. Oppressed magnates adhered. But the Strategos of the Anatolics murdered Phocas, hoping to replace him. Without Phocas, however, the movement melted away, and his assassin was tonsured.

The Bulgar-Butcher reestablished Roman suzerainty along the western Caucasus and was moving northwest of Lake Urmia to push back the Moslems when winter overtook him. Men and beasts froze, and the Emperor retired to Vaspurakan, whence he returned to New Rome with captives and hostages.

ITALY

In 970 the German monarch Otto I had been induced to withdraw from Roman Italy by the betrothal of Tzimisces' niece by marriage, the Porphyrogenita Theophano, to his son Otto II, who succeeded his father in 973. The union with this daughter of Romanus II did not still young Otto's desire to incorporate residual Roman Italy into his vast realm and expel the Moslems from Sicily. Consequently, in 982 he crossed the Roman border, conquered Longobardia, and advanced into Calabria.

At Stilo on the wild, precipitous, southern coast the ironclad men of the North collided with the sons of the Maghreb on a torrid July day. After a fierce engagement the mailed Christian knights killed the Sicilian Emir and routed the white-robed Moslems, who fled through beds of dried torrents and deep ravines. The Germans broke ranks and followed. But in the defiles and gullies the Moslems

From Gustave Schlumberger, L'épopée byzantine, Vol. II, ko received the photograph from M. C. Enlart

Byzantine church at Stilo—known as La Cattolica—of about the tenth century

rallied and turned on the pursuing German warriors. Many a blond Teuton fell under their scimitars or was driven into the blue waters of the Mediterranean to sink heavily beneath its smiling surface.

Otto was encircled by Moslems. His horse collapsed. A Jew gave him his own. The only avenue of escape lay seaward, where in the distance the officers of a Roman ship were observing the battle. Though fully armored, Otto rode into the azure waters and swam on horseback to the vessel. He was hoisted aboard. Without disclosing his identity he promised the captain a large reward to take him to the German base at Rossano. Here some of his paladins came aboard and while they covered him with their bodies he jumped into the sea and swam to land. Thus the ruler of Central Europe avoided possible detention in New Rome, an event that might have altered the course of history.

His expeditionary force wiped out, Otto II took the bitter road of retreat. The Moslems returned to Sicily to bury their fallen Emir and prepare for the succession. Roman authorities reoccupied the two provinces. German prestige was shaken. Danes and Wends returned to paganism and ravaged Saxony. Yet the young German potentate yielded to that medieval fata morgana of Italo-German unity that for centuries lured his countrymen to premature austral graves. He gathered another Italo-German host and was about to set out from Rome when he succumbed to dysentery (983).

With the Germans paralyzed by a minority and the Sicilian Moslems by internal strife, Roman borders spread to the Tronto on the Adriatic and to the Gulf of Policastro on the Tyrrhenian. But Moslem raids recommenced. Exposed Calabria, Greek in speech, faith, and customs, was loyal to the Empire. But the Italo-Lombard inhabitants of Longobardia, largely Latin in tongue and religion, especially in rural districts, yearned for autonomy, for, far from the searching eyes of their imperial master, Roman officials were often corrupt, grasping, and oppressive. As the tenth century drew to a close, Longobardians broke into repeated revolt.

Abetted by Sicilian Moslems, they again uprose in 1009 and were routed. Their leader, Meles of Bari, fled to the Pope, who gave him a castle on the Garigliano as a base for a renewed attempt. Moreover, the Pope mediated between him and some Norman lords. As a result, in 1017 Meles led a host of Lombards and Norman mercenaries into Longobardia but was defeated near ancient Cannae. The Pope and Meles (who soon died) then sought the aid of the German ruler Henry II, who was alarmed because his marches, the Lombard principalities, had again fallen under Roman hegemony. He decided to conquer all southern Italy and, accompanied by the Pope, invaded Longobardia at the head of sixty thousand men (1022). But he encountered a new and powerful city, Troy, built three years before on the site of an ancient town. Henry II laid siege, but stubborn resistance and dysentery among his troops forced him to abandon it.

Basil II, now sixty-eight, decided that the moment had come to oust the Moslems from Sicily and reestablish the Roman boundary on the Po. His vanguard seized Messina and the old Bulgar-Butcher was preparing to join the expedition when he was suddenly taken ill. Sensing his approaching end, he placed the diadem on the head of his brother Constantine VIII, his long silent colleague (1025). He died leaving the Empire at the zenith of her postheraclian power. On all her expanded frontiers, on the Save, the Cyrus, the Tigris, the Orontes, and the Garigliano, her armies were victorious. At home the magnates' power was bent and the treasury was replete with the booty of conquered nations.[3]

[3] This chapter is based largely on Schlumberger's monumental (in size, weight, and achievement) tomes on Nicephorus Phocas, John Tzimisces, and Basil II.

IX

Bureaucratic Ascendancy

1025–1072

Now sixty-five, Constantine VIII squandered the wealth that his brother had amassed in the vaults beneath the Great Palace, replaced efficient civil and military officers with his own cronies (mostly eunuchs), and blinded a number of the most powerful magnates, even those with long records of good service. Suddenly in 1028 he fell ill. The physicians intimated that death was near, and his thoughts turned to the succession. He had three daughters. The eldest, disfigured by smallpox, had early taken the veil. Zoë, now fifty, and Theodora, about forty-eight, had spent their lives in the gyneceum, condemned to celibacy because their uncle had feared that consorts might harbor imperial ambitions. Since a woman could not legally succeed to the throne, it was necessary for the preservation of the dynasty to find a husband for one of them. Constantine chose a kinsman, the City Prefect Romanus Argyrus, approaching sixty and of majestic appearance. Since he was married, he was arrested, accused of conspiracy, and given the choice between blinding or divorce and marriage to Zoë. His wife took the veil, and Argyrus was immediately divorced, created Caesar, and married to the Porphyrogenita, on whom traces of beauty still lingered. Three days later Constantine VIII died and Romanus III assumed the Augustan attributes.

He aspired to graft a new limb on the withering dynastic trunk. Charms, drugs, aphrodisiacs, pomades, and massages were tried. But nature had run its course. Meanwhile, while inflexible tax collection was ruining many farmers, Argyrus abolished the measure making the magnates responsible for their defaulted taxes. He also endeavored to reconquer the Emirate of Aleppo, which had thrown off the bonds of vassaldom. But the soldiers lacked confidence in his leadership and fled from their fortified camp to Antioch (1030).

Soon the glory of Roman arms was redeemed by George Mani-akes, a young officer of great stature and powerful voice, probably of Turkish origin, who had wandered into the Empire, entered the army, risen through the ranks, married, and acquired lands. With the clandestine help of a group of Edessenes, a detachment of picked men, and artillery he occupied three rampart towers of Edessa (lost in the reign of Heraclius) and withstood the on-slaughts of Edessenes, Aleppines, Fatimids, and the Emir of May-yafarikin until a Roman army arrived to complete the conquest (1032). The supposed letter of the Savior to Abgar was found in the ancient city and brought to the Sacred Palace, where Argyrus received it on his knees.

After his unsuccessful attempts to found a dynasty with Zoë, Argyrus appears to have discontinued an act that seemed purely symbolic. The unwanted wife espied among the palatine attendants a handsome, soft-eyed Paphlagonian youth, whose only blemish was an occasional attack of epilepsy. Her hungry heart was inflamed with love and pity. The lad, whose name was Michael, was at first terrified by her advances, but his brother Joannes, a highly placed eunuch, urged him to respond. Soon he lay with Zoë on the same couch. In this situation they were found by the Grand Eunuch of the gyneceum, an old and faithful functionary, who fainted from shock. Michael blushed with shame, but the Augusta pressed him close to her, calling him the grace and treasure of her eyes, the flower of beauty, the consolation of her soul. In April 1034 Argy-rus, who had treated the youth with especial marks of esteem, was found dying and incapable of speech in the Palace natatorium.

THE PAPHLAGONIANS

Before his body had grown cold Joannes persuaded the Patriarch to marry Zoë to Michael in the Golden Hall and crown the young Paphlagonian Basileus. Joannes conciliated the Senate with a distri-bution of dignities, the masses with gratuities. Michael IV ceased to play the lover, confined Zoë to the gyneceum under guard, and sought to purge his soul by religious austerities. Meanwhile, the government remained in the hands of Joannes, who removed, imprisoned, exiled, and expropriated higher officers, especially the most powerful members of the landed military aristocracy. He replaced them with relatives, naming one emasculated brother Domestic, another Duke of Antioch.

The appointment of incapable men to military posts bore funest fruit. The Patzinaks laid waste Danubian Bulgaria, inflicting a variety of exquisite tortures on their captives (1036). Aleppo refused the tribute. The vassal King of Georgia (as the southwestern Caucasian area was now called) revolted (1039). Moreover, after the death of the Armenian King of Kings his successor refused to transfer the kingdom to the Empire and crushed a Roman army at Ani (1041). On the other hand, in 1036 Serbs, who had thrown off the Roman yoke in the preceding reign, were again reduced to vassaldom.

Meanwhile, coastal cities of Roman Italy continued to be harassed by the Sicilan Moslems, who also aided disaffected Lombards in Longobardia. But in Sicily the descendants of the early Moslem invaders and of moslemized Christians, who owned most of the property, were in conflict with later Berber immigrants. Taking advantage of the situation, Roman troops invaded the island in 1037. Although driven out by the army of the Zirid ruler of Tunisia, suzerain of the island, they brought with them fifteen thousand Christians.

In 1038 George Maniakes landed in Sicily. Among his contingents was a troop of Varangians commanded by Harold Hardrada, seven and a half feet tall, future King of Norway and pretender to the throne of England, where near York he was to meet death in battle against King Harold in 1066. He has celebrated in verse his service for the Empire against Moslems in the Aegean, Patzinaks on the Danube, and with Maniakes in Sicily. The Roman force also included a few hundred Normans, who were filtering into southern Italy and offering their swords to the highest bidder. Maniakes seized Messina and reputedly annihilated 50,000 Moslems at Rametta and 60,000 at the foot of Mount Etna. In 1040 he took Syracuse. Here was discovered what was believed to be the body of the virgin Saint Lucy, said to be as fresh as on the day of her martyrdom in 303. It was reverently shipped to New Rome.

Maniakes was about to advance westward to complete the conquest of Sicily when he was recalled to New Rome and thrown into chains. He had reprimanded the incapable commander of the fleet, the Emperor's brother-in-law and a former calker, who now replaced him and soon lost all his conquests except Messina. Moreover, with Norman help the subject Lombards again uprose, defeated imperial forces in three furious battles (1041), and gained control of the greater part of Longobardia.

In 1040 the Bulgars, provoked by Joannes' refusal to accept the customary payment of taxes in kind, proclaimed Peter Delyan, possibly a grandson of Samuel, Tsar amid scenes of wild national enthusiasm. Michael IV, who was at Salonica seeking relief from dropsy at the tomb of Saint Demetrius, led his guards and the available troops against Peter but was routed. Peter moved southward to annex the Pindic Peninsula.

Abruptly, the sexagenarian Alusian, son of the last Tsar, appeared. He had been created Patrician and Strategos of Theodosiopolis, which he was forbidden to leave. But word of the Bulgarian revolt had so inflamed his ambition that he had traveled in disguise to Peter's headquarters at Ostrovo, where the boliads obliged Peter to accept him as colleague.

Peter sent him with forty thousand men to capture Salonica. Unable to take the city by assault, Alusian settled down to a siege. October 26 is the day of Salonica's patron saint, Demetrius. All day and night Salonicans prayed to him. In the morning men fervently seized their arms, sallied forth with the vision of the glorious young megalomartyr before them, and attacked the Bulgar camp, which Alusian, despite his years in the Roman army, had neglected to fortify. They are said to have killed twelve thousand Bulgars and captured twelve thousand.

Alusian fled back to Peter and at a banquet treacherously dug out his eyes and cut off his ears with a table knife. But he was defeated by the dying Emperor, now swollen with dropsy. Losing hope, he secretly offered to submit to the Anointed of God. Near Mosynopolis the Roman and Bulgarian armies deployed. Suddenly Alusian galloped from the Bulgarian ranks and threw himself at the Emperor's feet. He was created Magister, showered with wealth, and given a guarded home in New Rome.

The expiring Emperor extinguished the last sparks of rebellion and, barely able to hold the reins of his white charger, returned to New Rome in triumph. Casting aside the diadem, he retired to a monastery, and yielded the ghost in December 1041, expressing remorse at the murder of his predecessor.

Joannes had already selected another Michael, the son of his sister and of the former calker, to succeed to the imperium. The young man had been adopted by Zoë and created Caesar by Michael IV. A few days after his uncle's death he was crowned Basileus with Zoë's consent. Hardly was he on the throne than he banished Joannes. Then he had Zoë's still blond locks shorn and deported her to Prinkipo, the largest of the Princes' Islands (1042).

This act infuriated the capital masses, who, probably led by gildsmen,[1] assailed the Palace wall. Many of the guards went over to the populace. Michael V hastily brought Zoë back from Prinkipo and from the safety of the Kathisma presented her in conventual garb to his raging subjects in the Hippodrome. A hail of stones greeted him. Incensed by the connivance of the woman for whose rights they were fighting, the townsmen sought another person on whom to drape the robe of legitimacy.

Magnates, who had probably fomented the rebellion, led them to the convent of Petrion, where Zoë had immured her sister Theodora soon after her marriage to Argyrus. Terrified by the tumult and desiring to end her days in cloistral seclusion, she fled to the chapel altar. But her partisans dragged her from this sanctuary, arrayed her in imperial garments, placed her on a horse, and led her to Saint Sophia. Night had fallen, and amid flickering taper flames, resplendent mosaics, and richly dressed New Romans Theodora was crowned Zoë's associate to the acclamations, "Long live Theodora, our Mother!"[2] Michael V was declared deposed.

Meanwhile, the attack on the Palace continued. Deserted by his Varangians, Michael V lost heart, but his evirated uncle, the Nobilissimus Constantine, rallied the loyal guards, armed the palatine servants, placed archers and slingers at strategic points, and inflicted heavy losses on the assailants. Day and night the combat raged. As the third day dawned the mob crushed the exhausted defenders, entered the Palace precincts, and ran wildly through its stately

---

[1] Vryonis, *Dumbarton Oaks Papers*, 17 (1963).
[2] Schlumberger, *L'épopée byzantine* . . . (Paris, 1905), III, 367.

halls, seeking Michael V. But he, the Nobilissimus, and a few faithful friends had just taken ship at the Palace port for the monastery of Studion. The multitude hastened to Studion with murderous intent, but found Michael and Constantine, tonsured and clad as monks, clinging to the altar of the Church of the Forerunner. No one would profane the altar, but for hours the crowd howled insults and menaces. At length, an officer of Theodora arrived with a troop of soldiers, who cared little for the law of sanctuary (April 1042).

Michael and his uncle were seized by the feet, dragged through the mob, seated backward on mules, and taken to the Palace. Here the irons were sharpened to blind them. Michael begged for mercy, while Constantine accepted his fate with courage. Surrounded by a mob avid to see him suffer, he calmly stretched himself on the ground and uttered not a sound during the fearful torture. When it was over he arose without aid, the blood flowing from his empty sockets, giving signal proof that emasculation may rob a man of virility but not necessarily of pride and courage. Michael V had meanwhile been clawing the air, scratching his face, shrieking in terror. It was of no avail. Distant monasteries and death engulfed the blind pair. A year later Joannes was to die from the same penalty. The Paphlagonians, like a comet, had flamed and vanished.

MONOMACHUS AND MANIAKES

The scepter of Caesar lay in the withered hands of two old women. Zoë, who still retained a youthful complexion and figure, was interested in exotic perfumes and pomades, while Theodora's passion was numismatics. The Empire needed a man and Zoë, though sixty-four, not unwillingly entertained the idea of third nuptials. Constantine Dalassenus, the most popular magnate of the realm, incarcerated throughout the rule of the Paphlagonians, contemptuously refused. Another agreed but suddenly died.

Undaunted, Zoë recalled Senator Constantine Monomachus, a handsome, popular, wealthy, luxurious magnate, who had spent seven years in exile on the verdant isle of Lesbos, comforted by the love and fidelity of the gentle Sclerena of the progeny of Bardas Sclerus. Twice wed, he had not dared marry this young widow for

Mosaic in Saint Sophia, Istanbul, of Christ with Constantine IX Monomachus (reigned 1042–1055) and his consort, Zoé (d. 1050). Monomachus holds the usual offering and Zoé the certificate of orthodoxy

fear of ecclesiastical censure. Now, however, the Church made the necessary concessions. Monomachus made a brilliant entry into the capital, married the elderly Porphyrogenita, and was crowned Constantine IX (June 1042). Apparently viewing his elevation as a stroke of good fortune, he disbursed public funds with a lavish hand and debased the coinage.

He recalled Sclerena from Lesbos and established her in the Sacred Palace, where her charm, benevolence, soft voice, and exquisite diction soon conquered all hearts, even Zoë's. She received the new rank of Sebaste and appeared at all ceremonies beside the Emperor and the Augustae. Furthermore, Zoë exempted her husband from conjugal intimacy and did not disturb him when he was in the company of the fascinating companion of his exile. Nevertheless, in

1044 as he was proceeding through the City, a crowd demonstrated against Sclerena. Finally the Porphyrogenitae calmed the rioters. The foreign colony at New Rome may have been involved in this tumult, for Monomachus immediately ordered foreigners who had lived in the City fewer than thirty years to leave on pain of blinding. It is said that over a hundred thousand departed. After a few years the beautiful Sebaste was to succumb to pneumonia and to be buried in the sepulcher beside the one destined for her heartbroken lover in the elegant convent of Mangana.

The Emperor's love for Sclerena had more far-reaching results. Her brother, the Magister Romanus Sclerus, took advantage of his family's position to avenge himself on his famous neighbor, George Maniakes, whom he hated because of a boundary dispute. He ravaged his Anatolic estate, did violence to his wife, and induced the Emperor to deprive him of the Italian command, for which Michael V had released him.

Meanwhile, Maniakes had found most of Longobardia in the hands of Lombards and Normans, who had elected Argyrus, the son of Meles, their prince (February 1042). Maniakes had already commenced the reconquest when Monomachus' emissary insultingly degraded him in the presence of his troops. Maniakes' indignant soldiers smothered the imperial agent under a dung heap and hailed Maniakes Emperor. He crossed the Adriatic to Durazzo, where he was greeted as the savior of the Empire. The Serbian ruler of Zeta, who had recently defeated an imperial force of sixty thousand poorly led men, acknowledged him his suzerain and sent him auxiliaries. Maniakes took the Via Egnatia and at Ostrovo met the army of Monomachus, who had remained in New Rome. At the head of his troops Maniakes swept the opposing army into defeat. Suddenly he was struck by a spear and slipped to the ground, dead in the high tide of victory (1043). His memory lives on in legend, and forts are named after him in Edessa and Syracuse.

RUSSIANS

Since Tzimisces' crushing blows the Russians had lived in peace with the Empire. Their Metropolitan was appointed by the Patriarch of New Rome. Byzantine artists and missionaries flowed to

Russia, while young Russians joined the Roman army and Russian merchants sold their produce in the suburb of Saint Mamas. As intermediary between the Empire and the North the Russian confederation prospered. Kiev and Novgorod, whose bazaars displayed Byzantine gems, purple, brocades, and goldware, faintly reflected the splendors of New Rome.

Despite these intimate relations, the rude men of the North seem to have disliked the cultured New Romans, whose wealth and dreamlike capital they coveted. A quarrel in the bazaar at Saint Mamas, in which a Novgorod merchant was killed, furnished the pretext for another expedition against New Rome. The autonomous Prince of Novgorod, son and vassal of the Great Prince of Kiev, assembled a band of adventurers, including Scandinavians, Icelanders, Greenlanders, Hebrideans, and Orkneyans, embarked for New Rome, brushed aside the Black Sea squadron, and reached the mouth of the Bosporus, where Greek Fire annihilated the armada (1043).

ARMENIA

Monomachus continued Michael IV's efforts to force the Armenian King of Kings to deliver his realm to the Empire in accordance with the agreement of 1022. Two Roman armies, Moslem invasion, feudal chaos, and Roman promises at length induced the Bagratid to repair to the Great City. He was never to see his native land again. He became Magister, received a palace in New Rome, extensive lands, and a lavish pension (1045). The last state claiming suzerainty over all Armenians had expired. Its history since its foundation in 885 had been a series of feudal quarrels and foreign invasions (mostly Moslem) and its borders had shrunken from feudal encroachment. It was now transformed into Roman themes. Armenian nobles also exchanged their castles for land within the Empire. Never before had the Empire had such a strong frontier in the East. Ani became the seat of a Roman strategos, and Roman forces attacked the emirate of Tovin. Suddenly the greater part of the troops was recalled to New Rome (1047).

Averse to the monarch who squandered the Empire's wealth and gave incompetent civilians important commands, Macedonian regiments at Adrianople had flung the imperial mantle on the imposing figure of Leo Tornicius, Patrician, Bagratid, and kinsman of Monomachus, who had tonsured him. The new Emperor marched on the weakly held City and drove Monomachus' forces through the gates. The defenders fled from the ramparts and the gates stood open. Tornicius had only to enter. But, confident that the City would submit voluntarily and disliking to subject the inhabitants to the horrors of an assault, he did not let his troops follow. He was soon caught between the regiments returning from Armenia and Bulgarian contingents. Monomachus' gold fired his own men and suborned the dissidents. Deserted, Tornicius and the heart of the revolt, John Vatatzes, sought asylum in a church near Arcadiopolis but were torn from the altar. When they reached the site where they had encamped before the City three months earlier executioners came out and blinded them (Christmas Eve 1047).

PATZINAKS

In 1048 Patzinaks crossed the frozen Danube and were surrounded by imperial forces. The Emperor spared them, intending to settle them in Bulgaria and use them as mercenaries. The wild sons of the steppe soon uprose, occupied the confluence of the Osma and the Danube, and carried fire, sword, and torture to the gates of Adrianople. A new dismemberment of the Empire had begun.

To combat it the gouty Isapostol placed an inexperienced, ecclesiastical eunuch in command. For five years thousands of Roman soldiers were butchered while the Patzinaks transformed the lands between the Danube and the Aegean into a veritable hell, eviscerating even sucklings, burning, torturing, enslaving, pillaging, raping. Lacking confidence in their leaders, Roman troops readily took to flight. Finally, the Vicar of God gave the command to a professional officer, Nicephorus Bryennius. The demoralized army that he took over could no longer meet the Patzinaks in pitched battle, and he contented himself with wiping out individual plundering parties or making night attacks on the Patzinak camp. These tactics were crowned with success, and the Basileus again placed a eunuch in command. A disastrous defeat followed, and the Empire pur-

chased peace, leaving the Patzinaks at the Osma-Danube confluence.

SELJUK TURKS

By 1000 the decaying Abbasid Khalifate had lost Islam west of
the Jordan and had little influence in the East. Arabia, which had
recently thrown off the dominion of the Karmathian sectaries and
returned to premoslem disunity, ignored the Khalif of Bagdad.
Northern Mesopotamia and northern Syria formed the emirate of
Aleppo, which vacillated between allegiance to the Emperor and
the Fatimid Khalif of Cairo. Basra and the lower Tigris Valley
were independent. Armenia was lost. Azerbaijan and Media had independent dynasties. Khorasan, Gaznah, Transoxiana, and the Indus
Valley were united under a Turkish family, the Gaznavids. Buyid
dynasties ruled from the Caspian to the Persian Gulf. The Shiite
Buyid Sultan restricted the Sunnite Khalif's authority to his household. Only the right of investiture, by which Moslem princes legiti-
mized their rule, still lent the Abbasids a shadow of authority.
Almost two centuries of impotence and present dependence on
Shiite sultans had largely expunged Abbasid influence in Islam.

Soon after 950 Seljuk had led his Turkoman tribes from the
Kirghiz steppe to Transoxiana and embraced Islam. After 1000
these Irano-Turkish clans were permitted by the Gaznavid ruler to
cross the Oxus and settle in Khorasan. Strengthened by continuous
Turkoman immigration from Transoxiana, the Seljuks in 1038
made themselves masters of Khorasan, proclaimed Seljuk's
grandson Toghril (the Butcher) their chief, pushed the Gaznavids
eastward, and soon conquered the greater part of Iran and Azerbaijan, whence they hurled themselves against Armenia.

In this mountain country sturdy Armenian peasants, organized in
fighting groups by feudal lords, had for centuries held eastern invaders at bay. Monomachus abolished this militia, substituted a
money-tax for the body-tax, and replaced the hardy rustics, who
fought for their homes and terraced hills, with Roman mercenaries.
Moreover, Orthodox priests flocked into the country and endeavored to force the Armenians into religious conformity. Armenian
resistance to invasion was thus appreciably weakened.

The Seljuks ravaged Vaspurakan, wiped out a Roman army, captured the courtier-commander, flayed him alive, and stuffed his skin with straw. They pressed butchering into the Caucasus and upper Armenia, but were trapped by a Roman officer and almost exterminated (1048).

Infuriated by this defeat, Toghril hurled an enormous host into Armenia. The fierce multitude pushed as far as weak-walled Arzen, a commercial emporium thirty-five miles east of Theodosiopolis. The long-haired sons of Turkestan penetrated the city, where every house became a fortress. Six days the struggle raged. At length the Seljuks set fire to the city (1049). Over a hundred thousand persons are said to have perished rather than surrender. The survivors fled to powerful Theodosiopolis, whose name was changed to Arzen. This, in turn, became Erzerum (Arzen of the Romans).

A great but indecisive battle followed the sack of Arzen, and the Turks retreated. A truce was arranged whereby Monomachus agreed to build in New Rome a mosque in which prayers were to be said in Toghril's name. After completing the conquest of Persia proper Toghril returned to ravage the land of Ararat. Only triple-walled Manzikert withstood him. Here his mining, artillery, and assaults did not avail against the capable defense of an efficient Roman officer. Before he lifted the siege a Roman ballista hurled a sow into his camp with the proposal that if he take her to wife he might have Manzikert as dowry (1054).

The following year the Sunnite Toghril drove out the Shiite Buyid Sultan, entered Bagdad, and imposed his protection on the helpless Khalif, who bestowed on him the ancient Parthian title of Sultan and proclaimed him his Right Hand and presumptive son-in-law. Mosul and northern Mesopotamia yielded to him. His realm now stretched from the Oxus to the Euphrates and from the Caspian to the Persian Gulf.

NORMANS

In Italy the leader of the rebellious Lombards, Argyrus, soon discovered that in calling in the Normans the Lombards had exchanged the extortionate corruption of Roman officials for the cruel rapacity of allies who wanted Roman Italy for themselves. He consequently returned to Roman allegiance, became Patrician (1042), and finally Magister and Duke of Italy. The Normans thereupon became vassals of the Lombard Prince of Salerno, Capua, Amalfi, and Sorrento, who assumed the further title Duke of Apulia and Calabria. Five years later the German suzerain crushed him and declared the Normans of Campania and Apulia his own vassals.

The Normans nonetheless continued the conquest of Roman Italy, their numbers augmented by a steady immigration from Normandy. Their brutality goaded the Apulian population to insurge. The Pope, to whom the Normans had refused tribute, marched against them at the head of a German-Lombard army. The Normans cornered him at Civitate before he could join forces with Argyrus, routed his Lombards, but fought for hours against his outnumbered Suabians, who, wounded and unwounded, formed an iron wall until not a man was left (1053).

POPE AND PATRIARCH

Although both Orthodox and Latins believed in Christian unity, their practices had drifted apart in such matters as the sacramental use of leavened or unleavened bread, bearded or shaven priests, the admission of married men to the priesthood or the acceptance of only celibates, etc. Moreover, the Latins had added *filioque* to the Nicene-Chalcedonian creed, indicating the procession of the Holy Ghost from both Father and Son. The Latins asserted that this merely clarified a doctrine inherent in the creed, while the Orthodox maintained that the Pope had separated himself from his brother patriarchs by adding to the creed and insisted that only an ecumenical council had the right to amplify the decision of an earlier council, whose authority and inspiration would otherwise be challenged.

The differences between the churches were aggravated when after the early Norman conquests in Roman Italy the Latins forbade Orthodox usages. In reprisal the vigorous Patriarch of New Rome, Michael Cerularius, a former official, ordered the Latin churches in the City to adopt Orthodox practices. On their refusal he closed them (1052). As a result, papal legates came to New Rome in 1054 and after recriminations over differing religious procedures excommunicated Cerularius but not the Orthodox Church. Bowing to the will of the powerful Patriarch and the demonstrations of the indignant populace, Monomachus ordered the bull of excommunication to be burned, while a synod anathematized the legates but not the Papacy or the Latin Church.

There was thus no definitive breach in 1054. The Emperor continued to negotiate with the Papacy for cooperation against the Normans in Italy and to support the monastery at Monte Cassino, while Latin pilgrims passing through New Rome were well received. Indeed, although the Pope in 1080 supported the Norman invasion of the Empire, by the close of the eleventh century relations between the two Churches were generally amical. The root of their difficulties was not ritual or doctrinal, but the Papacy's claim to universal authority. While Orthodox prelates accorded it an honorary primacy, they rejected its assertion of supremacy, which for them resided in the ecumenical councils and the pentarchy of patriarchs.

About 1170 the Orthodox standpoint was enunciated by Michael of Anchialus, Patriarch of New Rome. He pointed out that the primacy of the Roman see was based less on its apostolic origin than on its location in the ancient capital. If the origin of a see were to determine its status, would not Antioch, whose see Saint Peter had founded before establishing Rome's, enjoy primacy? Indeed, would not Jerusalem, where Christ founded His Church, outrank all other sees? Since New Rome was now the imperial capital, Michael saw no reason why its see should submit to Old Roman authority.[3]

Michael of Anchialus also stated that he would prefer to have his Church under the secular rule of the Moslems rather than under the spiritual dominion of the Latins, for the former would not impose their faith on him and force him to separate himself from God. Much had happened between 1054 and the expression of this last sentiment about 1170. By then political events and especially popular contacts of crusading Latins and Orthodox populations had led

---

[3] As is known, the Papacy bases its claim to leadership on the words that Saint Matthew recorded Jesus as addressing to Saint Peter, ". . . thou art Peter and upon this rock I will build My Church . . . I will give unto thee the keys of heaven . . ."

This graceful church in Istanbul was perhaps erected and dedicated to Saint Theodore Tiro in the eleventh century. It has been converted into the mosque Molla Gürani, popularly known as the Kilisse Jami

to mutual antipathy. While the controversy of 1054 concerned mainly hierarchs, by the end of the twelfth century a deep popular abyss separated Latin and Orthodox communicants.

PSELLUS

Learning was the prime requisite for officials. They often lectured at the newly reopened university, where not only ancient Greece, but also Egypt and Babylonia were studied and to which students came from East and West.

Psellus, a gifted scholar and a high official, impregnated with Antiquity, was dean of the university and did not hesitate to oppose Platonic to the Aristotelian philosophy of the Church. Like Photius, he could lecture and write on many subjects—philosophy, history, grammar, rhetoric, music, archaeology, theology, astronomy, mathematics, militaria, physics, and medicine—and could inspire others to pursue them. He admitted that he expressed himself with natural beauty, that people listened to him with rapt attention, and that Monomachus was so entranced with the sound of his voice that he almost embraced him.[4] His learning colored diplomatic missives and he sought to crush foreign potentates under the weight of his intellect. He has been called the first great humanist.[5]

Educated laymen also continued the Hellenic tradition and were as familiar with Homer as with the Bible. The marked tendency to return to pure classical models in the eleventh century arrested the natural evolution of the written language. Thus, the cleft between literary and living Greek grew wider.

Zoë died in 1050 at seventy-two, and the court darkened as, one after another, learned ministers yielded their posts to bureaucratic nobles. Finally, even Psellus withdrew to a monastery to continue his history of the period and to return to office under more appreciative emperors. In January 1055 Monomachus bathed in the pond at the monastery of Saint George of Mangana, contracted pleurisy, and soon breathed his last.

Before he died Theodora's partisans had again torn her from conventual peace and proclaimed her Basilissa. The old lady replaced many officers with her eunuchs and continued to favor the bureaucracy over the military. The theme system began to collapse. Great military expeditions were avoided as much as possible and tribute was more extensively employed in dealing with barbarians.

While the Patriarch wanted Theodora to take a consort, her evirated entourage persuaded her to remain single. Soon she was attacked by a mortal intestinal disease. The elderly Patrician Michael Bringas, a retired official known as Stratioticus, swore to leave power in her advisers' hands, and the Basilissa adopted him as son and successor. After some hesitation the Patriarch anointed him Michael VI. Satisfied that her favorite eunuchs would retain their posts, Theodora died in August 1056.

ISAAC COMNENUS

Stratioticus, the instrument of Theodora's eunuchs, continued the antimilitary policy of his immediate predecessors, bestowing

---

[4] Psellus, *The Chronographia*, trans. by Sewter (New Haven, 1953), p. 131.
[5] Ostrogorsky, *History*, p. 290.

From H. G. Goodacre, A Handbook of the Coinage of the Byzantine Empire; *the coin is in the British Museum*

Cup-shaped coin of Isaac Comnenus (reigned 1057–1059) with drawn sword

largesses on populace and functionaries but omitting the customary donative to the army. Moreover, he was rude to a group of landed generals, who requested redress.

To save their class from further persecution Sclerus, Burtzes, Ducas, Bryennius, Argyrus, Botaniates, the battle-scarred Armenian Katakalon (the Burned), and others proclaimed the majestic Isaac Comnenus Emperor of the Romans before his troops on a Paphlagonian field in June 1057. Military malcontents flocked to his camp. He moved westward and defeated the army of Stratioticus. When he reached Chrysopolis, the popular Patriarch Michael Cerularius convoked prominent persons to Saint Sophia and informed Stratioticus that if he valued his life he must accept tonsure. The Chosen of God inquired what was offered him in exchange for the Empire. "The Kingdom of Heaven" was the stern reply.[6] He was shorn and taken to a monastery in the City, where he died in peace.

At dawn Katakalon, now Curopalates, took possession of the Great Palace. Later Comnenus ascended the richly carpeted deck of the imperial vessel and crossed to the City, surrounded by pleasure craft. The following day he was crowned by the Patriarch amid the glittering mosaics and multicolored marbles of Saint Sophia (September 1057).

Isaac Comnenus took over a sinking Empire. In the thirty-two years since the death of Basil II lax regimes, supported by the dynastic sentiments of the masses, had tolerated official corruption,

[6] Schlumberger, *L'épopée* . . . , III, 823, to which the writer is indebted for the account of the events between 1025 and 1057.

given tax remissions and largesses to powerful partisans, and encouraged the excessive construction of churches and monasteries. Income of the crown lands had passed to churches, monasteries, courtiers, and bureaucratic favorites. The wherewithal for elementary needs of the state had vanished into the pockets of those who held the reins of government. Consequently, while the long-haired Seljuks loomed in the east and the louse-eating Patzinaks in the north, the army had declined in numbers and quality. Frontier forts were neglected, arsenals were not replenished, and the navy rotted. The government persecuted military magnates and crushed free farmers, the fiscal and military backbone of the Empire, whom the emperors from Lecapenus to Basil II had sought to protect. Now they were so ruthlessly taxed that many lost their lands. Vast lay and monastic estates spread over the countryside and reduced them to tenants, who were bound to the estate by certain duties. Bearing a heavy tax and task burden, they lost interest in the welfare of the state and did not resist invaders. In their fate could be read the destiny of the Empire.

Comnenus set himself to save her. He introduced economy, reduced salaries, halted the flow into the pockets of corrupt courtiers or officials, expelled parasites, repossessed the crown property that his predecessors had transferred to private hands, and collected taxes from those who had theretofore been exempted. He stopped the acquisition of adjacent lands by pious institutions, limited their incomes, and confiscated their property to restore the finances and the free peasantry.

Enraged at these measures, monks, secular priests, populace, magnates, dispossessed courtiers and bureaucrats, even part of the army united under the leadership of the Patriarch, who assumed purple buskins and proclaimed the dominance of Church over State. Possibly he dreamed of heading a theocratic state. But he faced a man who did not fear public disapproval, and he was removed to the Island of Imbros (1058), where he soon died. His body was brought back to the City in solemn pomp. Miracles were said to occur at his tomb. His right hand was said to have remained lifelike. Even the Emperor came to pray at his grave.

In the north Hungarians crossed the middle Danube, while Patzinaks traversed the lower reaches of the river. After a successful campaign Comnenus was recrossing the Balkans when rain and

From *Spyridon Lampros*, Portraits of Byzantine Emperors;
the manuscript miniature is in the Bibliothèque Nationale, Paris

*Eudocia, consort of Constantine X Ducas (reigned 1059–1067) and of
Romanus IV Diogenes (reigned 1068–1071)*

snow suddenly fell. Many soldiers died of cold, drowning, or starvation, but the Vicar of God led them relentlessly forward to win-
ter-quarters. He too had suffered and not long after his return to
New Rome fell ill with pneumonia. A dark palace conspiracy led to
his abdication and the accession of the wealthy President of the
Senate Constantine Ducas. Still ailing, Comnenus was shorn and
relegated to the Monastery of Studion (November 1059). Here he
died a year later.

CONSTANTINE X DUCAS

Ducas became Basileus as Constantine X. His accession marked
the victory of the bureaucrats and the capital over the military and
the provinces. The crown properties that Comnenus had repossessed were returned to their previous holders, often completely
exempt from imperial taxes and control. Important offices were sold.
The sinecures and privileges that Comnenus had abolished were
restored. The collection of taxes was sold to publicans on a large
scale. The military aristocracy was repressed. Military small-holders
were obliged to pay taxes and permitted to purchase immunity from

military service. The theme system was thus subverted. Moreover, funds were withheld from the army and the most highly paid troops were dismissed. Many officers adopted the more profitable administrative career. Bureaucratic power had reached its apogee.

While Patzinaks were ravaging to the walls of the capital, Ducas continued the futile effort to force Armenians, notably those in Cappadocia, into the Orthodox Church, keeping their Catholicos under surveillance.

Meanwhile, Armenia, Georgia, and Anatolia were the theater of unpunished invasions by the Seljuks, against whom Ducas opposed poorly armed, half-trained Roman and Armenian bands.

Toghril, founder of Seljuk power and preserver of the Abbasid Khalifate, died in 1063, leaving his realm to his nephew Alp Arslan (Fearless Lion). The new ruler conquered the former Seljuk home beyond the Oxus and hurled his warriors into Albania, Georgia, and Armenia. Ani fell in 1065 and received a Turkish emir. The King of Kars, the last Armenian prince still on his own lands, transferred his realm to the Empire and received a fief in Cappadocia. The following year Alp Arslan again spent in Transoxiana and then conquered Aleppo and Jerusalem.

But the Sultan's Transoxian and Syrian activities did not free the Empire of his attentions. While some kindred Cumans fought under his banners, others wandered westward over the steppes and in 1064 crossed the lower Danube. Many settled in Danubian Bulgaria. Others pushed over the Balkans and spread havoc into Hellas. The inhabitants fled, cursing the ruler who did not defend his realm. But Ducas lacked the funds to raise an army. The Empire's wealth was in the hands of the nobles of the pen. Pestilence, however, killed many of the invaders, while the Bulgars and Patzinaks within the Empire drove others over the Danube. Still others were settled in Macedonia. While the Cumans were ravaging the Empire in the north, Alp Arslan, master of most of Albania, Georgia, and Armenia, invaded Anatolia, where there were no Bulgars or Patzinaks to oppose him. The Roman army, unpaid, underfed, and poorly equipped, offered little resistance. Trampling over the local militia, the Seljuks sacked Caesarea, crossed the Taurus, and ravaged fertile Cilicia, raping, enslaving, butchering. In northern Armenia the Empire retained only Manzikert and Erzerum. Yet the senatorial oligarchs took no action.

Ducas, now about sixty, sickened in October 1066 and for eight months wasted away. His three young sons were already Emperors, the youngest, who was born in the purple, enjoying precedence. Ducas gave his wife Eudocia tutelar rights, bestowed the Caesarate on his brother John, and imparted to him the state secret that the conspiracy that had deposed Comnenus in 1059 had transformed the Empire from a semi-hereditary military monarchy into an elective bureaucratic oligarchy; that the Empire was now regulated by agreements between Emperor, Patriarch, and Senate; and that he had weakened his dynasty and the Empire by giving the succession to his youngest son because the Senate desired a long minority to enhance its own power.

Moreover, the Senate now not only chose the Emperor, it shared with him the prerogative of selecting the Patriarch. Since 1043 the Patriarch no longer stemmed from the clergy but from the bureaucratic Senate, for the aristocrats of the pen feared that a cleric might oppose them. Through the Patriarch and the higher churchmen, who were now mere adjuncts of the bureaucracy, the Senate controlled the clergy. Thus, with Prince and Patriarch within its grasp, the bureaucratic aristocracy, similar to the senatorial oligarchy that Caesar had overthrown eleven centuries earlier, exploited the Empire and reduced it from the most powerful realm west of the Great Wall to a structure on the verge of collapse.

Lest the Senate violate the agreement of 1059, Ducas obtained from his wife Eudocia a written renunciation of remarriage and from the senators a statement of exclusive recognition of his three sons as rulers. He entrusted these documents to the Patriarch before his death in 1067.

Many felt that the bureaucrats were leading the Empire to doom and that only a strong military leader of the stamp of Isaac Comnenus could prevent collapse. There were popular murmurings.

Eudocia decided to forestall the imposition of a colleague on her or even the overthrow of the Ducas family by marrying, not Nicephorus Botaniates, for whom the public clamored, but a man who would owe his elevation to her. The Patrician Romanus Diogenes, a gifted general, had assumed the purple in Bulgaria, been betrayed, captured, and condemned to death. But the public demanded his pardon. The tall, handsome, tanned officer with ardent eyes was led before the Empress and profoundly impressed her. Might this be the man to share the bereaved imperial bed, protect her and her sons, and save the Empire? He was pardoned, permitted to withdraw to his Cappadocian estates, and on Christmas Day 1067 created Magister in Saint Sophia.

To wed him was more difficult, for the Patriarch held her pledge not to remarry and the Senate's undertaking to acknowledge no Emperor beside Ducas' three sons. A wily eunuch sought out the Patriarch, discoursed on the need for a courageous man, and intimated that the Empress wanted to marry the Patriarch's brother but dared not as long as the binding documents remained in his hands. Not only were the documents forthcoming, but the Patriarch took it upon himself to win over the senators. On New Year's Eve Eudocia and Diogenes were married in the Palace and on New Year's Day 1068 he was proclaimed Emperor Romanus IV.

ROMANUS IV DIOGENES

The state whose executive Diogenes became in 1068 bore only superficial resemblance to the powerful military monarchy that had endured from the reign of Heraclius to the death of Basil II in 1025. Its fiscal and military strength had been based on free farmers, who paid taxes to the central government, and small-holders, who served as soldiers in return for hereditary land grants. Emperors, notably Lecapenus, Constantine VII, and Basil II, had protected these farmers and small-holders against the tendency of great lay, monastic, and ecclesiastical estates to ingest their holdings. In the eleventh century, however, the scepter fell to weak rulers, who allowed, even encouraged, the absorption of small farms. Then it slipped into the control of magnate-bureaucrats and bureaucrat-ecclesiasts, who, controlling Church and Emperor, engulfed small farms for their own benefit, often ceasing to pay taxes thereon. Under this prehensile policy the agricultural revenue of the central government and the theme system, which had for centuries rendered Anatolia impregnable, collapsed. It was a shattering blow to the fiscal and military power of the central government. Thousands of lay and ecclesiastical lords collected taxes for themselves and assumed other public functions. The Empire was for practical purposes feudalized and came to resemble the weak feudal kingdoms of Europe.

With thousands of lords preventing direct control of his subjects, with the army now largely mercenary, with his own authority limited by the power and influence of the bureaucratic magnates, and with the military magnates also participating in the acquisition of small farms, it is doubtful whether Diogenes or any other man could have reversed the trend toward feudalization. Yet a return to the centralization of a half century earlier was the only salvation of the Empire. Instead, bureaucrats, military magnates, and the Ducas family nullified Diogenes' measures to save her and continued to gnaw at her vitals.

Beside these insidious foes within, Diogenes faced long-haired Seljuks and wilder Turkomans, who from Georgia and Armenia threatened to sweep the Empire out of Asia; bow-legged Patzinaks and Cumans, who menaced her Balkan territory; and Normans, who were engulfing her last Italian possessions. He crossed to Anatolia in the spring of 1068 and assembled the debris of the Roman army—Varangian guards (Northmen and Normans); Frankish guards (mostly Germans, the most reliable troops in the army); remnants of Macedonian, Cappadocian, and Bulgarian regiments; and auxiliary Cumans. These last soldiers of the Empire were a half-starved, ragged, horseless, shoeless crowd, whose arms included boarspears and agricultural implements. Those who saw them felt that they could not withstand the Seljuk onslaught, that the Empire was doomed. Undaunted, Diogenes enrolled new men, drilled, marched, and inspired the listless band into the semblance of an army. Overriding bureaucratic opposition, he provided them with pay, horses, and weapons.

At the head of his cavalry he surprised booty-laden Turks and took their spoils and captives. Sending a detachment to hold off the Seljuks near menaced Melitene and prevent the collaboration of the Armenians in the Empire with them, he crossed the mountains into the now hostile Emirate of Aleppo, which had recognized Seljuk sovereignty. He took the outer city of Manbij (the ancient Hierapolis), gateway to northern Mesopotamia, and was besieging the inner ramparts, erected by Justinian I, when the Seljuks attacked his camp. To such depths had military morale sunk under the rule of the pen that Roman regiments did not automatically support an attacked unit. The heartened Emir of Aleppo now joined the Seljuks, hoping to crush the Emperor, who had just taken the inner city. But Diogenes returned to his camp by night and the next day routed the combined enemy. He then repaired and garrisoned inner Manbij, which shielded the Empire from the south. His victories restored a measure of confidence to the Roman troops.

But soon word reached him that the Seljuks had sacked Amorium, that the imperial general at Melitene had been negligent, and that the alienated Armenians within the Empire had aided the invaders. Indeed, they were already offering to support the Seljuks in exchange for religious toleration. Yet the Armenian dissenters were less dangerous than the intriguers in Palace, Senate, and Army, who sought to prevent Diogenes' victory over the Seljuks, lest it confer on him a prestige that might enable him to sweep them from their sinecures. In the spring of 1069 Diogenes was again in the field, seeking to prevent the junction of Seljuks and Armenians. Holding his bickering troops together, he defeated the Seljuks near Caesarea. But his victories were offset by his subordinates' defeats and Armenian defection, which enabled the Turks to plunder prosperous Iconium.

Exempt from stifling imperial taxes, this city flourished at the head of a free community including three adjacent towns. This persistence of a measure of the freedom of the antique city-state was not accidental. While in thematic capitals like Cappadocian Caesarea or Trebizond or imperial fortresses like Melitene and Erzerum the influence of the central government was supreme, those cities where no higher imperial officers resided were threatened by the power of surrounding magnates. Hence, the central government allowed them an autonomy that enabled them to resist encroachment by the magnates. It was in a sense Antiquity holding back the Middle Ages.

In late 1069 Diogenes returned to New Rome, where he became practically the prisoner, not of the nobility of the pen but of that of the sword. The conspiracy was headed by the young nephew of Isaac I, Manuel Comnenus, who became Domestic and whose sister married Diogenes' son by his first wife. The results were disastrous. Comnenus was captured and his army dispersed by the Seljuks.

While Anatolia was at the mercy of Seljuks and wild Turkoman bands not under their control, the Emperor was still held captive in Constantinople. Here the bureaucrats had regained the upper hand and formed an imperial council including Psellus, the Caesar John

Ducas, and Nicephorus Paleologus, which endeavored to prevent Diogenes from taking the field. But his determination, public opinion, and ultimately the Empress (to whom the bureaucrats had intimated that he wanted to go off to war because he did not love her) broke down the resistance of the allied nobles of the pen and the sword.

In the spring of 1071 the Emperor rejoined the army on the Sangarius and found it demoralized by the calamities that had overtaken it during his captivity. Having dismissed many untrustworthy men and officers, he advanced to the Halys at the head of a host of Macedonians, Bulgarians, Varangians, Germans, Normans, Patzinaks, Cumans, Antiochenes, Cappadocians, and Armenians. Hardly had he crossed the Halys when fighting broke out between his foraging German troops and the inhabitants. It developed into mutiny. Having quelled it, he demoted the Germans from his immediate command to the rearguard. The army passed the scene of the recent defeat of Manuel Comnenus and stopped at Sebastea, where the Emperor reproached the Armenian princes of Sebastea and Tzamandos for their dealings with the Turks. Probably Cappadocian cities and magnates were also seeking accommodation with the Seljuks.

Diogenes continued on to Erzerum, where he ordered every soldier to provide himself with two months' provisions, for wasted Armenia could no longer feed a large army. It was his intention to cross Armenia, invade the Sultan's land, and impose peace on him. With this in mind he sent a strong detachment to seize the forts and occupy the passes north of Lake Van, while he advanced to take Manzikert, an important fortified town, which the Turks had recently captured. Alp Arslan, who was in Azerbaijan, outflanked and cut off the Roman detachments sent to the north of Lake Van. Meanwhile, Diogenes took Manzikert.

From here he advanced to meet the champion of Islam. At nightfall, while the Romans were fortifying their camp, the Seljuks suddenly appeared. All night they swarmed around the camp, filling the air with arrows and shrieks. At dawn the Cumans slipped out of the Roman camp to join their Turkish kinsmen.

Soon after, Diogenes issued forth and arranged his army in battle array. Skirmishing had already begun when suddenly the Caesar John's son Andronicus Ducas, commander of the reserves and agent of the bureaucrats, gave the signal for the rearguard to retreat. The Armenians followed. The betrayal became general. Soon the Emperor was left with only a loyal handful, the last defenders of the Roman Empire. Turks swarmed on every side, their scimitars flashing, their spears plunging. Diogenes was wounded. His pierced steed collapsed. He fell. A score of Seljuks were upon him (August 1071).[7]

The next morning the chained Roman Emperor, servile rings in his ears and in the garb of a simple soldier, was led before the triumphant Sultan and hurled to the ground, while Alp Arslan placed his foot on his neck. Even in this moment of traditional triumph the Sultan apparently did not realize the impotence to which bureaucratic policy had reduced the Empire. Possibly he viewed her as eternal and indestructible. However that might be, he urged the defeated monarch to rise, treated him with the honor due his unsullied valor and august rank, and concluded with him a treaty of peace and friendship. The Empire was to pay a ransom for his release and yearly tribute, cede certain cities, liberate Moslem captives, and furnish troops on request. To seal eternal friendship between the two states Diogenes was to give his daughter in marriage to the Sultan's son, with Armenia including Erzerum as her dowry. A fortnight after the battle of Manzikert, Diogenes, surrounded by his companions and a Seljuk guard of honor, took the road of return. He gazed sadly at the walls of Manzikert, soon to receive a Turkish garrison. At Erzerum, which Theodosius II had built six centuries before, Roman physicians treated his wounded hand.

At length he reached Colonea, now the Roman frontier station. But his trials were not over. The disaster had been exploited by the bureaucrats to restore the plentitude of their power. The Caesar John Ducas had suborned the Varangian guard; forced the Empress to take the veil; declared Diogenes deposed; proclaimed the reign of his young nephew Michael VII; and dispatched an army against Diogenes. Cornered at Adana, Diogenes capitulated on a solemn promise that he would not be harmed. Clad in a black monk's cowl, he rode out of the fortress on a donkey, was poisoned, but survived. Then by order of the Caesar his eyes were struck out in a manner to cause mortal infection. His head became

---

[7] For different versions of the battle see Cahen in *Byzantion*, 9, 2 (1934) and Jenkins, *Byzantium . . . 610–1071* (New York, 1966), pp. 369–373.

unrecognizably swollen. In this pitiable state he was sent to his wife on the Isle of Prote. No word of complaint issued from the last scion of Roman grandeur, and a few days later Eudocia buried his tragic remnant (1072). His dethronement and the consequent lapse of the treaty of friendship with Alp Arslan dealt a mortal blow to a state that was perhaps already irretrievably enfeebled by decades of demilitarization and feudalization. Cappadocia, the homeland of her most glorious emperors and bravest soldiers, lay defenseless at the Turks' feet. With it she lost her life blood.

X

The Comneni

1072–1185

THE tragic end of Diogenes symbolized the death of the powerful military monarchy of Heraclius. While public wealth continued to flow into the pockets of bureaucratic oligarchs, unpaid
mercenaries mutinied; Armenians established an independent state
in Cilicia; Croatia, Serbian Zeta, Trebizond, and probably Paphlagonia severed the imperial bond.

Meanwhile Roman Italy was gradually falling into the hands of
the Norman Robert Guiscard (the Crafty). Consecrated Duke of
Apulia and Calabria and future Duke of Sicily by the Pope in 1059,
he built a fleet and brought Brindisi, Tarento, Oria, and Reggio
under his sway. After a three-year siege he entered Bari in April
1071. For a decade isolated cities held out. Then imperial rule in
Italy lasped. Orthodoxy gradually succumbed to Catholicism and,
except in remote hill hamlets, Greek to Latin or Italian.

In the East it seemed that the bureaucrats' rump-Empire was
nearing her end. In Anatolia Turks raged through trim vineyards;
gentle groves of figs, nuts, olives, cherries, and mulberries; noble
oak and cedar forests; sturdy rhododendrons and mountain azaleas.
They wrecked beautiful, symmetrical, marble Hellenistic cities and
almost converted the Anatolian plateau into a steppe. Stripped of
most of its Greek-speaking inhabitants, inner Anatolia was lost to
the Empire beyond redemption. In Europe Patzinaks ravaged to the
walls of the City, exacting tribute, and the Hungarians recommenced their incursions.

Alp Arslan died in 1073, bequeathing to his son Malik Shah an
empire that stretched from the Oxus to the Mediterranean. Receiv-

ing from the Khalif the jealously guarded title of Commander of the Faithful, Malik increased his domain in all directions from Samarcand to Damascus. In Anatolia the Romans were driven to the seaboard.

The armies of Asia and Europe revolted, the former decorating Nicephorus Botaniates with the supreme symbols, the latter proclaiming Nicephorus Bryennius. Unpaid soldiers and Turkish adventurers flocked to their standards. Bryennius was defeated by young Alexius Comnenus, and Botaniates was acclaimed Emperor. Michael Ducas exchanged the imperial robe for the monastic cassock (1078). But bureaucrats continued to bore from within, Turks of Asia and Europe from without. Rebellion erupted. Bryennius still held Europe. Nicephorus Melissenus revolted in Asia, where his Turkish mercenaries occupied Nice and Bithynia. Against Bryennius Botaniates dispatched his Domestic Alexius Comnenus.

This officer of short but athletic build was now barely thirty, dark, handsome, dashing, gentle, shrewd, eloquent, talented, ambitious, and strong-willed. He was the son of Isaac's late brother John, who had rejected the bureaucrats' conditions for succession to his brother in 1059 despite the remonstrances of his ambitious wife Anna Dalassena. Botaniates created Alexius Nobilissimus and, after he had captured Bryennius and his successor Basilacius (who were blinded), President of the Senate.

Meanwhile, the twice-married Botaniates, though of advanced years, was not insensible to the charms of his predecessor's consort, Maria the Alan. It was said that neither Apelles nor Phidias had created anything more beautiful. Her marriage to Michael VII, now a monk, was dissolved and she was united to the elderly Augustus to the great indignation of the clergy and the pious.

But Maria apparently loved Alexius Comnenus, whom she adopted, thus associating him with the dynastic rights of her little son Constantine, whom Botaniates had excluded from the imperium. In the eyes of the populace the young Domestic thereby became the champion of legitimacy.

Warned by Maria that Botaniates was planning to blind them, Alexius and his brother Isaac fled to the army of Thrace. The Caesar John Ducas and others joined them. Alexius was proclaimed Emperor and assaulted New Rome. A gate was opened. There was street fighting, pillage, and massacre, which Alexius could not

From Spyridon Lampros, Portraits of Byzantine Emperors; *the manuscript miniature is in the Bibliothèque Nationale, Paris*

Nicephorus III Botaniates (reigned 1078–1081) and his wife, Maria

The manuscript miniature is in the Vatican Library

Alexius I (reigned 1081–1118) before Christ enthroned

prevent. The fleet went over to him. Botaniates abdicated and entered a monastery, indicating that his only regret was the future absence of meat from his diet (1081).

ALEXIUS COMNENUS

In the diminished Empire that Alexius inherited the social, economic, and military structure of Heraclius' state system had collapsed. Peasant proprietors and military small-holders had largely fallen prey to great lay, monastic, and ecclesiastical landowners, who had assumed much of the state's authority. Political leadership had passed from emperors to bureaucratic and military nobles. The Emperor no longer represented the Roman people but a class. Moreover, with the decline of independent cultivators and the subversion of the theme system with its national soldiers the army was again largely barbarized. The navy had also shrunken, and the fleets of Italian merchant republics had moved into the vacuum it left.[1]

Alexius had attained the throne of the disintegrating remnants of the Roman Empire only through the support of powerful groups—the army, the clergy, the navy, and the bureaucratic Ducas family. The Ducas faction had supported him because his wife was Irene Ducas, granddaughter of the Caesar John. But discord soon arose between her and the Emperor's mother Anna Dalassena, who urged him to divorce Irene and win over the party that had gathered around Maria and her little son. The Emperor's personal sentiments inclined toward the beautiful Alan. Consequently, he was crowned alone. But to divorce and exclude Irene required the concourse of the Patriarch Cosmas, the representative of the Ducas-bureaucratic faction, who refused either to collaborate or resign. Alexius followed the course of political expediency. Irene was crowned. Maria, her faith, her love, and her hopes dashed, but thankful that her child Constantine Ducas became Co-Emperor, withdrew to the Palace of Mangana.

---

[1] See Ostrogorsky's "Die Perioden der byzantinischen Geschichte" in *Historische Zeitschrift*, 163, 2 (1941). His theory of the complete disappearance of free peasants in the Empire's later centuries is further developed in his *Quelques problèmes d'histoire de la paysannerie byzantine* (Brussels, 1956). But Lemerle believes that there is no evidence to show that independent farmers did not continue to live beside dependent peasants. See his "Esquisse pour une histoire agraire de Byzance" in *Revue historique*, 219 (1958).

Another dilemma confronted Alexius. When his troops had taken the capital they had despoiled some churches. To appease the clergy the Emperor made a public confession and with the imperial family fasted forty days as penance.

The Emperor's brother-in-law Nicephorus Melissenus, who ruled the vestige of Roman Asia (strips along the Aegean, the Marmara, and the Black Sea), had suggested to Alexius before the capture of New Rome that they share the Empire, he keeping Asia, Alexius Europe. He now contented himself with the Caesarate, while the Emperor's brother Isaac became Sebastocrator.

NORMANS

A new danger had suddenly loomed beside bureaucrats and Turks of north and south—the Normans. Guiscard now held all Roman Italy, while his younger brother Roger was conquering Sicily for him. But the Duke of Apulia, Calabria, and Sicily was not content with these domains. He aspired to the crown of Constantinople.

He had succeeded in betrothing his daughter to the infant son of Michael VII and Maria, Constantine. When Botaniates seized the throne in 1078 Guiscard's daughter was put into a convent. Guiscard immediately became the champion of her rights and of the dethroned dynasty. He was about to cross the Adriatic when his Italian cities revolted. Two years later he had crushed the rebellion, found an imposter to pose as Michael Ducas, and suborned Ragusa to lend him ships. His son Bohemond secured the cities on the sheltered bay of Valona. Here Guiscard debarked in May 1081. He seized Corfu, whence he could control the entrance to the Adriatic, and navigated northward to attack Durazzo, the key to the Empire.

Alexius' situation was critical. The treasury was empty, the army reduced, scattered, and demoralized. The Seljuks were at Nice and Cyzicus. Having harassed them with ambushes and thus rendered their incursions less profitable, Alexius made peace with them and enrolled seven thousand of their warriors. He intrigued with Guiscard's Norman vassals and with the German monarch and granted exemption from customs duties throughout the Empire to his nominal vassal Venice for the support of her fleet, although it was in her interest to prevent the Normans from gaining a foothold on the Illyrian coast, whence they could close the Adriatic. The Venetian navy moved against the Norman fleet anchored near Durazzo and won a complete victory.

Thereupon Alexius determined to drive the Normans into the sea. Lest the bureaucratic malcontents seek to seize power during his absence, he placed the City and the Palace under the command of his brother Isaac and entrusted the government to his mother. He then concentrated his army at Salonica. It comprised the Bestiarites (a corps of courtiers), the Varangian Guard, the Excubitors, provincial troops, Alans, Cilician Armenians, Seljuks, Russians, Vardar Turks, Paulicians of Philippopolis, Bulgars, Serbs, Normans, Germans, Franks, and Englishmen (who had commenced to emigrate after the battle of Hastings).

With this motley host Alexius advanced to Durazzo, where George Paleologus was holding out against Guiscard. The Roman Emperor and the Norman Duke soon joined issue (October 1081). The fortunes of war seemed turning in favor of the Romans when suddenly their Serbian and Turkish auxiliaries, won over by Norman gold, withdrew from the field. Confusion ensued. The Emperor and his officers were unable to rally their fleeing soldiers. Nicephorus Paleologus, father of the defender of Durazzo, and Constantine Ducas, brother of Michael VII, fell. The army scattered.

The Emperor and his courtiers separated and fled. The defeated monarch, alone and hungry, wandered over mountains to Ochrida. From here he returned to Salonica to gather another army. But the reduced Empire offered little manpower. The remaining native troops were needed in their garrisons and funds were lacking to engage auxiliaries. Irene, Isaac, Anna Dalassena, and the Comnenian party made great personal sacrifices, but the total amount did not suffice. The demoralized taxpayers refused to contribute. Nor did the Church offer to help. Alexius resolved to seize its funds. Before a synod at Saint Sophia the Sebastocrator Isaac invoked an ancient canon permitting the employment of ecclesiastical wealth to ransom captives and pronounced the confiscation of the Church treasure.

The spring of 1082 found Guiscard master of Durazzo. He took the road to Castoria, which opened its gates to him. Many imperial soldiers, even officers, hoping for the spoil of the decayed Empire, deserted to him. He had reached the pinnacle of power. But Alexius induced his Norman and Lombard vassals to rebel and the German suzerain to besiege his ally, the Pope.

In black rage Guiscard returned to Italy, leaving Bohemond to consolidate and enhance their acquisitions. Alexius advanced against him and was twice routed. After a half century of oppressive bureaucratic rule the Roman military had lost the habit of victory. Bohemond continued the conquest of the western provinces. Ochrida, a foyer of Hellenism and the seat of the Archbishop of Bulgaria, capitulated. Alone the citadel, defended by a valiant Armenian, held out. Many mountain towns went over to the victors. Soon Bohemond extended Norman control to the Vardar and the Vale of Tempe. At the approach of winter in 1082 he invested Larissa, the gateway to Greece.

Meanwhile, with untiring energy Alexius had mustered another army and in the spring of 1083 advanced to relieve Larissa. Three defeats had taught him that his demoralized and conglomerate troops could not beat the Normans in open battle. He resorted to a stratagem. Near Trikala his brother-in-law Melissenus, conspicuously clad in imperial raiment and with a small force, rode within sight of the Norman camp. Thinking that he was the Emperor with the main army, Bohemond charged against him. Melissenus broke into flight. The Normans pursued. Meanwhile Alexius, who had lain hidden with the greater part of his host, seized the Norman camp. Bohemond was obliged to retreat to Castoria. Soon after, he returned to Italy to secure the arrears for his warriors. Alexius simplified his task by winning over part of the Norman army. Thus he recovered Castoria and Corfu, while Durazzo was retaken by the imperial and Venetian navies.

But, having crushed the revolt of his vassals, Guiscard again traversed the Adriatic with 150 ships (1084), defeated a Venetian fleet off Corfu, and retook the island. An epidemic broke out in his army and he died in the summer of 1085. His sons returned to Italy to fight over the succession. The Norman menace had passed.

PATZINAKS

During the Norman war Alexius' Paulician troops (established in the Philippopolis area by Tzimisces) had been insubordinate, and Alexius had mildly punished the leaders. They rebelled, made themselves masters of the upper Maritza Valley, and opened the Balkan passes to the Patzinaks. In the spring of 1086 these fierce tribesmen swept into the fertile Thraco-Macedonian plains and routed and killed the Domestic. The Anatolian army crossed to Europe and maneuvered them into the Balkans. With the return of spring the Patzinaks, who could raid only when fodder was available, reappeared. They were put to flight, and Alexius crossed the Balkans after them, but was discomfited near Silistria and fled back over the mountains. The Patzinaks were now assailed by the Cumans. These Central Asiatic tribesmen were more savage than the Patzinaks, whom they had pressed out of the Black Sea steppe about 1050. No commerce could pass through their territory, and the Russian confederation was cut off from the south.

When the Cumans retired the Patzinaks again crossed the Balkans, drove the weakened Roman forces before them, and approached the Great City. In this dark hour the clergy agitated against the unpopular Basileus because of his seizure of church property. Alexius countered with an apology before a congress of senators, generals, and prelates, invoking the similar conduct of David and Pericles in times of stress. He promised to refund the treasure by an annual levy on tax receipts and devalued the coin, thereby causing further financial confusion.

Again in the field, he was defeated by the Patzinaks, who were gradually isolating the capital. They made an alliance with the Emir of Smyrna, who had constructed a fleet to conquer New Rome. The existence of the Empire seemed at stake. While Constantine Dalassenus occupied the arms of the ambitious emir, Alexius joined forces with the dangerous Cumans on the banks of the Maritza. Lest they unite with the Patzinaks and rub out the Empire, he kept his own camp on the opposite bank.

In April 1091 the combined Roman and Cuman armies met the Patzinak host, just weakened by the desertion of five thousand men. They disrupted the Patzinak lines, overran their camp, massacred men, women, and children, and took a multitude of prisoners. That night, hearing shrieks in the Roman camp, the Cumans peered across the river and beheld a ghastly torchlight scene. The imperial soldiers, their blades dripping blood, were butchering the captives, three generations of Patzinaks. The renegade Patzinaks were settled east of the Vardar and furnished a corps to the Roman army. Only a few Patzinak tribes remained north of the Balkans.

Alexius returned to the Great City in triumph and, taking advantage of his enhanced fame, altered the succession. Childless in 1081, he had accepted Maria's son Constantine Ducas as his colleague and heir. Later he had affianced Constantine to his daughter Anna, born in 1083. Five years afterward Irene had borne him a son, John, but he had not proclaimed him his successor lest he alienate the powerful Ducas faction. Now, however, Constantine was forbidden to wear the purple buskins with the embroidered gold eagles and little John was solemnly crowned Emperor.

Meanwhile, Alexius had been occupied with the Serbian states, Rascia and Zeta, which, supported by Hungary, had not only thrown off imperial suzerainty, but were seeking to extend their control over the Serbs in imperial Dalmatia. After three years of warfare the Serbs yielded hostages and acknowledged nominal Roman overlordship (1094).

SELJUKS

During these bitter years of struggle against Normans, Patzinaks, and Serbs the Seljuk menace did not cease to glower on the Marmara. In the vast Seljuk empire that Malik Shah had inherited in 1072 his brothers, cousins, nephews, and generals formed subsidiary vassal states or ruled provinces as governors. They tended to make themselves independent. Malik could not prevent this centrifugence, for it was barely a century since the Seljuks had emerged from the mass of Eurasian Turks. They had no distinctive traditions, no especial bond of unity, and little conception of statecraft. Nor did the phantom Abbasid Khalifate offer them any unity other than that of Islam.

Following this centrifugal tendency, Suleiman, a kinsman of Malik, in 1077 proudly established himself as Sultan of Rum (the

Empire, specifically Anatolia). He held the greater part of Anatolia and was an ally of the Empire and a rival of Malik Shah. After his death in battle against the Seljuks of Syria in 1086 his emirs made themselves independent despite Malik's intervention. Had not the greater part of Alexius' forces been engaged in Europe at the time, he might have taken advantage of this internecine strife to attempt a measure of reconquest. It is doubtful, however, whether he could have expelled the masses of Turks who had settled in Anatolia after the battle of Manzikert. Though many were nominally Moslem, actually they seemed without deep religious feeling. Simple, tolerant, oblivious to privilege or organized society, they accepted Moslem or Christian dominion with equal equanimity.

An offensive by Alexius, however, would have been nullified by the Emir of Smyrna, Zachas. This half-hellenized Turk, formerly in Roman service, had founded a state of Aegean cities and islands. Aspiring to conquer the Empire, he sought to sever her communications with the West by his control of the Aegean; allied himself with the Patzinaks, who were to isolate New Rome by land; and leagued with the Emir of Nice, who was to advance on Nicomedia, which Alexius had recovered in 1086. Thus New Rome would be starved into submission. In anticipation of his impending greatness Zachas assumed the imperial title. But Dalassenus retook a number of his islands and cities and drove him back to Smyrna (1090). The Patzinaks were annihilated (1091). Malik Shah died (1092). Suleiman's son restored a diminished Sultanate of Rum, established his capital at Nice, became Alexius' ally, invited Zachas to a festival, and murdered him.

Meanwhile, Malik Shah's death was followed by a struggle for the succession. The Seljuk empire slipped into anarchy. Taking advantage of the confusion, Alexius recaptured Apollonia and Cyzicus and was planning the reconquest of Anatolia when abruptly his European provinces were invaded by a looting, murdering multitude—the Crusaders.

CRUSADERS

In the dark days when Patzinaks and Seljuks seemed on the point of annihilating the Empire, Alexius had appealed to the Pope for

mercenary auxiliary troops. He did not ask for a potentially perilous large army nor, with the existence of the Empire at stake, could
he have contemplated a crusade. Nevertheless, in the West a movement developed for a mass assault on Islam and the liberation of the
Holy Land. Thus, from the outset of the crusades there was a basic
divergence of aims between Empire and Crusaders.

Generally Moslems had treated Christian pilgrims to the Holy
Sepulcher well until 1009, when the mad Fatimid Khalif Hakim
destroyed the church over it. After his death in 1021, however, the
customary Moslem tolerance resumed. But the Turks' capture of
Jerusalem and the subsequent Turkish-Fatimid fighting hampered
access to the Sepulcher. In 1095, consequently, Pope Urban II
called on Latin Christians to direct their arms against Islam and free
the Holy Sepulcher, thereby attaining complete atonement. His appeal met with enthusiasm, especially in France. While many sought
only remission of sins, serfs also hoped to escape from bondage,
adventurers to make fortunes, malefactors to evade punishment.

The first to depart were the poor, the People's Crusade of Peter
the Hermit. Five groups marched east. The first two committed
such excesses on the way that the Hungarians annihilated them.
The third began to butcher Jews on the Rhine and was also scattered by the Hungarians. But two hosts, led by Walter the
Penniless and Peter the Hermit, reached New Rome in the summer
of 1096. Although provisioned by Alexius on their journey
through the Empire, they had pillaged.

Alexius received them with expedient forbearance, gave them
food and money, and urged them to await the next contingent of
Crusaders outside the city walls. Since, however, they began to loot
the suburbs, even sacking churches, he sent them over to Civitot, a
fort that he had built on the Marmara's Asiatic shore. They continued to maraud, even torturing Christians. Soon they began to
ravage in the Sultanate of Rum. The Emperor had warned Peter to
avoid contact with the Turks until properly supported, but Peter
lost control of his followers. About twenty-five thousand were
killed. The imperial fleet brought three thousand survivors to New
Rome to await the next Crusaders.

These, who formed the Princes' Crusade, were already streaming
eastward in plundering groups. Their leaders were feudal lords,
many of them ambitious to acquire lands and fortunes. Among

them were Godfrey of Bouillon, who led a contingent from Lorraine and who sought to exterminate the Jews in the German cities through which he passed; Raymond of Toulouse, who led the Crusaders of Provence; and Guiscard's son Bohemond of Tarento, who had lost most of his Italian lands to his brother and led Normans of Italy.

The advent of these armed hosts brought the danger of a sudden attack on the Great City. Though victualed by the Emperor, they pillaged, killed any who resisted, and murdered Orthodox priests. Fearing to jeopardize the City by intervention, Alexius treated them with tact, patience, and generosity and, moving through riot, arson, intrigue, and insolence, obtained from most of their leaders the promise to restore to the Empire any land that had been hers before the Turkish invasion that they might conquer and to acknowledge him as suzerain for any further conquests. His success was probably largely due to their realization that his food, fleet, army, and counsel were indispensable.

In the spring of 1097 the Crusaders commenced crossing to Anatolia. The moment was propitious for an attack on the Seljuks. Not only were the Seljuk states fighting among themselves, they were also warring with the Fatimids. In Anatolia the Seljuks, many of whose emirs accepted only the nominal authority of the Sultan of Rum, had achieved essentially a military occupation and had little control of the nomadic Turkoman herders. Thus, their rule might be terminated by taking their garrison cities.

Alexius directed the Latins' attack on Nice. Though he also crossed to Asia, he did not join them, as they wished, for with his small force he would have been at their mercy. But an imperial contingent accompanied them and an imperial fleet was transported to Lake Ascania. Realizing that they were cut off from Iconium, whither the Sultan had fled, and fearing Latin brutality, the Turks offered to surrender Nice to the Emperor. His Turkish mercenaries consequently penetrated the city, placed on the ramparts the silken Roman standards with Christ's monogram surmounted by a red dragon, and permitted the Crusaders to enter only in small groups. Thus Nice was spared pillage and massacre, but its food, wine, gold, silver, gems, and costly cloth were delivered to the Crusaders.

Later, at Dorylaeum the Crusaders scattered the united forces of the Sultan and his quondam rival, the Emir of Cappadocia, and continued their southward march almost unhindered. Alexius took advantage of the situation to retake Anatolia eastward to the source of the Sangarius and southward almost to the mouth of the Indus.

Yet it seemed impossible to halt the westward flow of Turks. In 1112 they were swarming around Nice, Abydus, Adramyttium, and many other towns, for the free peasants, who might have fought for their lands, had been largely replaced by serfs or slaves on large estates, who sympathized with the invaders. Although past sixty, his health broken by wars and other cares of state, Alexius took the field. After a series of victories he forced the Sultan of Rum (or of Iconium, his capital) to acknowledge his suzerainty. In Asia direct Roman rule now covered the Black Sea littoral, the land west and north of a line reaching from Sinope through Philomelium to Smyrna, and the Aegean seaboard as far as the Amanūs range (1116).

As for the Crusaders, having reached Cappadocian Heraclea in 1097, they separated. Normans and Lorrainers fought over Tarsus, which the Armenian and Roman inhabitants had delivered to them. Baldwin of Boulogne established himself at Edessa (1098). The main body moved on Antioch, which fell through treachery in June 1098. Three days later the relieving army of Kerboga, Atabeg of Mosul, arrived.

Many Crusaders fled from the city, met Alexius, who was marching toward Antioch, and told him that it had certainly fallen. His force was not strong enough to face the powerful Turkish Atabeg and his left flank was already exposed to Turkish attack. He consequently laid waste the countryside to hinder the Moslem advance, sent the inhabitants north, and retreated.

But the despair of the Crusaders in Antioch had yielded to zeal after the discovery of the lance said to have pierced the Savior's Side. They had sallied forth and defeated the Moslems. After months of wrangling over the city, Bohemond of Tarento retained it. The remaining Crusaders and the Latin fleet moved toward Jerusalem, which the Fatimids had recently retaken from the Turks. In June 1099 the warriors of the Cross beheld its glistening white domes. Five weeks later they stormed it and butchered every Jew and Moslem they found. At nightfall they sheathed their bloody swords and, sobbing with devout joy, assembled in and near the Church of the Holy Sepulcher.

Godfrey of Bouillon was elected Defender of the Holy Sepulcher with a domain including also Haifa, Jaffa, Ramleh, and Galilee. After beating off a Fatimid counterattack near Ascalon but without attempting to take Aleppo and Damascus, which would have cut Islam in two, twenty thousand Crusaders began the homeward journey, leaving two thousand men with the Defender. He died less than a year later and was succeeded by his brother Baldwin, Count of Edessa, who was anointed King of Jerusalem on Christmas Day, 1100.

Meanwhile, Alexius was occupied with the arrival of four major groups of Crusaders from Italy, France, Germany, and Scandinavia, who looted, murdered, even assaulted the Great City. He overlooked their misdeeds, exacted their recognition of him as overlord, and dispatched them against the Moslems. But the Latin invasion had united the Anatolian Turks, who annihilated the undisciplined multitudes.

Thus, the new Latin states, which had generally alienated the originally helpful Armenian, Syrian, and Nestorian Christians, were deprived of needed colonists. Nevertheless, like Bohemond with his Normans and Baldwin with his Lorrainers, Raymond of Toulouse with his Provençaux carved out a state for himself. With the aid of the imperial navy and Lebanese Christians he became Count of Tripoli under the Emperor's suzerainty and after a five-year siege took the peninsular town of Tripoli (1109).

Less satisfactory were the Empire's relations with the Antiochene Normans, who seized the recently acquired Roman littoral north of Tripoli and Roman Cilicia. Cilicia was important for the defense of Empire. As mistress of the Amanus range she could beat back invasion from Syria. Consequently, while the Atabeg of Mosul attacked the Principality of Antioch from the east, Roman forces moved into Cilicia. Cilician Romans, Syrians, and Armenians uprose against the Normans, and the Empire recovered the lost province.

Bohemond withdrew to Europe (1104), enlisted the Pope's support for a crusade against the Empire, and traveled through Italy and France, stirring ambitions and promising fiefs. With his Crusaders he crossed the Adriatic, landed at Valona in 1107, and besieged Durazzo. Alexius surrounded the invaders, while the Roman navy severed their communications with Italy. Famine descended on the Latin camp and after several desperate attempts to break through, Bohemond bent his knee as vassal of the Emperor. He acknowledged the cession of Norman Cilicia to the Empire and was permitted to hold Antioch and any future acquisitions in fief, while the Antiochene Patriarch was to be Orthodox and nominated by the Emperor. Bohemond could not bear the presence of the men to whom he had promised wealth and power. Humiliated, he left his army in the hands of his imperial lord, returned to Italy, and soon died. His successor refused to observe the treaty. At New Rome an assembly of senators and generals advised against further hostilities. Alexius concurred. His victory in Europe had not born fruit in Asia.

DOMESTIC POLICY

Returning from the Holy Land, where in 1100 he had helped King Baldwin take Sidon, Sigurd, King of Norway, desired to visit New Rome, the Miklagard of Nordic lore. He waited at the Dardanelles with his sixty vessels for a wind that would permit his silken purple sails to unfurl lengthwise and be viewed by the inhabitants of both Marmaran shores. Meanwhile, in the Great City Alexius was planning to do signal honor to a monarch of the race of his Varangian Guard, the bulwark of his throne. Sigurd was permitted to throw anchor off the Golden Gate, which was opened for his entry, a distinction theretofore accorded only to emperors. Mounted on golden-shod steeds and preceded by musicians and singers, the King and his paladins rode through streets carpeted with purple silk to the Palace of Blachernae, where they were to reside. Here they received from the Emperor presents of silver and red gold, for which Sigurd thanked the Emperor in Greek. There followed lavish festivities, games in the Hippodrome, and a distribution of priceless relics and costly gifts. Invincible in generosity as in battle, Sigurd presented the Emperor with ships of the finest Norwegian manufacture, permitted a large number of his men to join the Varangian Guard, and departed with warm friendship and happy memories.

In order to obtain more native troops, which the vestigial theme system supplied in only small numbers, Alexius imposed on those who held government estates and the right to collect their taxes the duty of supplying military contingents. He thus laid a feudal foundation for the revival of the Empire's military strength. This system, whereby magnates and others assumed the central government's fiscal and other authority, inevitably enfeebled the state.[2] Whether he had the power or the means to do otherwise is a moot question. He also raised money to enroll Russians, Scandinavians, Turks, Bulgars, Germans, Franks, and Englishmen and reconstituted the almost vanished cavalry, buying horses even in Syria.

For the reconstruction of army and navy, continual wars, and the Crusaders Alexius constantly needed funds. Yet some of the wealthiest provinces were lost, while others were ruined and depopulated. Moreover, bureaucratic rule had drained the treasury and created privileges and exemptions, which Church, aristocracy, and pious institutions continued to demand. Alexius' suppression of some of these prerogatives led many of the privileged to seek to dethrone him. Their conspiracies generally centered on the scions of former rulers or pretenders, such as Maria, Diogenes, Sclerus, Basilacius, the Bagratids, even the last Cretan emir.

The Emperor apparently sought to make the wealthy pay their share of the taxes and to spare the poor from extortion by appointing honest officials. But he did not reform the system whereby the collection of many of the taxes went to the highest bidder, who often offered twice the amount due. With authority to assess the taxes publicans generally extorted as much as possible, especially from the poor and defenseless.

In his efforts to spread the tax burden the Vicar of God distinguished between monasteries that abided by monastic principles and those that did not. Thus, he exempted Mount Athos from taxation and ceded to Christodulus the island of Patmos with extensive tax immunity. Moreover, he restricted the Patriarch's authority over monasteries and allowed bishops to visit them only if invited. As for those monasteries that did not observe the rules, he obliged them to contribute to the tax burden. The tendency of monasteries to acquire adjacent properties continued to be a problem. Sometimes the neighbor whose land a monastery coveted would be showered with

---

[2] The controversial subject of the feudalization of the Empire is exhaustively treated by Ostrogorsky, *Pour l'histoire de la féodalité byzantine* (Brussels, 1954).

gifts, invited to the monastery, offered a bath, and regaled with wines and culinary masterpieces. He would be told of the physical and spiritual benefits of the monastic life and of converse with the other world. Once he had become a novice and the monastery was in possession of his property, he might be informed that he was not fit for monastic life and dropped.

Upon his accession Alexius had his partisans to reward. The treasury being empty, he had transferred to them monasteries or other properties whose income they were to receive for life. This practice, already in existence by the end of the tenth century and which had flourished during the decades of bureaucratic rule, hampered reform. Often the holders of such grants established themselves near their pious institutions, ate meat, and engaged in other activities forbidden to nuns or monks. Frequently the superior's authority was undermined when the monks curried the favor of the new master, who held the purse strings and might provide greater material comfort. Nevertheless, Alexius tended to reform both the regular and secular clergy, the latter notably by the institution of clerical examinations.

He was equally concerned to suppress the Bogomils in the Balkan Peninsula. These dualistic sectaries were the spiritual descendants of those Paulicians who had been transported from the Taurus to Thrace in the eighth and tenth centuries. They took their name from Bogomil, who in the tenth century carried Paulician doctrines to the Bulgars, whence they spread as far west as the Pyrenees. Alexius failed to convert their leader Basil, who was consequently burned in the Hippodrome.

Moreover, when John Italus, a pupil of Psellus and the most cultivated mind of the period, expressed the belief that it was possible to have philosophical opinions independent of theology, a council condemned his teachings. Freedom of thought was restricted by the authority of the Scriptures and the Church Fathers.

The last days of the monarch who had saved and reunited the disintegrating remnants of the Empire, re-created army and navy, repulsed Normans, Patzinaks, and Seljuks, avoided major conflict with the Crusaders, regained part of Anatolia, and restored Roman rule in the Balkan Peninsula, were not peaceful.

His imperious mother Anna Dalassena had been allowed to share sovereign power with him for a period, but noticing his declining

patience, she withdrew to a convent, where she died, probably in
1105.

Her departure may have been due to the growing influence of
Alexius' wife Irene Ducas. Alexius and Irene had four girls and
three boys. The oldest child, Anna, her mother's favorite, had been
betrothed to the son of Michael VII, the little Co-Emperor Constantine, who, however, died before the marriage. In 1097 she married Nicephorus Bryennius. Meanwhile, the birth of her brother
John in 1088 and his elevation to the imperium four years later had
ended her prospects of becoming Empress. To gain the throne for
her, her mother tried to induce Alexius to degrade John and name
Bryennius Co-Emperor. Failing in this, Irene formed a faction aim-
ing at the elevation of Bryennius and Anna, despite Bryennius' disapproval. Alexius was aware of his wife's machinations and during
his last years always took her with him when he left the capital.

When in 1118 he fell ill Irene redoubled her efforts to alter the
succession. In August Alexius realized that death was at hand and
had himself transported to the Palace of Mangana. Taking advantage of his wife's momentary absence, he gave John his ring and
commanded him to assume supreme power. John bade his dying
father farewell, was acclaimed by his partisans, and galloped with
them to Saint Sophia, where he was crowned by the Patriarch.
After the ceremony he went to the Sacred Palace, where the Varangians admitted him on seeing the imperial ring.

Meanwhile, at Mangana, Irene was plaguing her expiring husband to elevate Bryennius. Suddenly a messenger reported that
their son had been crowned and had occupied the Sacred Palace.
Thinking that he had acted on his own initiative, Irene urged her
moribund spouse to create Bryennius Emperor. Alexius smiled and
raised his hands to thank God. Realizing that she had been outwitted, the Empress discharged a torrent of invective to accompany
her husband into the other world.

JOHN II

John II was thirty, short, homely, with very dark eyes, beard,
and complexion. He was mild, ascetic, devout, conscientious, courageous, a gifted statesman and general. His wife, Irene, the daugh-

From Spyridon Lampros, Portraits of Byzantine Emperors; *the enamel is in Saint Mark's, Venice*

Mosaic in Saint Sophia, Istanbul, of John II Comnenus (reigned 1118–1143) with the usual offering and his wife with the customary attestation of orthodoxy. Between them the Christ Child seems almost detached from the Virgin

ter of the sainted Hungarian King Ladislaus I, was equally modest, austere, pious, and charitable and became the mother of four boys and four girls.

Despite John's amiable qualities, his mother and sister plotted his downfall. Assassins failed to accomplish their purpose only because Bryennius refused to act, and Irene and Anna withdrew to a convent. In the conventual shadows Anna completed the history of her father's reign that her husband, who died in 1136, had begun—the *Alexiad*, an epic in prose.

Anna had studied rhetoric, philosophy, history, philology, geography, mythology, theology, medicine, and the natural sciences and was versed in the works of the great poets, historians, and philosophers of classical antiquity. She wrote the *Alexiad* in Attic Greek. This use of an antique language not entirely dead, yet not spontaneous, created an artificial medium, which was, however, employed by broadly educated persons with a profound knowledge of Hellenic history, mythology, and literature.

Irene, consort of Alexius I (reigned 1081–1118)

Spoken Greek had developed a literature of its own, notably epic poems, which were ardent, living pictures celebrating the feats of local heroes. Like the Homeric poems, the most famous of these local epics became national. Such were the Belisarius-Poems and the epic of Digenis Akritas, borderer of the peaceless Cappadocian frontier, whose feats are sung to this day.

EUROPE

Unlike his father, John did not have to fight to preserve imperial Europe. The Patzinaks were weakened. The Cumans were fighting the Russians and made only occasional incursions. The Russians, their realm divided by the law of equal succession and cut off from the Black Sea by the Cumans, had ceased to be formidable since the mid-eleventh century. Serbs and Normans were involved in feudal and dynastic strife. The Hungarians were seeking an outlet to the Adriatic. Germany was in the throes of civil war. The crusading spirit had lapsed.

Patzinaks

The Patzinaks, who had been almost wiped out in 1091, had with a new generation regained some strength. In 1122 they crossed the Danube and reached the southern slopes of the Balkans. The Emperor drove them into their wagon camp and, though wounded, dismounted and led his English guards against them. Protected by their long shields, they hacked their way into the Patzinak camp with their battle-axes and inflicted a crushing defeat on the barbarians. Many prisoners were taken. Some were sold. Others were given military fiefs within the Empire. The Patzinak peril was at an end.

Serbs

The vassal Serbs had again slipped into feudal anarchy. While their forbidding mountains and impassable forests fostered feudalism, they also prevented the Romans from subjecting them as they had the Bulgars. Nevertheless, taking advantage of Serbian chaos,

John intervened to strengthen Roman suzerainty over Zeta. Rascia, however, remained practically independent until about 1140 it fell under Hungarian influence.

Hungarians

For decades after they had settled in the fertile plains of the Theiss and Danube (884–895) the Hungarians had raided central and western Europe until, weakened by successive defeats by German rulers, they ceased marauding (about 970). Their Prince Stephen received from the Pope the title of Apostolic King in 1000, began the forcible conversion of his people to Christianity, and transformed the wild steppe tribes into a feudal kingdom. Avoiding the Crusade, the Hungarian King annexed Croatia in 1102. Ten years later he extended his suzerainty over the autonomous imperial cities of Dalmatia, Ragusa, Split, Trau, and Zara, since 1001 under Venetian supervision. After John had refused to expel his blinded brother the Hungarians invaded the Empire but were repulsed (1127–1129).

Venetia

The descendants of the modest lagoon-fishermen of the sixth century were the most prosperous merchants in the Occident, the intermediaries between East and West. As a result of a powerful navy, intimate relations with the Empire, and the unscrupulous pursuit of commercial supremacy, the silt and sand islets had become the Queen of the Adriatic. In 1000 the Doge crushed the Slavic pirates on the eastern shore of the Adriatic and was created Duke of Dalmatia by Basil II. In 1081 the Venetian navy wiped out the Norman fleet. As reward Venetian merchants received from Alexius the privilege of trading in the Empire without paying duties. This led to a stupendous development of Venetian commerce. Two decades later Venice extracted similar privileges from the newly founded Latin states in the Levant. As Venetian traders became merchant princes they tended to become pompous and arrogant. The large Venetian colony at New Rome became unpopular. For this reason and because he no longer needed the Venetian fleet to combat the weakened Normans John did not renew the trade treaty with Venice. It was a heavy blow to Venetian prosperity, and the Republic of Saint Mark ravaged imperial islands four years (1122–1126). The imperial fleet was too weak to cope with the Venetian navy, and John purchased peace by restoring Venetian commercial privileges.

Normans

In 1130 the Norman Count Roger II of Sicily, who had annexed the Norman possessions in southern Italy, was crowned King of Sicily. His assumption of the regal title incensed New Rome, for it seemed to confirm the loss of imperial Italy. Soon, however, the King of Sicily gave cause for greater concern. He claimed the Latin states in the Levant, notably Antioch. Were he to establish Norman power there, the Empire might be subjected to simultaneous Norman attacks from west and south. To prevent that the Basileus induced Pisa to exchange Norman for Roman alliance and subsidized a German invasion of Apulia (1137). Thus, John warded off the Norman peril.

ASIA

The Seljuk Sultan of Rum had little connection with the vast but centrifugal empire that Toghril and Alp Arslan had erected. While the Great Seljuk Sultan ruled beside the Abbasid Khalif, the assortment of potentates, sects, and races between Transoxiana and Yemen only occasionally and partially acknowledged his overlordship. In the twelfth century his actual domain included only Bagdad and Persia. He still fought futile, fratricidal wars to preserve the Seljuk empire, but for practical purposes it had ceased to exist. Thus, the Crusaders were able to defeat local Turkish rulers without having to face the full force of the Abbasid Khalifate. Nor did the Abbasid Khalif enjoy the authority or prestige to rally Asiatic Islam to a holy war against the Crusaders, who took advantage of the hatred between Arabs and Turks to carve out states.

The Seljuks tended to imbibe the culture of the peoples on whom they imposed their rule. Thus, the Seljuks of Anatolia, who retained the Iranian speech that their ancestors had acquired, adopted

many Greek customs. Having recovered from the defeat of Dorylaeum, the Sultan of Rum united with his rival, the Danishmend
Emir of Cappadocia, to crush later Crusaders. Thereby, he prevented the new Latin states from populating Syria and Palestine
with Latins. Possibly oblivious to the historical significance of this
achievement, he sought to take Mosul and Mesopotamia but lost his
life in the attempt (1107). Thereafter the Seljuks of Rum confined
their ambitions to Anatolia. As a result, their state took root, thus
constituting a permanent peril for the Empire.

With a view of the ultimate reconquest of Turkish Anatolia, John
drove the Turkish shepherds from the Meander Valley and adjacent areas in order to open the inland roads to Attalia and the
southern coast (1119–1120). Obliged to carry his arms to Europe,
he remained on the defensive in Asia, while the Sultan of Rum and
the Emir of Cappadocia fought each other. The Emir gained the
upper hand and soon attacked the Empire, capturing some Paphlagonian cities.

John took the field in 1130 but was interrupted by a conspiracy
of his brother, the Sebastocrator Isaac. Upon the failure of the
plot Isaac fled to the Danishmends; later to the Duke of Trebizond,
who had established a transient independence (1126–1140); and to
other Anatolian and Syrian courts in an effort to form a coalition
against John. Despite the agitations of Isaac's partisans in New
Rome, John carried on the war and by 1135 had moved the Roman
frontier southward and eastward.

Having prepared the road to reconquest, John in 1137 led an
army including Turks from reconquered Paphlagonian regions
against Cilicia, a large part of which had since 1071 been an independent Armenian state known as Lesser Armenia and ruled by the
Rupenid family. Many Armenian and Latin barons acknowledged
John as their suzerain and he took Tarsus, Adana, Mopsuestia, and
Anazarbus. The Rupenid fled and was later captured.

The Emperor aimed to extend imperial authority over the Armenians from the Taurus to beyond the Euphrates, now mostly ruled
by the Latin Count of Edessa. The Armenians were good fighters
and would form a powerful wedge in the southern flank of the
Anatolian Seljuks. First, however, John wished to enforce the
treaty of 1108, by which Bohemond of Antioch had become an
imperial liegeman. In August 1137, consequently, he laid siege to

Antioch. The Prince of Antioch, Raymond of Poitiers, acknowledged him his suzerain and agreed to install an Orthodox Patriarch.

In the spring of 1138 John commanded his Latin vassals to march
with him against the Atabeg of Mosul. He intended to capture
Aleppo, Shaizar, Hama, and Emesa and exchange them for Antioch.
He failed to surprise Aleppo, however, and turned to Shaizar, which
the imperial artillery began to batter down.

During the siege he reorganized the Roman army. Since the collapse of the thematic system the army consisted mostly of foreigners and there were no longer enough Romans to absorb them. John
consequently abandoned the effort to amalgamate the races and
grouped together men of the same speech and fighting habits.

Suddenly after occupying part of Shaizar the Basileus accepted a
large indemnity and an annual tribute from the besieged emir and
withdrew, possibly because his Latin vassals, the Prince of Antioch
and the Count of Edessa, had not collaborated but had spent their
time playing dice.

John made a resplendent entry into Antioch, installed himself in
the palace, and demanded possession of the citadel. The Latins
dared not refuse but instigated rioters, who butchered every Roman they found and threatened the Emperor's life. Outwitted, he
departed and led his army north. Despite this check, the reconquest
of Cilicia, the establishment of an Orthodox Patriarch at Antioch,
and the renewed luster of Roman arms enhanced the Emperor's
prestige and spelled failure for the plans of his brother Isaac, who
had been in the Holy Land intriguing. Deserted by his partisans, he
and his son became reconciled to John.

Meanwhile, the Danishmend Emirate of Cappadocia had recovered from its defeats and successional strife and invaded the Empire
(1138). John expelled the invaders and in the spring of 1139 advanced to Caesarea, the Danishmend capital, but having lost many
of his beasts of battle and burden and siege implements on the way,
made a difficult retreat, reaching New Rome in January 1141. Soon
after, the Danishmends again slipped into successional discord.
Isaac's son had deserted to the Turks, accepted Islam, and married a
daughter of the Sultan of Rum.

In the interim Antioch, threatened by the Atabeg of Mosul, implored John's aid. He set out in 1142. When he reached Attalia his
eldest son and colleague Alexius died. John's sons Andronicus and

Isaac accompanied the body homeward, but before they had reached the Great City Andronicus had also died. The bereaved monarch moved rapidly on Antioch, intending to restore imperial authority as far as the Euphrates and hinder communication between the Moslems of Anatolia and those of Syria. He summoned his unreliable Latin vassal to deliver Antioch to him. The Prince refused. John went into winter quarters in Cilicia, intending to besiege Antioch in the spring.

Soon after, while hunting wild boar he was scratched by a poisoned arrow. When it became apparent that he was doomed, he discussed the succession with the Grand Domestic Axuch, originally a Moslem captured at Nice in 1097 and sent to serve as page in the Sacred Palace. John and the young captive had become friends and been educated together. Axuch felt that John's elder son Isaac, who was in New Rome, was more fitted to succeed to the throne, but the Emperor favored his younger son Manuel, who was with him. Asserting that his choice had been prompted by conviction rather than affection, John II invested Manuel with the imperial crown and robe and invited the army to acclaim their new Emperor. Then, while a monk murmured prayers, John the Good died (April 1143).

MANUEL I

Manuel's first thoughts were for the safety of his throne. In New Rome his brother held the Sacred Palace and the treasury, while in Pontic Heraclea his ambitious uncle Isaac dwelt in exile. Before they knew of John's death Axuch arrested them and proclaimed Manuel's accession in the capital. When the young Emperor, who led the army northward, reached New Rome some months later he found that Axuch's regency had functioned so smoothly that he could release the two Isaacs.

Manuel was about twenty, tall, bearded, exceptionally dark, with soft eyes, and a charming manner. He was proud of his physical prowess and inclined to heroic deeds, sometimes to the point of neglecting his duties as a general. He admired the Latins, whom he favored in the army and the administration. The imperial majesty seems to have meant less to him than an opportunity to impress the

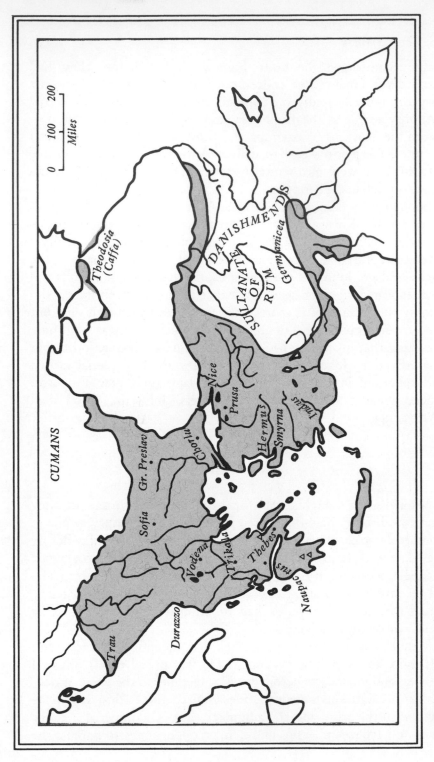

The Empire About 1180

fair sex with a brilliant exploit. Indeed, unlike his austere father, Manuel did not curb his romantic inclinations. He was soon imitated by his courtiers. Nor did the imperial dignity restrain him when a military wagon or camp constructions needed a helping hand. His interests ranged over theology, philosophy, geography, tactics, medicine, the natural sciences, and, above all, astrology. For the benefit of churchmen who disapproved of astrology he wrote a treatise designed to prove that it was permitted by Scripture.

In 1142 he had been betrothed to Bertha of Sulzbach, sister-in-law of the German ruler Conrad III, an ally against the menacing Normans. Bertha changed her name to Irene on entering the Orthodox Church and was married to Manuel in January 1146. The Empress was a devout, handsome, and charitable woman, apparently unloved by her husband. Chroniclers refer to her stiffness, lack of elegance, and failure to use cosmetics. She led a secluded life, devoting herself chiefly to charity and the education of their two daughters.

The Comneni were linked by marriage to the Empire's most powerful families, such as the Angeli, Axuchs, Cantacuzenes, Contostephani, Ducae, Paleologi, and Vatatzes. Manuel gave kinsmen the important military and administrative posts. While thereby preventing the renascence of the bureaucratic oligarchy, it made birth rather than worth the criterion for office. Thus, the army was led by courtiers more anxious for glory than solid military gains, while the finances, restored by Alexius and John II, fell into the hands of spendthrifts. Moreover, Manuel expanded the practice of granting land or other property to individuals, who in return for its income were obliged to render military or other service. The ownership of the properties was not involved, but the landowners and tenants on the grant passed in some measure from the control of the central government to that of the grantee, paying him their taxes, subject to his dispensation of justice, and looking to him for protection.

SECOND CRUSADE

When after his father's death Manuel moved north with his army, the Prince of Antioch permitted himself a few impertinent

Eleventh-century Byzantine marble relief of the Virgin

messages and invaded Cilicia. Manuel sent land and naval forces, which defeated the Latins and ravaged the Antiochene seaboard and countryside. Taking advantage of the situation, Zengi, Atabeg of Mosul, seized Edessa (1144). Menaced by the Turks, the Prince of Antioch hastened to New Rome, craved forgiveness at the tomb of John II, and was at length permitted to prostrate himself at Manuel's feet and renew his oath of fealty (1145).

But Manuel was also occupied with Turks and gave him little aid. The Danishmend realm had fallen into three parts (Caesarea, Sebastea, and Melitene) and the revived Sultanate of Rum was expanding against the Danishmends and the Empire. The Sultan frequently devastated Roman territory, carried off the inhabitants or drove them behind city walls, and threatened to cut the road to Cilicia. Manuel concluded an alliance with the Sebastean Danishmend, advanced to the Sultan's capital, Iconium, profaned an adjacent Moslem cemetery, and withdrew (1146). Of greater value were the construction and restoration of a line of forts to guard the invasion routes. Informed of the impending mutually menacing Second Crusade, Emperor and Sultan made peace, the Sultan returning the land that he had taken.

The fall of Edessa in 1144 and the jeopardy of the three remaining Latin states in the Levant shocked the West. At first the disunited Moslems had not been dangerous, and soon after the establishment of the Kingdom of Jerusalem in 1100 Venice, Pisa, and Genoa had, in exchange for trade concessions and a share of the booty of captured towns, aided it to stretch its borders from Beirut to the Gulf of Akaba. In 1127, however, Zengi became Atabeg of Mosul and consolidated and extended his dominion. The King of Jerusalem found that his conglomerate force of twenty-five thousand barons, knights of religious orders, Maronites, Armenians, and Moslems could not hold off the formidable Turkish Atabeg. Indeed, the kingdom's military strength lay less in its army than in the powerful fortresses of its barons and military orders, whose obedience to the king was, however, not always certain. Realizing his inability to stem Zengi's rising power, the King of Jerusalem in 1133 allied himself to the equally menaced Atabeg of Damascus.

This alliance was of inestimable value to the Latin states, which were weak because of their feudal and financial structure, because they formed only a ruling class over a hostile Moslem mass, and because they seemed unable to adapt themselves to the environment. Indeed, Latin warriors still made war in full armor despite the burning sun and sand. Nor could the small influx of fresh Crusaders check a steady decline, for they were often adventurers who aroused the mistrust of the local Latins or disturbed their commercial intercourse with the Moslems by greed or fervor. Thus, the loss of Edessa to Zengi seemed to foreshadow the extinction of the Latin states in the Levant. Two years later, however, Zengi was assassinated and his state split asunder.

But the fall of Edessa had already had its effect in the West. On Christmas Day of 1145 King Louis VII of France announced to his vassals that he was taking the Cross. Only the eloquence of Saint Bernard of Clairvaux overcame their repugnance to the long journey. He also persuaded the German ruler Conrad III to join the Crusade.

The entry of this monarch into the ranks of the Crusaders was a blow to New Rome, for since the reign of Alexius the German alliance had served to check the hostile Normans. Now, however, the Empire would confront the simultaneous peril of Crusaders and Normans.

While North German Crusaders attacked the pagan Slavs east of the Elbe and Dutch and English Crusaders took Lisbon from the Moslems, German Crusaders moved pillaging eastward. They were with difficulty restrained by Roman forces and supplied from the imperial commissary. Manuel urged Conrad to cross the Dardanelles to Asia and intimated that he would consider it a hostile act for the Germans to march on New Rome. Ignoring the warning, Conrad and his army arrived before the City in 1147, refused to hold future conquests in fief from the Emperor, and after much marauding and some fighting against Roman forces finally crossed to Asia. Advancing on Iconium, the unwieldy host soon suffered from thirst, hunger, and harassment. During a seven-day retreat the discouraged, horseless, starving mass was an open target for Turkish horse archers and suffered heavy losses before reaching Nice.

Meanwhile, Louis VII and his Crusaders were on the way, ravaging what the Germans had spared. The French king also refused to cross the Dardanelles to Asia and was received by the Emperor with every mark of honor. Manuel's prime concern, however, was to move the Crusaders to Anatolia, for many were more anxious to seize New Rome than to combat Moslems. Moreover, the Normans had already invaded Greece. This assault on the Christian Empire diverted her from aiding the Crusaders and probably doomed whatever prospects of success the Crusade had.

However that might be, the rumor of a German victory over the Turks, possibly bruited by the Roman government, animated the French to cross to Asia. Joining forces with Conrad and the debris of his host, Louis moved toward the Holy Land through imperial territory, inflicting greater punishment on Christians than on Moslems. The outraged natives leagued with Turks and often ambushed Crusaders in the mountains north of Attalia. At that city Louis and his barons chartered a fleet and abandoned the mass of the Crusaders, many of whom left their bones to molder in dim valleys in their efforts to reach the Holy Land.

In the interim Conrad had fallen ill and retired to New Rome, where apparently Manuel's medical skill restored him to health. Taking ship, he joined the kings of France and Jerusalem in the Holy Land and attacked, not the inimical Zengid Atabeg of Aleppo, but the recent ally, the Atabeg of Damascus. The effort failed (July 1148), and Louis and Conrad departed. The Second Crusade was over. The failure of an enterprise led by the two mightiest monarchs of the West momentarily discredited crusades, relieved Manuel of the nightmare of further mass invasions, deprived the Latin states of the colonists they needed, and enhanced the Empire's influence over them.

NORMANS AGAIN

While Manuel had been trying to avert hostilities with the Crusaders and channel their activities to the benefit of the Empire, he faced a Norman invasion. Although the King of Sicily, Roger II, had not succeeded in directing the Crusade against New Rome, the German monarch's participation in it enabled him to attack the Empire without incurring a German countermove. Consequently, as soon as the Crusaders were on their way, the Normans struck at the Pindic Peninsula. They seized Corfu, plundered Thebes and Corinth, and carried off to Palermo the most skillful silk weavers.

Determined to drive them from Corfu and to invade Apulia, Manuel extended Venice's commercial privileges to Rhodes and Cyprus in return for the use of her navy and in 1148 assembled his army under the Grand Domestic John Axuch and his fleet under his brother-in-law, the Grand Duke Stephen Contostephanus. Before the expedition had reached Corfu, however, Manuel recalled part of it to punish invading Cumans. Later, at New Rome he spent Christmas with Conrad III, who was returning from the ill-fated Crusade. The two monarchs agreed to attack the Normans in the spring. Manuel was to regain Apulia and Calabria as a dowry for his German wife.

Meanwhile, Romans and Venetians had debarked on Corfu and besieged the town. After a riot between Roman and Venetian soldiers, to quell which Axuch sent his guard, the Venetians withdrew to an adjacent island, burned Roman vessels, seized the imperial galley, draped that part of it reserved for the Emperor in purple, crowned a Negro, and rendered him imperial honors. Manuel overlooked the Venetian actions, took personal command of the reunited fleets, entered the town of Corfu in the summer of 1149, and was thus free to invade Italy.

But Roger II had not been inactive. He had encouraged Serbian Rascia to revolt and the Hungarians to attack the Empire. Manuel marched north to deal with them, leaving Axuch to invade Italy. But the Venetians were as loath to have the Romans on the western side of the Adriatic as they were to have the Normans on the eastern shore. They preferred to have the mouth of the Adriatic under divided sovereignty and delayed the embarkation long enough for the autumnal storms to destroy part of the fleet and prevent passage.

Roger also subsidized insurrection against Conrad in Germany and endeavored to incite a Latin crusade against the Orthodox Empire. The ground was well prepared for such an attack, since the survivors of the Second Crusade attributed their disasters to Manuel, much as the men of the First Crusade had blamed Alexius for their great losses rather than their own incompetence. The French king supported the Norman plan and sent Bernard of Clairvaux to rally Conrad, who, however, was not disposed to join an expedition designed to enhance Norman power. Moreover, the Pope, who for the moment feared Norman more than German puissance, sided with Conrad. Thus, the idea of a Latin crusade against Manuel was abandoned. On the other hand, the death of Conrad in 1152 transformed the Roman-German alliance against the King of Sicily into rivalry, for his successor opposed a Roman restoration in Italy.

Nevertheless, Manuel was determined to regain Roman Italy, which Norman oppression had rendered ripe for revolt. Consequently, Michael Paleologus with an army of mainly Italian mercenaries and exiled or discontented Norman barons invaded Norman Italy in 1155 and in a few months had restored imperial rule from Ancona to Tarento. The following year, however, the new King of Sicily, William, defeated the Romans at Brindisi. The imperial restoration collapsed and in 1158 a peace was concluded leaving the Empire a few coastal towns.

Yet, like Justinian I, Manuel drained the treasury and weakened the Empire in Asia to restore imperial authority in the West. He had friendly relations with the Papacy and wrote of his desire to restore political and religious unity. He subsidized North Italian cities in their successful struggle against the German sovereign Frederick Barbarossa. He also aided Henry the Lion, Barbarossa's rival in Germany. Possibly these interventions prevented the formation of a crusade against the Empire.

MERCHANT REPUBLICS

The relationship between the Empire and the merchant republics, Venice, Genoa, and Pisa, was such as to permit the Emperor to influence their policies by his hold on their commerce and citizens. They had large colonies in Constantinople and other imperial cities, where they shared the tax burden with the natives and were liable for defensive military service. When one of these republics veered toward alliance with the Empire's enemies its commerce and colonies suffered. Thus, when in 1162 Genoa made a treaty with Barbarossa, Pisans and Venetians sacked her quarters in New Rome with the connivance of the imperial authorities.

As for Venice, she lent the Empire her navy and the Empire made trade concessions that raised Venetian prosperity to unprecedented heights. Mistress of the Adriatic and exercising sovereignty in Dalmatia, Venice controlled the wine and wheat markets of Apulia, which she needed for her own use. The imperial ports of the Peloponnese, the Aegean, and the Marmara were at her disposal. Her ships navigated the Black Sea and penetrated the Sea of Azov to the mouth of the Don, where they collected the products of the steppes and the East. Throughout the Levant Moslem and Christian cities were open to Venice, who more and more replaced the Empire as the intermediary between Asia and Europe. Manuel's reoccupation of Ancona and Dalmatia aroused Venice's fears lest her supremacy in the Adriatic be challenged. For a time common opposition to Barbarossa prevented a breach, but in 1171 Manuel arrested Venetians on imperial soil and confiscated their enormous wealth. In retaliation the Republic of Saint Mark ravaged imperial coastal cities.

Lacking Venice's protected position, it was not until the eleventh century that Pisa and Genoa gained communal independence and not until the First Crusade that they spread their mercantile activities to the eastern Mediterranean, for the Crusaders needed the fleets of Italian merchant cities to take and hold powerful cities. Indeed, so vital was the assistance of the merchant cities to the Crusaders' states that they were granted special extraterritorial space in every Levantine Latin city. Although these distant colonies tended to become independent, it was only the authority of the mother republic that suffered, not the commerce of her citizens. While their ships and those of other Italian and western Mediterranean cities transported pilgrims and Western products to the Levantine Latins, their homeward cargos included dyes, silks, spices, pearls, perfumes, ivory, gold brocades, and other products of the Near and Far East and Africa, generally channeled through Bagdad, Damascus, and Alexandria.

SERBS AND HUNGARIANS

Manuel's reign was troubled by Serbian revolts. The mountainous country prevented the deployment of large forces and facilitated ambush, thus rendering complete conquest impracticable. Nevertheless, a campaign in the leafless autumn generally sufficed to unseat a rebellious yupan or constrain him to fulfill his imperial obligations—a contingent of two thousand men for European wars and five hundred for Asiatic campaigns.

Hungary supported Serbian revolts because with her Slovaks and Slovenes and her suzerainty over Croatian and Dalmatian Slavs, she sought to supplant the Empire as protectress of the Slavs. Moreover, the Roman-German alliance had led to a Norman-Hungarian entente. In 1151 Manuel crossed the Save, ravaged the Hungarian countryside, and led off a host of captives. The Hungarian king asked for peace, but the following year Conrad's death freed him from the dread of a simultaneous Roman-German attack. Years of intermittent fighting and diplomatic efforts followed. Finally, in 1167 near the Save, fifteen thousand Germans and Hungarians faced the conglomerate Roman army under the Emperor's nephew Andronicus Contostephanus, whom Manuel had forbidden to engage in battle because the stars were not favorable. Contostephanus thought better of it and the opposing forces collided. At first it seemed as if the compact German-Hungarian mass must carry the day, but when Contostephanus threw in his reserves, the enemy formation broke.

This victory terminated the Hungarian wars and assured imperial control of Bosnia, Dalmatia, a strip of Croatia, and Sirmium. The lord of these territories, Bela, heir to the Hungarian throne, resided at New Rome. Apparently intending to unite Hungary to the Empire, Manuel gave him the name Alexius, the title of Despot (theretofore used only by emperors), and the affianced hand of his daughter Maria and declared him joint heir to the imperium despite the indignation of the court. When a son was born to Manuel, however, he dissolved the betrothal and demoted Bela-Alexius to Caesar. In 1172 Bela-Alexius ascended the Hungarian throne and left the Empire in possession of Dalmatia.

THE ARMY

The military labors of Alexius and John II had borne fruit and the Roman army had regained proficiency. It was maintained by rigid discipline. Punishments such as thrashing, nose-slitting, and blinding were still used. Even officers were subject to prison, corporal punishment, or a ride seated backward on an ass and dressed as a woman.

The chief problem was recruitment. To check the diminution of the number of free natives, Manuel liberated at public expense all persons born free but fallen into servitude. Moreover, following a millenary policy, he established prisoners of war in military colonies and invited foreign peoples to settle in the Empire. Whether native troops still exceeded foreigners is unknown. Even if they did not, the situation would not have been as grave as in the fourth and fifth centuries when the foreigners had been chiefly Germans, whereas now there were so many different nationalities that concerted action was unlikely.

The Roman army was divided into light and heavy infantry and light and heavy cavalry. The light infantryman was an archer, while the heavy infantryman carried a sword, a shield, and and a battle-axe and was used for sieges, mountain fighting, and to storm entrenchments. In the cavalry Arabian and Hungarian horses were preferred. The light cavalry, mostly Turks and Patzinaks, was armed with bows and swords and was employed for scouting or skirmishing. The heavy cavalryman wore a coat of mail, in clear weather often covered with a tunic, and carried a sword, a lance, and a mace.

THEOLOGY

The Byzantine passion for theological dispute flamed during Manuel's reign. Was the sacrifice on the Cross dedicated to all Three or only to the other Two Members of the Trinity? A council in 1156 declared it to be to all Three and distributed the necessary depositions and excommunications.

Soon another controversy flared up. When Christ said, "My Father is greater than I," did He mean Himself as a man, as the Holy Ghost, or as a theandric being? Did not these words indicate an inferiority to the Father? If Christ were inferior to the Father, then His action and influence were more or less human, for one and the same person could not be simultaneously equal and inferior to the God Who had engendered him. These ideas of Demetrius had gained the support of many churchmen when Manuel intervened.

This Church of the Virgin Pammakaristos (All Blessed) was built or reconstructed in New Rome about 1050 by the parents of Alexius I. In 1305 the mortuary chapel on the right was added. It became the Patriarchal Church after the fall of the city in 1453 and was converted to the Victory Mosque (Fetiye Jami) in 1591, when the minaret was erected

He dissuaded many priests but could not convince Demetrius and his group. A council in 1166 decreed that the quotation in question referred only to Christ's human nature.

Manuel's ecclesiastical activities were not confined to the preservation of orthodoxy. Throughout his reign he vainly negotiated for reunion with the Latin, Syrian, and Armenian churches. Moreover, he tried to facilitate the conversion of Moslems within the Empire, such as the Vardar Turks.

He was also concerned over the infringement of pious institutions on private property. He forbade them to increase their holdings further, but, lest this render him unpopular, confirmed them in their actual possessions, even if held illegally.

This mosaic icon of the Virgin and Child dates from 1065, when the parents of Alexius I gave it to the Church of the Virgin Pammakaristos. It is now a treasured possession of the Patriarchal Church of Saint George in Istanbul

ART

Unrivaled in Christendom, Byzantine art shone with a brilliance that it could probably not have attained had not iconoclasm freed Hellenism from ecclesiastical restrictions. Yet Byzantine art continued to flow in two streams, one free, secular, Hellenistic, and progressive, the other dogmatic, monastic, Oriental, and traditional. They were both, however, refined, creative, colorful, decorative, and expressive. Indeed, influenced by the secular, ecclesiastical art retained much of Antiquity's grace, beauty, and elegance.

In the eleventh century besides the traditional Byzantine formalism there appeared a gentle, personal, intimate, even tender trend. This style flowered under the Comneni. Manuscript miniatures, however, tended to revert to hierarchic standards and to lose both individual fancy and antique inspiration. Their figures stiffened into the only three permitted types—angelic, biblic, and apostolic.

On the other hand, Byzantine architects built ever lighter and more elegant edifices. The drums and domes of the cruciform churches became more graceful; the brick exteriors were enlivened with niches, blind arcades, slim columnets, bibolate and tribolate windows. The interiors were masterpieces of color with marble mosaic pavements, colored marble columns contrasting with lacy white capitals, and multihued mosaic walls with golden backgrounds.

LEVANTINE LATINS

Had Manuel continued the work of Alexius and John II and attempted to regain the Tauric frontier, his reign might have marked a turning point. But his Italian and Hungarian enterprises led him to neglect the East in a manner reminiscent of Justinian I.

After the Second Crusade the County of Edessa was dismembered by the Sultan of Rum, the Atabeg of Aleppo, and neighboring emirs. The last Count's widow sold its vestige to the Empire, but Manuel did not garrison it in strength and it also fell to the Moslems (1151).

In Cilicia the Rupenid Thoros expelled the Romans and restored

Armenian independence. Occupied in the West, Manuel paid the Sultan and later the new Prince of Antioch, Reginald of Chatillon, to attack the sturdy Armenians. After taking a few forts, which he turned over to the Templars, Reginald joined Thoros, invaded imperial Cyprus, pillaged towns, churches, and monasteries, mutilated Orthodox priests, butchered some islanders, and abducted others for ransom (about 1155).

Normally Levantine Latins would have applauded an assault on the Empire. But the failure of the Second Crusade, the likelihood that there would not soon be another, the Moslem partition of Edessa, and the progress of Nuraddin, Atabeg of Aleppo, who had taken Damascus in 1154, convinced them that they needed the Empire's protection. As a result, the King of Jerusalem requested an imperial marital alliance. After long negotiations Manuel accorded him his niece and took the field, ostensibly against the Turks (1158). From Seleucia he fell upon the unsuspecting Armenians, drove Thoros into the Taurus, restored Roman rule in Cilicia, and set up camp near Mopsuestia. Thoros later came to crave Manuel's pardon and do him homage.

Realizing that his turn was next, the Prince of Antioch obtained permission to come to the imperial camp. His head, arms, and feet bare, a rope around his neck, and holding his sword by its point in the hope that the Emperor might deign to grasp its pommel, he and a group of barefooted monks walked through Mopsuestia to the Roman camp. In the imperial tent on a raised throne sat the Emperor encircled by generals, dignitaries, and foreign ambassadors. Reginald's followers fell on their knees and stretched suppliant arms toward the enthroned monarch, while the penitent prince prostrated himself before him. Manuel allowed this performance to last long enough for their humiliation to sink into the Antiochenes' memories and to impress the envoys with the fear and respect that the Empire inspired. Before receiving imperial permission to do homage Reginald had to agree to surrender the citadel of Antioch upon request, furnish a contingent to the imperial armies upon command, and accept an Orthodox Patriarch.

Unaware of the reconciliation, the King of Jerusalem requested an audience with the Emperor, presumably to ask for Antioch in fief. To mitigate his disappointment Manuel had intended to receive him with exceptional honors, but Baldwin III rode past a point in the camp at which everyone except the Emperor was supposed to dismount. He was consequently received with less than the planned distinction but permitted to sit beside the Basileus, albeit on a lower throne. Whether on this occasion the King swore fealty is a moot question.[3]

Manuel now announced that he would visit Antioch. Fearing that he might expel them, the Latins spoke of a plot to assassinate him. He was, however, determined to impress the seal of his suzerainty on them, exacted hostages, disarmed the Latin participants in the procession, and donned the customary coat of mail under his robe.

Crowned, bearing the imperial symbols, and clad in an imperial cloak stiff with gems, the Emperor rode into the carpeted, bedecked, beflowered city to the sound of drums, hymns, and trumpets (spring 1159). On foot and disarmed, holding his bridle and stirrups, were the Prince of Antioch and other Latin vassals, surrounded by the martial Varangian Guards. Behind him rode the unarmed King of Jerusalem.

Manuel remained a week in Antioch and distributed lavish gifts to people and barons, that all might know that submission to the Empire was preferable to enmity. Fetes, games, tournaments, and hunting parties followed one another. Roman courtiers and Latin knights jousted. The Emperor himself descended into the arena and unhorsed two Latin adversaries. Later, while hunting, the King of Jerusalem fell from his horse and broke his arm. Kneeling beside him, Manuel set it.

The festivities concluded, Manuel led the Latins against the Atabeg of Aleppo-Damascus. Nuraddin liberated six thousand Latin prisoners, mostly captured during the Second Crusade, and agreed to support Manuel in an attack on Rum. This solution was agreeable to Manuel, who preferred not to crush the potentate whose power had led the Latins to submit to the Empire. Moreover, such was apparently Manuel's haste to return to the Great City that, instead of taking the road through imperial territory from Attalia, he moved from Seleucia through Rum. At first the Turks tried to dispute the way, but seeing that the Romans were not bent on conquest, sold them provisions.

[3] For a cogent discussion of the question of Latin vassaldom to the Empire see Lamonte in *Byzantion,* 7, I (1932).

From Spyridon Lampros, Portraits of Byzantine Emperors; *the manuscript miniature is in the Vatican Library*

Manuel I (reigned 1143–1180) and his consort, Mary of Antioch

Manuel's wife died early in 1160. On Christmas Day of 1161 he married Mary, the beautiful daughter of the late Prince of Antioch, Raymond of Poitiers. This marriage gave Mary's mother, whose husband, Reginald of Chatillon, had been captured by the Turks, protection against Turkish attacks and the ambitions of the King of Jerusalem. But, although Roman contingents generally helped beat back Nuraddin, Manuel was too occupied in the West to retain large forces in the East. As a result, Roman influence in the Antioch area waned. The Cilician Armenians again revolted and in 1170 the Latin Patriarch returned to Antioch.

On the other hand, the Kingdom of Jerusalem had moved closer to the Empire, for the Atabeg of Aleppo-Damascus had sent a force to decadent Fatimid Egypt. Were he to consolidate his hold on that country, Jerusalem's situation would be serious, since with the Egyptian fleet he might isolate the Latin states from the West. Having failed to dislodge the Atabeg's forces, the King of Jerusalem, Amalric, married an imperial princess in 1167 and two years later a Roman-Jerusalemite force made an abortive attack on Egypt.

The situation of the Latin states was critical. The Cilician Armenians had in 1168 entered into alliance with Nuraddin. Three years later the powerful Atabeg took Mosul, thus restoring the Syro-Mesopotamian realm of his father Zengi. His Kurdish emir Saladin had fortified his position in Egypt by wiping out the Fatimid Khalif's Nubian and Armenian mercenaries. As the Khalif's Vizir he held Egypt and in 1170 took Jerusalem's port on the Gulf of Akaba. This triple enhancement of Nuraddin's power, Egypt, Mosul, and the Armenian alliance, seemed to foreshadow the end of the Latin states.

In search of help the King of Jerusalem journeyed to New Rome (1171). He was received with pomp, solemnity, cordiality, and generosity and was permitted to view the sacred relics of the Passion. Amid the festivities that followed Manuel and Amalric concerted another attack on Egypt. When, however, the Roman fleet reached Acre, the King's expeditionary force was not ready. The opportunity to crush Saladin passed.

MYRIOCEPHALUM

In 1162 the Sultan of Rum, hoping to free himself to crush the Danishmends and perceiving that Manuel was anxious to war in the West, came to New Rome to cement peace. He was entertained with lavish magnificence. Gifts were heaped upon him and sumptuous repasts that were sent to the palace of his sojourn were served in gold and silver dishes, which remained his property. He agreed to make his subjects respect the imperial frontier and to furnish contingents to the imperial army. The Emperor, who was fighting the Hungarians, continued to shower him with gifts and subsidies, while the Sultan crushed the Danishmend emirs and his subjects continued to invade the Empire. At length Manuel realized that his course had enabled the Sultan to consolidate his state to a point where it menaced the security of the Empire without halting Turkish raids.

To terminate this situation he advanced with a powerful force from Fort Myriocephalum on the dusty road toward Iconium (autumn 1176). The Turks had burned crops and villages and poisoned wells but had not attacked. Instead, the Sultan had offered favorable peace terms. Manuel convened his military council. His veterans urged peace, but his younger kinsmen and intimates advocated war. Manuel concurred with the younger officers, and the army headed for a mountain pass, where the Turks lay in ambush. The road was so narrow and the defile so steep that the column extended ten miles and it was impossible for the van and rearguard to join. Manuel knew of the Turks' ambush but let his van enter the pass.

The Turks waited until the rear of the Roman line had also entered the defile. Then from heights on either side they fell upon the long thin column. The Roman van under John and Andronicus Angelus and the bulk of the army beat them off and seized a hill, which they fortified. Meanwhile, the Turks had shot down Roman transport beasts. Their cadavers and the wagons blocked the road and separated Manuel and the rearguard from the rest of the army. Manuel deserted his troops and sought safety in headlong flight. Assailed from all sides by Turkish bowmen, the ranks of the Roman rear broke. The leaderless troops retreated to a contiguous height but reached there in such disorder and in such a cloud of dust that men and horses tumbled over an unseen precipice on the yonder side. Further resistance seemed useless and, following the Emperor's example, the men fled precipitately through lateral valleys. But there too the Turks lay in ambush and shot them down mercilessly.

His shield studded with arrow holes and his helmet dented, Manuel broke through the enemy lines. Joined by a dozen other fugitives, he fled from valley to valley until he reached the van, still entrenched on the hill taken at the beginning of the battle. Soon after, Andronicus Contostephanus arrived with the debris of the rearguard. Night fell. A despondent silence hung over the foodless, surrounded Roman camp, where kinsmen and comrades were making farewells before the morrow's massacre. The officers grouped themselves around the dejected Emperor, who suddenly announced that he would abandon the troops. His officers were astounded, and Contostephanus protested. Abruptly through the night rang biting words of reproach. It was the army speaking through the voice of a common soldier. Manuel bowed to its will and remained. At dawn Turkish arrows began to rain on the Roman camp.

Suddenly the attack stopped. An emir approached, presented Manuel with a completely accoutered horse and the Sultan's peace terms—a large indemnity and evacuation of the fortresses of Dorylaeum and Sublaeum, which hampered Turkish incursions into the fertile valleys of the Sangarius and the Meander. Manuel gladly accepted such lenient terms, possibly inspired by the reputation of the Roman army. Safely back in his capital, however, he refused to abandon the fort of Dorylaeum. But the weakened army remained on the defensive. Hope of crushing Rum was abandoned. The Turkish invasions continued, and the Romans were insensibly pushed from the upper Meander and Sangarius valleys.

After this defeat Manuel turned more than ever to astrology. Even when he fell gravely ill in the spring of 1180 he disbelieved the physicians who warned him of approaching death. The stars foretold fourteen years of life and natural cataclysms. To prepare for the latter he constructed subterranean quarters and demolished wings of the Palace of Blachernae just inside the land wall, to which he had transferred the imperial residence. Only in September did he realize that death was near and at the Patriarch's insistence disavowed astrology. Then, dressed as a monk and troubled about his young son's future, Manuel died and was interred in the Church of the Pantocrator under the stone upon which the Body of the Savior was said to have reposed after the Descent from the Cross.

He had largely undone the patient labor of partial reconstruction of his father and grandfather. The cost of his misdirected foreign policy and and his many campaigns had imposed a heavy burden on the taxpayers. As a result, many peasants had exchanged their freedom for a magnate's protection from extortionate tax-collectors. This trend, his own grants of public functions to private persons in distributing fiefs, and the outright usurpation of public functions by magnates in peripheral regions further diminished the authority of the central government and feudalized the Empire. She now seemed to function largely for the benefit of the military nobility and was a fragile structure.[4]

ANDRONICUS I

Alexius II, son of Manuel's second marriage, was now eleven. Crowned Emperor at two, he had in March 1180 married the nine-year-old daughter of the King of France. He was to reign under the regency of his mother, assisted by the Patriarch and imperial kinsmen. The young Emperor's mother, Mary of Antioch, not yet forty and once acclaimed as the most beautiful woman of her time, had been tonsured together with the moribund Manuel. To the people of New Rome she symbolized her late husband's hated predilection for Latins. It was rumored that the carefree Protosebastor Alexius, now thirty-eight and first cousin of Alexius II, was her lover. However that might be, the government was soon in his hands.

A nationalist conspiracy to do away with him centered on the Caesarissa Maria, the surviving daughter of Manuel's first nuptials. Originally intended to succeed him as the consort of Bela-Alexius, she had in 1180 at the age of twenty-seven been married to the seventeen-year-old Rainier (changed to John) of Montferrat. The

---

[4] For the period between 1081 and 1180 this chapter is largely based on Chalandon's outstanding works.

plot failed and Maria and her husband fled to the Patriarchate. Supported by secular and regular clergy, they formed a fighting force of native and foreign inhabitants of the capital. The Protosebastor called in Anatolian troops, who after a day-long battle in the Augustaeum drove Maria's partisans into Saint Sophia. She accepted generous terms and returned to the Palace.

The nationalists' hopes then converged on Andronicus Comnenus, son of John II's ambitious brother Isaac. Born about 1120, Andronicus developed into a handsome, black-bearded man of herculean stature, an outstanding athlete, an intrepid warrior, an elegant arbiter of fashion, an eloquent and persuasive speaker, an ardent worshiper of Venus. He was irreligious but superstitious, ambitious but adventurous, martial but unmilitary, outspoken and unrestrained but false and boasting. Violent, rebellious, and unscrupulous, his intimacy with his niece, his neglect of his military duties, his dealings with foreign foes, and his attempts to assassinate Manuel had finally led the latter to incarcerate him. Nine years (1155–1164) he languished in a tower. With the aid of his faithful wife he twice escaped. The first time he was recaptured. The second time he reached the court of a Russian prince on the Dniester.

Manuel found it expedient to pardon him and sent him to Cilicia to combat the Armenians. Andronicus courted and abandoned the Empress' sister in Antioch, fled to Jerusalem with army funds, and at Acre became enamored of a kinswoman, the twenty-two-year-old Theodora. She had been married to the King of Jerusalem at thirteen and had been a widow for some years. When word reached them that the Emperor had commanded his vassals to blind Andronicus they fled to the Moslems. For thirteen years they wandered from court to court. Finally an emir gave Andronicus a fortress in Colonea near the Roman frontier. From here he raided the Empire, took captives, and sold them to the Turks. Manuel's officers finally captured Theodora and their two children. Heartbroken, Andronicus decided to submit to the Emperor.

In 1180 the now white-bearded but robust sexagenarian returned to court with a long chain wound around his body. When admitted to the presence of his cousin, he threw himself to the floor, shed tears, and implored pardon. Visibly moved, the Emperor urged him to rise, but Andronicus insisted that as punishment for his crimes he be dragged by the chain to the foot of the throne. He was magnanimously treated and assigned residence near Sinope on the Black Sea.

It seemed that the fires of ambition that had flamed so high in his youth had died down, and he remained in his Pontic retreat until the pressing solicitations of the Caesarissa and the nationalist party, the imprisonment of his two legitimate sons (who had been involved in the nationalist conspiracy), and the urgings of his legitimate daughter finally roused him. Or possibly he simulated indifference to allow the situation to ripen. In any event, in 1182 he denounced the government and declared himself the only friend of the Romans and the champion of Alexius II. Then at the head of his tenant farmers, a few Turkish mercenaries, and some regulars he began the march through Anatolia. The population hailed him. The provincial generals remained neutral. The fleet and the Varangian Guard declared for him.

Only the Latins in New Rome, whose numbers had risen to sixty thousand during Manuel's reign, stood by the Empress. But the capital masses uprose, freed Andronicus' sons, arrested and blinded the Protosebastor, and, led by priests and monks, attacked the Latin quarters, massacred many Latins, and indiscriminately destroyed their homes, churches, hospitals, and monasteries (May 1182).

Andronicus entered the capital hailed as the liberator of the Empire. He put to death Mary of Antioch, the Caesarissa, and Montferrat, became associate Emperor with feigned reluctance in 1183, and, soon after, had Alexius II strangled. The boy Basileus' bride thus became a widow before she had been a wife. Andronicus married her and created his son John associate Emperor. His power seemed assured. It was based on the support of the people, in contrast to the older Comnenian line, which had been sustained by the nobility, to which it was linked by marriage and consanguinity. Manuel had paid little attention to administration. With the higher civil and military posts in the hands of his kinsmen the abuses of the bureaucratic oligarchy had been repeated by generals, officials, or landowners exploiting the Empire.

Inheriting a depopulated realm verging on economic collapse, Andronicus came to terms with Venice, agreeing to compensate her citizens for Manuel's seizure of their property and permitting them to reoccupy their quarters. Above all, he set about to curb the cor-

From Spyridon Lampros, Portraits of Byzantine Emperors; *the fifteenth-century manuscript from which this was taken is in the Biblioteca Estense, Modena*

John II, Manuel I, Alexius II, Andronicus I, Isaac II, Alexius III
(reigned 1118–1203)

rosive power of his kinsmen and to restore justice and prosperity. Disregarding birth or influence, he appointed functionaries for integrity and ability. To those whom he left in office he gave the choice of honesty or death. He abolished the sale of offices and paid his officials sufficient salaries. He revised the tax registers on an equitable basis, protected the weak, and provided for the poor. Under his powerful impulsion new life was infused into the administration and the provinces. It became apparent that the people had suffered, not from the demands of the state, but from the extortion of officials. The Empire, which had appeared withered at Manuel's death, began to revive. But Andronicus' reforms met with bitter resistance from the aristocracy. He harshly put down conspiracies and risings except for the rebellion of Isaac Comnenus on Cyprus, for whose suppression he lacked naval power.

Besides his internal enemies he had to combat Turkish, Hungarian, and Serbian invasion. Moreover, in 1184 the son of the German sovereign was betrothed to the daughter of the King of Sicily. Assured against German attack, the Normans made another attempt to conquer the Empire. They seized Durazzo, advanced to Salonica, and invested it by land and sea. The city fell, and seven thousand Salonicans were slaughtered. Leaving a strong garrison, the Normans marched on New Rome.

Here the masses, disappointed that the massacre of the Latins had not restored prosperity, disliking Andronicus' marriage to the French widow of Alexius II, outraged by his permission to rebuild Latin churches in the capital, and blaming him for the loss of Cyprus and Salonica, turned against their champion. Lest the nobles use the masses for their own purposes, Andronicus started executing those in prison and arresting others.

One of the latter was Isaac Angelus, an impulsive, red-haired man. When in September 1185 an official with a small guard arrived before his palace and summoned him to surrender, he seized a sword, killed the functionary, jumped on the dead man's horse, and brandishing his bloody sword, galloped to Saint Sophia. His relatives joined him. The populace was soon won over, sacked the abodes of Andronicus' ministers, and released the imprisoned magnates. At Saint Sophia the clergy adhered to the revolt. Isaac Angelus was crowned and carried in triumph toward the Great Palace. The crowd was already battering at the gate when Andronicus, who had been in the country, debarked at Bucoleon. When the mob broke through, Andronicus discarded his purple boots and reembarked at Bucoleon with his child-wife and his mistress, a beautiful flutist. He was driven back by a sudden wind, and Angelus turned him over to the masses whose interests he had championed. He remained dignified throughout the vile indignities and tortures that they inflicted on him until at length he breathed his last in the Hippodrome. The masses had joined the magnates to terminate the last great effort at social reform and the salvation of the Empire.

XI

The Angeli

1185–1204

CARRIED to the throne by the capital masses, Isaac II Angelus was hailed by the nobles as health after disease, spring after winter, the calm after the storm. They had good reason. Angelus reversed Andronicus' course and practically delivered the Empire to them. Though occasionally capable of decision, he was generally indolent and irresponsible. Unlike Andronicus, he did not husband the imperial wealth. The simplicity of Andronicus' court gave way to luxury and extravagance. Much was spent on Angelus' fabulous wardrobe, actors, buffoons, old wines, exotic dishes, delicate perfumes, rare pomades, and ostentatious largesses to assure his popularity. Soon the finances were in disarray. Government posts were sold as if they were vegetables. Taxes were increased despite declining prosperity and the coin was debased. Officials were unpaid and slipped back into extortionary habits.

Meanwhile, the force that Andronicus had assembled under Branas cut the Normans to pieces in two battles (1185), and they evacuated Salonica, Durazzo, and Corfu. But the Roman navy met disaster when it sought to retake Cyprus from Isaac Comnenus. The Empire had lost control of the Aegean to pirates and the Italian merchant republics.

THIRD CRUSADE

The situation of the Levantine Latin states was precarious. They had not colonized the countryside with Latins. Their religious persecutions had alienated the native Jews and Christians. The Moslems remained unassimilated. Thus, they had no demographic basis, while the independence of the barons and the militarized religious orders tended to weaken the central power.

Furthermore, between 1168 and 1183 a brilliant and gallant Kurd, Saladin, had become ruler of Egypt, Nubia, Yemen, Damascus, and Aleppo, had deposed the Fatimid dynasty, and had proclaimed Egypt's spiritual submission to the Abbasid Khalif. Since King Guy of Jerusalem could not restrain his barons from plundering Moslem caravans, Saladin made war. On a torrid summer day in 1187, not far from the Sea of Galilee, he crushed the thirsty Jerusalemite army and captured the King with so many Latin warriors that the price of a Latin slave sank to that of a pair of sandals. Alone the Count of Tripoli and his men cut their way through the Moslem host. Two months later the city of Jerusalem capitulated on generous terms. Only Tyre, Tripoli, and Antioch remained in Latin hands.

Tyre was about to capitulate when Conrad of Montferrat arrived from New Rome, organized the defense, and sent to Europe for aid. A Norman squadron saved Tripoli. The Pope preached the Third Crusade. The first to respond was the German sovereign Barbarossa, who marched eastward with a huge host and entered the Empire in July 1189. His understanding with the King of Sicily and his negotiations with Serbs, Bulgars, and Rum alarmed Angelus, who, however, reached agreement with him for the transportation of his host across the Dardanelles. A few months later Barbarossa drowned and his army scattered (1190).

In the interim ships and Crusaders from all over Europe had reached the Holy Land. Richard I of England took Cyprus from Isaac Comnenus, and sold it to the released King of Jerusalem, Guy de Lusignan. Richard then joined the King of France, Philip Augustus, at the siege of Acre, which finally capitulated in 1191. It became the capital of the Kingdom of Jerusalem, which, together with the County of Tripoli and the Principality of Antioch, retained a hold on the seaboard. Without demographic or territorial power, however, these Latin states depended on the navies of the Italian merchant cities for their existence. Indeed, their original religious and political purposes were overshadowed by their commercial importance. Thus, though Saladin died in 1193 and his empire dissolved in diadochan war, the Latins did not attempt to recapture Jerusalem.

VLACHS AND BULGARS

Angelus' attempt to increase the financial burdens of Vlachs (Rumans, scions of latinized Thraco-Illyrians) and Bulgars provoked them to revolt. For centuries the Vlachs had herded in the uplands. Now they united with Bulgars and Cumans, gave them a dynasty, and established a kingdom between the Danube and the Balkans with its capital at Trnovo (1185–1186).

Angelus took the field against them but soon wearied of warfare, turned the army over to his uncle, the Sebastocrator John Ducas, and then to his brother-in-law, the Caesar John Cantacuzene. After the latter's defeat public opinion forced Angelus to give the command to Branas, the prime general of the Empire. Branas, however, advanced to the Great City. Angelus' army issued forth. His brother-in-law, the Caesar Conrad of Montferrat, charged at the head of Latin knights and caused a possibly purchased panic in Branas' force. Branas died fighting. The capital had again defeated the provinces. Angelus permitted the Latins to plunder New Rome's environs to punish the residents for supporting Branas. The Latins, however, committed such excesses that the inhabitants of the capital attacked their quarters. This time they found manned barricades. After two days' fighting the Emperor was able to restore order (1187).

With Vlacho-Bulgars as well as Serbs preserving their independence, Roman magnates usurping authority in the provinces, the vestige of Andronicus' centralized civil service vanishing, provincials overtaxed and exposed to invasion, and pretenders arising to defend local interests, the Empire was rapidly disintegrating. In 1195 the Basileus' brother Alexius and a group of nobles seized, blinded, and incarcerated him during a campaign against the Vlacho-Bulgars.

Even more than his brother the gouty Alexius III distributed to the nobles the Empire's wealth, including the campaign funds. He disbanded the expeditionary force, while Vlachs, Bulgars, Cumans, and Patzinaks ravaged the European provinces. Meanwhile, Alexius neglected army, navy, and police, increased taxes, sold offices and justice, and ruined commerce with the monopolies he sold. Roads, bridges, aqueducts, harbors, and fortifications fell into disrepair. The antipathy between weak and powerful, provinces and capital, starving taxpayers and extortionate bureaucrats grew apace. Pindic Greeks, religious dissenters, and unassimilated Slavs and Vlachs came to hate and reject the oppressive central government. The Empire appeared to be dissolving.

Pretenders rose on every side, many of them actual or self-styled members of the Comnenus family. In New Rome fat John Comnenus entered Saint Sophia, placed a crown on his head, was acclaimed Basileus by his partisans, entered the Great Palace, seated himself on the throne, and appointed his ministers, while the adherent rabble pillaged the palaces of the wealthy. That night Alexius III and his followers returned and beheaded his corpulent rival (1201). In Asia pretenders were often supported by the Turks. Resistance to them consumed the greater part of the Emperor's military effort and eventually led to war with Rum, which, however, was soon involved in fratricidal strife and ceased to be dangerous.

FOURTH CRUSADE

The weakness of the Empire and the Seljuks was not unobserved in the West, where Moslems and Orthodox Christians were equally abhorred. The hatred of the Orthodox stemmed from the religious schism and rivalry; the tendency to blame the "Greeks" for the Crusaders' disasters; the massacre of Latins in Constantinople in 1182; and Venice's ambition to supplant the Empire in order to assure her commercial position in the Levant. It was not, however, aversion to the Orthodox that led Pope Innocent III in 1198 to preach the Fourth Crusade. He realized that if the shrunken Latin states in the Levant were not to be brushed into the sea by a future Moslem revival advantage must be taken of the Moslem discord that followed Saladin's death.

Most of the Crusaders were French and Flemings, but there were also many Germans. It was decided to travel by sea. Venice agreed to transport the Crusaders with nine months' provisions and to furnish fifty armed galleys in exchange for a stipulated sum and half of the spoil.

The Crusaders intended to attack Alexandria, the heart of Moslem power, and from there to advance into the Holy Land. They assembled in Venice in June 1202 but were unable to pay the agreed amount. The aged, vigorous, and probably unblind "blind" Doge Henry Dandolo quartered them on the sultry Lido, where they were practically his prisoners and where provisions were at famine prices. He intimated that he would let them starve on the sandbank unless they compensated for the deficiency by capturing Zara for Venice. This wealthy Dalmatian metropolis was under the suzerainty of the King of Hungary, who had also taken the Cross and whose possessions were consequently under the Pope's protection. This mattered little to Dandolo, but the suggestion that they break their vow incensed many Crusaders. Nevertheless, after lengthy negotiations between their leader Boniface of Montferrat and the Doge it was agreed to attack Zara. In a solemn ceremony at Saint Mark's in 1202 Dandolo took the Cross for the assault on the Christian city. Some of the fifty thousand Crusaders escaped, but the great mass obeyed. Three months later Zara, despite the crucifixes on its walls, had been stormed and sacked.

In the interim, Alexius Angelus, son of the deposed and blinded Isaac II, had escaped to the court of his brother-in-law Philip of Suabia, the German ruler, who urged the Venetians and the Crusaders to restore Isaac. They signed a treaty with Alexius for the conquest of New Rome and in June 1203 debarked at Chalcedon.

In July Venetian galleys, each towing a transport with mailed knights and horses, moved over to Tophana. The next day the Western host seized the tower of Galata and severed the chain that blocked the entrance to the Golden Horn. The Venetian fleet entered the harbor and sank the neglected imperial ships. While the Crusaders, who preferred to fight on land, unsuccessfully attacked the ramparts of Blachernae, Dandolo with hide-covered, fireproof ships assailed the weaker wall of the Golden Horn. Their mangonels spitting stones, the Venetian vessels advanced through a stone hail and moored close to the wall. While some warriors threw up scaling ladders on the narrow strip of land between the river and the wall, others rushed across gangplanks to the top of the wall, drove off the Varangians, seized twenty-five towers, and burst into the City. But Varangians and Pisans pushed them back. They covered their retreat by starting fires and abandoned the wall.

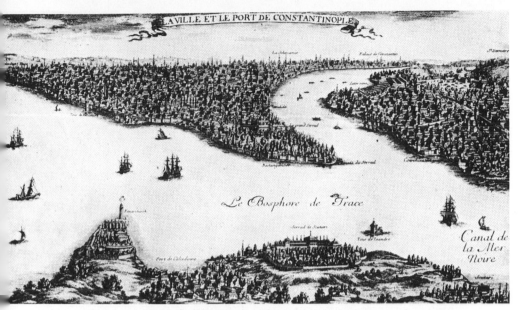

From *Robert Byron,* The Byzantine Achievement; *the original is in Guillaume Joseph Grelot,* Relation nouvelle d'un voyage de Constantinople, *which was published in Paris in 1680*

General view of New Rome bordered by the Golden Horn, the Bosporus, and the Marmara

That night Alexius III fled from the City with a sack of precious stones and ten thousand pieces of gold. In the morning the blind Isaac II was led forth from his dungeon and acclaimed Emperor by the assembled troops. Thus, the Latins' avowed purpose had been accomplished. They asked Isaac to ratify his son's concessions to them, namely payment of two hundred thousand silver marks, a year's provisions, transportation to Egypt, maintenance of five hundred knights in the Holy Land for the rest of his life, and spiritual obedience to the Pope. The blind Basileus expressed doubt that the convention could be fulfilled but promised to make every effort to do so. The Crusaders were permitted to escort Alexius into the Queen City, and Isaac agreed to associate his son in the imperium provided they withdrew to the yonder bank of the Golden Horn. They accordingly settled in the Jewish quarter, the present Pera.

Alexius IV's prime task was to raise the money to pay them. It was difficult to do so in a state whose treasury had been rifled for eighteen years. Alexius made a partial payment and agreed to remit the remainder after receipt of the provincial revenue in the spring.

Until then the Latins would remain on the left bank of the Golden Horn at the Empire's expense.

There was soon friction between Latins and Romans. A band of armed Latins broke into the mosque in the Moslem district and robbed the worshipers. When Romans came to the rescue of the Moslems the Latins set fire to the City in various places. Two days and two nights the flames raged, consuming many lives and works of art. Fearing reprisals, members of the Latin merchant colonies fled across the Golden Horn. In November 1203 Dandolo demanded immediate payment on pain of war. His insulting demand, the fire, the fact that churches had been stripped to pay the Latins, the report that New Rome was to be placed under the spiritual authority of the Pope, the Latins' interruption of the City's commerce, and their raids and arson in the suburbs increased resentment against them and Alexius, who had brought them. Popular indignation ran high, and it was without great difficulty that in February 1204 Alexius Ducas seized power. A few days later Isaac II and Alexius IV were dead.

Alexius V faced an almost hopeless situation—a diminished, demoralized, disorganized army, no navy, an empty treasury, a chaotic, burned city, and rebellious nobles, who resented the heavy contributions that he exacted. The new Emperor punished looting Latin bands at the head of his cavalry, heightened the harbor wall, and strengthened the land gates. Seeing the new vigor, Dandolo requested an audience with Alexius at a monastery outside the walls. Alexius consented. While he was at the monastery a troop of Latin horsemen swept down from an adjacent hill and only the Varangians' timely warning enabled him to escape. After the failure of this coup the Crusaders voted to assault the City, and a treaty between them and Venice provided for the division of the spoils. The Holy Land was apparently forgotten.

In April 1204 Venetian vessels assailed the Golden Horn wall of the city that had for centuries sheltered Christendom. After a heavy bombardment the Latins swarmed against the Romans from gangplanks and scaling ladders. But they encountered a determined defense, and hours later the Doge gave the signal to withdraw.

The heavy losses gave rise to discontent, and priests were called upon to kindle hatred against the Orthodox. The Emperor was termed a traitor and a murderer worse than Judas. The Pope's wish to unite the Churches was mentioned. The recent repulse was described as divine punishment for Latin sins. As a result, prostitutes were expelled from the Crusaders' camp, confessions were made, and communion was taken.

Three days later the ships again moved across the Golden Horn. All morning a fierce battle raged. Two of the transports planted their gangplanks firmly against a tower. The Latins rushed across, cut down the defenders, and seized it. Scaling ladders were thrown up and soon four more towers were in Latin hands. Three gates were battered down. Mailed knights charged through, heading for Alexius' purple tent. As the sun was sinking, the Emperor and his last troops met the Latin charge. After a bitter battle they broke. The Emperor retreated to the Palace of Bucoleon. The Crusaders butchered everyone they met regardless of sex or age. Another fire broke out, destroying more houses than there were in the three largest cities of France. Darkness checked the Crusaders' further advance and they bivouacked near the part of the walls that they had taken. The Varangians agreed to cease fighting on their promise of immunity. Alexius V and thousands of others fled through the Golden Gate.

When the sun rose the Soldiers of the Cross, who had sworn not to shed Christian blood, steeped themselves in loot, rape, murder, and other atrocities. Nuns, maidens, and matrons were abused and violated. Persons suspected of hidden wealth were tortured. The emperors' tombs were sacked. Exquisite cruelties were inflicted on Orthodox priests. On every side could be heard the shrieks and groans of the raped, the martyrized, and the dying. Dazed survivors, including the Patriarch without shoes, money, or luggage, fled through the Golden Gate. Churches were profaned. Saint Sophia's altars were broken up and a prostitute was seated on the patriarchal throne. Priceless masterpieces of Hellenic, Hellenistic, and Byzantine art were destroyed. After the three days allotted for the sack had passed, a number of Crusaders were hanged for failing to turn in the booty that they had taken. The spoil was then heaped up in churches, divided, and carted off. Antique bronze masterpieces were unhesitatingly melted down. These included the Hercules of Lysippus and the time-honored wolf with Romulus and Remus, al-

This portion of a column to which Jesus is said to have been tied and scourged apparently escaped the notice of Latin relic hunters and is reverently preserved in the Patriarchal Church of Saint George in Istanbul

though the quadriga of Lysippus was sent to Venice and the serpent column of Delphi was spared, perhaps because it was of inferior metal. It still stands where it was placed by Constantine I.

But if the Crusaders did not appreciate Hellenic beauty, they prized Christian relics, of which New Rome had a greater number than the rest of Christendom. To them a relic meant good fortune, forgiveness of sins, and intercession with God. Among the relics were the supposed: stone on which Jacob had rested his head; rod that Moses had changed into a serpent; head and arm of John the Baptist; shirt and girdle of the Virgin; hair and first teeth of Jesus; parts of the garment He had worn and bread He had blessed at the Last Supper; drops of blood that He had sweat at Gethsemane; tear of His; purple robe of His; blood gathered from the purple robe; crown of thorns; True Cross; sponge; Holy Sepulcher; finger of doubting Thomas; head and arm of Saint James; crown of the head of Saint Mark; body of Saint Andrew. The fame and wealth that these relics brought to the recipient Western churches and institutions stimulated the demand for relics and soon a steady supply began to flow westward. While their beautiful reliquaries were at first barely noticed, in time they began to inspire Latin artists.

After the disposal of the booty came the division of the Empire in accordance with the pre-assault treaty. Baldwin, Count of Flanders, was elected Emperor of the Latin Empire of Romania and a Venetian was named Patriarch. Baldwin obtained five-eighths of the City, southern Thrace, adjacent land in Anatolia, and the islands Samothrace, Lesbos, Chios, Samos, and Cos. Boniface of Montferrat became King of Salonica, vassal of Baldwin, and received southern Macedonia and northern Thessaly. The Duchy of Athens took shape in Attica and Boeotia. The Principality of Achaia covered the greater part of the Peloponnese. Other fiefs were assigned to a host of barons.

In recognition of Venetian power Dandolo owed no homage to the Latin Emperor and assumed the title "Lord of one quarter and a half of the Empire of Romania." Venice had the right to choose three-eighths of the territorial spoil. Dandolo selected the Adriatic and Ionian coasts and islands; the Peloponnese (which the Venetians called Morea because its contour faintly resembles a mulberry leaf); Crete, Euboea (which the Venetians called Negroponte), and most of the other Aegean islands; important cities in Thrace, on the Dardanelles, and the Marmara; and finally, three-eighths of Constantinople, including Saint Sophia. But Venice lacked the colonizing and military strength to hold all these territories and contented herself with Ragusa, Durazzo, Peloponnesian ports, Ionian and Aegean islands, Crete, and a few strategic cities. She thus held the sea route to Constantinople; was practically the mistress of the Latin states, which were open to her traders free of duty; and was the arbiter of Eurasiatic commerce. Constantinople became her chief branch, where she allowed friendly merchant cities to trade subject to the former rents and duties, excluding Genoa until the peace of 1218. Venice grew still wealthier and replaced Constantinople as the first city of Europe.

XII

The Lascarids

1204–1259

THE Latins' hope of acquiring the entire Empire upon the fall of her capital was not fulfilled. A Roman magnate established himself at Philadelphia, another in the Meander Valley, another near Miletus, another on Rhodes. The vigorous bastard Michael Angelus Ducas Comnenus ruled a domain reaching from Durazzo to the Gulf of Corinth, which came to be known as the Despotate of Epirus.[1] A grandson of Andronicus I, aided by the Queen of Georgia, had already before the fall of New Rome established himself at Trebizond, assumed the titles Grand Comnenus and Emperor, and become master of the Black Sea coast from the Caucasus to the Sangarius.

Theodore Lascaris, a short man about thirty with a forked beard and an ocular defect, having failed to rally the Varangians for a last stand, left New Rome, crossed to Asia, and, supported by landed magnates, selected Nice as his interim capital. This regular Hellenistic city, built by Antigonus about 315 B.C., lay in a fertile plain at the foot of Mount Olympus and on the shore of Lake Ascania. It had a regular supply of lake fish, was strongly fortified, and was at the junction of important roads. Here Lascaris began to rebuild the shattered Empire. But already in 1204 the Latins, aided by the Grand Comnenus and Armenians of the Troad, defeated him and took Nicomedia, Abydus, Adramyttium, and Lopadium. Suddenly in 1205 they withdrew to Europe.

A major battle had occurred at Adrianople. The Latins had not only committed excesses, rebuffed the advances of Roman mag-

---

[1] Henceforth *Epirus* will refer to the Despotate.

nates in Thrace, and insulted the Orthodox religion, but had responded to the amical overtures of the Vlach Tsar of the Bulgars by informing him that unless he address them as a slave his master, they would reduce him to his former servile status. As a result, a host of Vlachs, Bulgars, and Cumans had joined the Romans of Thrace, crushed the Latins, and captured Baldwin, who soon died.

In 1206 the Orthodox Patriarch of New Rome, who had fled to the Bulgars, resigned. His Venetian successor's election had taken place before his abdication and was consequently considered uncanonical by the Orthodox churchmen who had remained in the Latin Empire. They proposed to Pope Innocent III that he permit them to elect a patriarch of their own besides the Latin Patriarch and leave them their language, liturgy, customs, and traditions. With Orthodox fortunes at low ebb it was perhaps the psychological moment to inaugurate the reunion of the Churches. But the Orthodox appeal apparently remained unanswered. As a result, most of the bishops fled to Nice and elected a Patriarch-in-exile, who in 1208 crowned Theodore Lascaris Emperor. The opportunity to unite the Churches had passed, although Lascaris continued to seek union.

In the interim, the Latins had resumed their attack on Lascaris, who was obliged to leave them in possession of northwestern Anatolia. But he took part of Paphlagonia from the Comneni. In 1211 he confronted the Sultan of Rum, an ally of the Latins, near Antioch on the Meander. The Sultan rode at the Emperor, unhorsed him, and shouted to his servants to carry him off. But from the ground the Equal of the Apostles swung his sword at the legs of the Sultan's huge mare and brought him down. A soldier decapitated him, and the Moslems fled.

Alexius III, who had accompanied the Sultan in the hope of regaining the throne from his son-in-law Lascaris, was captured and relegated to a monastery. Earlier Alexius III had blinded Alexius V, who had wanted to make common cause with him against the Latins. The blind man had later fallen into the hands of the Latins, who had hurled him from the Pillar of Theodosius in Constantinople.

When Theodore Lascaris died at forty-eight in 1222 in customary monastic garb he left to his son-in-law John III Vatatzes a state reaching from east of the Sangarius on the Black Sea to the Aegean

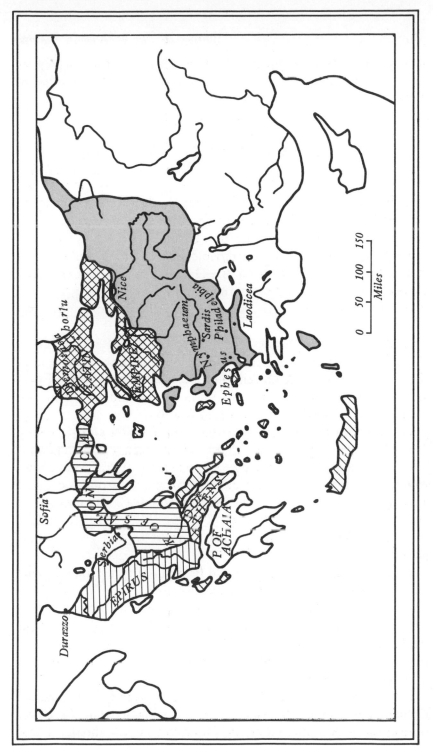

The Empire And Her Latin Neighbors About 1214

between Adramyttium and the Meander, held together largely by the common bonds of the Orthodox faith, Greek language, imperial tradition, and Byzantine civilization.

JOHN III VATATZES

Vatatzes, an epileptic Thracian, faced rebellion by two of Lascaris' brothers, supported by the Latins. In a short time he swept the Latins from Anatolia except for Nicomedia and a strip opposite Constantinople, reconquered Lesbos, Chios, Samos, Icaria, and Cos, imposed his suzerainty on the Roman ruler of Rhodes, and gained a foothold on the north shore of the Dardanelles. He was thus in a position to contemplate the reconquest of the Queen City. But two other monarchs shared that ambition—a fellow Roman Emperor and the Bulgarian Tsar.

In 1224 Theodore, Despot of Epirus, crushed the Latin Kingdom of Salonica, made Salonica his capital, and was crowned Emperor of the Romans by the Archbishop of Ochrida. Hailed by the European Romans as a deliverer from Latin heresy and barbarism, his realm reached from the Adriatic to the Maritza.

Vatatzes urged upon him the necessity of union and suggested that, while retaining the imperial title and sovereignty of the European provinces, he acknowledge the seniority of his Asiatic colleague. Theodore refused. Indeed, when Vatatzes' troops occupied Adrianople and seemed on the point of taking Constantinople he forced them to withdraw (1225). Theodore then advanced to the Great City and was, in turn, forced to retire by the Tsar of Bulgaria, John Asen II.

In 1228, when the eleven-year-old Baldwin of Courtenay became ruler of Constantinople, John Asen proposed to the Latin barons that his little daughter marry Baldwin and that he become regent for his young son-in-law. As a wedding gift he offered to conquer the Thracian territory held by Theodore. The Latins rejected the proposal and chose the elderly titular King of Jerusalem, John of Brienne, regent and Emperor.

Two years later John Asen defeated, captured, later blinded Theodore, and annexed a large part of his realm from the lower Maritza to the Adriatic, including Durazzo and Adrianople. Theodore's brother retained Salonica and Thessaly, while a kinsman was soon to establish himself as Despot of a reduced Epirus and to take Thessaly. The rivals for the Great City were thus reduced to Vatatzes and John Asen.

After Vatatzes had repelled Brienne's attack, he sought John Asen's alliance. The two monarchs met at Gallipoli, which Vatatzes had recently recaptured from the Venetians (1235). The Basileus' eleven-year-old son and heir and the Tsar's nine-year-old daughter were betrothed; the archbishopric of Trnovo became a patriarchate; and military collaboration against the Latins of Constantinople was concerted. The Tsarina, Mary of Hungary, escorted by the Basileus, accompanied her daughter to Lampsacus, where the Empress Irene and young Theodore received them. Here the Patriarch performed the wedding ceremony and Irene took the children home to Nymphaeum.

Vatatzes and the Tsarina recrossed the Dardanelles and he and John Asen opened the campaign against the Latins. The Emperor retained the southern part of their conquests, the Tsar the northern portion. They laid siege to Constantinople by land and sea but were thwarted by the Venetian and Achaian fleets with heavy reinforcements (1235–1236).

John Asen soon realized that he was aiding a strong state to replace a conveniently weak neighbor. Moreover, Brienne's death in 1237 led him to hope that he might acquire the City by peaceful means. He consequently abandoned the alliance with the Emperor and demanded the return of his daughter. When she wept at her separation from her young husband and the kindly imperial family he slapped her face. He then combined with Cumans and Latins to attack the imperial territory that he had recently helped to reconquer. He was besieging Chorlu when he received word of the deaths of his wife, son, and the newly created Patriarch. Seeing divine punishment for his conduct toward the Equal of the Apostles, he abandoned the siege, asked his forgiveness, and returned his daughter to him.

In 1241 John Asen II died and Bulgaria fell into weaker hands. Taking advantage of the situation, Vatatzes annexed the greater part of southern Bulgaria in an almost bloodless campaign in 1246, stretching Roman borders to the Maritza and the Vardar. The same year he entered Salonica in a triumph. Later he conquered Thracian towns still under Latin rule, Epirote territory in Macedonia and Albania, and extended his suzerainty over Epirus. In Europe the Empire now stretched from the Black Sea to the Adriatic and but for the Venetian, Pisan, and Genoese navies might have regained her capital.

MONGOLS

While Vatatzes was in Europe in 1243, he received a grave report, which he did not divulge. A Mongol horde had defeated the Sultan of Rum. Vatatzes returned without delay to Nymphaeum. The Mongol menace had originated before 1200 on the bleak, windswept plateau between the Great Wall and Lake Baikal when it occurred to a young chieftain to range his horsemen in battle formation instead of sending warrior against warrior. He united the Mongol and Tatar (probably mongolized Turks) tribes, established his capital at Karakorum, and assumed the name Jenghiz Khan (1206). With two hundred thousand horsemen he pierced the Great Wall and after a horrible five-year struggle and the slaughter of millions became overlord of northern China. Extending their dominion westward into Central Asia, the Mongols absorbed numerous Turks and in 1220 collided with the powerful Turkish Shah of Khwarazm, whose domain reached from Mesopotamia into northern India. The Mongols conquered Khwarazm, reducing populous cities to blackened mounds. They had no apparent ideal or purpose other than rapine and tribute and butchered with equal ferocity fighting men and playing babes, those who resisted and those to whom they had promised safety. When Jenghiz died in 1227 he was master of an empire stretching from the Sea of Japan toward the Persian Gulf.

Already before his death the Mongols, who tended to spread in all directions, had pushed into the Black Sea steppe, crushed the united Cumans and Russians, and laid Great Bulgary under tribute. They returned in the 1230's and amid frightful massacres subjugated a large part of Russia, successively annihilated Polish, German, and Hungarian armies in 1241, and then retired from Central Europe because of successional problems. Other Mongols defeated the Sultan of Rum and his vassal, the Emperor of Trebizond, sub-

From Spyridon Lampros, Portraits of Byzantine Emperors; *the fifteenth-century manuscript is in the Biblioteca Estense, Modena*

Alexius IV, Alexius V, Theodore I, John III, Theodore II, John IV, Michael VIII, Andronicus II, Michael IX (1203–1328)

jecting them to tribute. Then they turned to other enterprises. Vatatzes met the Sultan at Tripolis on the Meander and agreed that if the Mongols renewed their onslaught Emperor, Sultan, and Emperor of Trebizond would stand together (1243).

Vatatzes also negotiated intermittently with the Pope for the reunion of the Churches. He established small-holdings for soldiers, settled Cuman military colonies in the Empire, and strengthened the frontier fortifications. He built asyla and hospitals, amassed a reserve of gold, fostered industry and agriculture, and sought to relieve poverty. He restrained the magnates and protected the peasants and the middle classes. He and his successor revised the school system and founded municipal libraries, which seem to have become lending libraries. Theology, philosophy, rhetoric, versification, mathematics, logic, physics, astronomy, and medicine flourished. Manuals were published, which became textbooks for awakening Europe. The arts continued in the noble Byzantine tradition, although much creative strength had been lost by the dispersal of Byzantine artists after the fall of New Rome.

Meanwhile, Vatatzes had lost his wife and in 1244 married Constance of Hohenstaufen, the twelve-year-old daughter of the brilliant Holy Roman Emperor Frederick II. Constance, who became Anna, brought with her an Italian lady-in-waiting in whom the Basileus showed great interest and whom he permitted to wear purple buskins. After protests by a vigorous abbot near Ephesus her name vanished from the court chronicles.

As Vatatzes grew older his epileptic seizures became more frequent. Eventually in October 1254 they became extremely violent and in a tent in the Palace gardens of Nymphaeum a great Roman Emperor died at the age of sixty-two. He had restored army, navy, and letters to a measure of their former glory, reduced taxes, consolidated Roman Asia and restored its prosperity, reconquered a large part of the Balkan Peninsula, transformed Rum, Bulgaria, and the Holy Roman Empire into allies, and reduced the Latin state of Constantinople to a living corpse. A half century after his death miracles were attributed to his remains at Magnesia and to this day he is venerated as Saint John the Merciful.

THEODORE II LASCARIS

His son Theodore II, a studious, sensitive, epileptic, irascible man of thirty-two, took his mother's name, Lascaris, to stress the continuity of the dynasty.

When word of Vatatzes' death reached Bulgaria the Tsar crossed the Balkans and annexed the land between the Rhodope and Ochrida, which was mainly inhabited by Bulgars. In the dead of winter Theodore II traversed the Dardanelles and in two hard campaigns reconquered the lost lands. Perceiving that Theodore's energy equaled his father's and that he controlled his army so well that he could lead it through snow and ice, the Tsar sued for peace. Soon after, Theodore's daughter married the new Tsar. The Basileus also made a marital alliance with the Despot of Epirus and extorted Durazzo and the fortress Serbia, the keys to the Despotate.

At home Theodore confronted the perennial problem of the magnates' power. When the monarch preponderated the people were generally protected and prosperous and the Empire was strong. When the centrifugal magnates gained the upper hand, however, the people were often oppressed and the Empire was a prey to foreign aggression. Theodore's effort to curb the magnates' power led his general Michael Paleologus to fear blinding and to flee to the Sultan of Rum, whose territory had again been invaded by the Mongols. The Sultan gave him the command of his Christian troops.

But the Mongol flood was irresistible, and the Sultan appealed to the Basileus for help. Theodore received him at Sardis, accorded him a Roman corps, and obtained Laodicea and Chonae and the return of Paleologus, who was restored to his former position after renewed oaths of fealty. Despite Roman aid, the Sultan fell under Mongol suzerainty. To obtain lenience he painted his own portrait on the soles of a pair of shoes and offered them to Hulagu, the Mongol ruler of Persia, expressing the hope that his master would honor his slave's head by placing his august feet thereon.

Early in 1258 Hulagu invested Bagdad. After three weeks the Khalif capitulated. He was put into a sack and trampled to death by steppe horses, while the eight hundred thousand inhabitants are said to have been butchered. Hardly a stone of the Holy City was left

standing. Incalculable treasures of art, science, religion, and literature were lost. Thus ended the Abbasid Khalifate of Bagdad. Alone
the Christians, who assembled in their churches, were spared, for
the present Mongol policy was to cultivate Christians and crush
Islam. In pursuance of this course Mongol emissaries concluded a
treaty of amity with Theodore.

In August 1258 Theodore II, who had continued his father's negotiations for the reunion of the Churches, died. He left the Empire
to his seven-year-old son John IV under the regency of his friend
George Muzalon, a man of modest origin. Realizing the magnates'
power and the insecurity of his own position, he publicly offered to
relinquish his post to their candidate. Paleologus, however, assured
him of the magnates' loyalty, asked him to continue in office, and a
few days later murdered him. Paleologus became successively
Grand Duke, Despot, and Emperor (probably in January 1259).
Little John was to be blinded and imprisoned in a Bithynian fortress
despite the resistance of the Patriarch and a rising of mountain men
around Nice.

XIII

The Paleologi

1259–1448

MICHAEL VIII Paleologus was thirty-three, strong, shrewd, courageous, unscrupulous, popular, and related to the Ducae, the Comneni, and the Angeli. He was also quick-witted. When accused of treason and urged by the Metropolitan of Philadelphia to submit to the Latin custom of the ordeal he had declared himself prepared to accept the red-hot iron from the pure hands of that pious pontiff.

He faced peril in the Balkan Peninsula. The Despot of Epirus had made marital and military alliances with the Prince of Achaia and the King of Sicily and was threatening to sweep the Empire from Europe. Paleologus dispatched his brother, the Sebastocrator John, who defeated the allies on the Pelagonian Plain near Castoria and captured the Prince of Achaia (1259).

Having reduced the borders of the Despotate of Epirus, Paleologus turned to the Latin state of Constantinople, protégé of Venice. In order to neutralize the Venetian fleet he granted Genoa free trade in the Empire, absolute control of Smyrna, the right to establish colonies with extraterritorial rights in New Rome and other imperial cities, and the exclusion of Genoa's enemies (except Pisa) from imperial markets and waters, including the Black Sea. Genoa, in turn, accorded free trade to the Emperor's subjects and naval support except against the Pope or friendly states.

Paleologus' costly concessions proved unnecessary. In July 1261 the Caesar Alexius Strategopulus was reconnoitering near Constantinople with possibly only a thousand men when he learned that the Venetian squadron and a large part of the Latin garrison were off

μιχαηλ
ςος βασι
τωρ. ρῶ

ἐν χω τῶ δω
λε. ὁ αὐτοκ
ρατωρ. δουκα
ἀγγελος. κο
νος. ὁ παλαιο
λ'ΓΟΣ.

*Photo by Arthur Schneider, Munich; the manuscript miniature
is in the Bayerische Staatsbibliothek, Munich*

Michael VIII Paleologus (reigned 1259–1282)

the isle of Daphnusia in the Black Sea. He entered the City before dawn and was greeted with joyous shouts, "Long live the Emperors Michael and John!" The Latins fled and, perhaps under cover of a truce, many of them with their families embarked on the returning Venetian fleet.

Three weeks later Paleologus, the highest dignitaries, and the imperial guard knelt before the walls. From a tower of the Golden Gate the Metropolitan of Cyzicus rendered thanks for the deliverance, reverently holding the icon of the Pathfinding Virgin said to have been painted from life by Saint Luke and found in Jerusalem by the consort of Theodosius II over eight centuries earlier. Then, preceded by sacred relics, Paleologus, less as Emperor than as a Christian, entered the City on foot, exposed to the rays of the summer sun, while the Kyrie Eleison echoed through the streets. At Saint Sophia a solemn ceremony marked the homecoming of Orthodoxy.

But the sacred city of soft zephyrs and tideless waters had changed. Her religious relics were scattered, her works of art destroyed, her riches dissipated, her churches stripped, her palaces burned or ruined. The timber of the Great Palace had been used for heating and its lead roofs for coinage. Blachernae, the residence of the Latin prince, was grimy and littered with filth. Extensive parts of the City were heaps of rubbish. Her commerce was controlled by Italian merchant cities, whose fleets dominated even her home waters.

Furthermore, the restoration of the City, the strengthening of its defenses, the reestablishment of a sumptuous court, the construction of a fleet, the maintenance of greater armed forces, and the gifts and subsidies of Paleologus' foreign policy soon consumed the treasure amassed by the Lascarids. The two main sources of revenue, the land tax and the customs duties, proved insufficient to meet his needs and he resorted to confiscations and debasement of the coinage. Moreover, the extortionate practices of the collectors of the land tax so oppressed the provincials that they often fled from the Empire or called in the Turks. As for the customs duties, the Genoese and the Venetians enjoyed respectively full and partial exemption. As a result, Romans were unable to compete with them. Thus, the economic prosperity of the Lascarid period slipped away, while the provincials' resentment at the heavy taxation for the beautification of the capital fostered separatist sentiments.

The Empire's actual domain comprised western Anatolia, some Aegean islands, and a band of European territory bordered by the Marmara, the Black Sea, the Balkan range, a strip of the Adriatic, and the Aegean. She also acquired Monemvasia, Mistra, Maïna, and Hierakion (Geraki) in the Peloponnese in exchange for the release of the Prince of Achaia.

Paleologus sent part of his army to reconquer Achaia and some of his ships to join the Genoese fleet and seize the Aegean possessions of Venice. The campaign ended in 1263–1264 with the defeat of the Romano-Genoese fleet in the Gulf of Nauplia and of the imperial army in Achaia. As a result, while the Romans and Genoese retained control of the northeastern Aegean, the southwest remained under the Venetians and other Latins. They preyed on each other's shipping and were soon joined by professional pirates. Convoys became necessary.

NEIGHBORS

Famous since ancient times for its vineyards and mild climate, Trebizond was the capital of a state controlling the southeastern Black Sea littoral. Its ruler styled himself Great Comnenus and Emperor of the Faithful Romans. On the northern shore of the Black Sea he held sway over Gothia and Cherson, whence steppe produce flowed through Trebizond to Anatolia, Syria, and Mesopotamia. As a result of the Mongols' destruction of Bagdad in 1258 and the later establishment of the Mongol capital at Tabriz, much Far Eastern traffic passed through Trebizond, which also found an easy sale for its textiles, silver, and other minerals and attained unprecedented prosperity.

Politically the Trapezuntine Empire had fallen under Seljuk and then under Mongol suzerainty. Although the latter soon lapsed, dynastic dissension and the magnates' pretensions weakened the state. Consequently, when in 1281 Paleologus finally succeeded in making the Trapezuntine Emperor his son-in-law, the latter abandoned a title whose identical claim had prevented friendship between the two states. Thereafter he more modestly called himself Emperor and Autocrat of all the East, the Iberians, and the Transmarine Provinces.

With the rulers of Epirus and of Thessaly (which after 1271 had its own Despot at Neopatras and which had a large Vlach population) Paleologus attempted both warfare and intermarriage but was unable to reach lasting agreement because they sought to preserve their separate identity and he aimed to reabsorb them into the Empire. Thus, they were usually aligned with the Empire's foes.

His constant aim to restore the Empire also prevented satisfactory relations with the Slavic states. His alliance with Hungary, however, kept the hostile Serbs in check.

Against the Bulgars he at first had no such counterweight. Early in his reign they invaded the Empire. Paleologus counterattacked and among other towns took Anchialus and Mesembria. The Bulgars returned with twenty thousand Tatars of the Golden Horde, whose domain reached from east of the Aral to the Carpathians. Paleologus met them, but apparently his troops panicked at the sight of the Tatars (1264). Almost alone, he escaped to his exposed capital, while the invaders delayed to ravage Thrace. After another Tatar invasion in 1271 Paleologus gave the Tatar leader Nogai a natural daughter in marriage. Through this alliance he checked the Bulgars.

With the Seljuks in Anatolia he preserved peace during the greater part of his reign. This was largely due to his good relations with the Mongol Ilkhan of Persia. The Mongols' westward sweep had in 1260 been decisively halted in Palestine by the Mamelukes (Cuman and other Turkish steppe-dwellers, who had formed the bodyguard of Saladin's scions in Egypt, had in 1250 established their own sultan, and had in 1261 restored in Cairo the Abbasid Khalifate, which performed ceremonial functions until the Osmanli conquest in 1517). The Mongols nonetheless remained a strong power and retained their hold on Persia. In 1265 their Ilkhan Abaga was baptized and married an illegitimate daughter of Paleologus. Until his death in 1281 Abaga generally restrained the Sultan of Rum, thus relieving Paleologus of the need to maintain large forces in Anatolia.

In fact, the Roman frontier in Anatolia was no longer as strong as it had been under Vatatzes, for Paleologus had restricted the privileges and reduced the fiefs of the tax-free borderers established by

Vatatzes. As a result, the hardy farmer-soldiers insurged. They were defeated, and their military holdings to a large extent yielded to great feudalized estates. Consequently, Turkish and Mongol bands moved easily into imperial territory. Many settled in the Meander Valley, where Paleologus ceded them a strip of pasture land in 1264.

However unfortunate his policy toward the borderers, Paleologus had succeeded in encircling the Empire's potential foes, Rum, Bulgaria, and Serbia, with a restraining ring of Mongols, Tatars, and Hungarians.

CHARLES OF ANJOU

The Latins had inflicted deep wounds on the Empire but had been unable to create a viable order in the East. Nevertheless, three Latin powers still desired to overthrow the Empire—the Papacy, which excommunicated the Genoese because of their alliance with the Empire and preached a crusade for the recovery of New Rome; Venice, which offered Crusaders free passage; and the ruler of southern Italy and Sicily, known as the King of Sicily. Were these three powers to unite, they would probably carry the states of the Balkan Peninsula with them and make a crushing assault on the Empire.

The Sicilies had in 1194 come into the possession of the ruling family of the Germanies, the Hohenstaufens, to whom the Papacy seemed irrevocably opposed. It persevered in its opposition even after the personal union of the Germanies and the Sicilies had ended in 1258 when Frederick II's natural son Manfred became King of Sicily.

Already in 1264 Manfred intrigued with the Genoese podesta in New Rome to seize the City. Although the podesta seems to have acted on his own responsibility, Paleologus expelled the Genoese of the capital to Thracian Heraclea. This action was perhaps motivated by a desire to withdraw the costly concessions made to the Genoese, by their apparent reluctance to risk their galleys in battle, by the growing animosity between Romans and Genoese, and by the hope of befriending Venice by offering her a commercial position similar to that which Genoa had occupied. Venice, however, seems to have expected to reconquer her quondam supremacy in New Rome as a member of the impending coalition with the Papacy and Sicily and rejected Paleologus' proposals. As a result, probably in 1267, he permitted the Genoese to settle at Galata on the yonder bank of the Golden Horn, stipulating, however, that it remain unfortified. The following year Venice, anxious to trade until the coalition should come into being, signed a less advantageous treaty than she might have earlier. Paleologus had thus lessened the likelihood of her adherence to a hostile alliance and was in a position to exploit Veneto-Genoese rivalry.

In the interim, important events had taken place in Italy. Determined to oust the Hohenstaufens from the Apennine Peninsula, the Pope had declared a crusade against Manfred and supported the King of France's brother Charles of Anjou against him. Charles defeated and killed Manfred in 1266, took over his realm, and established himself as the preponderant power in Italy. The event was fraught with peril for the Empire, since the Pope, Charles, and Venice might now unite against her.

Indeed, already in 1267 the Pope, Charles, the Prince of Achaia, and the Latin Emperor Baldwin met at Viterbo; confirmed Charles' overlordship of Achaia and his tenure of Corfu, the Epirote coast between Valona and Butrinto, and other fiefs; and agreed on the partition of the Empire. The assault on New Rome was later set for 1270. At that time, however, Charles' armada was deflected southward by his brother's crusade against Tunisia. That expedition ended with the French king's demise, an advantageous treaty for Charles, and the destruction of a large number of Latin vessels by a storm. Thus, New Rome was for the present safe from attack.

Both before and after the assault on Tunisia Charles actively prepared for the offensive against the Empire. He constructed ships; made alliances with Hungary, Serbia, Bulgaria, and Thessaly; negotiated with Rum, Armenia, and the Mongols of Persia; produced a pseudo John IV Lascaris to claim his rights; occupied Durazzo; became King of Albania; extended his suzerainty over Epirus; sent large forces to vassal Achaia; exerted his influence to keep the papal throne vacant for three years, lest the Papacy and Paleologus reach agreement on the reunion of the Churches; and sought to engage the aid of Venice, which was beginning to fear his power. In the interim Baldwin enlisted Burgundian and Navarrese support. The planned onslaught was, however, delayed by the war with Genoa that erupted in 1272 after Charles had seized Ghibelline Genoese and their property within his dominions.

Meanwhile, Paleologus had not been inactive. He arranged imperial marriages with the ruling families of Epirus, Thessaly, Bulgaria, and Hungary. He negotiated with the kings of France and Castile, tightened his relations with Genoa, sought to extend the treaty with Venice, and supported the Ghibellines of northern Italy against Charles. Above all, he proposed the reunion of the Churches to the Papacy. It was not until Gregory X ascended the vacant papal throne in 1271 that this matter could progress. To Paleologus his Church, like his army, was an instrument of policy and he sought to check Charles with the Papacy as he had checked Serbs, Bulgars, and Seljuks with Hungarians, Tatars, and Mongols. But while he was willing to acknowledge papal ecclesiastical supremacy to ward off Latin aggression, the Orthodox clergy and communicants were not.

Paleologus had already had difficulties with his Church. He had been excommunicated by the Patriarch for his cruel and perfidious treatment of little John IV. While he had managed to remove the Patriarch, it was only in 1268 that absolution was pronounced over the prostrate Emperor in a candlelight ceremony in Saint Sophia. Now it seemed to the Orthodox devout that he wanted to deprive their Church of its freedom, orthodoxy, and supremacy and subject it to a Church that they regarded as impious, heretical, and presumptuous and that persecuted their coreligionaries still under Latin rule.

Nevertheless, when in 1273 papal legates reached New Rome the Emperor demanded that the Orthodox clergy recognize the Pope's primacy and appellate jurisdiction and mention his name in the liturgy. He indicated that these were insignificant concessions since the Pope could not exercise his primacy from distant Rome, since his appellate jurisdiction would be merely theoretical, and since the liturgical mention of his name was unimportant. The Patriarch and the clergy rejected his request. Undaunted by violent opposition, Paleologus removed the Patriarch and found churchmen willing to sanction reunion provided there were no interference with Orthodox rites and practices. Thus, in July 1274 Orthodox representatives appeared at the Council at Lyon and in a solemn ceremony the

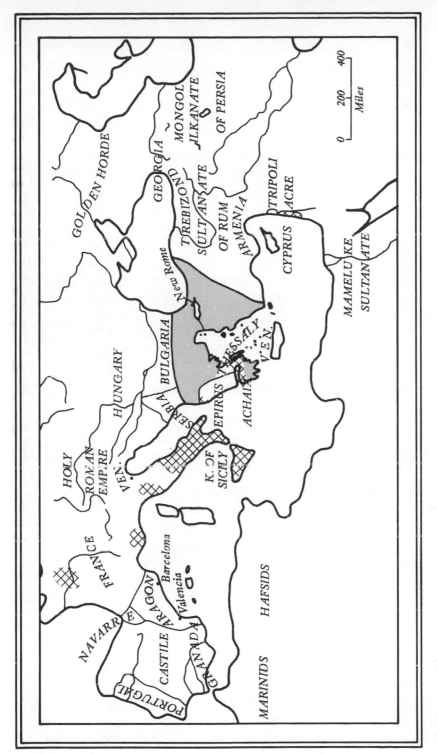

The Empire About 1280

Imperial, Bulgarian, and Serbian Churches were united with the Latin Church under the primacy of the Pope.

Paleologus had achieved a diplomatic success but had split the Orthodox Church asunder. To enforce the reunion he resorted to exile, confiscation, incarceration, flogging, torture, blinding, other mutilations, even executions. He nonetheless encountered the bitter resistance of the public, the regular and secular clergy, magistrates who would not condemn his religious opponents, officers who refused to attack the Orthodox despotates, and members of the imperial family who sought to overthrow him. Nor did the demands for submission by the successors of Gregory X render Paleologus' task easier. Moreover, the Despot of Thessaly proclaimed himself the leader of the Orthodox, welcomed refugees from the Emperor's persecutions, and in 1277 summoned a council, which anathematized Pope, Patriarch, and Emperor.

Whatever Paleologus' domestic difficulties, he had deprived Charles of the moral support of the Pope, who forbade him to attack the Empire. Paleologus, however, had taken the offensive. His forces advanced in Albania, capturing Berat. In the Peloponnese they reconquered Laconia and Arcadia. And under the leadership of a young Italian, Licario, whom Paleologus created Grand Duke, the Empire recaptured from the Latins and Venetians most of Euboea and a number of other islands, thus regaining control of the Aegean (1273–1278).

In 1281, however, under pressure of Charles' troops the cardinals elected the leader of the French faction Pope Martin IV. With his approval Charles, Venice, and the titular Latin Emperor signed a treaty providing for a powerful assault on the Empire in April 1282. In support of it the Pope excommunicated Paleologus and demanded that he surrender the Empire. Thus, the policy of Gregory X, who had sought to unite Christendom by a common crusade against Islam, was reversed. The formal union of the Churches was destroyed and Christians were to fight Christians.

Indeed, hostilities had already begun in 1280 in Albania, where Charles' forces had driven the Romans into Berat and invested it. A Roman relief column arrived in March 1281, put the Angevins to flight, and reoccupied Albania and northern Epirus as far south as Janina. Charles retained the coastal towns from Durazzo to Butrinto. Moreover, the Balkan states were preparing to join in the fray against the Empire. The Serbs took the Macedonian fortress Skoplje.

Furthermore, Turkish emirs pushed down the Meander Valley and in 1280 took Tralles. Thus, at a time when Latins, Slavs, Vlachs, even Greeks were on the verge of an overwhelming onslaught on the Empire, Paleologus was obliged to leave part of his army in Anatolia.

With foes closing in from all sides, the days of the Empire and of Paleologus—now bitterly hated by his subjects—seemed numbered. Charles, King of Sicily, Arles, Albania, and Jerusalem, lord of extensive areas in France, northern Italy, and Greece, supported by the Papacy, Venice, and other states, appeared on the point of becoming the most puissant potentate of the Occident.

Paleologus spared no effort to halt the ruthless Angevin. In his desperate search for possible allies he fixed on two in particular— Peter III, King of Aragon and husband of Manfred's daughter Constance, who asserted the Hohenstaufen claim to the Sicilian crown; and the inhabitants of the island of Sicily, who bitterly resented Charles' rapacious rule. Paleologus and Peter, however, differed in their objectives. While the Emperor sought to involve Charles in Sicilian hostilities in order to deflect his impending assault on the Empire, Peter wanted to invade Sicily only after Charles' forces were committed against the Empire. Paleologus nevertheless supplied Peter with funds for the enlargement of his navy. He also contributed gold to enable the Sicilians to obtain arms and organize revolt. With Charles' armada scheduled to move from various ports the beginning of April 1282, the timing of the Sicilian insurrection was of vital importance to the Empire.

The end of March, Sicilians were waiting near the Church of the Holy Ghost outside Palermo to attend vespers. Frenchmen appeared and began to take liberties with the women. An indignant husband stabbed a Frenchman. When the others sought to avenge him Sicilians armed with daggers and swords killed them. At that moment church bells began to summon to vespers. As the bells tolled Sicilians ran through the streets of Palermo shouting, "Death to the French!" French men, women, and children, even inmates of monasteries were massacred. The movement spread and eighty thousand French are said, perhaps exaggeratedly, to have been butchered. Angevin rule of the island was at an end.

Whether the rising at that moment was fortuitous or whether Paleologus had outwitted both Charles and Peter is unknown. In any event, the Pope, whom the Sicilians asked to be their overlord, excommunicated them. Charles issued an ordinance reforming the island's administration and crossed the Strait of Messina with a formidable host to visit exemplary punishment. He was, however, delayed by the valiant defense of Messina. Finally, in August 1282 Peter debarked at the other end of the island to claim Sicily for his wife and himself. Fearing to be caught between the advancing Aragonese and defiant Messina, Charles withdrew to the mainland. The Aragonese, bent on further conquest, followed. Charles' dream of a great Mediterranean empire and Paleologus' twenty-year nightmare passed. For 170 years Western powers and pretenders were to continue scheming to conquer the Empire, but their projects failed to materialize.

So hated was Paleologus that when he died at fifty-eight on an expedition against Thessaly, his son and colleague Andronicus II interred his body secretly (1282). Thus ended the reign of the man who had recovered the Great City, held the Slavic states at bay, and broken in two a powerful state that for two centuries under different dynasties had sought to annihilate the Empire.[1]

GENOA AND VENICE

The first care of Andronicus II, who was now twenty-four, was to convoke a synod, which expelled the churchmen who had favored union with the Latins. Thereafter monks gradually came to control the Church, whose influence on the state increased.

Less easily solved was the financial problem. The costly diplomatic struggle with the King of Sicily and the military efforts to restore the Empire in the Balkan Peninsula had exhausted the finances. Andronicus succeeded in increasing the revenue, notably by exacting a share of the harvest of every farm laborer and by recuperating income-yielding properties granted to churches, mag-

---

[1] This section is based largely on Chapman, *Michel Paléologue* (Paris, 1926); Geanakoplos, *Emperor Michael Palaeologus and the West* (Cambridge, Mass., 1959); and Runciman, *The Sicilian Vespers* (Cambridge, G.B., 1958).

The so-called Palace of Constantine VII Porphyrogenitus (reigned 912–959) adjoining the inner side of the land wall of New Rome, once part of the complex known as the Palace of Blachernae, and dating possibly from the twelfth century

nates, and monasteries. He decreased expenditures by practically abolishing the navy, thus making the Empire dependent on the Genoese. He also reduced the army to a few thousand men, paring the national regiments, while retaining the foreign troops. This dismissal of native soldiers deprived possible provincial pretenders of support but also weakened the fiber of the nation. Moreover, a large part of the economies achieved was consumed by tribute that might have been unnecessary had the Empire's military power not been curtailed. Under Michael VIII her political influence had been felt from Spain to Persia. The reduction of her armed forces marked her descent to a minor state.

While Michael had sought to preserve a balance between Genoa and Venice, Andronicus sided unreservedly with Genoa. The results of this course were soon to be felt. In 1291 the last Latin cities in the Levant fell to the Mamelukes. Venice's commerce suffered, and she determined to compensate herself by tearing the Black Sea trade from Genoa. A fierce naval war broke out in 1294. A Venetian squadron defeated the Genoese in the Bosporus, burned Genoese Galata, and ravaged other suburbs of Constantinople. As a result, Andronicus allowed the Genoese to retaliate against the Venetians in the capital. The Empire thus became involved in war with Venice. Genoa made peace in 1299, but Venice continued to wage war against the defenseless Empire until 1302. The Empire then paid an indemnity, ceded a number of Aegean islands to Venice, and restored her former commercial privileges. Two years later the Genoese admiral Zaccaria took the imperial island of Chios and established his own rule.

As a result of the war with Venice, Genoa had obtained from Andronicus the right to surround Galata with a wall. Thus, a strong Latin city under a powerful podesta took shape next to the Orthodox capital. The less important Venetian colony within the capital was headed by a bailo. Both in New Rome and in the provinces the memory of the Venetians' conduct in 1204 and their present desire to overthrow the shadow Empire rendered them unpopular. Their commerical activities were consequently subjected to many official and popular hindrances.

As for Pisa, her commerce in the East had begun to dwindle after Genoa broke her naval power in 1284. Besides Genoa, Venice, and Pisa, Ragusa, Ancona, Trani, Bari, Sicily, Amalfi, Florence, Marseille, Montpellier, Beziers, Narbonne, Barcelona, Tortosa, and Valencia also had colonies in Constantinople. The principal market however, was no longer within the City but in Genoese Galata. Here could be found the multiple manufactures of New Rome; wools, alums, and gallnuts from Anatolia; putty from Chios; henna and laudanum from Cyprus; Greek and Cretan wines; flax from Greece and Alexandria; grain from Thrace, Bulgaria, and the Crimea; Oriental spices, dyes, and aromatics from Trebizond and Tana; furs from Tana and Caffa; silks from Persia; Oriental weaves from Cyprus and Armenia; wax from Greece; soaps from Cyprus, Rhodes, Apulia, Ancona, and Venice; Italian olive oil; gold and silver thread from Lucca and Genoa; Neapolitan nuts; Spanish figs; woolens from Tuscany, France, and Flanders; and linens from Champagne. But peaceful exchange was continually interrupted by Latin strife. Thus, in 1324 a fleet from Guelf Genoa attacked Ghibelline Galata and was destroyed only after it had dislocated the Black Sea trade. In 1328 the Venetians blocked the Bosporus until paid a large sum of money.

THE BALKAN PENINSULA

During the latter half of the twelfth century Nemanya had united the Serbs and founded a dynasty. Roman suzerainty had lapsed on the fall of New Rome. In 1217 the Pope recognized the Serbian ruler as king, and two years later the Orthodox Patriarch authorized an autocephalous archbishopric for Serbia. But the new kingdom was subject to dynastic struggles and partitions and until 1282 had remained confined between the Morava and the coastal range. In that year Milutin became king and seized Skoplje from the Empire. An era of prosperity began. Furs and flour were exported and ancient mines were again exploited. German and Italian immigrants established industries. Moreover, Milutin strengthened his army with foreign mercenaries and expanded Serbian borders at the Empire's expense. Andronicus sought peace. His sister, the widow of the Emperor of Trebizond, having refused to marry Milutin, Andronicus gave him his five-year-old daughter Simonis as wife with the already conquered lands north of the Ochrida-Prilep-Stip line as dowry (1299). Byzantine civilization began to impregnate Serbian life.

As for byzantinized Vlach-Slavic Bulgaria, after the extinction of the Asen dynasty in 1280 it slipped into feudal anarchy and became vassal to the Tatars. About 1300 it revived, threw off Tatar dominion, attacked the Empire, and by the peace of 1307 obtained Mesembria, Anchialus, and points south of the Balkan range.

After the extinction of the Angelus line in Epirus and in Thessaly in 1318 Andronicus established imperial influence in Epirus and nominal authority in northern Thessaly. Thessaly as a state disintegrated. Some of its Roman magnates established principalities of their own. Albanians occupied other areas. Venice took the port of Pteleon. But the greater part of the former Despotate with its capital, Neopatras, fell to the Catalan Duchy of Athens.

In the Peloponnese the Romans extended their territory at the expense of the Latins. Moreover, in 1317 Andronicus granted Monemvasia commercial privileges to enable it to compete with the Venetian ports of Coron and Modon.

TURKS AND CATALANS

While the Empire was struggling to preserve her possessions in Europe, she faced fresh assaults in Asia. These attacks did not come from the Mongol-dominated, disintegrating Seljuk Sultanate of Rum, but from Turkish emirs and wild Turkoman tribes, who had swept into Anatolia as a result of the Mongol upheaval. The growing feudalization of the Empire had led to a decline of the military small-holdings and the Turks did not encounter the hardy borderers defending their lands as in the days of Vatatzes. Nevertheless, until 1296 the Roman forces coped with the assailants. Then unpaid Roman mercenaries mutinied and the Turks swept forward. Andronicus sent his son, the Emperor Michael IX, with Alans from the lower Danube, where they had found refuge from the Tatars. They were, however, more effective pillaging the natives than repelling the Turks. In 1302 Michael withdrew, and the Turks pushed down the Meander and Hermus valleys, took to the sea, invaded Rhodes, Samos, Chios, and other islands, even reached the Marmara. The surviving Greeks fled from the highlands that Alexander the Great had opened to their forebears sixteen centuries before. Their once flourishing homeland, the backbone of the Empire's financial and military strength, became a pasture for wild Altaic nomads. Some cities held out against the torrent, notably Heraclea on the Black Sea, Nicomedia, Nice, Prusa, Sardis, Magnesia, Phocaea, Philadelphia, and Smyrna.

To stem the Turkish tide Andronicus engaged the Catalan Grand Company. These Spanish mercenaries had been employed by the Aragonese King of Sicily. Also in his employ was an Italo-German, Roger Blum, who had hispanicized his name to de Flor. He had been expelled from the Knights Templar because at the fall of Acre in 1291 he had deserted his fellow Templars and because his galley had rescued only persons able to pay a high price. He had distinguished himself in the service of the King of Sicily, but on the conclusion of peace in 1302 the question arose whether he should be delivered to the Grand Master of the Temple for punishment. To preclude this he offered to remove the unruly Catalans from Sicily. He and sixty-five hundred Catalans entered imperial service and in 1303 their galleys anchored off New Rome.

They were received with honor, generosity, and lavish hospitality. Flor was created Grand Duke and married the Emperor's niece. Soon Catalans and Genoese of Galata were fighting, and the Grand Drungary was killed trying to separate them. In 1304 the Catalans crossed to Cyzicus, pillaged it, and fought against imperial Alan troops. At length they took the field, gained a series of victories over the Turks, and relieved Philadelphia. But their chief interest was rapine and they made war indiscriminately against Romans and Turks. Moreover, as Grand Duke, Flor levied heavy contributions on Anatolian cities and Aegean islands and put to death imperial governors unable to supply the sums demanded. In the enveloping catastrophe some cities refused entry not only to Turks, but also to Catalans and imperial officials. Magnesia, which Flor attacked, possessed itself of his treasure and repelled his furious onslaughts. At length he ruefully obeyed Andronicus' order to cross the Dardanelles, leaving a wide belt of devastation on his way north. The Catalans went into winter quarters at Gallipoli, where they were reinforced by more Spanish adventurers anxious to share in their golden harvest.

Flor visited New Rome to demand pay. But his rapacity had reduced the imperial revenues from Asia. Moreover, the Bulgars were assailing the Empire. Thus, although Andronicus had imposed new taxes, sold his wife's jewels, and sent his plate to the mint, he was unable to meet Flor's demands. Flor went to see Michael IX in Adrianople, where he was assassinated by an Alan general, whose son the Catalans had killed in Cyzicus. The Alans then massacred all but three of his three hundred Catalan horsemen (spring 1305) When the news reached the Catalans at Gallipoli they stormed Heraclea, burning the men alive, violating and cruelly murdering the women, and impaling the children. After the Genoese had destroyed their fleet the Catalans enrolled a body of light Turkish cavalry and near Fort Aprus charged against the army of Michael IX. The Roman mercenaries gave way and Michael led his reserve against the foe. He was unhorsed and carried off the field by his guardsmen. The Romans retreated to Demotica. The Catalans took Rhaedestus and butchered men, women, and children.

Their success attracted more Turks to their standards and their host swelled. For two years they ravaged Thrace to the walls of New Rome, destroying its towns, cutting down vineyards and fruit trees, torturing, butchering, or selling its inhabitants into slavery. Soon they could no longer live off the land. They failed to take Kavalla and went into winter quarters on the Cassandrean peninsula, emerging in the spring of 1308. They sacked Mount Athos but were unable to storm Salonica. They tried to return to Thrace but were beaten back by imperial forces. They then inflicted themselves on helpless, largely feudalized Thessaly for a year. In 1310 they entered the service of the Latin Duke of Athens, killed him with most of his knights on the banks of the Cephisus, and in 1312 placed themselves under the protection of the King of Sicily, who sent them his son to be Duke of Athens. Catalan dominion over the Atheno-Theban duchy was to last until 1388 and its brutality lingers in popular memory.

Meanwhile, after the battle of the Cephisus the Turkish allies of the Catalans decided to return to Asia and obtained free passage through the Empire on condition that they refrain from pillage. Guarded by three thousand imperial cavalrymen, they proceeded toward the Dardanelles, where fighting broke out. Michael IX was defeated and the Turks devastated Thrace. At length Philes Paleologus raised a corps of veterans, who routed the Turks in a pitched battle, stormed their camp, put most of them to the sword, and sold the survivors into slavery (1314).

In the interim Roman Asia was sinking beneath the Turkish flood. On Cyprus the Knights of the Hospital of Saint John of Jerusalem (today also known as the Knights of Malta), who had settled there after the fall of Acre, were dissatisfied with Lusignan rule. They obtained from the Pope permission and nine thousand ducats to invade imperial Rhodes, made a sudden assault on the island, and remained its sovereign rulers from 1309 until 1522.

CIVIL WAR

The Empire's vestigial provinces were no longer linked to the central authority by a common administration but through the person of a governor, who was generally a relative or courtier of the Emperor.

Moreover, the feudalization of the Empire continued almost unhindered. The estates of magnates, churches, and monasteries, all paying limited amounts of taxes, grew and almost obliterated minor nobles and free peasant proprietors. As these secular and ecclesiastical estates became larger, they often assumed the state's legal and financial authority, while the surviving free peasants were so heavily taxed that they frequently welcomed invaders or fled to the mountains. In consequence, the state's authority grew weaker and its income smaller.

Furthermore, fiefs that had originally been granted for life had since the reign of Michael VIII become heritable, while their obligation to provide soldiers had tended to be ignored. Thus, with the growing power of magnates and monasteries and the corresponding decline of the central authority and of independent, militarized countrymen, the Empire lost the two main bases of her strength— her centralized administrative structure and her native warriors.

The decline of the Empire's financial power was accompanied by a progressive debasement of the currency. The Roman gold coin, once the unquestioned medium of international commerce, was replaced by the gold specie of Italian merchant republics. Prices rose together with taxes and reduced many to penury and hunger.

To the public misfortunes were added those of the imperial family. Andronicus II had lost his first wife Anna of Hungary (mother of the Co-Emperor Michael IX) in 1284 and had married Yolande (who became Irene). She was the daughter of the Marquess of Montferrat, who transferred his titular right to the kingdom of Salonica to her. In the Empire's twilight Irene wished to divide the imperial vestiges among her sons as if they were private property. When the Emperor refused to abandon the tradition of imperial unity she indignantly withdrew to Salonica.

Of more tragic nature was the Emperor's experience with his grandson Andronicus, the son of Michael IX and Co-Emperor since an early age. This handsome young man apparently employed assassins to do away with a rival in love. By mistake his brother was murdered. The news reached Michael IX at his residence in Salonica, where he died a week later (1320). Old Andronicus decided to exclude his grandson from the succession. Thereupon young Andronicus, supported by John Cantacuzene and other nobles, to whom he distributed land, privileges, and tax-exemptions, raised his standard at Adrianople and marched on New Rome. The unpopular old Emperor yielded, acknowledged his grandson's right to the

On the site of earlier sanctuaries, possibly reaching back before the reign of Justinian I, the Church of the Holy Savior in Chora is near the ruins of the Palace of Blachernae and the walls of New Rome. Several times rebuilt, repaired, and restored, the last Byzantine restoration was about 1310. Transformed into a mosque (Kariye Jami) after the Turkish conquest of 1453 and now a museum, its impressive marble mosaics and wall paintings were reconditioned by the Byzantine Institute of America in the 1950s

succession, and left him in command of Thrace and part of Macedonia. Fighting broke out again, interrupted by intrigues and armed truces. Serbia supported old Andronicus and Bulgaria his grandson. At length in 1328 Andronicus III entered New Rome, deposed Andronicus II, but allowed him to remain in the Palace until 1330, when he was tonsured. Two years later the imperial monk died at the age of seventy-two.

DUSHAN AND CIVIL WAR

Andronicus III was a likable man in his thirties with little patience for court and ecclesiastical ceremonies, many of which he suspended. He enjoyed hunting and left the government in the hands of his handsome Grand Domestic John Cantacuzene, who was about three years older and to whose support he largely owed his throne.

To protect the Empire from Latin and Turkish pirates and to overcome her naval and commercial dependence on Genoa Cantacuzene and other magnates contributed funds to enlarge the fleet. With the new navy the Empire recaptured the putty island of Chios from the Genoese Zaccaria and imposed her suzerainty on the Genoese lord of the alum city of Phocaea (1329 and 1340). She was soon to lose both.

Two rising powers threatened the Empire's existence, the Serbs and the Osmanli Turks. Andronicus sought to ward off the Serbian peril by an alliance with the Bulgars, but in 1330 the Serbs crushed the Bulgars on the banks of the Struma. Thereupon Andronicus took Anchialus, Mesembria, and frontier fortresses from his defeated ally. But the Serbian and Bulgarian rulers formed a marital alliance, and Bulgaria regained the seized territory (1332).

Dominant in the Balkan Peninsula, the Serbs did not pursue a policy of racial consolidation but of territorial aggrandizement. They did not seek union with the kindred, though Catholic Croats and the kindred, though Bogomil Bosnians and a natural outlet on the Adriatic. Apparently dazzled by the lure of Salonica and Constantinople, they occupied northern Macedonia and the greater part of Albania. Cantacuzene and Andronicus offset these losses by reannexing Thessaly and Epirus in 1334 and 1337 almost without fighting.

In 1341 Andronicus died. The crown devolved on his nine-year-old son John V, whose mother, Anne of Savoy, assumed the regency. Cantacuzene's position was difficult. He did not wish to infringe on the rights of the late Emperor's son, but the interests of the Empire, the urgings of his friends, his reluctance to abandon the governance of the realm, the enmity of the Empress and her faction, and consequently his personal safety seemed to indicate that he should assume the imperial insignia.

Meanwhile, Turks and Serbs invaded the European provinces and the Bulgars threatened. With troops recruited at his personal expense Cantacuzene restored peace and was absent planning to extend imperial suzerainty over the Latins in the Peloponnese when his foes in the capital struck. He was declared a public enemy, his mother was incarcerated, his partisans were seized, his home was wrecked, and his estates were pillaged. Supported by Thracian magnates, Cantacuzene assumed the sacred purple at Demotica as John VI but acknowledged the precedence of Anne and young John V (1341).

For six years civil war raged. A large part of the government's power had passed to the landed magnates, who now also dominated the towns. Without the central government to protect them the rural and urban masses had slipped into misery, and the civil war soon took on the aspect of class war. The regency, supported by monks and masses, encouraged social hatred of Cantacuzene and the magnates. Insurrections against Cantacuzene erupted in the countryside, in Salonica, Adrianople, and other cities. The Zealots, as the populists were known (not to be confused with the religious Zealots, who sided with Cantacuzene) confiscated the property of magnates, churches, and monasteries and cruelly put to death many of the wealthy. Cantacuzene's cause seemed lost.

With two thousand men he retired to Serbia and concluded an alliance with her ruler Stephen Dushan. After the new allies had failed to take Serres in 1343 Cantacuzene's followers declined to five hundred. At this low point in his fortunes Thessaly and Epirus recognized his as Emperor. His governor of the two despotates, John Angelus, soon extended his domains at the expense of the Catalan holdings in Thessaly. As a result of these successes, Dushan, who did not wish the civil war to end, transferred his alliance to the regency. The regency also obtained the support of Turks and Bulgars. To the latter it ceded an area on the upper Maritza including Philippopolis. Cantacuzene, on the other hand, secured the aid of the Osmanli Turks. While unable to take Salonica from the practically independent Zealots or Macedonia from Dushan, he reconquered Thrace, entered New Rome in February 1347, and was recrowned by the Patriarch. Not until 1350, however, did the Zeal-

John VI Cantacuzene (reigned 1341–1354, d. 1383) as Emperor and monk. On the scroll is written "Great God of Christians"

From Spyridon Lampros, Portraits of Byzantine Emperors; *the manuscript miniature is in the Bibliothèque Nationale, Paris*

ots yield Salonica, when John V and John VI made their triumphal entry.

But their Empire had suffered irreparable losses of men, money, and territory. Moreover, Dushan, who now possessed almost all Macedonia except Salonica, had given solemn notice of his intention to take over the Empire when in 1346 he had the newly created Serbian Patriarch crown him Emperor of the Serbs and Romans. He completed the conquest of Albania and took Epirus and Thessaly. He had thus reduced the Empire's territory by over half and almost doubled the area of his own realm, which now reached from the Danube to the Gulf of Corinth and from the Adriatic to the Aegean. It was, however, not a nation but a Serbian state with Roman, Bulgarian, Vlach, and Albanian minorities. Half his subjects were Greek-speaking and continued to live under Roman laws, although Serbian nobles had replaced Roman magnates. To fulfill his dream and his title Dushan needed only take Constantinople. Lacking a fleet, he approached the Republic of Saint Mark, which, however, preferred to have the enfeebled Empire on the Bosporus.

OSMANLI

Meanwhile, in Asia, while the Roman vestiges had continued to sink under the confused blows of ephemeral Turkoman chieftains or Seljuk emirs, a new, purposeful power was rising to menace Bithynia—the Osmanli. About 1240 Turkomans from between the Caspian and the Aral under Ertughrul had been granted borderlands around Dorylaeum by the Sultan of Rum. At what time they accepted Islam is a controversial question. In any event, in 1281, when Ertughrul's son Osman succeeded him, the Osmanli (sons of Osman), as they came to be called, were not only Moslems, but also Ghazis (fighters for the faith, a military order).

Osman welcomed other Ghazis, Turkish shepherds, Tatar or Turkoman immigrants, and Christian peasants or townsmen, allowing those who so desired to retain their faith. His good treatment and inflexible justice facilitated conquests and Osmania grew. When the Seljuk Sultanate of Rum came to an end about 1307 Osman was one of ten emirs who established themselves on its ruins and those of the Empire and paid tribute to the Mongol Ilkhan of

Persia. He continued to capture Roman forts and gradually spread his realm to the Marmara and the Black Sea. The imperial cities, Nice, Prusa, and Nicomedia, were too strong to storm and he adopted the attrition tactics of the Turks on the Aegean, building forts in their vicinity, ravaging the countryside, capturing towns-people who ventured outside the walls, and in general ruining their trade, industry, and agriculture. As a result, starving Prusa capitulated on generous terms to Osman's son Orkhan in 1326 during the civil war between the two Andronici. Osman was buried there and as Brusa became the holy city and capital of the Osmanli.

In an effort to loosen the Osmanli grip on Nice Andronicus III crossed to Asia but was wounded and defeated (1329). Two years later Nice, the city of the Creed, capitulated on terms permitting those who so wished to depart and allowing religious relics and writings to be sent to New Rome. In 1337 Nicomedia, its commerce ruined and with no hope of relief, accepted Osmanli rule. Already before its fall Orkhan had crushed his Turkish neighbors on the west. His realm thus reached from the Black Sea east of the Sangarius to the Aegean, including Pergamum on the south.

Within these borders Orkhan sought to fuse Romans and Turks into a nation. The honesty and tolerance of the Osmanli as well as the security and prosperity that accompanied their expansion had aided their conquests. It was believed, however, that their state would cohere only if the Romans were assimilated to the Turks through Islam. Forcible conversion was not desired. Indeed, with such powerful neighbors as the emirs of Karaman, Kermian, and Sarakhan, it would have been dangerous to weaken the state by attempting it. Orkhan consequently adopted a series of measures to attract Christians to Islam. He restricted military service and fiefs in conquered areas to Moslems. In place of military service he imposed a heavy head tax. He permitted Moslem men to marry Christians but forbade Christian men to marry Moslems. As a result, for one reason or another, many Christians adopted Islam and mingled with the generally clean, sober, and hospitable Osmanli. While the Romans accepted the religion and language of the Turks, the latter adopted many Roman laws and customs. Thus, at this period, when the Roman influence was still strong, Osmanli women were not considered inferior beings and did not wear the veil. In cities, however, many Romans retained their faith and speech.

Orkhan organized an efficient fighting force. He formed a regular militia by the judicious distribution of moderate military fiefs, which provided future military generations and precluded the rise of a feudal aristocracy. When a campaign began irregular horse and foot were summoned, the horse to serve as scouts or advance guard, the foot to be placed in the front line of battle to tire the foe, break his ranks, or draw him into pursuit.

If he pursued he ran into disciplined, almost immovable Janissaries. This elite corps, created probably in 1330,[2] was composed of men taken from their Christian parents when about eight years old as captives or tribute. They were transformed into a celibate Moslem brotherhood, isolated from the rest of the community, lodged in the Sultan's[3] palace, and educated as members of his family. The absence of other ties, generous emoluments, and other advantages bound them to the Sultan in undivided allegiance. Admirably trained, enjoying war as a change from barrack monotony, able to act as both infantry and cavalry and to use the scimitar, the lance, and the bow, they were formidable fighters of unshaken fidelity, not battling for booty but for their beloved Sultan's safety.

Some Janissaries became officials and were, like their military brethren, efficient and faithful servants of the Sultan. Indeed, the nucleus of Osmanli power resided in the Sultan's household, indissolubly bound to him by education, religion, and ideals. With trained, educated, cohesive civil and military establishments and clear objectives Osmanli rulers built an enduring state.

Meanwhile, the Seljuk and Turkoman emirs of western Anatolia subjected the Romans who still clung to isolated coastal cities and Aegean islands, even those in Thrace, to frequent raids. In inner Anatolia the only imperial city to hold out was Philadelphia. Founded by the King of Pergamum about 150 B.C., this handsome city now stood as an island of Hellenistic culture in a billowing Turkish sea.

For the Empire the Osmanli constituted a great danger, and both Andronicus III and Cantacuzene were generally in alliance with

---

[2] See Papoulia, *Ursprung und Wesen der "Knabenlese" im osmanischen Reich* (Munich, 1963).

[3] It would seem that Orkhan was the first Osmanli ruler to adopt the title of sultan. *Enzyklopaedie des Islam*, IV, 589.

Seljuk emirs. In 1344, however, Cantacuzene outbid the regency for Orkhan's alliance, giving him his daughter in marriage. Ten years later Orkhan was to extend his frontier eastward to include Ankara.

JOHN VI CANTACUZENE

Upon entering New Rome in 1347 Cantacuzene restrained his embittered partisans and Osmanli mercenaries, who wished to massacre the Paleologi and their adherents. Instead, he decreed a general amnesty and declared himself the colleague of John V, thus excluding his own sons from the succession. John V, now fifteen, married Cantacuzene's daughter Helen, thirteen, and was to share in the government when he reached twenty.

Cantacuzene must have been deeply saddened by the condition to which the civil war had reduced the Empire that he had governed with such care. Pressed between Serbs and Osmanli on land and Genoese and Venetians on sea, her territory comprised only Thrace from Sozopolis on the Black Sea to Kavalla on the Aegean, Salonica, a strip of Thessaly and Epirus, some Aegean islands, part of the Peloponnese, and a few Anatolian cities. Thrace resembled a desert, and its remaining inhabitants were too impoverished to pay taxes. Indeed, the wealth, commerce, industry, agriculture, and population of the Empire were deeply diminished. Then in 1348 a plague known as the Black Death swept out of Central Asia to the Black Sea and was carried to New Rome in Genoese galleys. It was said, possibly with exaggeration, to have wiped out eight-ninths of the City's inhabitants.

The smaller the Empire grew the more difficult she became to govern. This was because the centralized Roman officialdom had practically vanished, and many of its functions had been taken over by local magnates. Nor was the Emperor the autocrat of yore. He was now little more than the strongest magnate. To prevent the various parts of the Empire from breaking away and to strengthen the hold of his dynasty, Cantacuzene established autonomous areas under members of his family. His younger son, Manuel, became Despot of the Peloponnese. His elder son, Matthew, controlled the Adrianople area, and John V was given the Rhodope region.

The impoverishment of the Empire reached into the Palace of Blachernae. Table service was no longer of gold and silver but of lead and earthenware. The gems of the imperial diadem and robes had been replaced by glass. The Great Palace had long since been abandoned and was falling into ruins. The serviceable part of it was used as a prison, while women washed clothes in its fountains and animals grazed on its grounds. Even Saint Sophia was in need of repair, but the funds that the Great Prince of Moscow sent for its restoration were used to pay Osmanli mercenaries.

The diminished revenue made it impossible to balance the budget, and Cantacuzene took vigorous steps to restore the Empire's shattered economy. To encourage agriculture he taxed foreign grain. To recover the Empire's lost commerce was more difficult, for the Genoese, who collected 87 per cent of the customs duties on the Bosporus, fiercely resisted any infringement on their monopolies. In order to deal with them Cantacuzene needed a navy, for the one that he and Andronicus III had built was no more. With great difficulty he collected funds from the magnates and began to build a fleet. Moreover, he lowered the customs duties on most of New Rome's imports and thus diverted merchant ships from Galata. The Galatese made war and in 1349 destroyed the imperial fleet. The Empire thus remained under Genoa's commercial dominion.

Soon after, war erupted between Genoa and Venice over Genoa's attempt to monopolize the Black Sea trade. Cantacuzene supported Venice and in 1352 a great but indecisive naval battle took place in the Bosporus. After the Venetian withdrawal Cantacuzene had no choice but to confirm all Genoa's privileges at Galata and elsewhere in the Empire.

In retaliation Venice loaned John V a large sum to overthrow Cantacuzene and obtained his promise to cede her the Island of Tenedos. Supported by Serbs and Bulgars, John V attacked Adrianople. Orkhan sent Osmanli troops to help Cantacuzene, who routed his young colleague (1352). Later John V and a few soldiers debarked at New Rome during Cantacuzene's absence. The Empress Irene repelled them and he fled to Galata. Until this point Cantacuzene had not sought to displace the Paleologus dynasty. Now, however, he made his son Matthew Co-Emperor and heir to the throne (1353).

The Church of Saint Sophia in Mistra, built about 1350 by the Despot Manuel Cantacuzene

But Cantacuzene's position was rendered difficult by his Osmanli allies, who had established themselves at Gallipoli and refused to withdraw. There were thus already murmurings against him when on a stormy December night in 1354 a large ship requested refuge at New Rome's port of Heptaskalon. No sooner were the gates opened than two Genoese galleys pushed in from behind and landed John V with troops. Cantacuzene was at the Palace of Blachernae. His Turkish and Catalan guards were at the Golden Gate, which he had transformed into a powerful citadel. They could have coped with the situation. At worst, they could have held the Golden Gate until reinforcements arrived from Matthew. But Cantacuzene forbade them to resist, abdicated, and, adopting the name Brother Joasaph, entered the monastery of Mangana, while his wife took the veil.

Brother Joasaph later retired to Mount Athos and devoted himself to memoirs and theological research. It was rumored that he visited Rome to resume with the Pope the discussion of the reunion of the Churches, which he had sought to achieve as Emperor. Many years later—in 1383—he died in the Peloponnese and was buried with his sons in Mistra.

His sons did not follow their father's example. The Emperor

Matthew maintained himself in the Rhodope region until 1357, when he was captured fighting the Serbs. They turned him over to John V, who imprisoned him until he yielded to his father's urgings and abdicated. He retired to Mistra, where his brother Manuel ruled as autonomous Despot of the Peloponnese. He was to succeed him in 1380 and to die two or three years later. At this time, when elsewhere the Empire seemed in dissolution, in the Peloponnese Manuel's development of its economic resources, his stout resistance to Turkish incursions, and his encouragement of Hellenic artistic and intellectual efforts gave imperial rule a faint afterglow of glory.

HESYCHASM

There were two tendencies in the imperial Church—the monastic and intransigent Zealots, who believed in a strong Church dominating the State, and the Moderates, who believed that the Church should cooperate with the State. After the ninth century the Moderates had generally occupied the patriarchate, while the Zealots formed the opposition, giving haven to conspirators and discontented, spreading rumors, and under the watchword of orthodoxy rallying the masses against the Emperor. During the early fourteenth century the Zealots gained the upper hand. Thereafter monks generally occupied the higher ecclesiastical posts, and the patriarchate became the especial domain of Athonites.

At Athos a mystic practice known as *hesychia* (silence) had developed. The aim of the hesychasts was to acquire total union with God. Alone in his cell, the monk held his breath, sank his chin, and regarded his navel. His mind was emptied of earthly knowledge and entered into ecstatic contemplation of the light of God, the same that shone around Christ at the Transfiguration on Mount Tabor. Soon degrees of contemplative ability were established—the beginners, the successful, the past successful, and the perfect.

When Barlaam, a Calabrian abbot, visited the sacred mount he denounced these mystical activities as heretical, asserting that man could not view the uncreated light of Mount Tabor. Two councils decided the matter in favor of the Hesychasts, but the controversy continued to rage. Hence Cantacuzene convoked a third council in

1351. It definitively decided that the light of Tabor corresponded to that of Athos. Neither was created but emanated from the Divine Energy, not from the Divine Essence. Thus was upheld the prestige of Mount Athos, where in these sad times men, broken in the struggle to save the Empire, sought refuge in God. Monastic retirement never offered more solace than now, when the sacred Empire seemed sinking under the blows of implacable fate.

JOHN V

John V gave the island of Lesbos in fief to the Genoese adventurer who had helped him to power. Meanwhile the Osmanli had continued to expand from Gallipoli and soon colonized Thrace as far as Rhaedestus. In 1362 Orkhan died at an advanced age, leaving a firmly established state and the unfinished campaign for the Balkan Peninsula to his son Murad. The time seemed ripe for its conquest. Its various Greek, Vlach, Latin, Slavic, and Albanian inhabitants did not form compact national states. Their boundaries had been drawn by conquest, not nationality. Thus, with often hostile foreign elements in their populations, the Balkan states could not offer united national resistance. In fact, many of the oppressed inhabitants of these feudalized states welcomed Osmanli justice and efficiency.

With Adrianople as their goal the Osmanli took Chorlu, Demotika, and Kirk Kilisse, thus neutralizing the imperial forces in New Rome, the Serbs, and the Bulgars. They then advanced on Adrianople and defeated the Roman garrison in a bloody battle. On the morrow the townspeople opened the gates of the city that was to become the Sultan's European capital. The campaign was concluded with the seizure of Philippopolis from the Bulgars (1363).

To assimilate the conquered Christians Murad gave his soldiers the right to enslave military captives who did not become Moslems and forbade Christians to bear arms. It is not certain whether it was he or a successor who introduced into Europe Christian boy-tribute for the Janissary corps. He transferred many Europeans to Asia and Asians to Europe and bestowed extensive estates in the newly conquered areas on his generals. Thrace and other imperial territory became known as Rumelia (land of the Romans). The

Osmanli were thus firmly established in the Balkan Peninsula, while the Empire, deprived of the revenue and manpower of Thrace, was definitively broken.

John V tried to rally Serbs, Bulgars, and Hungarians. But the disunited Bulgars went over to the Osmanli, whereupon imperial forces seized Anchialus (1364). Nor was John able to reach an accord with the Serbs, who since Dushan's death in 1355 had also slipped into chaos. Having also failed to obtain help from the Italian merchant republics, John journeyed to Hungary in 1366 to appeal to her king. He was informed that help would be forthcoming only after the Orthodox Church had submitted to the Papacy. On the Emperor's return the Bulgars detained him until his cousin Count Amadeo of Savoy with a Latin fleet had seized Mesembria and Sozopolis and forced them to free him.

John now undertook to obtain Western help through the reunion of the Churches and in 1369 in a solemn ceremony in Rome accepted the Latin faith. The conversion, however, remained personal. It did not affect the Orthodox Church nor did it produce Western help. On the contrary, on his return journey John was detained in Venice as an insolvent debtor. His son Andronicus IV, regent in New Rome, made no effort to liberate him. But his younger son Manuel, Despot of Salonica, collected funds and hastened to Venice to obtain his father's release. John returned to his capital with lowered prestige.[4]

In 1371 near the Isker the Osmanli broke Bulgar resistance and in a nocturnal battle near the Maritza crushed the Serbs. Thus, Murad was lord of the Balkan Peninsula. In order to preserve the debris of the Empire John acknowledged himself his vassal and gave him his son Manuel as hostage (1373).

Manuel, a well built man of medium height with blond hair and finely chiseled features, was devout, kindly, courageous, and perseverant. He was an accomplished warrior and man of letters, as versed in ancient literature as in Christian theology. Even while serving the Sultan as hostage or vassal and suffering the hardships of mountain campaigns, he composed letters, orations, and theological treatises in Attic style. It was probably in 1391 that he wrote that the pangs of cold, thirst, and hunger were insignificant compared

---

[4] For a different account of John's experiences in Italy see Halecki, *Un empereur de Byzance à Rome* (Warsaw, 1930).

with those he felt when he saw the ruins of dead Anatolian cities, whose very names had been forgotten.

In 1373, while John V was serving Murad in Anatolia, their sons rebelled in Europe. Murad crossed the Dardanelles, trapped them at Demotika, and blinded his son. Although his son died as a result, Murad insisted that John inflict the same penalty on Andronicus. John had the operation performed with boiling vinegar in a manner leaving Andronicus vision. He also elevated Manuel to the rank of Emperor and made him heir to the throne.

Later, Andronicus escaped with Genoese aid. Genoa wanted the Island of Tenedos, the key to the Dardanelles, which John had promised to Venice. In order to secure this valuable outpost Genoa supported Andronicus' siege of New Rome. Andronicus also obtained Osmanli aid and took the City, dethroned and imprisoned his father and brother, and made his young son Co-Emperor John VII (1376). Andronicus IV rewarded Genoa with Pera above Galata, but the Venetians occupied Tenedos. After an exhausting war between the two merchant republics it was agreed to depopulate by transplantation, defortify, and neutralize the island (1382).

Meanwhile, in 1379 John V and Manuel II had escaped. With Venetian and Osmanli help they recaptured New Rome. But Andronicus and the Genoese held out in Galata. After two years' fighting a compromise peace was concluded. Apparently in conformity with Murad's wishes the Empire was partitioned. John V retained the City and part of Thrace. Andronicus IV and John VII were recognized as heirs to the throne and given the Marmaran coast with Selymbria as their capital. From here they occasionally attacked the territory of John V, generally with Genoese help. John V's son Michael governed the Black Sea cities, while in 1384 his son Theodore became Despot of the Peloponnese, where Hellenism was shedding its last rays.

Thus, the Emperor Manuel II was deprived of the succession, possibly even of his appanage, Salonica. In 1382 he clandestinely left New Rome with his followers and resumed the rule of Salonica, acting as an independent monarch. Although his father recognized the Sultan as his overlord, Manuel resisted Osmanli pressure in Macedonia. Soon tidings of his victories stirred New Rome. Patriots took ship to join his army of liberation. But in September 1383 the tide turned. The Turks took Serres. Before the end of the

The icon is in the Byzantine Museum, Athens

Fourteenth-century icon of Jesus, from Salonica

year they had invested Salonica by land. Despite the defeatism, lack of cooperation, and social discords of the Salonicans, Manuel and his devoted band held off the Turks. As the years passed, however, the Salonicans became rebellious. Alliance with the Despot of the Peloponnese and the Latin lord of Corinth, an appeal to Venice, and the proclamation of the union of the Churches proved fruitless. Confronted with the insurgence of the Salonicans, who were weary of the long siege, Manuel and his adherents at length departed in April 1387. The townsmen thereupon opened the gates to the Osmanli.

The now landless Emperor Manuel found a haven on Lesbos, the domain of the Genoese Gattilusio family. Later he went to Brusa to make peace with Murad and then to New Rome, where he became reconciled with his father, who again recognized him as heir to the throne.[5]

While these events had been transpiring in the Empire, Murad continued to extend Osmanli borders in Anatolia. In 1387, accompanied by Roman, Bulgarian, and Serbian contingents, he advanced on Konia, capital of the powerful Emir of Karaman. A number of Serbs disobeyed his orders and plundered the countryside. He executed them. But Murad was unable to defeat the Emir and withdrew.

In Europe events were more decisive. His troops had taken Sofia and entered Albania. In Serbia, however, the indignation over his infringement on what was considered a warrior's right to pillage led to a rising of Serbs, Bosnians, and Albanians and the defeat of an Osmanli army. Vlachs and Bulgars joined the insurrection. Murad won over a number of Serbs, made agreements with other members of the Slavic league, and then met the insurgent Serbs, Bosnians, Vlachs, Bulgars, and Albanians at Kossovo (Blackbird Field) in 1389. He was assassinated by a Serb. Later his left wing was beaten back, but his son and successor Bayazid rallied the Osmanli and won a crushing victory.

Bayazid immediately gave orders that his brother, who had fought with conspicuous gallantry, be strangled, lest there be successional strife. Giving the defeated Slavs lenient terms of vassalage, Bayazid crossed to Asia and annexed the emirates of Kermian,

[5] The last three paragraphs are based chiefly on Dennis, *The Reign of Manuel II Palaeologus in Thessalonica, 1382–1387* (Rome, 1960).

Sarakhan, Aidin, and Menteshe. The acquisition of maritime emirates brought the birth of an Osmanli navy.

With Slavic resistance broken and Seljuk power curtailed, the Empire was completely dependent on the Sultan, who in 1390 permitted John VII, whose father Andronicus IV had died five years earlier, to seize the throne. Manuel II, however, recovered it for his father John V a few months later.

As hostage-vassal the humiliating task fell to Manuel II to accompany the Sultan on his expedition against valiant Philadelphia, which had withstood Turkish assaults for a century. When the Philadelphians saw the Roman Emperor in the enemy ranks they capitulated on generous terms (1390). Thus, Anatolia's last free relic of Hellenism, Romanism, and Christianity passed honored into Osmanli hands. After annexing the remnant of the Emirate of Tekke with the seaport Attalia, Bayazid advanced against Konia, capital of Karaman, but failed to take it.

In the interim, John V had begun to rebuild Cantacuzene's citadel at the Golden Gate, which he had demolished thirty-six years earlier, using marble blocks of the ruined Church of the Holy Apostles and other churches for the purpose. Bayazid, however, commanded that the work cease, intimating that his hostage Manuel II might otherwise lose his eyes. This was John V's last humiliation. In 1391 the man who had helplessly beheld the Empire's tragic decline into vassalage died at the age of sixty.

But although she was politically impotent, though her economic life was partially paralyzed, though many of her poor were unemployed, though the sources of her revenue had largely vanished, though the population of her cities had dwindled, the Empire was, even in her twilight, still a great cultural center. Students from distant lands still came to her schools. Her teachers still expounded the philosophies of Plato and Aristotle in Attic Greek. Her historians continued the labors of Herodotus and Thucydides and used archaic names for races unknown to Antiquity, calling the Bulgarians Scyths, the Serbs Triballi, the Turks Persians, Bayazid the Satrap. Byzantine grammarians even purified the language of Greek authors of the Alexandrian and the early Roman periods. Poets, both in Attic and vulgar Greek, sang the deeds and loves of ancient and Byzantine heroes in the Homeric manner, and popular literature spread from epic and lyric romances to history. But, whether in

Attic or Byzantine Greek, the intellectual life of the dying Empire continued to beat intensely. Theologians polemized, philosophers opposed Platonic to Aristotelian theories, philologists commentated classical authors, jurists continued the labors of Justinian I and Leo III, scientists pressed their researches, poets found fresh inspirations, and physicians composed manuals of medicine, which were used in Western Europe until the seventeenth century. Often a scholar might produce works in theology, philosophy, astronomy, history, rhetoric, and grammar and might be equally adept in prose and verse. The free Hellenic spirit was breaking through Christian conventions. It seemed as if, sensing approaching death, the Empire was struggling to pass on her last treasures.[6]

MANUEL II

Manuel II, now about forty and unmarried, escaped from the court of his cousin—he and Bayazid were both grandsons of John VI Cantacuzene—and hastened to New Rome. The Empire that he inherited included only the City and part of the Peloponnese. Bayazid had apparently intended to detain him and acquire the pearl of the Bosporus by ruse or through dissension within the City, for her walls were too strong for him to storm and his navy was inadequate for a complete blockade. Thwarted, he called upon Manuel to surrender the City or face annihilation. Upon Manuel's refusal Osmanli troops advanced ravaging to its walls (1394) and the Sultan forbade his subjects to trade with the City. These were the tactics that Osman and Orkhan had used to reduce Nice, Brusa, and Nicomedia. Food soon became scarce.

Meanwhile, the Emir of Karaman had attacked Osmania while Bayazid was absent in Europe. With fabulous speed the Sultan returned to Asia, defeated the formidable emir on the foodless Anatolian tableland, and annexed his domain. A campaign in northern Anatolia brought Osmanli arms to the source of the Halys and to Samsun on the Black Sea. All Anatolia west of the Taurus now obeyed the Osmanli (1395).

---

[6] The fourteenth-century statesman and scholar Cydones, however, was concerned about the decline in the pursuit of learning in the Empire and wrote of Latin cultural superiority. Sevcenko, *Speculum*, 7 (1932).

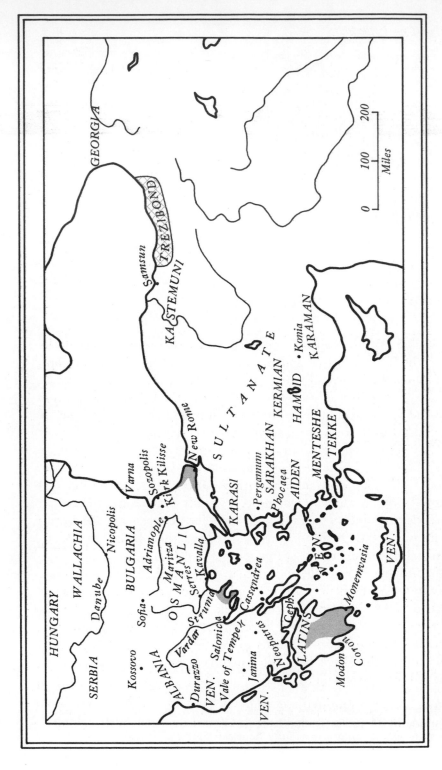

The Vestigial Empire About 1400

Simultaneously with Bayazid's Anatolian conquests the Osmanli took Thessaly, invaded the Peloponnese, established their direct rule over most of Danubian Bulgaria, and extended their authority over Wallachia. The Pope thereupon preached a crusade, and King Sigismund of Hungary led a host of Latin knights into Danubian Bulgaria. Wallachia joined them. Soon the Crusaders were encamped before Nicopolis on the southern bank of the Danube. Bayazid, who was still besieging New Rome, marched north with his Moslem and Christian forces.

Upon his approach Sigismund, who understood Osmanli fighting habits, suggested that Vlach and Hungarian infantry engage the Turks and that the chivalry of Europe form the second line. The Latin knights rejected this proposal as an affront and, their rich armor glittering, rode full-tilt at the foe. They overwhelmed the Osmanli irregulars, swept forward, were encircled, and surrendered. The Vlachs withdrew across the Danube and the Hungarians were put to flight by the sudden appearance of the Sultan's Serbian vassals.

Informed that the Crusaders had massacred their prisoners, Bayazid had ten thousand Latin knights beheaded. Of his remaining captives those under twenty were converted and became Janissaries, those with great wealth were ransomed, and the rest were enslaved. Sigismund and the Grand Master of the Knights Hospitaler escaped to New Rome by sea. Thus ended the last great enterprise of European chivalry.

It seemed to foreshadow the death of the Empire. The Osmanli ravaged the Peloponnese and abducted thirty thousand persons. They also continued to harass New Rome and urged the inhabitants to accept Osman clemency and deliver their City. So dark did the Empire's future appear that John VII endeavored to sell his claim to the imperial crown to the King of France.

Manuel II, however, appealed to Christian princes to save his sacred City. Finally, in 1399 a small fleet bearing Marshal Boucicaut and over a thousand men from France, Genoa, Venice, Rhodes, and Lesbos anchored in the Golden Horn. Uniting forces, Manuel and Boucicaut cleared the suburbs of Turks, defeated a Turkish squadron, and reprovisioned the City. But forces sufficiently large for an offensive were required and, since a Turkish assault did not seem imminent, Manuel decided to seek Western aid personally. To pre-

From Spyridon Lampros, Portraits of Byzantine Emperors; *the manuscript miniature is in the Louvre*

Manuel II (reigned 1391–1425), his wife, Helen, and their sons John, Theodore, and Andronicus

clude an attack on the City by John VII and the Osmanli he named John regent, and in December 1399 he and Boucicaut embarked for the West on Venetian galleys. They left his wife Helen Dragases, the daughter of a Serbian prince of the Vardar Valley, with his brother in Mistra.

At Venice the Doge awaited Manuel at the entrance to the lagoon on the glittering state galley, the *Bucentaur*. Possibly the sumptuous fetes, magnificent receptions, and promises of assistance kept Manuel from harking back three decades when he had come to Venice to rescue his father from his creditors. Riding west, Manuel and his elegant cortege were welcomed at Padua, Vicenza, and Pavia with lavish hospitality and assurances of aid. From the fertile Po Plain the Basileus crossed the Alps into France, everywhere welcomed and honored.

At length, in June 1400 the imperial horseman approached Paris. At Charenton the highest dignitaries of the kingdom welcomed the cavalcade with solemn pomp. Manuel rode slowly through the velvet-clad assemblage. His majestic figure; his noble features, in which the agony of the Empire seemed graven; and his prematurely white, but flowing hair and beard made an indelible impression. He greeted the red-robed cardinals of France, who rode out to meet him. A little farther, the pale Charles VI advanced at the head of an elegant entourage. The royal trumpets sounded and the crowd cheered. The King of France doffed his headgear. Not to be outdone in courtesy, the Emperor did likewise. They dismounted, embraced, and rode together into Paris. Months were spent in splendid functions, consummate banquets, brilliant hunting parties, and solemn religious ceremonies in Latin and in Greek (to the indignation of the intolerant). Both monarchs endeavored to surpass each other in marks of esteem and goodwill. Above all, Charles promised to give Manuel French reinforcements.

When Charles VI lapsed into insanity Manuel visited King Henry IV of England (December 1400). Here he was also cordially received, lavishly entertained, and promised substantial help, which did not materialize. He returned to Paris, where Charles had recovered his sanity. Though the months lengthened into seasons and the Emperor still waited, no French expeditionary force took shape. Yet Manuel was touched by the spontaneous friendship of the French King and his court, while Manuel's grace, culture, and affability endeared him to his hosts. But when a tactless theologian of the Sorbonne presented Manuel with a treatise on the double procession of the Holy Ghost Manuel responded with a refutation of 157 chapters. Two years passed and Manuel still awaited the promised aid, but the King seemed helpless, while contending factions struggled for power. Suddenly news of the battle of Ankara reached the Emperor.

TIMUR

The fourteenth century witnessed the dissolution of Mongol dominion. The khanate of Central Asia split asunder. The khanate of Persia dissolved into rival dynasties. The Mongol rulers were driven out of China. Alone the Golden Horde, though weakening, maintained its Eurasian domain.

In 1369 Timur, an olive-skinned Moslem of Turko-Tatar lineage, whose left leg had been lamed by an arrow, fought his way to the rule of his native Transoxiana, the land of lush pastures, fertile orchards, flourishing industries, and international trade routes. He spent a decade consolidating his control and then crossed the Oxus to conquer Persia. For two decades he battled and butchered, not sparing infants, the aged, or the infirm and erecting pyramids of human heads after taking cities. At Isfahan, the city of roses, he is said to have slaughtered seventy thousand persons. He also attacked the Golden Horde and impelled it on the path of decline. In India he commanded his troops to massacre a hundred thousand captives. The order is said to have been executed within an hour. By 1400 he ruled from the Indus to the Euphrates and from the Jaxartes to the Persian Gulf, while the Golden Horde, Central Asia, and Hindustan acknowledged his supremacy.

Soon he entered into rivalry with Bayazid, invaded Osmania, and stormed Sivas with his cutomary brutality. He then moved southward, destroying and exterminating, crushed a Syro-Egytian Mameluke army, sacked Aleppo and Damascus, but turned away from Egypt because of a locust plague. Instead, he advanced on Bagdad, looted it, and erected 120 pyramids of human heads.

Then the old and ailing Grand Emir again moved into Anatolia to meet Bayazid. They joined battle at Ankara in July 1402. Bayazid's irregular Turko-Tatars deserted to the kindred enemy. His contingents from Aidin and Karaman saw their fugitive emirs in the enemy ranks and also defected to Timur's red horsetails. Bayazid nonetheless hurled his left wing against the Asiastic horde but was unable to break its lines. Timur's horse then swept his decimated left wing and the bulk of his army into flight. Bayazid's loyal Serbs did their best to stem the Mongol flood. It was in vain. The Serbian leader urged Bayazid to flee. He scorned the advice. Thereupon the Serbs cut their way through the swarming Asiatic mass. Bayazid, his Janissaries, and the remnants of his broken battalions held out on a knoll. Throughout the long hot day this mailed square beat off the invaders. Amid the pointed helmets and the heaving sabers of his faithful Janissaries Bayazid tirelessly wielded his battle axe. Under the overwhelming Mongol assault his unparalleled warriors fell one by one. The survivors closed ranks to shield him. Night fell, but the shrinking Osmanli square fought on. At length, Bayazid tried to fight his way through the enemy lines but was unhorsed and captured.

Timur pushed westward, took Brusa, tortured, butchered, or enslaved the inhabitants, and destroyed the city. He captured the Serbian wife, daughters, and harem of Bayazid, on whom he inflicted many humiliations without breaking his spirit. Irritated, Timur compelled him to witness his Serbian wife serving naked at his victor's table. The scene apparently drove Bayazid to suicide.

Meanwhile, Timur's barbarous hordes ravaged the countryside, burned the cities, and murdered or enslaved the inhabitants. In December 1402 they reached Smyrna, which the Knights Hospitaler of Rhodes had seized in 1344 and which not even Bayazid had been able to take, for it could be reinforced by sea. Timur took it in a fortnight amid the customary carnage, the Grand Master and the surviving knights fleeing by sea. As Timur approached Ephesus, a procession of children came out of the city, chanting verses of the Koran in his honor. He ordered his horsemen to trample them to death.

On the ruins of Anatolian Osmania, Timur restored the dispossessed emirs or their heirs, notably in Karaman, Tekke, Menteshe, Sarakhan, and Kastemuni, while he encouraged Bayazid's sons to struggle over the succession. Satisfied that he had destroyed Osmanli power, he returned to Samarcand in 1403 and died two years

later at the age of seventy. His artificial empire insensibly disintegrated.

RETURN OF MANUEL II

Anxious to take advantage of the situation created by the battle
of Ankara, Manuel left Paris in November 1402, showered with
gifts, including an escort of two hundred men. Winter fell upon
them, but the Emperor pushed on and in January 1403 reached
Genoa, now under the protection of the King of France. He entered the city under a brocade canopy carried by scarlet-clad
townsmen. After ten days of festivities and discussions with the
governor, his friend Boucicaut, Manuel took the road to Florence,
Ferrara, and Venice, obtaining a few galleys. He stopped to get his
wife and children from Mistra, was met at Gallipoli by John VII
with the imperial fleet, and returned to his capital in 1403, bringing
the galleys, a short-lived pension from the King of France, broken
promises of aid, and pleasant memories. But he hoped that, as a result of the battle of Ankara, he might consolidate the Empire's
position even without Western assistance.

The Osmanli empire was in disarray. Bayazid's son Suleiman held
the Balkan Peninsula and was at war with his brothers, who held
what remained to the Osmanli in Anatolia. There seemed no prospect of a Christian coalition to expel the Turks from Europe.
France, the Papacy, and the Germanies had other preoccupations.
The Genoese and Venetian fleets had helped transport the Osmanli
army fleeing from Timur to Europe. Hungary was weakened by a
foreign dynasty. And in the Balkan Peninsula, except for a feeble
Bulgarian rising, the subjected peoples did not insurge against the
Osmanli.

In the circumstances the Empire concluded an alliance with Suleiman against his brothers and received or was promised territory
on the Black Sea, the Bosporus, the Marmara, and the Aegean, including Salonica. In 1406 at Cosmidion on the Golden Horn Manuel and Suleiman faced the latter's brother Musa, who had the support of Serbs and Bulgars. Manuel induced Musa's Slavic allies to
desert, and Musa was defeated. Three years later, however, Musa
routed and slew Suleiman. He then took Salonica and Suleiman's

other territorial cessions to the Empire and invested New Rome. But Manuel had rebuilt the imperial navy and in coalition with Venice, Genoa, and Galata sank Musa's fleet.

Manuel then entered into alliance with another of Bayazid's sons, Mohammed, helped transport his troops to Europe, and, together with Serbs, joined him in crushing Musa in 1413. Thus, the state that Timur thought effaced was substantially reconstituted a decade later. He had not perceived that its existence did not depend on a ruler's transient ability, as with his own artificial state, but on the civil and military organization of the Janissaries, in whom the tradition of state survived regardless of disaster, the death of an able sovereign, or the accession of an incapable one.

Mohammed's triumph brought peace to the Empire and the restitution of Suleiman's cessions. Since the reign of Cantacuzene Salonica and the Peloponnese had been almost independent principalities, and Manuel undertook to strengthen their bonds with the capital. He embarked with six galleys and a miniature army. At Salonica he appointed his son Andronicus Despot to succeed the deceased John VII. Later he set oars for Corinth to reorganize the Peloponnese, which was suffering from the effects of Turkish devastation and feudal strife.

He was presented with proposals for the replacement of foreign soldiers by natives and the simplification of the tax system by the philosopher Plethon. This interesting individual, who had moved from New Rome to Mistra, sought to regenerate the ancient Greek spirit. He even referred to the Deity as Zeus. Indeed, it was discovered with horror after his death that he had abandoned the Christian faith.[7] Such was his philhellenism that he urged the Emperor to assume the exclusive title of Basileus of the Hellenes. Without accepting a suggestion that would have infringed on the Empire's ancient universality,[8] Manuel rebuilt a ruined wall six miles across the Isthmus of Corinth in twenty-five days. Nineteen centuries earlier the

---

[7] Runciman, *The Fall of Constantinople* (Cambridge, G.B., 1965), pp. 14–15.

[8] Beck sees no denial of Roman universalism in Plethon's proposal. On the contrary, he believes that his Greek national pride was based on it. He points out that Plethon was as much Roman as Greek in outlook and that he viewed the reviving Peloponnese as a base for imperial reconquest. *Byzantinische Zeitschrift*, 53, 1 (1960).

For another viewpoint see Masai, *Pléthon* . . . (Paris, 1956), pp. 42–46.

Greeks had built it to repel Xerxes, and both Valerian and Justinian I had repaired it. Manuel also endeavored to restore imperial authority in the Peloponnese, exiling the most rapacious magnates to New Rome, replacing feudal assessments with imperial taxation, and enhancing the authority of his son Theodore II, Despot of the Peloponnese since 1407. Having extended imperial suzerainty over the Latin Prince of Achaia, Manuel departed. After entertaining Mohammed aboard the imperial galley off Gallipoli he returned to New Rome as if in triumph (1416).

Meanwhile, Mohammed was pacifying and consolidating his reduced state. In Europe the task was not difficult, for Osman justice, tolerance, and efficiency had led many to accept Osman rule. In Asia, however, the restored emirs of Karaman, Kastemuni, and Aidin had taken advantage of the civil war to attack the Sultanate. Mohammed annexed Aidin and part of Kastemuni and made peace with powerful Karaman. He died in 1421, having firmly reestablished the Osmanli state, more by peaceful means than by war.

Hoping to save his two younger sons from death at the hands of his nineteen-year-old son and successor Murad II, he had directed that they be entrusted to his friend and ally Manuel II. Murad refused to deliver them. Manuel was now over seventy and steeped in thoughts of the other world. He consequently let his son John VIII determine the course to pursue. It was decided to follow Manuel's successful policy of 1403 and support a pretender to the Sublime Porte (the name of the entrance to the Sultan's lofty tent), extract territorial concessions from him, and play the role of arbiter between a European and an Asiastic sultanate. But Murad defeated and executed the pretender, and the Osmanli besieged New Rome, using cannon for the first time, but with little effect (1422). Led by dervishes, the Turkish troops assaulted the walls. Their ladders were broken, and a sortie seized their siege material. Before sundown a thousand Moslems had fallen. Another claimant arose, and Murad abandoned the siege. His generals broke through the Isthmian Wall and ravaged the Peloponnese. In 1423 the Despot of Salonica, Andronicus, despairing of holding the starving city and possibly suffering from leprosy, transferred the Despotate to the Venetians, who promised to feed and defend the inhabitants. Seven years later they were to lose it to Murad II.

In 1424 the Empire ceded to Murad a few Black Sea towns,

agreed not to rebuild the Isthmian Wall, and consented to pay tribute. The following year Manuel II died at seventy-seven in the monastery of the Pantocrator, where he had lived since his stroke in 1422, praying and writing.

JOHN VIII

John VIII succeeded to the pitiful relic of the economically ruined Empire. But neither this shadow state nor its Church renounced the universal roles that had once been theirs. Thus, when the Grand Duke Basil of Moscow refused to recognize the Emperor as spiritual overlord of the Orthodox World because he was a vassal of the Sultan, the Patriarch of New Rome chided him (1390's). He pointed out that Church and Imperium were inseparable; that Christians could consequently not have a Church without an Emperor; that Saint Peter and the councils had recognized only one Emperor; that regardless of the appropriation of the title by other Christian rulers, there could be only one Emperor, whose decrees held throughout the world and who was to be revered by all Christians; and that, though his realm might be encircled by the infidel, he still received from the Church the same consecration as Emperor and Autocrat of the Romans, that is, of all Christians.[9]

Yet the smaller the state became, the more its sovereignty was divided. Thus, John VIII shared direct regional rule with his brothers Theodore, Andronicus, Constantine, Thomas, and Demetrius. Of these princes the most worthy seems to have been Constantine. He defeated the Latins and by 1432 had brought under Roman rule the entire Peloponnese except for the four Venetian footholds.

The contrast between this expansive vitality of the Peloponnese and the dying capital was striking. So diminished was the population of New Rome that ruins abounded. Vacant houses were used for firewood, and large areas were now copses, orchards, vineyards, or tilled soil. The once flourishing trade had moved to Galata. Only the powerful ramparts sheltered the feeble Roman remnant from the Turks. Yet despite losses, poverty, misfortunes, and humiliations, the people of New Rome were proud of their religion, their

[9] Barker, trans., *Social and Political Thought in Byzantium* (Oxford, 1957), pp. 194–196.

Fourteenth-century mosaic of Christ in the former Church of the Holy Savior in Chora, now the Kariye Museum. It will be noted that the fourteenth-century portrayal of Christ is gentler than that of the eleventh century (cf. the mosaic of Christ of Daphni, p. 74)

civilization, and their Basileus, to them still the prime potentate of the world. Court and religious ceremonies preserved the solemnity of yore, but the gems were false and the sacred vases brass. The Varangian guardsmen had been supplanted by Cretans. The Hippodrome no longer vibrated to chariot races, nor resounded to the tread of triumphant soldiers and captured barbarians. Instead, there were displays of archery and horsemanship.

BYZANTINE ART

If New Rome was no longer the great political focus, it was with its many churches and sacred relics still the holy city of Eastern Christians. And it was still a great cultural center. During the thirteenth century ecclesiastical art fused with the secular. The cold solemnity of stiff, sacred compositions yielded to picturesque elegance. Indeed, the union of Hellenistic and Christian led in the fourteenth and fifteenth centuries to the last great era of Byzantine art, infinitely more human and expressive than the others.

Before death enshrouded her the tragic vestige of the Empire appeared to be making a supreme effort to give to the world as many creations of her fecund genius as possible. By now gold, silver, ivory, and enamel had largely yielded to wood, while mosaics and luxurious marble had to a great extent given way to mural paintings. But painting seemed a more suitable medium for the Paleologue era. It rendered dramatic movement and expression better. The concord of Hellenistic, Oriental, and Christian breathe a new spirit into Byzantine art, far distant from the classic majesty of the tenth century. The persons of the frescos are singularly alive and expressive. They are painted with realism and keen observation of nature but retain the grace and elegance of the past. The Virgin is no other than a young, gentle, refined Byzantine woman. The figures are no longer set against solid backgrounds but against picturesque Hellenistic landscapes or structures. Deep, rich colors harmonize with bright, luminous hues. Touches of light contrasting with shadows give the effect of relief to the faces. New religious themes are depicted, old ones are transformed, and in the faces, gestures, and attitudes there is something infinitely tender and pathetic.

Fabrics are still of luxurious material. They reveal the grace, realism, elegance, creativeness, decorative sense, freedom of style, and profound knowledge of color of the Paleologue age.

Even icons are affected by the new spirit and charm by the colors, the nobility of the style, and the harmony of the composition. Serene saints become human and are delicately placed in picturesque landscapes. Alone illuminations seem unaffected by the new spirit.

Byzantine architects continued to create and improve graceful domed and cruciform churches, occasionally even domed basilicae, whose exteriors become ever more elegant.

Old and broken as was the Empire, her art seemed in the first flush of youth, ardent, sincere, emotional. It has been said that the force that permitted this ancient art to be reborn again and again was the continual struggle within it of two hostile cultures, the Oriental and the Occidental, which bestowed on it the incalculable powers engendered by continual combat. Byzantium continued the stupendous task undertaken by Alexander the Great—the fusion of East and West.

Fourteenth-century mosaic of the Dormition of the Virgin in the former Church of the Holy Savior, Chora, now the Kariye Museum

TRAPEZUNTINE EMPIRE

To the East lay a remnant of the Empire—Trebizond. Since 1282, when a Trapezuntine Emperor had married Michael VIII's daughter and restricted his title to avoid infringing on the universal pretensions of the Roman Emperor, relations between the two states had been amical. New Rome generally retained some influence in Trapezuntine affairs through marital unions. The Comneni still wore the Trapezuntine diadem, although there was much intra-dynastic strife. There was also much rivalry between the scions of the Pontic nobility and those of the guardsmen who had come from New Rome in 1204. The former controlled the countryside, while the power of the latter lay in the capital. These factions were usually involved in Comnenian family conflicts, constantly seeking to place a child or a woman on the throne.

Taking advantage of these civil wars and the weakened central power, Turkomans made many inroads into the Trapezuntine Empire and seized land for pastures. The Genoese also waged occasional war against her from their colony at Caffa. The Osmanli were apparently planning to extend control over her when the battle of Ankara supervened in 1402.

At this time the Empire of Trebizond still stretched 180 miles along the coast and 40 miles inland. Despite the unceasing struggle for existence, she remained an outpost of culture. Official documents were composed in Attic Greek. The academy of sciences and the observatory were famous. Churches and monasteries flourished. The wine and the water were good. Trapezuntine women and both sexes of the Comnenian family were renowned for their beauty. In 1428 John VIII married Maria, daughter of the Trapezuntine monarch.

CHURCH REUNION AND CRUSADE

Two years before his death Manuel II advised John VIII to employ the project of ecclesiastical reunion to obtain Latin help when needed but never to consummate the reunion, which the alienation

From *Robert Byron*, The Byzantine Achievement; *the medal, which is in the British Museum, was made by Pisanello during the Emperor's sojourn in Italy (the original is in Guillaume Joseph Grelot,* Relation nouvelle d'un voyage de Constantinople)

John VIII Paleologus (reigned 1425–1448)

of East and West had rendered impossible.[10] Yet, since John VIII had neither land nor gold with which to purchase Western aid, he decided to offer the Papacy's inflexible prerequisite—ecclesiastical submission. After protracted negotiations he departed for Italy in 1437, leaving his brother Constantine as regent. With his brother Demetrius, the Patriarch, and other Eastern prelates he attended the Council of Ferrara. After prolonged discussions, controversies, and flight from the plague, the union of the Churches was proclaimed in the Cathedral of Florence in 1439. The Pope was recognized as Vicar of Christ, while the Eastern Church was permitted to preserve its own rites. Other Eastern Christians, including spiritual descendants of Nestorians, Monophysites, and Monotheletes, adhered to the union.

When John returned to New Rome with two Latin galleys and a Latin guard of three hundred men he was greeted with insult. His subjects refused to submit to the Papacy. Not only did reunion bring domestic discord to the expiring Empire, it lowered her pres-

[10] Berger de Xivrey in *Mémoires de l'Institut National de France: Académie des Inscriptions de Belles-Lettres* (Paris, 1853), p. 178.

tige among Eastern Christians. The Russians and the patriarchs of Antioch, Jerusalem, and Alexandria rejected union.

Meanwhile, Murad II had reincorporated the emirates of Kermian, Aidin, Menteshe, and Hamid into Osmania but had failed to defeat Karaman. In Europe his bitterest rivals were the Hungarians. Had they been Orthodox, they might have rallied the Balkan Christians and expelled the Osmanli from Europe. But antipathy between Catholic and Orthodox led many Balkanians to prefer Osman rule. For years the Osmanli had raided Hungarian territory.

About 1440 reports of the defeats that the Hungarian hero Hunyadi, was inflicting on the Osmanli stirred Christendom and gave impulse to the Pope's call for a crusade. Crusaders joined Hunyadi, who in 1443 advanced conquering deep into the Turkish realm. The tide seemed turning. In Albania Scanderbeg uprose against the Turks. In Greece the Despot Constantine rebuilt the Isthmian Wall and advanced northward, supplanting Osman suzerainty over the Florentine Duke of Athens and Thebes. This Hellenic revival at a time when the Empire was in her death throes led many to evoke such names as Themistocles, Pericles, and Epaminondas and to hope that under Constantine the great reconquest might begin.

In 1444, however, the Sultan annihilated the crusading host at Varna. Undeterred, Constantine carried his arms as far as the Pindus, encouraging the Vlachs and Albanians of Thessaly to hope for liberation from Turkish rule. Determined to crush this budding Greek upsurge, Murad advanced against Constantine at the head of 60,000 men and drove him behind the Isthmian Wall (December 1446). Turkish cannon breached it and the Turks poured through, took Corinth, ravaged the Peloponnese, burned Patras, abducted 60,000 persons, and subjected Constantine to tribute.

Murad then moved against Scanderbeg but failed to take his capital. In 1448 Hunyadi reappeared, hoping to join Scanderbeg and drive the Turks eastward, but met defeat at Kossovo. The Balkan Peninsula thus remained firmly in Osmanli hands and any hope of overland relief of New Rome was abandoned.

Ten days after the battle of Kossovo John VIII died. Although he had successively married Anne of Muscovy, Sophia of Montferrat, and Maria of Trebizond, he had remained childless. A deputation consequently traveled to Mistra to carry the imperial diadem to his brother Constantine. In March 1449 Constantine XI entered the Golden Horn on a Catalan ship amid popular acclaim.

XIV

The End

1448–1453

TALL, slender, just, tolerant, unselfish, honorable, and magnanimous, Constantine XI was forty-four, twice a widower, childless, and an efficient general and administrator. Continuing the Paleologue policy of giving imperial sons or brothers autonomous despotates, he divided the Peloponnese between his brothers Thomas and Demetrius. Thus, only New Rome, vestigial Thrace, and some islands were under his direct rule.

Murad II died in 1451 and was succeeded by his son Mohammed II. The new Sultan, nineteen, pale, highly strung, and secretive, had piercing eyes, an exceptionally aquiline nose, and thick lips. He had often said that his first care after his accession would be the conquest of Constantinople, a potential peril in the heart of Osmania. Now he bent all his energies to that purpose, making peace with Hunyadi and the still redoubtable Emir of Karaman.

In 1452 he seized imperial territory on the European side of the Bosporus and built a triangular fortress opposite a Turkish fort on the Asiatic bank. Surmounting it with bronze bombards able to discharge stone balls of six hundred pounds, he controlled the Bosporus and could sever New Rome's indispensable Black Sea grain shipments. His fleet moved to Gallipoli to cut off help from the West; a Turkish army marched into the Peloponnese to prevent the Emperor's brothers from coming to his aid; and the bombards of the new Bosporan fort sank a Venetian vessel carrying barley from the Black Sea. The crew was beheaded and the captain impaled to discourage further attempts to provision the City. Imperial cities on the Marmara and the Black Sea were taken.

Although it was clear that any Western ruler who might intervene would do so, not to save the dying Empire, but to supplant her and although the Orthodox clergy and communicants overwhelmingly opposed union with the Latin Church, yet the only possible source of help lay in the West. Consequently, under Constantine's auspices Greek and Latin churchmen in December 1452 celebrated the reunion of the Churches in Saint Sophia. Constantine hoped that this act would bring the direly needed reinforcements from Latin Christendom.

While the reunion was being solemnized at Saint Sophia, the populace was seeking the will of God from a revered monk, Gennadius. He asked them why one should place one's trust in Italians instead of in God and predicted that the loss of Orthodoxy would be followed by that of the City. Thereafter Saint Sophia was shunned as the haunt of demons. The popular attitude was expressed in a statement attributed to the Grand Duke Notaras to the effect that he would rather see the Turkish turban in the City than the Latin miter. Thus, in the hour of greatest peril Constantine was alienated from his subjects.

In defense of the City, however, nobles and people rallied to the Emperor, who displayed the same vigor that he had as Despot of the Peloponnese. On the almost four miles of the partially ruined land walls, where the fiercest attack was expected, New Rome was sheltered by the crenelated inner wall of Theodosius II. It was forty feet high and fifteen feet thick and had ninety-six projecting towers. Fifty feet in front of it stood the crenelated outer wall, which was twenty-seven feet high and two to six feet thick and also had projecting towers. Fifty feet beyond the outer wall was a six-foot breastwork, which bordered a moat sixty feet wide. The inner wall, the main defense, was in such a state of neglect that Constantine decided to make the chief stand at the outer wall. The moat was cleared and its bridges were destroyed. The huge chain to bar the mouth of the Golden Horn was put into place. All able-bodied men were called to arms. Weapons and provisions were collected.

In the spring of 1453 Mohammed set out from Adrianople. His host outnumbered the City's population, which had declined from the estimated eight hundred thousand of her heyday to fewer than fifty thousand. He is believed to have had between a hundred

From Archäologisches Institut des Deutschen Reiches, Vol. 6

Reconstruction of Land Walls of New Rome

fifty and two hundred thousand regulars and irregulars. The latter, both Moslem and Christian, were booty-hunters, who were used as shock troops and were continually reinforced by fresh loot-seekers. In addition, a multitude of Moslem holy men provided for spiritual fervor.

Furthermore, over the roads leading to New Rome oxen were

dragging enormous bronze bombards, the greatest collection of artillery that the world had seen. The barrel of one, the Basilique, the creation of a Christian founder, was twenty-seven feet long and three feet in diameter. The largest bombard in the world, it could project a fifteen-hundred-pound stone ball a mile. It was hauled by sixty oxen with two hundred men supporting it, for cannons were not yet placed on wheels.

On April 5 the men on New Rome's land wall saw an enormous cloud of dust approaching. Above the ominous rumble of men, beasts, wagons, and bombards could be heard the menacing roll of drums, the shrill notes of fifes, and the sharp clash of cymbals. On the morrow the Turks began to dig a trench from the Marmara to the Golden Horn, three-fourths of a mile from the wall. Behind it they formed a mound, which they topped with a palisade with large loopholes. They also made massive molds and cast new bombards. Having no carriages, they embedded the fourteen batteries of four bombards each in earth and blocks of wood. Three quarters of a mile behind the trench, on the edge of the Lycus Valley, the young Sultan's lofty red and gold tent was erected amid those of his faithful Janissaries. Opposite his tent, where the Lycus passes into the City, the wall was weak. It was here that he intended to concentrate the attack, and here he placed the formidable Basilique battery. Turkish forces crossed the Golden Horn and encircled neutral Galata. Soon, possibly three hundred fifty Turkish ships concentrated in the Bosporus.

To oppose the greatest armament of the age Constantine had about five thousand Romans, including enrolled monks, burghers, and artisans; about three thousand Cretan, Latin, and Turkish mercenaries and volunteers; and twenty-seven ships to defend twelve and a half miles of wall. The blockade had prevented his obtaining enough arms and provisions. Moreover, the recoil of his few bombards did more harm to the wall than to the foe.

In conformity with the dictates of the Koran to offer peace before making war, Mohammed II called on Constantine XI to surrender the City. The successor of a long line of civilizers and conquerors had done everything possible for the defense and left the fate of the Empire in God's hands.

On April 12 Mohammed ordered the bombardment to commence. There followed blinding flashes, an indescribable roar, a great quaking, and an enormous cloud of black smoke and dust. Scores of huge stone balls crashed into the walls, shaking them to the foundations, cracking them, tearing gaping holes out of them, scattering stone and masonry, and creating havoc among the defenders. For a week the bombardment continued, the Basilique discharging seven times a day and once at night. Supplementing the bombards, catapults slung stones, ballistae shot darts, and culverins hurled stone balls, while archers, arbalesters, arquebusiers, and escopetters fired at the defenders. The bombards did the greatest damage. Theretofore their potentialities had not been realized and they had been used as a secondary weapon. Mohammed II was the first to employ them to open the way for an assault, in preparation for which his men were filling the moat.

During the cataclysmic bombardment the Romans, who had taken their positions in the enclosure between the inner and outer walls, suspended bales of wool in front of the outer wall and struggled to repair the damage. But the bombards destroyed faster than the Romans could mend. From towers and crenelations Roman catapults, ballistae, fusils, and culverins returned the Turkish fire, while Roman archers, arbalesters, arquebusiers, and escopetters shot at the Turks filling the moat. Wherever the wall was in peril or in need of repair the Emperor was present, encouraging his men with his valor, vigor, and good cheer. But anguish must have gripped the hearts of these last Romans as they beheld the gaping, irreparable wounds in their venerable walls.

In the Lycus Valley the bombardment was heaviest. Here, at the end of a week the moat was partially filled, the breastwork and the outer wall were in ruins, and two towers of the inner wall had crumbled. But on the ruins of the outer wall the indefatigable Romans had built a barricade of beams and tree trunks, attached and reinforced by branches, vine cuttings, fascines, ladders, crates filled with straw, and stones from the demolished wall. It was cemented together with earth and clay and faced with several layers of hides, which were continually watered to protect them from flaming arrows and firebrands. In front were bales of wool to soften the impact of the bombard balls. On top a row of earth-filled barrels formed the crenelation. This improvised barrier had the advantage

Moat and walls of New Rome today

that bombard balls could imbed themselves in it without necessarily shattering it.

Pleased with the effects of the bombardment, the Sultan ordered assault. Suddenly, after nightfall on April 18, the weary defenders at the barricade in the Lycus Valley were startled by Turkish war whoops and the roll of drums. The Turks were crossing the partly filled moat, clambering over the wrecked breastwork, and rushing toward them. The alarm bells on the walls sounded. Church bells took up the toll. People rushed to the walls to help in the defense, while priests hastened to their altars. The Turks tried to set fire to the barricade. From behind their barrels of earth the Romans beat them off and extinguished the blazes. With long hooks the Turks pulled down the barrels and showered the exposed but mailed Romans with darts and stones, while others tried to climb up ladders. The Romans hurled missiles of all kinds on the Turks and over-turned their ladders. Four hours the nocturnal battle lasted, fierce, murderous, implacable. Then the Turks withdrew. Bombardment and almost daily assaults continued. When the defenders were not fighting they were repairing the defenses.

The Sultan did not limit his attacks to the land wall. He knew that in 1204 the successful assault had been made on the weak harbor wall. His fleet's prime offensive purpose was to break through the boom blocking the Golden Horn. But behind the boom were ten large vessels under the command of the Grand Duke Notaras. From these high galleys the defenders poured all kinds of projectiles on the assailants and drove them off with jeers.

On April 20 an imperial transport bringing corn from Sicily and three large Genoese ships carrying arms and provisions from the Pope appeared in the Marmara. A tremor of joy ran through the suffering citizens, who thought that they were the van of a relieving crusade. A breeze was carrying the four vessels gently toward the Golden Horn when suddenly 150 Turkish galleys with the Sultan's best mailed effectives rowed out from their Bosporan base. The admiral, the Bulgarian Baltoglu, called upon the four ships to lower their sails. Watching from walls, house tops, and the Hippodrome, the people of New Rome prayed for a miracle. The Christian ships continued their course. The Turkish navy bore down on them, raining arrows and fire darts. The leading galleys tried to board the higher Christian vessels but were repulsed.

Suddenly, almost at the mouth of the Golden Horn, the Christian ships were becalmed. Under the eyes of the Sultan, who viewed the combat from beneath the walls of Galata, the Turkish galleys surrounded the four ships and bombarded them with stones and fire darts. It was of no avail, and Baltoglu again gave the order to board. He ran the bow of his galley against the poop of the imperial transport and attempted to board her. Other Turkish galleys attached themselves to the Christian vessels. Three hours the Turkish soldiers struggled to reach their decks or set them aflame. The mailed Christian men-at-arms beat them off with battle-axes, while the Christian crews extinguished the firebrands and dropped rocks on the Turkish galleys. Above the cracking of timbers could be heard agonizing and blasphemous cries of pain and rage. When one Turkish galley was disabled another took her place.

The Sultan, infuriated that a hundred fifty Turkish galleys could neither sink nor capture the four vessels, spurred his horse into the shallow waters off Galata and, trembling with rage, blasphemed his admiral, crews, and combatants and made vile menaces. His entourage joined him and soon a steady stream of invective and profanity was flowing out to the fighting Turks. Yet they had fought bravely and many had fallen on their decks or sunk into the depths with crushed skulls and maimed bodies.

To add to their misfortunes a wind sprang up. The sails of the Christian vessels swelled. They broke through the frailer Turkish galleys. The watching Romans thanked God for a miracle. The enraged Sultan shouted impossible orders, but his wounded admiral pretended not to hear. He had sacrificed enough. The Turkish navy withdrew, and the Christian ships passed triumphantly over the loosened boom amid transports of joy. The wrathful Sultan wanted to impale Baltoglu. His officers dissuaded him, but he deprived the hapless Bulgar of post and property and administered the bastinado to him.

Yet it mattered little whether the Turks controlled access to the Golden Horn or not, for no further succor came. Day and night the Turkish bombards continued to pulverize the land walls, especially in the Lycus Valley, where the breach grew ever wider. Feverishly the last defenders of Antiquity, incessantly under a hail of ancient, medieval, and modern missiles, filled the gaps with rocks, logs, clay, earth, and barrels of stones and fought off masses of red-fezzed and white-turbaned Turks. So resolute was their resistance that Mohammed determined to attack the City from the Golden Horn in order to draw men from the land wall. The difficulty was to reach the Golden Horn. Unable to pass the boom, he built a wooden road from the Bosporus over the hill of Pera to the Golden Horn and transported seventy-two ships over it.

With this squadron on the opposite bank of the Golden Horn under the protection of Turkish bombards the Romans had to take men from other parts of the wall to defend the three and a half miles of the harbor wall. Moreover, the Christian fleet was in danger of being attacked from two sides. It was decided to burn the squadron at night. The plan is said to have been betrayed to the Sultan by Genoese of Galata, and the Turkish shore batteries sank the leading ships. The Turks impaled those Christian sailors who succeeded in swimming to shore. In reprisal the Emperor executed 260 Turkish prisoners. Soon after, Mohammed threw across the Golden Horn a barrel bridge from which another battery of bombards attacked the City.

The situation was desperate. The walls were unceasingly bombarded. The fleet was fired on from Pera Hill. And the dwindling defenders at the crumbling walls had to fight off continual assaults. Food was running low. There was discord between Genoese and Venetians and between imperial and Latin officers. But the Emperor was everpresent to restore as much concord as possible. April passed into May. The assaults against the breaches grew fiercer. The defenders labored and fought febrilely. But fresh Turkish irregulars arrived from Asia to replace those who had fallen.

The Latins offered Constantine ships to escape from the City, rally the Romans in the Peloponnese, perhaps unite with Skanderbeg, and attack the Turks from the rear. The Emperor replied that he would never abandon the clergy, the churches, his throne, and his people and that, if necessary, he would die with them. It was, however, decided to seek the expected Venetian fleet and urge the admiral to come with haste. At night a small brigantine with twelve men aboard slipped out of the Golden Horn, glided silently through the Marmara and the Dardanelles, and searched the Aegean for the Venetians.

In the interim the Sultan's Serbian miners had dug a tunnel under the walls. Subterranean noises alarmed the City. Roman engineers dug a counter-mine into the tunnel and burned the props. The Serbs were buried alive. The Sultan's miners dug thirteen more tunnels. Each one was discovered. Water was let in or the miners were suffocated by smoke or mephitic gases or set aflame with Greek Fire.

On the morning of May 18 the defenders saw on the edge of the partly filled moat in the Lycus Valley a huge rolling tower covered with three layers of camel hides. The tower, which was connected with the Turkish lines by a protective leather arbor, was provided with ballistic machines, earth to fill the moat, and scaling ladders. From it the Turks hurled projectiles of all sorts on the Romans, thus impeding the repair of the wall, whose breach in the Lycus Valley grew ever wider, while the moat was rapidly filling up. Under cover of the tower's barrage the Turks attacked with scaling ladders. All day the battle raged. At twilight the Turks withdrew, while the weary Romans labored through the night, repairing the widened breach, clearing out the moat, and burning the tower with its garrison. Undismayed, the Sultan ordered the construction of other towers, which the Romans burned by night.

On May 23, after an absence of twenty days, the little brigantine was seen moving swiftly toward the City. Hearts beat faster. At last there would be words of help from Christendom. Turkish ships set out to crush the valiant vessel, but she eluded them and glided triumphantly into the Golden Horn amid the expectant joy of the City. But the faithful twelve of the brigantine reported that the Venetian fleet was not to be found. They had returned to die with their comrades for the glory of God and the honor of Christendom.

The agony continued. Wherever the walls were demolished or the moat filled the Emperor was at hand. In the Lycus Valley bombard balls of twelve hundred pounds were pulverizing the wall, sending tremors through the City, even to the ships in the Golden Horn. The ring around the City grew ever tighter. Yet all attempts to take her by land, sea, underground, or with towers, all the ingenuity of Antiquity, the Middle Ages, and the incipient modern era broke against the resistance of the heirs of a double tradition reaching back two millennia to Leonidas and Horatius.

Early on the morning of May 25 the Emperor discussed in council the measures to take in view of the imminent general assault. All present realized that the City would fall and urged him to depart in order to preserve the imperial tradition. But Constantine declared that he would not leave the City. He would be a good shepherd and lay down his life for his flock. But he sent off the ladies of the court.

The same day in the Turkish camp the Sultan announced the general assault, proclaimed three days of pillage, and promised his combatants all the men, women, and children in the City. He reminded them that three large breaches had been made in the land wall, notably in the Lycus Valley, where the moat was largely filled and the wall destroyed over a length of twelve hundred feet. He further pointed out that not only were the dwindling Romans enfeebled after six weeks of continual fighting and repairing, but that the Osmanli fleet would draw many of them away from the land wall.

On May 28 he harangued his officers. He is reported to have described the beauty and riches that would soon be theirs, the glory of conquering the most famous city in the world, the piety of fulfilling an ancient Islamic prophecy, and the pleasures of Paradise for those about to fall. He dwelt on the small number of defenders, their insufficient equipment, and the facility of access to a city whose moat was filled and whose walls were demolished.

Within the city abandoned by Christendom the last Romans confided in the mercy of God. On May 28 a solemn procession carried sacred icons and relics to the walls and the breaches. Later the Emperor addressed his court and his officers, recalling the ancient duty of Romans to die for their faith, country, sovereign, and families. He reminded them that they were scions of antique Hellenic and Roman heroes and that they did not place their faith in masses of men and machines, but in God. As for himself, he was determined, if need be, to die in defense of the Empire. In accordance with Byzantine custom, the military leaders embraced one another and asked forgiveness for any offense. In the evening the Emperor and all who could leave the walls attended services at Saint Sophia. The myriad tapers flickered uncertainly, lighting the mosaics and the drawn faces of the worshipers, Orthodox and Catholic, who had sunk their differences in the face of impending tragedy in what was the funeral ceremony of a state born over twenty-two centuries earlier on the left bank of the Tiber.

The Emperor rode slowly from Saint Sophia to the Palace of Blachernae, where he asked pardon of anyone whom he might have offended. Soon after midnight he mounted his Arabian mare and rode to the wall. From a tower he gazed across the moat and saw the Turks moving the bombards and assault equipment nearer to the walls.

Abruptly—it was one o'clock on the morning of May 29, 1453— he saw the Turkish masses advancing along the whole line. Simultaneously the Turkish fleets, provided with towers and scaling platforms, attacked from the Golden Horn and the Marmara. The wild Turkish war cry rent the night, while from the City rose the strains of the Kyrie Eleison as every man hastened to his post. The crisis had come.

The Emperor sped to the Lycus Valley, where only a makeshift barricade separated the Empire from extinction. Possibly fifty thousand of the Sultan's Moslem and Christian irregulars, armed with bows, slings, arquebuses, muskets, or scimitars, fired at the defenders and rushed screaming across the filled moat and the outer enclosure with scaling ladders, while trumpets, flutes, and cymbals cut the air. In a moment hundreds of ladders were placed against

Ruins of New Rome's walls. The top of the so-called Palace of Constantine VII Porphyrogenitus is visible next to the structure with the bush

the barricade and the wall and the motley irregulars commenced climbing up. The Romans fought with the vigor and valor of their ancient renown, overturned ladders, hurled stones, discharged bows, muskets, and culverins into the dense mass, and broke the elan of the charge. When the irregulars turned to flee, military police with iron maces and loaded whips drove them back into battle. The Sultan was using them to exhaust the strength of the besieged. At length, after two hours of fighting he permitted the survivors to withdraw.

The Romans, who had fought or labored fifty days and nights, hoped to spend the last hours of the night resting. But the irregulars had hardly retreated when the shining breastplates of the disciplined Anatolian regulars appeared. While fifes, drums, and trumpets summoned the Turks to the assault, alarm bells on the walls called the Romans to their posts. A shot from the monster bombard brought down part of the barricade. Under cover of dust and smoke the regulars, crying "Allah, Allah," poured through the breach. At the head of a valiant band the Emperor drove them back over the ruined barricade. Night was fading into dawn and the Empire still lived.

Despite heavy losses, Mohammed ordered a third general assault before the sun had risen. He accompanied his Janissaries as far as the moat in the Lycus Valley. The big bombard hurled another enormous ball at the broken barricade, creating a covering cloud of dust. As bombards roared and fifes, drums, and trumpets sounded, a rain of missiles from bows, slings, muskets, and arquebuses fell on the embattled Romans. Then fresh, invincible Janissaries rushed against them, shouting "Allah, Allah." The supreme moment had come. The alarm bells sounded on the walls, the church bells in the City. Women and children brought stones to the fighters and prayed that the City be saved.

At the tragic Lycus breach the Emperor and his fighters halted the onrushing Janissaries with a wall of pikes, swords, and axes. The Genoese Giustiniani, the leader of the Latins, was wounded and decided to leave the enclosure. The Emperor besought him not to depart, lest the Italians lose heart. But Giustiniani withdrew and was followed by many other Latins. Constantine XI and his little band of Romans remained steadfast at the breach.

Informed that the Turks had entered a postern gate, Constantine left the breach for a few minutes. Taking advantage of his absence, the Janissaries surged forward, pressed back the Romans by weight of numbers, and soon enveloped them on three sides. The Emperor returned and saw the white-capped Janissaries thronging into the inner exclosure. He dismounted, discarded the most obvious imperial insignia, drew his sword, and with three officers dashed into the swelling flood of Janissaries.

The sun rose and shone for the last time on a Roman Emperor, almost alone, without hope or fear, fighting against the best warriors in the world. He fought on until he fell under their blows. The good shepherd had died for his flock and with him the Roman Empire.

Epilogue

OF the five thousand Roman combatants who had fought beside Constantine XI to stem the onrushing torrent of history, over four thousand had fallen. They were the last of a line of heroes reaching back to the dawn when Greek gods were men. With them the last spark of Antiquity flickered out.

As the Turks rushed over their dead bodies and the sickening cry "The City is taken" rose, two streams of fugitives formed. One moved toward the port, hoping to find safety aboard a ship or to cross to Galata. But that city's gates were closed. Others, believing an old prophecy that the Moslems would advance as far as the Great Church and then be smitten by the Angel of God, fled to Saint Sophia. Meanwhile, the Turks, infuriated by the stubborn resistance, began to butcher everyone regardless of age or sex. As the sun rose higher, their rage abated and they put to death only infants, invalids, and the aged. Of the survivors many preferred suicide to violation and misuse by Turks, sale at auction, and transportation to rude provincial abodes.

To the Grand Duke Notaras, who had commanded the Roman reserves, the Sultan offered the post of governor of the City on condition that he accept Islam and give him his young son as page. Notaras refused. His son and son-in-law were killed in front of him and then he was executed. He met this fate with resignation.

In 1460 Mohammed terminated the rule of Constantine XI's bickering brothers, the Despots Thomas and Demetrius, over the Peloponnese. Thomas found refuge in Rome, where he died in 1465, while Demetrius died a monk in Adrianople in 1470.

Meanwhile, in 1461 the Sultan had invested Trebizond with overpowering naval and military forces. Protesting that he had broken no treaty, the Emperor David Comnenus nonetheless surrendered the state that his house had ruled for two and a half centuries. The Janissaries took over the city and divided the inhabitants into those who became slaves of the Sultan and his ministers, those who were to recolonize Constantinople, and those who were to populate the Trapezuntine countryside. Moreover, Mohammed selected 800 youths for the Janissary corps and 700 for himself.

David and his sons were later murdered by order of Mohammed, who refused the corpses burial and reduced the bereaved Empress to poverty. Nicephorus, claiming to be David's son, fled to inaccessible Maïna, where he was chosen First Senator. In this hereditary post his descendants governed the autonomous peninsula until expelled by the turbulent nobles in 1675. The last of his progeny and seven hundred followers migrated to Genoa, which gave them lands in Corsica.

In 1472 Zoë-Sophia, daughter of the Despot Thomas, married Ivan III, Grand Duke of Moscovy. Ivan adopted the double-headed eagle of the Paleologi, thus proclaiming Moscovy the political heiress of the Empire. A number of Romans accompanied Sophia, thereby strengthening the influence of Byzantine civilization in Russia, where some of its features survived until the twentieth century. In a sense Moscow became a third Rome and Russia carried the Empire's missionary and civilizing task eastward to the Pacific. She also assumed the duty of expelling the Turks from Europe but was thwarted by the Western powers, notably Britain.

Meanwhile, as once popes had succeeded emperors as leaders of the Christians in the West, the patriarchs of Constantinople took the place of the vanished emperors among the Christians under Turkish rule. During the dark centuries of the submersion of Greeks, Slavs, and Vlachs the Orthodox Church kept alive their memory of separate nationality and of the states that they had once formed, thus preserving a framework for survival and for the national resurrections of the nineteenth and twentieth centuries.

While the states of southeastern Europe thus owe their rebirth to the Empire's last living institution and while the Slavs from the Adriatic to the Urals received the essential elements of their culture from her, the Turks were indebted to her for much of their political and military organization.

But the influence of the dead Empire spread far beyond the Greek, Vlach, Slavic, and Turkish worlds. Not only had she for centuries championed Christianity, stood as a bastion of civilization against continually threatening Barbaria, broken the Arab assault on Europe, and delayed the Turkish torrent, she also gave birth to the most brilliant civilization of the Middle Ages and preserved for the West the works and traditions of Antiquity. It is difficult to conceive of the Renaissance without these and without the unceasing flow of Byzantine ideas and artistic inspiration.

The properties that enabled the Empire to survive and flourish despite almost continual assaults probably lay largely in the militarized free peasantry that came into being in the seventh century and the elastic defense of which it was capable; her absolute form of government, permitting rapid decisions and action; her centralized administration, enabling her to concentrate her power; her efficient armed forces; her skilful foreign policy, which deployed to great advantage the power and prestige of her age, wealth, religion, military strength, and antique civilization; a social structure that permitted able men to rise from humble ranks even to the post of Emperor; her ability to assimilate aliens; her stable currency; her prosperous economy; and her impregnable capital.

These positive properties were offset by certain weaknesses. They included religious intolerance, which alienated Syrians, Egyptians, and Armenians and deprived the Empire of the support of many hardy heretics; excessive state control of commercial and industrial enterprise, which retarded the development of the middle class; official corruption; the failure to evolve a system of pacific succession to the throne; the occasional succession of children or incapable persons; the excessive growth of monasticism and the concomitant decline of revenue, land under cultivation, and ablebodied men for the armed forces; the tendency of churches, magnates, and monasteries to deprive free farmers and peasant-soldiers of their land; the assumption of public functions by private persons; the consequent decline of the central authority and the collapse of the military system based on free farmer-fighters. Indeed, by 1100 the social, political, and military system of the Empire probably resembled the feudal kingdoms of the West more than it did the Empire of 1000. Such a state found it difficult to maintain a navy and in due course came under the naval and commercial domination of Italian merchant republics. Yet so skilled were imperial statesmen that the Empire did not completely disappear until the eve of modern times.

Appendix I:

Abridged List of Roman Emperors

49–44	Caesar	286–305	Maximian
43–14	Augustus	292–306	Constantius I
14–37	Tiberius	293–311	Galerius
37–41	Caligula	305–313	Maximin Daia
41–54	Claudius	305–307	Valerius Severus
54–68	Nero	306–312	Maxentius
69–79	Vespasian	306–337	Constantine I
79–81	Titus	311–324	Licinius
81–96	Domitian	337–340	Constantine II
96–98	Nerva	337–350	Constans I
98–117	Trajan	337–361	Constantius II
117–138	Hadrian	350–353	Magnentius
138–161	Antoninus Pius	361–363	Julian
161–180	Marcus Aurelius	363–364	Jovian
180–192	Commodus	364–375	Valentinian I (West)
193–211	Septimius Severus	364–378	Valens
211–217	Caracalla	375–383	Gratian (W)
218–222	Elagabalus	375–392	Valentinian II (W)
222–235	Alexander Severus	379–395	Theodosius I
235–238	Maximin	383–388	Magnus Maximus (W)
238–244	Gordian III		
244–249	Philip	392–394	Eugene (W)
249–251	Decius	395–408	Arcadius
251–253	Gallus	395–423	Honorius (W)
253–259	Valerian	408–450	Theodosius II
253–268	Gallienus	409–410	Priscus Attalus (W)
268–270	Claudius II	421	Constantius III (W)
270–275	Aurelian	423–455	Valentinian III (W)
276–281	Probus	450–457	Marcian
281–283	Carus	455	Petronius Maximus (W)
284–305	Diocletian		
		455–456	Avitus (W)

457–461	Majorian (W)
457–474	Leo I
461–465	Libius Severus (W)
467–472	Anthemius (W)
472	Olybrius (W)
473–474	Glycerius (W)
474–480	Julius Nepos (W)
474	Leo II
474–491	Zeno
475–476	Romulus (W)
491–518	Anastasius I
518–527	Justin I
527–565	Justinian I
565–578	Justin II
578–582	Tiberius II
582–602	Maurice
602–610	Phocas
610–641	Heraclius
641	Constantine III
641	Heracleon
641–668	Constans II
668–685	Constantine IV
685–695	Justinian II
695–697	Leontius
697–705	Tiberius III
705–711	Justinian II
711–713	Philipicus
713–715	Anastasius II
715–717	Theodosius III
717–741	Leo III
741–775	Constantine V
775–780	Leo IV
780–797	Constantine VI
797–802	Irene
802–811	Nicephorus I
811	Stauricius
811–813	Michael I Rangabé
813–820	Leo V
820–829	Michael II
829–842	Theophilus
842–867	Michael III
867–886	Basil I
886–912	Leo VI
912–913	Alexander
912–959	Constantine VII
919–944	Romanus I Lecapenus
959–963	Romanus II
963–969	Nicephorus II Phocas
969–976	John I Tzimisces
976–1025	Basil II
1025–1028	Constantine VIII
1028–1034	Romanus III Argyrus
1034–1041	Michael IV
1041–1042	Michael V
1042	Zoë and Theodora
1042–1055	Constantine IX Monomachus
1055–1056	Theodora
1056–1057	Michael VI Stratioticus
1057–1059	Isaac I Comnenus
1059–1067	Constantine X Ducas
1068–1071	Romanus IV Diogenes
1071–1078	Michael VII Ducas
1078–1081	Nicephorus III Botaniates
1081–1118	Alexius I Comnenus
1118–1143	John II Comnenus
1143–1180	Manuel I Comnenus
1180–1183	Alexius II Comnenus
1183–1185	Andronicus I Comnenus
1185–1195	Isaac II Angelus
1195–1203	Alexius III Angelus
1203–1204	Isaac II Angelus
1203–1204	Alexius IV Angelus
1204	Alexius V Ducas
1204–1222	Theodore I Lascaris
1222–1254	John III Vatatzes
1254–1258	Theodore II Lascaris
1258–1261	John IV Lascaris
1259–1282	Michael VIII Paleologus

1282–1328	Andronicus II Paleologus
1295–1320	Michael IX Paleologus
1328–1341	Andronicus III Paleologus
1341–1391	John V Paleologus
1341–1354	John VI Cantacuzene
1353–1357	Matthew Cantacuzene
1376–1379	Andronicus IV Paleologus
1390	John VII Paleologus
1391–1425	Manuel II Paleologus
1425–1448	John VIII Paleologus
1448–1453	Constantine XI Paleologus

Appendix II: Races

This note concerns only peoples mentioned in this work. Humanity is generally divided into three main groups—Caucasoid, Mongoloid, and Negroid. The Caucasoids, in turn, are usually subdivided into Mediterraneans, Alpines, and Nordics. Interfecundation has given rise to numerous intermediary strains. Nevertheless, with many exceptions the Mediterraneans still predominate in the area of the Middle Sea, the Alpines in the highlands to the north, and the Nordics in the northern plains, the British Isles, and Scandinavia.

The Mediterraneans are usually slight, brunet, and long-headed. A primordial Hamito-Semitic language group has been discerned among them. The most eminent Hamites are the ancient Egyptians, who seem already to have been of conglomerate lineage when the first rays of history fall on them. The last living trace of their idiom lingers in Coptic liturgy, while in Atlas valleys some Berbers retain spoors of hoary Hamitic. The Semites include Phoenicians, Assyrians, Chaldeans, Hebrews, Arameans (whose language was used by Jesus), and the farflung Arabs. Moreover, the Turkomans east of the Caspian, many of whom began to move into Anatolia in the eleventh century, are apparently basically Mediterraneans, although linguistically related to Mongoloids.

The Alpines tend to be dark-haired, thick-set, and broad-headed. They apparently had early contact with Nordics, whose idioms they often use. They may be divided into three types:

1. Occidental, the shorter strain with a large Mediterranean admixture;

2. Dinaric or Illyrian, of taller stature and with much Nordic blood, a source of many of the Empire's soldiers and emperors;

3. Armenoid, tall with prominent curved nose and high sloping forehead, such as the Khaldians in precimmerian Armenia, who tended to impose their nasal and cranial characteristics on the peoples with whom they interbred.

The Nordics are generally tall, blond, and long-headed. They speak related Indo-European language and are often divided into an eastern and a western group.

Within the eastern group are:

(a) the Aryans, who about 1500 B.C. invaded India and imposed the caste system and their language, whose purified form is Sanscrit;

(b) the Iranians (Medes, Persians, Parthians, Bactrians, etc.), who tend to be round-headed and who mantled the Iranian tableland during the second prechristian millennium, subduing its unidentified occupants;

(c) perhaps the Cimmerians (possibly Iranians), who seven centuries before Christ merged with the native Armenoid Khaldians, gave birth to the Armenian nation (the name of a Cimmerian tribe), and imposed their tongue;

(d) many tribes of the vast Eurasian plain, who accepted the vague dominion of the probably Iranian Scyths;

(e) the related Sarmatians, who during the first prechristian century supplanted the Scyths. (Ages later vestigial Sarmatians, the Alans, retreated to the security of the Caucasus, where they are known as Ossetes and to this day use their ancestral Scytho-Iranian language.);

(f) the Slavs, who began to emerge from the general area of the Pripet marshes early in the Christian Era and spread over a large part of Europe, absorbing such conquerors as the Nordic Russians and the Mongoloid Bulgars.

Among the western Nordics are:

(a) the ancient Greeks, who entered the Aegean area in successive waves, beginning possibly two millennia before Christ;

(b) the Macedonians, originally indistinguishable from other Greeks but who differentiated from them as a result of divergent geographical and ethnological conquests;

(c) the Phrygians, who entered Anatolia from Thrace before 1500 B.C. and ultimately overthrew the Hittites;

(d) many Thracian and Illyrian tribes of mixed Nordic, Alpine, and Mediterranean blood, who in historic times used Nordic vernaculars and whose last relic lives on in Albanian;

(e) the Italic tribes, who descended into the Apennine Peninsula before 1000 B.C., conquered the Mediterraneans, and imposed their dialects;

(f) the Celts, of whom the Gauls swept into France, Spain, the Po Valley, and Illyria about 500 B.C. and in the third prechristian century into Macedonia, Thessaly, Thrace, the Black Sea steppe, and Anatolia;

(g) other Celts, the Brythons, who probably in the fourth prechristian century crossed the Channel to the island that has been named after them. (Three linguistic vestiges remain: Welsh; the almost extinct

Cornish; and Breton, which British Celts took to Brittany, where they joined Gallic kinsmen between A.D. 400 and 600.);

(h) the North Germans, who moved into Scandinavia during the second prechristian millennium, and slew the possibly Mongoloid natives or drove them into the mountains, where they perhaps blended into the giants of Teutonic mythology and after struggling three thousand years against cold and want finally expired, while the North Germans multiplied to such an extent that after the eighth Christian century they migrated far and wide, entering history with such names as Rus, Norsemen, Normans, Vikings, or Varangians, even reaching forgotten America;

(i) the East Germans, including Goths, Gepids, Vandals, and Burgundians, who settled between the Oder and the Vistula about 500 B.C. and were destined to centuries of wanderings, conquests, and ultimate extinction, the last Gothic remnant lingering in the Crimea until the sixteenth century;

(j) the West Germans, who in Caesar's time dwelt east of the Rhine and included such tribes as the Suevi (Quadi, Lombards, Alamanni, Marcomanni), Franks, Saxons, Frisians, and Thuringians.

The Mongoloids are generally divided into Malaysians, Amerindians, and Mongolians. The Mongolians, in turn, are divided into two linguistic groups, the Sinitic and the Ural-Altaic.

Our concern is with the Ural-Altaians, who in prehistoric times spread over northern and central Eurasia. The relationship between Uralic and Altaic is disputed. They seem unrelated to Sinitic, while Uralic has similarities with Indo-European. Moreover, early Uralians, such as the Finns and the Hungarians, whose habitat appears to have been between the Baltic and the Urals, were possibly not Mongolians but Mediterraneans. Early in the Christian Era the Hungarians apparently moved eastward across the Urals and later southward into the steppes. Mingling with Turkish and Iranian nomads, they adopted their way of life, were in due course driven westward, and when they reached their present home about 900 were already a mixed race.

As for the Altaians, they may be linguistically divided into Turks, Tungus, and Mongols. Centuries before Christ Chinese sources refer to the Hiungnu, who were probably mixed Altaians, including the ancestors of the Huns and the Turks. They came to exercise a vague dominion between the Great Wall and the Caspian. Early in the Christian Era the Hiungnu empire succumbed to the Tungus. Huns were propelled westward and White Huns southward. But many of the Hiungnu, notably the Turks, remained in the Altai Mountains. In the sixth century the Turks overthrew the Tungus, spread their rule to the

Caspian, and drove the kindred Avars into Europe. Thus the name *Turk* came to designate the scattered racial or linguistic descendants of the Hiungnu, such as the early Bulgars, the Patzinaks, Turkomans, Seljuks, and Osmanli. In the thirteenth century the Mongols extended their rule over the related Turks, who, however, tended to absorb them.

There follows a courageous attempt to identify the peoples mentioned in this book racially and linguistically in that order. In many cases only the dominant strain is indicated. Where the linguistic term is repetitive a broader classification is used and occasionally the more common linguistic category replaces the racial.

Abasgians, Georgians
Alamanni, West Germans, Indo-European
Alans, Sarmatians, Iranian
Albanians, Illyrians, Indo-European
Altaians, speakers of Turkic, Tungu, and Mongol
Antae, Slavs with Altaic infusion
Arabs, Mediterraneans, Semitic
Armenians, Armenoids, Indo-European
Avars, Turko-Mongols(?), Turkic
Balts, Nordics, Indo-European
Basques, Caucasoids, linguistically unidentified
Bastarnae, East Germans interbred with Sarmatians, Indo-European
Bavarians, Nordics, Germanic
Bedouins, Arabs
Berbers, Caucasoids, Hamitic
Bosnians, Nordics, Slavic
Bulgarians, Huns/Slavs, Slavic
Burdas, Turks(?)
Burgundians, East Germans, Indo-European
Celts, Nordics, Indo-European
Cimmerians, Nordics, Iranian(?)
Croats, Nordics, Slavic
Cumans, Turks
Dacians, Nordics (Thracians), Indo-European
Danes, North Germans, Indo-European
Dorians, Hellenes, Greek
Egyptians, Mediterraneans (mixed), Hamito-Semitic
Finns, Mongolians or Mediterraneans, Uralic
Franks, Nordics, Germanic
Frisians, West Germans, Indo-European
Gauls, Nordics, Celtic

Georgians, Mediterraneans, language unidentified
Gepids, East Germans, Indo-European
Golden Horde, Tatars
Goths, East Germans, Indo-European
Greenlanders, Nordics, Norse
Hebrideans, Nordics, Norse/Celtic
Hellenes, Nordics, Greek
Herules, North Germans, Indo-European
Hungarians, originally Mongolians or Mediterraneans, Uralic
Huns, Caucasoids/Mongoloids, Altaic
Iberians of Western Europe, Mediterraneans, language unidentified
Iberians of Caucasus, Georgians
Icelanders, Nordics, Norse
Illyrians, Nordics/Alpines, Indo-European
Iranians, Nordics, Indo-European
Isaurians, Armenoids(?), language unidentified
Italics, Nordics, Indo-European
Jews, Mediterraneans, Semitic
Kabars, Turks
Khaldians, Armenoids, Indo-European
Khazars, Turks(?)
Kurds, Nordics, Iranian
Kushans, Caucasoids, Iranian
Laconians, Hellenes, Greek
Latins, Nordics, Indo-European
Lazi, Georgians
Libyans, Berbers, Hamitic
Lombards, West Germans, Indo-European
Macedonians, Nordics, Indo-European
Marcomanni, West Germans, Indo-European
Medes, Nordics, Iranian
Megarians, Dorians, Greek
Mongols, Mongolians, Altaic
Moors, Berbers, Hamitic
Moravians, Nordics, Slavic
Normans, Nordics, Indo-European
Nubians, Negroids, Macro-Sudanic
Orkneyans, Nordics, Norse
Osmanli, Turkomans (mixed), Turkic
Ostrogoths, East Germans, Indo-European
Parthians, Nordics, Iranian
Patzinaks, Mongolians, Turkic

Persians, Nordics, Iranian
Phoenicians, Mediterraneans, Semitic
Phrygians, Nordics (mixed), Indo-European
Picts, Mediterraneans or Protonordics(?)
Quadi, West Germans, Indo-European
Rugians, East Germans, Indo-European
Rumans, Vlachs
Russians, North Germans/Slavs, Indo-European
Sabines, Nordics, Italic
Saracens, Arabs
Sarmatians, Nordics (mixed), Iranian
Saxons, West Germans, Indo-European
Scirians, East Germans, Indo-European
Scyths, Nordics (mixed), Iranian
Seljuks, Mediterraneans(?), Iranian
Serbs, Nordics, Slavic
Slavs, Nordics, Indo-European
Slovaks, Nordics, Slavic
Slovenes, Nordics, Slavic
Suevi, West Germans, Indo-European
Syrians, Mediterraneans, Semitic
Tatars, Mongolians(?), Turkic
Thracians, Nordics, Indo-European
Thuringians, West Germans, Indo-European
Tungus, Mongolians, Altaic
Turkomans, Mediterraneans(?), Turkic
Turks, Alpines(?), Altaic
Vandals, East Germans, Indo-European
Varangians: Russians, Scandinavians, Icelanders, Anglo-Saxons
Visigoths, East Germans, Indo-European
Vlachs, Latinized Illyrians, Ruman
Wallachians, Vlachs
Wends, Slavs
White Huns, Mongols(?), Turkic

Bibliography

The first part of this bibliography lists the works consulted under six general headings. The second part lists additional works by chapter.

Part One
A. Reference Works

Association Internationale des Etudes Byzantines. *Dix années d'études byzantines: Bibliographie internationale,1939–1948.* Paris, 1949.

Barker, Ernest, trans. and ed. *Social and Political Thought in Byzantium from Justinian I to the Last Palaeologus.* Oxford, 1957.

Bussard, René. *Topographie historique de la Syrie antique et médiévale.* Paris, 1927.

Byzantinische Quellen zur Länder- und Völkerkunde, 2 vols. Leipzig, 1912.

Cambridge Ancient History, Vols. 7–12. Cambridge, G.B., 1928–1951.

Cambridge Medieval History, Vols. 1–4. Cambridge, G.B., 1957 (reprints).

Cambridge Medieval History, Vol. 4, 1–2. Cambridge, G.B., 1966–1967.

Colonna, Maria E. *Gli storici bizantini dal IV al XV secolo:* Vol. 1, *Storici profani.* Naples, 1956.

Dictionnaire des antiquités grecques et romaines, 5 vols. Paris, 1877–1919.

Dictionnaire d'archéologie chrétienne et de liturgie, 15 vols. Paris, 1903–1953.

Dictionnaire de droit canonique. Paris, 1924 ff.

Dictionnaire d'histoire et de géographie ecclésiastiques. Paris, 1912 ff.

Dictionnaire de théologie catholique, 15 vols. Paris, 1909–1950.

Dölger, Franz, and Schneider, A. M. *Byzanz.* Bern, 1952.

Encyclopaedia of Islam. New York, 1960 ff.

Encyclopaedia of Religion and Ethics, 13 vols. New York, 1908–1927.

Enzyklopaedie des Islam. Leiden, 1913 ff.

Fliche, Augustin, and Martin, Victor. *Histoire de l'Eglise . . .* , Vols. 1–15. Paris, 1935–1959.

Gerland, Ernst. *Das Studium der byzantinischen Geschichte vom Humanismus bis zur Jetztzeit.* Athens, 1934.

Hefele, Carl J. von. *Conciliengeschichte,* Vols. 1–7. Freiburg i.B., 1873–1890.

Honigmann, Ernst. *Die Ostgrenze des byzantinischen Reiches von 363 bis 1071.* . . . Brussels, 1935.

Hunger, Herbert, ed. *Byzantinische Geisteswelt.* . . . Baden-Baden, 1958.

Janin, Raymond. *Constantinople byzantine: Développement urbain et répertoire topographique.* Paris, 1950.

Jones, A. H. M. *Cities of the Eastern Roman Provinces.* Oxford, 1939.

Krumbacher, Karl. *Geschichte der byzantinischen Literatur . . . (527–1453).* Munich, 1897.

McEvedy, Colin. *The Penguin Atlas of Medieval History.* Manchester, G.B., 1961.

Paetow, Louis J. *A Guide to the Study of Medieval History.* New York, 1931.

Paulys Realencyclopädie der classischen Altertumswissenschaft. Stuttgart, 1894 ff.

Philippson, Alfred. *Das byzantinische Reich als geographische Erscheinung.* Leiden, 1939.

Reallexikon für Antike und Christentum. Stuttgart, 1950 ff.

Reallexikon der Vorgeschichte, 15 vols. Berlin, 1924–1932.

Robert, Louis. *Etudes anatoliennes.* Paris, 1937.

———. *Villes d'Asie Mineure.* Paris, 1935.

Spruner von Merz, Karl. *Hand-Atlas für die Geschichte des Mittelalters . . .* , Theodorus Menke, ed. Gotha, 1880.

Vidal de la Blache, Paul M. J. *Atlas historique et géographique.* Paris, 1960.

Zachariä von Lingenthal, K. E. *Geschichte des griechisch-römischen Rechts.* Berlin, 1892.

B. *Political and Military Matters*

Alastros, Doros. *Cyprus in History.* . . . London, 1955.

Andréadès, André. "La vénalité des charges, est-elle d'origine byzantine?" *Nouvelle revue historique du droit français et étranger,* 45, 1921.

Baynes, Norman H. "The Emperor Heraclius and the Military Theme System." *English Historical Review,* 67, 264, 1952.

Bratianu, G. I. *Privilèges et franchises municipales dans l'empire byzantin.* Paris, 1936.

Bréhier, Louis. *Le monde byzantin: La vie et la mort de Byzance.* Paris, 1947.

Bury, John B. *The Constitution of the Later Roman Empire.* Cambridge, G.B., 1910.

Charanis, Peter. *The Armenians in the Byzantine Empire.* Lisbon, 1963.

———. "Coronation and Its Constitutional Significance in the Later Roman Empire." *Byzantion,* 25, American Series 1, 1940–1941.

Deanesly, Margaret. *A History of Early Medieval Europe, 476 to 911.* London, 1956.

Diehl, Charles. *Byzance: Grandeur et décadence.* Paris, 1938.

———. *Figures byzantines,* 2 vols. Paris, 1925–1927.

———. *Les grands problèmes de l'histoire byzantine.* Paris, 1947.

——— and others. *L'Europe orientale de 1081 à 1453.* Paris, 1945.

——— and Marçais, Georges. *Le monde oriental de 395 à 1081.* Paris, 1936.

Dölger, Franz. *Byzantinische Diplomatik: 20 Aufsätze zum Urkundenwesen der Byzantiner.* Ettal, 1956.

———. *Byzanz und die europäische Staatenwelt.* . . . Ettal, 1953.

Dvornik, Francis. "The Circus Parties in Byzantium. . . ." *Byzantina-Metabyzantina,* 1, 1, 1946.

Finlay, George. *History of Greece* . . . B.C. *146 to* A.D. *1864,* Vols. 1–4, Henry F. Tozer, ed. Oxford, 1877.

Gelzer, H. *Abriss der byzantinischen Kaisergeschichte.* Munich, 1897.

Gfrörer, A. F. *Byzantinische Geschichten,* Vol. 2. Graz, 1874.

Gibbon, Edward. *The History of the Decline and Fall of the Roman Empire,* 7 vols. John B. Bury, ed. London, 1896–1902.

Grousset, René. *L'Empire du Levant: Histoire de la question d'Orient.* Paris, 1949.

Guilland, Rodolphe. ". . . Le domestique des Scholes." *Revue des études byzantines,* 8, 1950.

Hill, Sir George. *A History of Cyprus,* Vol. 1. Cambridge, G.B., 1940.

Jenkins, Romilly. *Byzantium* . . . A.D. *610–1071.* New York, 1966.

Levtchenko, Mitrofan V. *Byzance* . . . , trans. by Pierre Mabille. Paris, 1949.

Manojlovic, G. "Le peuple de Constantinople," trans. by Henri Grégoire. *Byzantion,* 11, 2, 1936.

Maricq, A. "La durée du régime des partis populaires à Constantinople." *Académie Royale de Belgique, Bulletin de la classe des lettres* . . . , 5th Series, 35, 1, 1949.

Miller, William. *Essays on the Latin Orient.* Amsterdam, 1964 (reprint).

Oman, C. W. C. *The Art of War* . . . A.D. *378–1515*. John H. Beeler, ed. Ithaca, 1960.

Ostrogorsky, George. *History of the Byzantine State*, trans. by Joan Hussey. New Brunswick, N. J., 1957.

———. *Pour l'histoire de la féodalité byzantine*, trans. by Henri Grégoire. Brussels, 1954.

———. *Quelques problèmes d'histoire de la paysannerie byzantine.* Brussels, 1956.

Pertusi, A. "Nuova ipotesi sull'origine dei 'temi' bizantini." *Aevum*, 27, 2, 1954.

Previté-Orton, Charles W. *A History of Europe from 1198 to 1378.* London, 1951.

Setton, Kenneth M. "Of the Importance of Land Tenure in the Byzantine Empire from the Fourth Century to the Fourth Crusade." *American Journal of Philology*, 74, 3, 295, 1953.

Stadmüller, Georg. *Geschichte Südosteuropas.* Munich, 1950.

Vasiliev, A. A. *History of the Byzantine Empire, 324–1453*, 2 vols. Madison, Wis., 1961 (reprint of 1952 ed.).

Walter, Gérard. *La ruine de Byzance, 1204–1453.* Paris, 1958.

C. Civilization

Adontz, N. "Les fonds historiques de l'épopée byzantine, Digénis Akritas." *Byzantinische Zeitschrift*, 29, 1929–1930.

Baynes, Norman H. *The Byzantine Empire.* London, 1946.

———. *Byzantine Studies and Other Essays.* London, 1955.

——— and Moss, St. L. B. *Byzantium: An Introduction to East Roman Civilization.* Oxford, 1948.

Bréhier, Louis. *L'art byzantin.* Paris, 1924.

———. *L'art chrétien: Son développement iconographique.* Paris, 1928.

———. *Le monde byzantin: Les institutions de l'empire byzantin.* Paris, 1949; *La civilisation byzantine.* Paris, 1950.

———. *La sculpture et les arts mineurs.* Paris, 1936.

Browning, Robert. "Byzantine Scholarship." *Past & Present*, 28, 1964.

Byron, Robert. *The Byzantine Achievement.* . . . New York, 1929.

Byzantinische Geschichtsschreiber: Vol. 5, . . . *Das sogenannte Strategikon des Kekaumenos*, trans. and ed. by Hans-Georg Beck. Graz, 1956.

Charanis, Peter. "How Greek Was the Byzantine Empire?" *Bucknell Review*, 11, 3, 1963.

Dalton, Ormonde M. *Byzantine Art and Archaeology.* Oxford, 1911.

Diehl, Charles. *Choses et gens de Byzance.* Paris, 1926.

———. *Etudes byzantines.* Paris, 1905.

———. *Manuel d'art byzantin,* 2 vols. Paris, 1925–1926.

Dölger, Franz. . . . *30 Aufsätze zur Geschichte, Kultur und Sprache des byzantinischen Reiches.* Ettal, 1961.

Downey, Glanville. *Constantinople in the Age of Justinian.* Norman, Okla., 1960.

Ebersolt, J. *Les arts somptuaires de Byzance.* Paris, 1923.

———. *Le Grand Palais de Constantinople et le Livre des Cérémonies.* Paris, 1910.

———. *La miniature byzantine.* Paris, 1926.

———. *Monuments d'architecture byzantine.* Paris, 1934.

———. *Orient et Occident,* 2 vols. Paris, 1928–1929.

———. *Sanctuaires de Byzance.* Paris, 1921.

Goodacre, Hugh G. *A Handbook of the Coinage of the Byzantine Empire.* London, 1957.

Grabar, André. *Byzantine Painting.* Geneva, 1953.

Guilland, Rodolphe. "Les eunuques dans l'empire byzantin. . . ." *Revue des études byzantines,* 1, 1943.

Hamilton, J. Arnott. *Byzantine Architecture and Decoration.* New York, 1934.

Haussig, Hans-Wilhelm. *Kulturgeschichte von Byzanz.* Stuttgart, 1959.

Hussey, Joan. *The Byzantine World.* London, 1961.

———. *Church & Learning in the Byzantine Empire, 867–1185.* London, 1937.

Iorga, Nicolae. *Histoire de la vie byzantine* . . . , 3 vols. Bucharest, 1934.

Kitzinger, Ernst. "The Hellenistic Heritage in Byzantine Art." *Dumbarton Oaks Papers,* 17, 1963.

Krischen, Fritz. "Die Landmauer von Konstantinopel." *Archäologisches Institut des Deutschen Reiches,* Vol. 6. Berlin, 1938.

Labarte, Jules. *Histoire des arts industriels au moyen âge* . . . , 2 vols. Paris, 1873–1875.

Lampros, Spyridon. *Portraits of Byzantine Emperors* (in Greek). Athens, 1930.

MacDonald, William L. *Early Christian & Byzantine Architecture.* New York, 1962.

Mango, Cyril. "Antique Statuary and the Byzantine Beholder." *Dumbarton Oaks Papers,* 17, 1963.

Masai, François. *Pléthon et le platonisme de Mistra.* Paris, 1956.

Mavrogordato, John, trans. and ed. *Digenes Akrites.* Oxford, 1956.

Miller, D. A. *The Byzantine Tradition.* New York, 1966.

Millet, Gabriel. *Monuments byzantins de Mistra.* . . . Paris, 1910.
Rice, D. Talbot. *Art of the Byzantine Era.* New York, 1963.
———. *Byzantine Art.* Oxford, 1953.
———. *Constantinople.* New York, 1965.
Tyler, Royall, and Peirce, Hayford. *Byzantine Art.* London, 1926.

D. Religion

Adeney, Walter F. *The Greek and Eastern Churches.* Edinburgh, 1908.
Alexander, Paul J. *The Patriarch Nicephorus of Constantinople: Ecclesiastical Policy and Image Worship in the Byzantine Empire.* Oxford, 1958.
Bevan, Edwyn. *Hellenism and Christianity.* London, 1921.
Bréhier, Louis. *La querelle des images.* . . . Paris, 1904.
Charanis, Peter. *Church and State in the Later Roman Empire: The Religious Policy of Anastasius the First, 491–518.* Madison, Wis., 1939.
Chastel, Etienne. *Histoire du Christianisme* . . . , Vols. 1–3. Paris, 1881–1882.
Choukas, Michael. *Black Angels of Athos.* Brattleboro, Vt., 1934.
Conybeare, Fred C. . . . *the Paulician Church of Armenia.* Oxford, 1898.
Duchesne, Louis M. O. *L'Eglise au VIe siècle.* Paris, 1925.
———. *Histoire ancienne de l'Eglise.* Paris, 1911.
Dvornik, Francis. *The Ecumenical Councils.* New York, 1960.
———. *The Photian Schism: History and Legend.* Cambridge, G.B., 1948.
Every, George. *The Byzantine Patriarchate, 451–1204.* London, 1947.
Fliche, Augustin. *La chrétienté médiévale (395–1254).* Paris, 1929.
Fortescue, Adrian. *The Orthodox Eastern Church.* London, 1929.
Gardner, Alice. *Theodore of Studium.* . . . London, 1905.
Geffcken, Johannes. *Der Ausgang des griechisch-römischen Heidentums.* Heidelberg, 1920.
Gill, Joseph. *The Council of Florence.* Cambridge, G.B., 1959.
Halecki, Oskar. *Un empereur de Byzance à Rome* . . . *1355–1375.* Warsaw, 1930.
Hannay, James O. *The Spirit and Origin of Christian Monasticism.* London, 1903.
Harnack, Adolf von. *History of Dogma,* 7 vols., trans. by N. Buchanan and others. London, 1896–1899.
Hergenröther, Josef. *Photius, Patriarch von Konstantinopel* . . . , 3 vols. Regensburg, 1867–1869.

Jugie, Martin. *Le schisme byzantin.* . . . Paris, 1941.

Kidd, Beresford J. *History of the Church to* A.D. *461,* 3 vols. Oxford, 1922.

Lacarrière, Jacques. *Men Possessed by God: The Story of the Desert Monks of Ancient Christendom,* trans. by Roy Monkcom. Garden City, N. Y., 1964.

Marin, L. *Les moines de Constantinople (330–898).* Paris, 1897.

Michel, Anton. *Humbert und Kerullarios,* 2 vols. Paderborn, 1924–1930.

Mohler, Ludwig. *Kardinal Bessarion* . . . , Vol. 1. Paderborn, 1923.

Norden, Walter. *Das Papsttum und Byzanz* . . . . Berlin, 1903.

Ostrogorsky, Georg. *Studien zur Geschichte des byzantinischen Bilderstreits.* Breslau, 1929.

Owsepian, G. *Die Entstehungsgeschichte des Monotheletismus.* Leipzig, 1897.

Runciman, Steven. *The Eastern Schism.* Oxford, 1955.

Sarkissian, Karekin. *The Council of Chalcedon and the Armenian Church.* London, 1965.

Stanley, Arthur P. *Lectures on the History of the Eastern Church.* London, 1883.

Stewart, John. *Nestorian Missionary Enterprise.* . . . Edinburgh, 1928.

Vasiliev, A. A. "Il viaggio dell'imperatore bizantino Giovanni V Paleologo in Italia (1369–1371)." *Studi bizantini e neoellenici,* 3, 1931.

Viller, M. "La question de l'union des églises . . . (1274–1438)." *Revue d'histoire ecclésiastique,* 17–18, 1921–1922.

Wigram, William A. *The Separation of the Monophysites.* London, 1923.

Zöckler, D. Otto. *Askese und Mönchtum.* Frankfurt a. M., 1897.

E. Economy

Bratianu, George I. *Etudes byzantines d'histoire économique et sociale.* Paris, 1938.

Brentano, Lujo. "Die byzantinische Volkswirtschaft." *Schmollers Jahrbuch,* 41, 2, 1917.

Charanis, Peter. "On the Social Structure and Economic Organization of the Byzantine Empire in the Thirteenth Century and Later." *Byzantinoslavica,* 12, 1951.

Dölger, Franz. *Beiträge zur Geschichte der byzantinischen Finanzverwaltung besonders des 10. und 11. Jahrhunderts.* Leipzig, 1927.

Heyd, Wilhelm von. *Histoire du commerce du Levant au moyen âge,* 2 vols. Leipzig, 1923.

Jones, A. H. M. *The Later Roman Empire, 284–602: A Social, Economic and Administrative Survey*, 2 vols. Norman, Okla., 1964.

Launay, L. de. *L'or dans le monde*. Paris, 1907.

Lemerle, Paul. "Esquisse pour une histoire agraire de Byzance. . . ." *Revue historique*, 219, 1958.

Lopez, Robert S. "The Role of Trade in the Economic Readjustment of Byzantium in the Seventh Century." *Dumbarton Oaks Papers*, 13, 1959.

———. "The Trade of Medieval Europe: The South." *Cambridge Economic History of Europe*, Vol. 2. Cambridge, G.B., 1952.

Ostrogorsky, George. "Agrarian Conditions in the Byzantine Empire in the Middle Ages." *Cambridge Economic History of Europe*, Vol. 1. Cambridge, G.B., 1941.

Runciman, Steven. "Byzantine Trade and Industry." *Cambridge Economic History of Europe*, Vol. 2. Cambridge, G.B., 1952.

Vryonis, Jr., Speros. ". . . Guilds in the Eleventh Century." *Dumbarton Oaks Papers*, 17, 1963.

Zakythinos, D. A. *Crise monétaire et crise économique à Byzance du XIIIe au XVe siècle*. Athens, 1948.

Zoras, Giorgio. *Le corporazioni bizantini* . . . . Rome, 1931.

F. Other Peoples

Allen, W. E. D. *A History of the Georgian People*. London, 1932.

Anastasijevic, Dragutin N. "L'hypothèse de la Bulgarie occidentale" in *L'art byzantin chez les slaves: Les Balkans: Premier Recueil dédié à la mémoire de Théodore Uspensky*. Paris, 1930.

Arnold, Thomas W. *The Caliphate*. Oxford, 1924.

Barthold, W. *Histoire des Turcs d'Asie Centrale*, trans. by M. Donskis. Paris, 1945.

Bloch, Raymond. *Le mystère étrusque*. Paris, 1958.

Behn, Friedrich. *Römertum und Völkerwanderung*. Stuttgart, 1963.

Bryce, James B. *The Holy Roman Empire*. New York, 1932.

Caro, Georg. *Genua und die Mächte am Mittelmeer* . . . *1257–1311*, 2 vols. Halle, 1895–1899.

Chalandon, Ferdinand. *Histoire de la domination normande en Italie et en Sicile*, 2 vols. Paris, 1907.

Childe, V. Gordon. *The Aryans: A Study of Indo-European Origins*. London, 1926.

Christensen, Arthur. *L'Iran sous les Sassanides*. Copenhagen, 1944.

Coon, Carleton S. *The Races of Europe*. New York, 1939.

Dennett, Jr., Daniel C. *Conversion and the Poll Tax in Early Islam.* Cambridge, Mass., 1950.

Diehl, Charles. *Une république patricienne, Venise.* Paris, 1916.

Dunlop, D. H. *The History of the Jewish Khazars.* Princeton, 1954.

Dvornik, Francis. *The Making of Central and Eastern Europe.* London, 1949.

———. *The Slavs: Their Early History and Civilization.* Boston, 1956.

Eicke, Hermann. *Geschichte der westgotischen Könige seit Alarichs Tod.* Leipzig, 1944.

Gaudefroy-Demombynes, Maurice. *Mahomet.* Paris, 1957.

Gfrörer, A. F. *Byzantinische Geschichten,* Vol. 1. Graz, 1872.

Gibbons, Herbert A. *The Foundation of the Ottoman Empire . . . (1300–1403).* Oxford, 1916.

Giese, Friedrich. "Das Problem der Entstehung des osmanischen Reiches." *Zeitschrift für Semististik,* 2, 1924.

Glubb, Lt.-Gen. Sir John B. *The Great Arab Conquests.* Englewood Cliffs, N. J., 1963.

———. *The Empire of the Arabs.* London, 1963.

Grousset, René. *L'empire des steppes: Attila, Gengis-Khan, Tamerlan.* Paris, 1939.

———. *Histoire de l'Arménie des origines à 1071.* Paris, 1947.

Guldescu, Stanko. *History of Medieval Croatia.* The Hague, 1964.

Halphen, Louis. *Charlemagne et l'empire carolingien.* Paris, 1947.

——— and Sagnac, Philippe. *Les barbares des grandes invasions aux conquêtes turques du XIe siècle.* Paris, 1948.

Hitti, Philip H. *History of the Arabs. . . .* London, 1956.

———. *History of Syria . . . .* London, 1951.

Huart, Clement I. *Histoire des Arabes,* 2 vols. Paris, 1912–1913.

Iorga, Nicolae. *Geschichte des osmanischen Reiches,* Vol. 1. Gotha, 1908.

———. *Histoire des Roumains de la péninsule des Balcans. . . .* Bucharest, 1919.

Jirecek, Constantin. *Geschichte der Serben,* 2 vols. Gotha, 1911–1918.

Kretschmayr, Heinrich. *Geschichte von Venedig,* Vols. 1–2. Gotha, 1905–1920.

Lane-Poole, Stanley. *A History of Egypt in the Middle Ages.* London, 1901.

———. *Saladin and the Fall of the Kingdom of Jerusalem.* London, 1926.

Laurent, Joseph. *L'Arménie entre Byzance et l'Islam depuis la conquête arabe jusqu'en 866.* Paris, 1919.

Lopez, Robert. *Storia delle colonie genovesi nel Mediterraneo.* Bologna, 1938.
Macartney, Carlile A. *Hungary.* . . . Edinburgh, 1962.
―――. *The Magyars in the Ninth Century.* Cambridge, G.B., 1930.
Manandian, Y. A. "A Brief Survey of the History of Ancient Armenia." *Armenian Quarterly,* 1, 2, 1946.
Mayani, Zacharie. *Les Etrusques commencent à parler.* Paris, 1961.
McGovern, William M. *The Early Empires of Central Asia.* Chapel Hill, N. C., 1939.
Mehmed Fuad, Köprülü. *Les origines de l'empire ottoman.* Paris, 1935.
Menendez Pidal, Ramon, comp. *Floresta de leyendas heroicas españolas,* Vol. 1, Madrid, 1942.
Miller, William. *The Latins in the Levant: A History of Frankish Greece, 1204–1466.* New York, 1908.
Morgan, Jacques de. *Histoire du peuple arménien.* . . . Paris, 1910.
Muir, William. *The Caliphate* . . . , T. H. Weir, ed. Edinburgh, 1924.
Niederle, Lubor. *Manuel de l'antiquité slave,* Vol. 1. Paris, 1923.
Nutting, Anthony. *The Arabs* . . . . New York, 1964.
O'Leary, De Lacy. *A Short History of the Fatimid Khalifate.* London, 1923.
Pallottino, Massimo. *Etruscologia.* Milan, 1963.
Papoulia, Basilike D. *Ursprung und Wesen der "Knabenlese" im osmanischen Reich.* Munich, 1963.
Pares, Bernard. *A History of Russia,* Richard Pares, ed. New York, 1960.
Pittard, Eugène. *Les races et l'histoire.* . . . Paris, 1924.
Prawdin, Michael (pseud. for Michel Charol). *Tschingis-Chan und sein Erbe.* Stuttgart, 1957.
Rice, Tamara Talbot. *The Seljuks in Asia Minor.* London, 1961.
Rostovtzeff, M. *Iranians and Greeks in South Russia.* Oxford, 1922.
Runciman, Steven. *A History of the First Bulgarian Empire.* London, 1930.
Saunders, J. J. *A History of Medieval Islam.* New York, 1965.
Schevill, Ferdinand, and Gewehr, Wesley M. *The History of the Balkan Peninsula.* . . . New York, 1933.
Seton-Watson, Robert W. *A History of the Roumanians.* . . . Cambridge, G.B., 1934.
Setton, Kenneth M. *Catalan Domination of Athens, 1311–1388.* Cambridge, Mass., 1948.
Slatarski, W. N. *Geschichte der Bulgaren:* Vol. 1, . . . (679–1396). Leipzig, 1918.
Spinka, Matthew. *A History of Christianity in the Balkans: A Study of the Spread of Byzantine Culture among the Slavs.* Chicago, 1933.

Spuler, Bertold. *Iran in früh-islamischer Zeit.* Wiesbaden, 1952.

Sykes, Brig.-Gen. Sir Percy. *A History of Persia,* 2 vols. London, 1930.

Temperley, Harold W. *History of Serbia.* London, 1917.

Thompson, E. A. *A History of Attila and the Huns.* Oxford, 1948.

Tournebize, F. *Histoire politique et religieuse de l'Arménie depuis les origines des Arméniens jusqu'à la mort de leur dernier roi (l'an 1393).* Paris, 1900.

Vasiliev, A. A. *The Russian Attack on Constantinople in 860.* Cambridge, Mass., 1946.

Vernadsky, George. "The Date of the Conversion of the Khazars to Judaism." *Byzantion,* 25, American Series, 1, 1940–1941.

———. *The Origins of Russia.* Oxford, 1959.

Voinovitch, Louis de. *Histoire de Dalmatie . . . (1409).* Paris, 1934.

Watt, W. Montgomery. *Muhammad: Prophet and Statesman.* London, 1961.

Wittek, Paul. *The Rise of the Ottoman Empire.* London, 1938.

Wolff, Robert L. "The 'Second Bulgarian Empire': Its Origin and History to 1204." *Speculum,* 24, 2, 1949.

Part Two
Introduction
I Constantine and New Rome/*306–337*

Alföldi, Andrew. *The Conversion of Constantine and Pagan Rome,* trans. by H. Mattingly. Oxford, 1948.

Batifol, Pierre. *La paix constantinienne.* Paris, 1914.

Baynes, Norman H. *Constantine the Great and the Christian Church.* London, 1931.

Boak, Arthur E. R., and Sinnigen, William G. *A History of Rome to 565* A.D. New York, 1965.

Burckhardt, Jacob C. *Die Zeit Constantin's des Grossen.* Leipzig, 1880.

Coleman, Christopher B. *Constantine the Great and Christianity. . . .* New York, 1914.

Dannenbauer, Heinrich. *Die Entstehung Europas: Von der Spätantike zum Mittelalter:* Vol. 1, *Der Niedergang der alten Welt im Westen.* Stuttgart, 1959.

Delbrück, Hans. *Geschichte der Kriegskunst im Rahmen der politischen Geschichte,* Vol. 2. Berlin, 1909.

Dörries, Hermann. *Konstantin der Grosse.* Stuttgart, 1958.

Dvornik, Francis. "Emperors, Popes and General Councils." *Dumbarton Oaks Papers,* 6, 1951.

Eusebius of Caesarea. "The Life of Constantine," trans. by E. C. Richardson, in *A Select Library of Nicene and Post-Nicene Fathers of the Christian Church*. New York, 1890.

Firth, J. B. *Constantine the Great.* . . . New York, 1905.

Gerland, Ernst. "Byzantion und die Gründung der Stadt Konstantinopel." *Byzantinisch-Neugriechische Jahrbücher*, 10, 1933.

Grosse, Robert. *Römische Militärgeschichte von Gallienus bis zum Beginn der byzantinischen Themenverfassung*. Berlin, 1920.

Heuss, Alfred. *Römische Geschichte*. Brunswick, Germany, 1960.

Holsapple, Lloyd B. *Constantine the Great*. New York, 1942.

Huttmann, Maude A. *The Establishment of Christianity and the Proscription of Paganism*. New York, 1914.

Jones, A. H. M. *The Later Roman Empire, 284–602: A Social, Economic and Administrative Survey*, 2 vols. Norman, Okla., 1964.

Kraft, Heinz, *Kaiser Konstantins religiöse Entwicklung*. Tübingen, 1955.

Lot, Ferdinand. *La fin du monde antique et le début du Moyen Age*. Paris, 1951.

McFayden, Donald. *The History of the Title Imperator under the Roman Empire*. Chicago, 1920.

Maurice, Jules. *Constantin le Grand: L'origine de la civilisation chrétienne*. Paris, 1924.

Mommsen, Theodor. *Römische Geschichte*, 3 vols. Berlin, 1920–1923.

Petit, Paul. "Libanius et la VITA CONSTANTINI." *Historia*, 1, 4, 1950.

Piganiol, André. *L'empereur Constantin*. Paris, 1932.

———. *L'empire chrétien (325–395)*. Paris, 1947.

———. "L'état actuel de la question constantinienne, 1939/49." *Historia*, 1, 1, 1950.

Schwartz, Eduard. "Constantin," in *Meister der Politik* . . . , Erich Marcks and Karl A. von Müller, eds. Stuttgart, 1922.

Scullard, Howard H. *From the Gracchi to Nero*. New York, 1959.

Seeck, Otto. *Geschichte des Untergangs der antiken Welt*, Vols. 1–3. Berlin, 1921.

Stein, Ernst. *Geschichte des spätrömischen Reiches:* Vol. 1, . . . *(284–476 n. Chr.)*. Vienna, 1928.

Syme, Ronald. *The Roman Revolution*. Oxford, 1939.

Vogt, Josef. *Constantin der Grosse und sein Jahrhundert*. Munich, 1960.

II Christians and Pagans / 337–399

Allard, P. *Julien l'Apostat*, 3 vols. Paris, 1906–1910.

Ammianus Marcellinus. *Rerum Gestarum,* trans. by J. C. Rolfe, 3 vols. London, 1935–1939.

Bidez, Joseph. *La vie de l'empereur Julien.* Paris, 1930.

Boissier, Gaston. *La fin du paganisme . . . ,* 2 vols. Paris, 1913.

Dannenbauer. *op. cit.* in I.

De Camp, L. Sprague. *The Ancient Engineers.* New York, 1963.

Delbrück. *op. cit.* in I.

Geffcken, Johannes. *Kaiser Julianus.* Leipzig, 1914.

Huttmann. *op. cit.* in I.

Jones. *op. cit.* in I.

Kaegi, Jr., W. E. "Research on Julian the Apostate, 1945–1964." *Classical World,* 58, 8, 1965.

Negri, Gaetano. *L'imperatore Giuliano l'Apostata.* Milan, 1902.

Piganiol, André. *op. cit.* in I.

Seeck. *op. cit.,* Vols. 4–5, in I.

Stein. *op. cit.* in I.

III *Romans and Germans* / 400–498

Bury, John B. *A History of the Later Roman Empire . . .* (A.D. *395 to* A.D. *565*), Vol. 1. London, 1923.

Byzantinische Geschichtsschreiber. Vol. 4, . . . *Abschnitte des Priskos und Menander Protektor,* trans. by Ernst Doblhofer. Graz, 1955.

Dannenbauer. *op. cit.* in I.

Delbrück. *op. cit.* in I.

Demougeot, E. *De l'unité et de la division de l'Empire romain, 395–410 . . . .* Paris, 1951.

Gordon, C. D., trans. and ed. *The Age of Attila: Fifth-Century Byzantium and the Barbarians.* Ann Arbor, 1960.

Grosse. *op. cit.* in I.

Hodgkin, Thomas. *Italy and Her Invaders,* Vols. 1–3. Oxford, 1892–1896.

Jones. *op. cit.* in I.

Lot. *op. cit.* in I.

——— and others. *Les destinées de l'Empire en Occident (395–888):* Vol. 1, *De 395 à 768.* Paris, 1940.

Seeck. *op. cit.,* Vol. 6, in I.

Stein, Ernst. *Histoire du Bas-Empire:* Vol. 2, . . . *(476–565),* J.-R. Palanque, ed. Paris, 1949.

———. *op. cit.* in I.

IV The Lure of Hesperia / 498–610

Barker, John W. *Justinian and the Later Roman Empire*. Madison, Wis., 1966.

Bury. *op. cit.*, Vol. 2, in III.

Byzantinische Geschichtsschreiber. op. cit. in III.

Chassin, L. M. *Bélisaire* . . . . Paris, 1957.

Dannenbauer. *op. cit.* in I.

Delbrück. *op. cit.* in I.

Diehl, Charles. *Etudes sur l'administration dans l'Exarchat de Ravenne (568–751)*. Paris, 1888.

——. *Justinien et la civilsation byzantine au VIe siècle*. Paris, 1901.

Goubert, Paul. *Byzance avant l'Islam*, 2 vols. Paris, 1951–1956.

Grosse. *op. cit.* in I.

Hartmann, Ludo M. "The Early Mediaeval State: Byzantium, Italy and the West." *Historical Association*, Gen. Ser., G, 14, 1949.

——. *Untersuchungen zur Geschichte der byzantinischen Verwaltung in Italien (540–750)*. Leipzig, 1889.

Higgins, Martin J. "International Relations at the Close of the Sixth Century." *Catholic Historical Review*, 27, 3, 1941.

Hodgkin. *op. cit.*, Vols. 4–5, in III.

Holmes, W. G. *The Age of Justinian and Theodora*, 2 vols. London, 1912.

Janssens, Y. "Les Bleus et les Verts sous Maurice, Phocas et Héraclius." *Byzantion*, 11, 2, 1936.

Jones. *op. cit.* in I.

Lemerle, Paul. "Invasions et migrations dans les Balkans depuis la fin de l'époque romaine jusqu'au VIIIe siècle." *Revue historique*, 121, 1954.

Lot. *op. cit.* in I.

—— and others. *op. cit.* in III.

Martroye, F. *L'Occident à l'époque byzantine: Goths et Vandales*. Paris, 1904.

Procopius of Caesarea. *History of the Wars; Secret History; Buildings*, trans. by H. B. Dewing, 7 vols. London, 1914–1940.

Rubin, Berthold. *Das Zeitalter Iustinians*, Vol. 1. Berlin, 1960.

Schubart, Wilhelm. *Justinian und Theodora*. Munich, 1943.

Stein. *op. cit.*, Vol. 2, in III.

——. *Studien zur Geschichte des byzantinischen Reiches, vornehmlich unter den Kaisern Justinus II u. Tiberius Constantinus*. Stuttgart, 1919.

Teall, John L. "The Barbarians in Justinian's Armies." *Speculum,* 40, 2, 1965.

Thiess, Frank. *Die griechischen Kaiser* . . . . Hamburg, 1959.

Time, April 1, 1966, p. 42.

Vasiliev, A. A. *Justin the First.* Cambridge, Mass., 1950.

V *The Heracliads/610–716*

Brooks, E. W. "Who Was Constantine Pogonatus?" *Byzantinische Zeitschrift,* 17, 1908.

Bury, John B. *History of the Later Roman Empire* . . . *395* A.D. *to 800* A.D., Vol. 2. London, 1889.

Cankova-Petkova, Genoveva. "Bulgarians and Byzantium during the First Decades after the Foundation of the Bulgarian State." *Byzantinoslavica,* 24, 1, 1963.

Charanis, Peter. "On the Question of the Hellenization of Sicily and Southern Italy during the Middle Ages." *American Historical Review,* 52, 1, 1946.

Darko, Eugenio. "La militarizzazione dell'impero bizantino." *Studi bizantini e neoellenici,* 5, 1939.

Gaudefroy-Demombynes, Maurice, and Platonov, Sergei F. *Le monde musulman et byzantin jusqu'aux croisades.* Paris, 1931.

Grégoire, Henri. "An Armenian Dynasty on the Byzantine Throne." *Armenian Quarterly,* 1, 1, 1946.

Hodgkin. *op. cit.,* Vol. 6, in III.

Lemerle. article cited in IV.

Lot and others. *op. cit.* in III.

Ostrogrosky, George. "The Byzantine Empire in the World of the Seventh Century." *Dumbarton Oaks Papers,* 13, 1959.

Parlangèli, O. "L'importanza dell'elemente greco nella storia linguistica dell'Italia meridionale," in *Akten des XI. Internationalen Byzantinistenkongresses.* . . . Munich, 1960.

Pernice, Angelo. *L'imperatore Eraclio.* . . . Florence, 1905.

Randa, Alexander. "Byzanz und der Donauraum." *Der Donauraum,* 3, 3, 1958.

Stein, Ernst. "Ein Kapitel vom persischen und vom byzantinischen Staate." *Byzantinisch-Neugriechische Jahrbücher,* 1, 1920.

Thiess. *op. cit.* in IV.

VI *The Iconoclasts/717–867*

Adontz, N. "L'âge et l'origine de l'empereur Basile I (867–886)" and

"La portée historique de l'oraison funèbre par son fils Léon VI le Sage." *Byzantion*, 8, 2, 1933.

Ahrweiler, Hélène. "L'Asie Mineure et les invasions arabes (VIIe–IXe siècles)." *Revue historique*, 227, 1962.

Bury, John B. *A History of the Eastern Roman Empire* . . . (A.D. *802–867*). London, 1912.

———. *op. cit.* in V.

Byzantinische Geschichtsschreiber. Vol. 6, . . . *aus der Weltchronik des Theophanes*, trans. and ed. by Leopold Breyer. Graz, 1957.

Canard, M. "La prise d'Héraclée et les relations entre Harun ar-Rashid et l'empereur Nicéphore Iier." *Byzantion*, 32, 2, 1962.

Charanis. article cited in V.

———. "Nicephorus I, the Savior of Greece from the Slavs." *Byzantina Metabyzantina*, 1, 1, 1946.

Diehl, Charles. *Etudes sur l'administration dans l'Exarchat de Ravenne* (*568–751*). Paris, 1888.

Dvornik, Francis. *The Photian Schism.* . . . Cambridge, G.B., 1948.

———. *Les Slaves, Byzance et Rome au IXe siècle.* Paris, 1926.

Finlay, George. *History of the Byzantine Empire from DCCXVI to MLVII.* London, 1920.

Freshfield, Edwin H., trans. . . . *The Ecloga.* . . . Cambridge, G.B., 1926.

Gaudefroy-Demombynes and Platonov. *op. cit.* in V.

Hodgkin. *op. cit.*, Vols. 6–8, in III.

Lemerle. article cited in IV.

Lombard, Alfred. . . . *Constantin V* . . . . Paris, 1902.

Ohnsorge, Werner. *Das Zweikaiserproblem* . . . . Hildesheim, 1947.

———. "Das Kaisertum der Eirene und die Kaiserkrönung Karls des Grossen." *Saeculum*, 14, 2, 1963.

Ostrogorsky, Georg. "Über die vermeintliche Reformtätigkeit der Isaurier." *Byzantinische Zeitschrift*, 30, 1929–1930.

Theiss. *op. cit.* in IV.

Vasiliev, A. A. *Byzance et les Arabes:* Vol. 1, . . . (*820–867*). Brussels, 1935.

Vogt, Albert. *Basile Ier* . . . . Paris, 1908.

VII The Early Macedonians / 867–963

Byzantinische Geschichtsschreiber. Vol. 10, . . . *Die Zeit von 959 bis 976 in der Darstellung des Leon Diakonos*, trans. by Franz Loretto. Graz, 1961.

Constantine Porphyrogenitus. *De administrando imperio:* Vol. 1, trans. and ed. by Gy. Moravcsik and R. J. H. Jenkins, Budapest, 1949; Vol. 2, commentary by Francis Dvornik and others, R. J. H. Jenkins, ed. London, 1962.

——. *Le livre des cérémonies,* 3 vols., trans. and ed. by Albert Vogt. Paris, 1935–1940.

Dvornik, Francis. *Les Slaves, Byzance et Rome au IXe siècle.* Paris, 1926.

——. works cited in VI.

Finlay. *op. cit.* in VI.

Gaudefroy-Demombynes and Platonov. *op. cit.* in V.

Gay, Jules. *L'Italie méridionale et l'empire byzantin . . . (867–1071),* Vol. 1. Paris, 1904.

——. "Le patriarche Nicolas le Mystique et son rôle politique," in *Mélanges Charles Diehl,* Vol. 1. Paris, 1930.

Lampros, Spyridon P. "Leo und Alexander als Mitkaiser von Byzanz." *Byzantinische Zeitschrift,* 4, 1895.

Oikonomides, N. "La dernière volonté de Léon VI au sujet de la tétragamie" and "La 'préhistoire' de la dernière volonté de Léon VI au sujet de la tétragamie." *Byzantinische Zeitschrift,* 56, 1 and 2, 1963.

Rambaud, Alfred. *L'empire grec au dixième siècle: Constantin Porphyrogénète.* Paris, 1870.

Runciman, Steven. *The Emperor Romanus Lecapenus and His Reign: A Study of Tenth Century Byzantium.* Cambridge, G.B., 1929.

Schlumberger, Gustave. *Un empereur byzantin au dixième siècle: Nicéphore Phocas.* Paris, 1890.

Vasiliev, A. A. *Byzance et les Arabes:* Vol. 2, . . . (867–959). Brussels, 1950.

Vogt. *op. cit.* in VI.

VIII Fighting Emperors / 963–1025

Anastasijevic, Dragutin N. "L'hypothèse de la Bulgarie occidentale." *L'art byzantin chez les Slaves: Les Balkans: Premier Recueil dédié à la mémoire de Théodore Uspensky.* Paris, 1930.

Byzantinische Geschichtsschreiber. op. cit. in VII.

Canard, M. "Deux documents arabes sur Bardas Skléros." *Studi bizantini e neoellenici,* 5, 1939.

Charanis, Peter. "The Monastic Properties and the State in the Byzantine Empire." *Dumbarton Oaks Papers,* 4, 1948.

Finlay. *op. cit.* in VI.

Gaudefroy-Demombynes and Platonov. *op. cit.* in V.

Gfrörer, A. F. *Byzantinische Geschichten,* Vol. 3. Graz, 1877.

Psellus, Michael. *The Chronographia*, trans. by E. R. A. Sewter. New Haven, 1953.

Schlumberger, Gustave. *L'épopée byzantine à la fin du dixième siècle:* Vol. 1, *Guerres contre les Russes, les Arabes, les Allemands, les Bulgares, luttes civiles contre les deux Bardas, Jean Tzimisces, les jeunes années de Basile II, le Tueur de Bulgares* (*969–989*), Paris, 1896; Vol. 2, *Basile II, le Tueur de Bulgares*. Paris, 1900.

———. *op. cit.* in VII.

IX *Bureaucratic Ascendancy | 1025–1072*

Byzantinische Geschichtsschreiber. Vol. 5, . . . *Das sogenannte Strategikon des Kekaumenos*, trans. and ed. by Hans-Georg Beck. Graz, 1956.

Cahen, Claude. "La campagne de Mantzikert d'après les sources musulmanes." *Byzantion*, 9, 2, 1934.

———. "La première pénétration turque en Asie Mineure (seconde moitié du XIe siècle)." *Byzantion*, 18, 1948.

———. "Le problème ethnique en Anatolie." *Journal of World History*, 2, 2, 1954.

Finlay. *op. cit.* in VI.

Gaudefroy-Demombynes and Platonov. *op. cit.* in V.

Gay. *op. cit.*, Vol. 2, in VII.

Gfrörer. *op. cit.* in VIII.

Hussey, Joan. *Ascetics and Humanists in Eleventh-Century Byzantium*. London, 1960.

———. "The Byzantine Empire in the Eleventh Century: Some Different Interpretations." *Transactions of the Royal Historical Society*, 4th Series, 32, 1950.

———. "Michael Psellus, the Byzantine Historian." *Speculum*, 10, 1935.

Laurent, Joseph. "Byzance et les Turcs Seldjoucides dans l'Asie occidentale jusqu'en 1081." *Annales de l'Est*, 28, 2, 1913.

Mädler, Heinrich. *Theodora, Michael Stratiotikos, Isaak Comnenos* . . . . Plauen, 1894.

Neumann, Carl. *Die Weltstellung des byzantinischen Reiches vor den Kreuzzügen*. Leipzig, 1894.

Ostrogorsky, Georg. "Die Perioden der byzantinischen Geschichte." *Historische Zeitschrift*, 163, 2, 1941.

Polemis, D. I. "Notes on Eleventh-Century Chronology (1059–1081)." *Byzantinische Zeitschrift*, 58, 1, 1965.

Psellus. *op. cit.* in VIII.

Schlumberger, Gustave. *L'épopée byzantine à la fin du dixième siècle:* Vol. 3, *Règnes de Constantin VIII, de Zoé . . . avènement d'Isaac Comnène (1025–1057).* Paris, 1905.

X *The Comneni* / *1072–1185*

Beck, Hans-Georg. "Alexios Komnenos zwischen Normannen und Türken." *Akten des XI, Internationalen Byzantinistenkongresses. . . .* Munich, 1960.

Bréhier, Louis. *L'Eglise et l'Orient au Moyen Age: Les Croisades.* Paris, 1928.

Brown, Horatio F. "The Venetians and the Venetian Quarter in Constantinople to the Close of the Twelfth Century." *Journal of Hellenic Studies,* 40, 1920.

Buckley, Georgina. *Anna Comnena . . . .* London, 1929.

Byzantinische Geschichtsschreiber. Vol. 3, *. . . des Bischofs Eustathios,* trans. and ed. by Herbert Hunger; Vol. 7, *. . .* (*1118–1180*) *aus dem Geschichtswerk des Niketas Choniates,* trans. and ed. by Franz Grabler; Vol. 8 *. . .* (*1180–1195*) *aus dem Geschichtswerk des Niketas Choniates,* trans. and ed. by Franz Grabler. Graz, 1955–1958.

Chalandon, Ferdinand. *Les Comnène: Jean II . . .* (*1118–1143*) *et Manuel I* (*1143–1180*). Paris, 1912.

———. *Essai sur le règne d'Alexis Ier Comnène* (*1081–1118*). Paris, 1900.

———. *Histoire de la première Croisade. . . .* Paris, 1925.

Classen, P. "Treueid für Komnenos." *Akten des XI. Internationalen Byzantinistenkongresses. . . .* Munich, 1960.

Cognasso, Francesco. "Partiti politici e lotte dinastiche in Bisanzio alla morte di Manuele Comneno." *Memorie della Reale Academia delle Scienze di Torino,* 2nd Series, Vol. 62, Torino, 1912.

Comnena, Anna. *The Alexiad . . .* , trans. by E. A. S. Dawes. London, 1928.

Danstrup, John. "Manuel's Coup against Genoa and Venice. . . ." *Classica et Mediaevalia,* 10, 2, 1949.

Halphen, Louis. "Le rôle de 'Latins' dans l'histoire intérieure de Constantinople à la fin du XIIe siècle." *Mélanges Charles Diehl,* Vol. 1. Paris, 1930.

Lamma, Paolo. "Comneni e Staufer. . . ." *Istituto storico italiano per il medio evo, Studi storici,* 14–18, 22–25, 1955–1957.

La Monte, John J. "To What Extent Was the Byzantine Empire the Suzerain of the Latin Crusading States?" *Byzantion,* 7, 1932.

Laurent, Joseph. "Byzance et l'origine du sultanat de Roum," in *Mélanges Charles Diehl*, Vol. 1. Paris, 1930.

Leib, Bernard. *Rome, Kiev et Byzance . . . (1088–1099)*. Paris, 1924.

Runciman, Steven. *A History of the Crusades*, Vols. 1–2. Cambridge, G. B., 1952–1953.

Setton, Kenneth M., ed. *A History of the Crusades*, Vols. 1–2. Philadelphia, 1955.

Tivcev, P. "Le règne de l'empereu̇r de Byzance, Andronic Ier Comnène (1183–1185)." *Byzantinoslavica*, 24, 1, 1962.

Wirth, P. "Wann wurde Kaiser Alexios II Komnenos geboren?" and "Kaiser Manuel I Komnenos und die Ostgrenze. . . ." *Byzantinische Zeitschrift*, 49, 1956, and 55, 1962.

XI *The Angeli / 1185–1204*

Byzantinische Geschichtsschreiber. Vol. 8, . . . *(1180–1195) aus dem Geschichtswerk des Niketas Choniates;* Vol. 9, . . . *Nikolaos Mesarites . . .* , trans. and ed. by Franz Grabler. Graz, 1958.

Cognasso, Francesco. "Un imperatore bizantino della decadenza: Isacco II Angelo." *Bessarione*, 31, 1915.

Daly, William M. "Christian Fraternity, the Crusaders and the Security of Constantinople, 1097–1204. . . ." *Mediaeval Studies*, 22, 1960.

Gardner, Alice. *The Lascarids of Nicaea. . . .* London, 1912.

Luchaire, Achille. *Innocent III: La question d'Orient*. Paris, 1907.

Pears, Edwin. *The Fall of Constantinople, Being the Story of the Fourth Crusade.* London, 1885.

Runciman. *op. cit.*, Vol. 3, 1954, in X.

Setton. *op. cit.*, Vol. 2, 1962, in X.

Villehardouin, Geoffroi de. *La conquête de Constantinople*, trans. and ed. by Edmond Faral, 2 vols. Paris, 1938–1939.

XII *The Lascarids / 1204–1259*

Gardner. *op. cit.* in XI.

Gerland, Ernst. *Geschichte des lateinischen Kaiserreiches von Konstantinopel:* Vol. 1, *Geschichte der Kaiser Balduin und Heinrich, 1204–1216.* Homburg v. d. Höhe, 1905.

Janin, R. ". . . Les tentatives d'union des Eglises (1204–1208)." *Echos d'Orient*, 36, 169, 1933.

L'Huillier, P. "La nature des relations ecclésiastiques greco-latines après la prise de Constantinople par les croisés." *Akten des XI. Internationalen Byzantinistenkongresses . . . .* Munich, 1960.

Longnon, Jean. *L'empire latin de Constantinople et la principauté de Morée*. Paris, 1949.
Luchaire. *op. cit.* in XI.
Miller, William. *Trebizond, the Last Greek Empire*. London, 1926.
Nicol, Donald M. *The Despotate of Epiros*. Oxford, 1957.
Pappadopoulos, Jean B. *Theodore II Lascaris*. . . . Paris, 1908.
Runciman. *op. cit.* in XI.
Setton. *op. cit.* in XI.
Stiernon, Lucien. "L'origine du Despotat d'Epire." *Revue des études byzantines*, 17, 1959.
Vasiliev, A. A. "The Foundation of the Empire of Trebizond (1204–1222)." *Speculum*, 11, 1, 1936.
Villehardouin. *op. cit.*, Vol. 2, in XI.

XIII The Paleologi/1259–1448

Atiya, Aziz S. *The Crusade of Nicopolis*. London, 1934.
Bakalopulos, A. "Les limites de l'empire byzantin depuis la fin du XIVe siècle jusqu'à sa chute (1453)." *Byzantinische Zeitschrift*, 55, 1, 1962.
Beck, H.-G. "Reichsidee und nationale Politik im spätbyzantinischen Staat." *Byzantinische Zeitschrift*, 53, 1, 1960.
Berger de Xivrey, Jules. "Mémoire sur la vie et les oeuvres de l'Empereur Manuel Paléologue." *Mémoires de l'Institut National de France: Académie des Inscriptions et Belles-Lettres*, Vol. 19, 1853.
Chapman, Conrad. *Michel Paléologue, restaurateur de l'empire byzantin*. Paris, 1926.
Charanis, Peter. "Internal Strife in Byzantium in the Fourteenth Century" and "The Strife among the Palaeologi and the Ottoman Turks, 1370–1402." *Byzantion*, 15–16, American Series, 1–2, 1940–1943.
Cirac Estopañan, Sebastian. *La unión, Manuel II Paleólogo*. . . . Barcelona, 1952.
Cydonès, Démétrius. *Correspondance*, trans. by Giuseppe Cammelli. Paris, 1930.
Dade, E. *Versuche zur Wiedererrichtung der lateinischen Herrschaft in Konstantinopel . . . 1261 bis etwa 1310*. Jena, 1938.
Dennis, George T. "The Reign of Manuel II Palaeologus in Thessalonica, 1382–1387." *Orientalia Christiana Analecta*, 159, 1960.
————. "The Second Turkish Capture of Thessalonica: 1391, 1394 or 1430?" *Byzantinische Zeitschrift*, 57, 1, 1964.

Dölger, Franz. "Johannes VII, Kaiser der Rhomäer, 1390–1408." *Byzantinische Zeitschrift*, 31, 1931.

Geanakoplos, Deno J. *Emperor Michael Palaeologus and the West*, 1258–1282. . . . Cambridge, Mass., 1959.

Gerola, Giuseppe. "L'aquila bizantina e l'aquila imperiale a due teste." *Felix Ravenna*, New Series, 4, 1, 1934.

Grégoras, Nicéphore. *Correspondance*, trans. and ed. by R. Guilland. Paris, 1927.

Halecki, Oskar. "Angora, Florence, Varna and the Fall of Constantinople." *Akten des XI. Internationalen Byzantinistenkongresses* . . . . Munich, 1960.

———. *The Crusade of Varna*. . . . New York, 1943.

———. *Un empereur de Byzance à Rome*. Warsaw, 1930.

Loenertz, Raymond-J. "Jean V Paléologue à Venise (1370–1371)." *Revue des études byzantines*, 16, 1958.

Miller, William. *The Latins in the Levant*. London, 1908.

———. *op. cit.* in XII.

Parisot, Valentin. *Cantacuzène, Homme d'Etat et Historien*. Paris, 1845.

Runciman, Steven. *The Sicilian Vespers*. . . . Cambridge, G.B., 1958.

Schlumberger, Gustave. *Un empereur de Byzance à Paris et à Londres*, Paris, 1916.

———. *Expédition des . . . catalans en Orient*. . . . Paris, 1924.

Setton. *op. cit.* in XI.

Sevcenko, Ihor. "The Decline of Byzantium Seen through the Eyes of Its Intellectuals." *Speculum*, 7, 1932.

Zakythinos, D. A. *Le despotat grec de Morée*, Vol. 1. Paris, 1932.

XIV The End / 1448–1453
Epilogue

Babinger, Franz. *Mehmed der Eroberer*. . . . Munich, 1953.

Byzantinische Geschichtsschreiber. Vol. 1, . . . *Der auf den Fall Konstantinopels 1453 bezügliche Teil des dem Georgios Sphrantzes zugeschriebenen "Chronicon Maius"*; Vol. 2, . . . *Aus dem Geschichtswerk Laonikos Chalkokondyles*, trans. and ed. by Endre von Ivanka. Graz, 1954.

Chavardès, Maurice and Marilène. *La chute de Constantinople (29 mai 1453)*. Paris, 1963.

Cinq-Centième Anniversaire de la prise de Constantinople. L'Hellénisme contemporain, 2nd Series, 7, Athens, May 29, 1953.

Iorga, Nicolae. *Geschichte des osmanischen Reiches*, Vol. 2. Gotha, 1909.

Kritovoulos. *The History of Mehmed the Conqueror*, trans. by C. T.
    Riggs. Princeton, 1954.
Miller. *op. cit.* in XII.
Pears, Edwin. *The Destruction of the Greek Empire and the Story of
    the Capture of Constantinople by the Turks.* London, 1903.
Runciman, Steven. *The Fall of Constantinople, 1453.* Cambridge, G.B.,
    1965.
Schlumberger, Gustave. *Le siège, la prise et le sac de Constantinople par
    les Turcs en 1453.* Paris, 1914.

Salbaroli, Ravenna

*Mosaic of Virgin and Child in the sixth-century church
San Apollinare Nuovo, Ravenna*

Index

Map Index

* B = Back endpaper.
† F = Front endpaper.

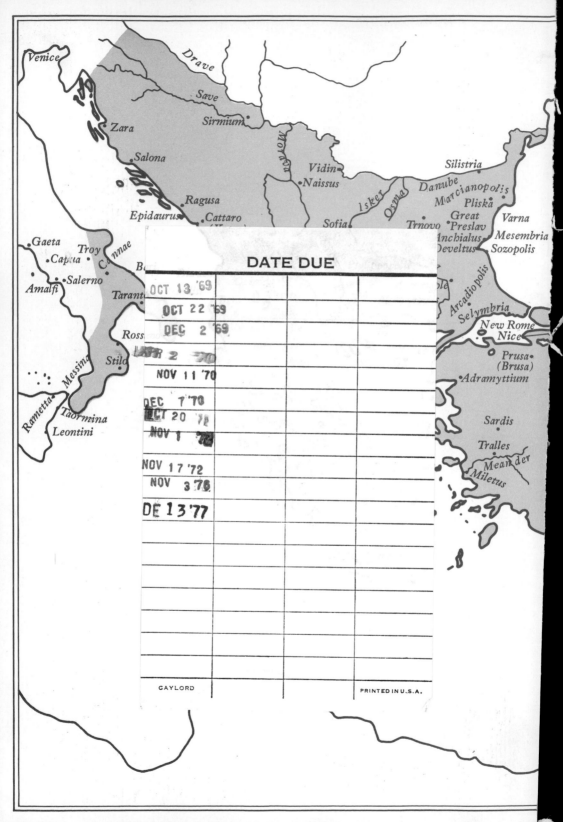

THE EMPIRE ABOUT 1025